THE SECOND VATICAN COUNCIL

Otto Hermann Pesch

THE SECOND VATICAN COUNCIL

PREHISTORY – EVENT – RESULTS – POSTHISTORY

TRANSLATED BY
DEIRDRE DEMPSEY

MARQUETTE
UNIVERSITY

PRESS

MARQUETTE STUDIES IN THEOLOGY

NO. 82

ANDREW TALLON, SERIES EDITOR

LIBRARY OF CONGRESS CATALOGING-IN-PUBLICATION DATA

Pesch, Otto Hermann, author.
[Zweite Vatikanische Konzil. English]
The Second Vatican Council : Prehistory - Event - Results - Posthistory /
Otto Hermann Pesch ;
Translated by Deirdre Dempsey.
pages cm. — (Marquette studies in theology ; No. 82)
Includes bibliographical references and index.
ISBN 978-1-62600-702-4 (pbk. : alk. paper)
1. Catholic Church—Doctrines. 2. Vatican Council (2nd : 1962-1965 :
Basilica di San Pietro in
Vaticano) I. Dempsey, Deirdre, 1956- translator. II. Title.
BX1751.2.P39413 2014
262'.52—dc23
2014012460

*Marquette University Press wishes to express very special thanks to
Dr. Markus Wriedt
for his editing this volume for English translation.*

♾The paper used in this publication meets the minimum requirements of the
American National Standard for Information Sciences—
Permanence of Paper for Printed Library Materials, ANSI Z39.48-1992.

Association of American
University Presses

MARQUETTE UNIVERSITY PRESS
MILWAUKEE

Member of Jesuit University Presses

TABLE OF CONTENTS

PREFACE TO THE AMERICAN EDITION

BY

Otto Hermann Pesch

T his book intends to explain the history of the Second Vatican Council, the controversies with regard to the elaboration of the texts, and the results along with the story of their reception in the Roman Catholic Church. It does so not only independently from the various national contexts, but also without any presupposition of preceding information. The presentation does not at all presuppose any fore-knowledge about what a council is and what kind of authority it has. Since this is not only rather unknown to non-Catholics but also to true Catholics we will proceed this way. Everything will be explained whenever basic knowledge cannot be presupposed.

Nevertheless, it is fairly evident that the book has been elaborated in a specific context: that of Germany and, more generally, of Europe. More specifically, the book appears in the context of an academic lecture course for hearers of all faculties and other interested parties, but mostly a Protestant audience. More accurately, the lecture course is given by a Roman Catholic theologian at the Faculty of Protestant Theology at the University of Hamburg/Germany, which is a very particular exception within the denominational Theology Faculty System in Germany.

How to adapt the specific Germany-concerned passages within the presentation of the Council? Since it was not possible to replace these examples by analogous experiences for the American audience, the German context was not changed. The reader may take these passages as a German voice, and with it a memory of certain ecclesiastical and pious roots which still nurture American Catholic environments.

A specific problem occurred with regard to "German academic perfectionism" to put it in the phrase of the famous American historian Anthony Grafton, whose book on the Footnote became translated as *The Tragic History of the German Footnote*. Since it was completely impossible to reproduce the "academic apparatus" within the notes, the editors have, with my full approval, decided to proceed very differently from Continental customs. Quotations of the conciliar texts derive from the official translations as available on the World Wide Web. Other documents, for instance papal encyclicals or commentaries, are mentioned in the text with their year and can be found on the internet as well. Finally, you will find in the appendix a list of publications on the Council available in English which contain all necessary information for further inquiries. The translation of Deirdre Dempsey, Ph.D. follows 5th edition of 2001.

The Council ended on the 8th of December 1965. For those who are younger than 50 years, the Council is an event of history, and for the generation between 50-70 years old, the Council was mostly forgotten. I do not know whether or not there is a Bishop still alive who was a member of the Council. Also, the theologians who have done the tremendous work of preparing the drafts and the final texts are mostly dead, except some young theologians at that time, including Hans Küng and Joseph Ratzinger, now Pope Benedict XVI. Last but not least, these theologians also include some cooperating students of the Gregorian University, such as Karl Cardinal Lehmann, now bishop of Mainz, Germany. Therefore, it seems to be a trick of the Holy Spirit that the so-controversial reconciliation of the Society of St. Pius X had the effect of suddenly making the Second Vatican Council a topic of conversation.

In this context, the author is very happy that his book can appear on the American scene just in this moment. The author is even happier, perhaps a little bit proud, that this book comes out in the years of the 50th anniversary of the Council (1962 – 1965), and in the memory of the release of the Dogmatic Constitution *unitatis redintegratio*. One can imagine what great many books and articles will appear, and what conferences will be held which tell the story of the Council under various viewpoints and present retrospectives of its reception.

It is due to the merit of a few people around Marquette University in Milwaukee, Wisconsin that this could become possible. Thus, at the end of this preface the author wants to thank first of all his colleague (and former student in Hamburg) Marcus Wriedt, professor at the Goethe University Frankfurt in Main, Germany and, for more than 10 years, regular visiting professor for Historical Theology at Marquette University. He inaugurated the idea of this translation and has promoted its way through his contacts to the relevant and competent persons in the academic and editorial field. In particular he has supervised the necessary American adaptions.

No less I have to thank Deirdre Dempsey, Ph.D. for the strenuous work of translation. She worked on the recommendation of Marcus Wriedt, and, as far as I can judge, she has transformed my German text into an elegant English, easily read. When first reading the English text, I became aware how complicated, against all my intentions and my self-understanding, my German text is. I am very glad to have found such a competent translator. I had very few occasions to correct little misunderstandings.

In this thanksgiving, I include all the colleagues and cooperators who have helped Markus and Deirdre during the process of the elaboration of the translation: Paul Monson, Markus Wriedt's teaching assistant for a couple of years, and Patrick Sperber and Christin Neugeborn, his German counterparts in Frankfurt.

Last but not least, I thank Andy Tallon, Ph.D., and his team from Marquette University Press for their patience and the courage to publish this book; I hope that this courage does not end in disappointment.

"May fresh air come into the Church!" This phrase of Pope John XXIII is reported to have been said a couple of months before the opening of the Council. Of course, for the time being, this is a legend. Nevertheless, the wish is substantiated. May this book contribute to its fulfillment!

29th of June 2011
Feast of Peter and Paul the Apostles
Otto Hermann Pesch

EDITOR'S PREFACE

abent sua fata libelli – if ever the sentence of the antique rhetorician Terentius Maurus (2nd century AD) can be proven, it is with the history of this translation. The story starts in the mid-70s of the last century when I became a student of Otto Herman Pesch. Not understanding why and barely knowing that his professorship had certain uniqueness in the German academic system, I was thrilled by his vast knowledge of theology and all the stories about the "making of" many great books. Later he trained me in methods for accurately reading the sources and judging the arguments of strange and far-away authors. He became one of the advisors of my theological doctorate and a dear friend for now more than 35 years. In 2002, when I became joint appointed regular visiting professor for Historical Theology at Marquette University in Milwaukee, Wisconsin, it was clear that this vocation symbolized the more than 30 years of training and collegial advice I had received gratefully from the Professor of Hamburg.

Otto Hermann Pesch, born 1931 in Cologne, became a theologian and religious member of the Dominican Order. Trained especially during his years in Munich by the most esteemed Catholic ecumenist, he became himself a theologian in the ecumenical age that started with Vatican II. Though he departed and became laicized, he devoted his academic work to the intellectual understanding of the reformation, especially the theological work of Martin Luther, from a loyal and critical Catholic perspective. Out of this work came more than 50 books, which made him one of the rare theological "million sellers" – at least in Germany. To find him a professorship in Germany became an adventure. Since the state-church regulations constitute confessional departments, it seemed impossible to introduce a Roman Catholic to a faculty of Protestant Theology. Nevertheless in 1975 – while Pesch was at Harvard – the German episcopate, represented by Joseph Cardinal Volk from Mainz in clandestine consultations, accepted the offer to the Catholic theologian from the University of

Hamburg by silent consensus, and allowed thus the continuation of Hermann Pesch's academic career outside the limitations of canon law until 1997. After his retirement, Pesch returned to Munich and spent most of his time writing an extensive 2 volume Catholic Dogmatic based on his ecumenical experiences.

To translate this work of nearly 3000 pages, I had neither power nor resources. However, as part of my obligations at Marquette, I was partly responsible for the program of Luther Studies in a Catholic Context that was founded by Kenneth Hagen in the mid-70s of the last century. To initiate further discussions and to provoke another stimulus to the ecumenical debate, I suggested Otto Hermann Pesch be invited in 2006 as distinguished speaker of the annual Père Marquette Lecture. Pesch gladly accepted and combined this invitation with a longer tour through the US, giving talks on Ecumenical Theology and the Vatican Council. Out of this re-union of the 'older' Professor with his 'younger' disciple in the ecumenical spirit of the last century there arose the idea to initiate a first translation of his work for the English-speaking world.

With some naïveté, we started this work financially supported by Hermann Pesch's longtime friend, Bishop Karl Cardinal Lehmann from Mainz. He supported us not only financially, but also spiritually. Nevertheless, it took much more time to finish this translation than we had originally intended.

With a certain delay which has to be blamed partially on adverse circumstances, but also partially to my transatlantic travels and the final transition back to Germany, we are glad to present the translation of Deirdre Dempsey, Ph.D., my wonderful colleague from the Marquette Theology Department. She did not just translate the German original – she also introduced me regularly to the great variety of American Catholicism. Unfortunately, we were not able to include these wonderful talks in the book.

However, we need to clarify its accentuation. It is without doubt a German book with a particular German background. As such, it contains a large number of particularities, and in the wider horizon of the global ecumenical movement, the German problems and debates shrink and become less important. Nevertheless, they might retrospectively explain several difficulties, coming from German perspectives, with ecumenical approaches, for example, from the US. The long ongoing debate on the Common Declaration on Justification filled

German newspapers in 1999, but were hardly noticed in other parts of Christianity outside Germany.

The book is written by a witness – not an eyewitness but a time-witness from a narrow inner-catholic perspective – to the Vatican Council and an active member of the Roman Catholic-Protestant dialogue for nearly 45 years. His great experience and his personal fate have certainly left some scars and spots within the manuscript. Though it was written as the result of classes given mainly to Protestant students of theology, it performs its message in more perspectives. It certainly informs about the history of the second Vatican Council. It gives insights in the discussion whose results have been promoted as constitution and doctrinal advice to the Catholic world of the mid-20th century. With this, it tries to evoke understanding of the inner-Catholic debate to non-Catholics or even hostile Protestants who have no clue about the world *intra muros* of the council. In addition, it is an emphatic cry for a greater ecumenical engagement – at least in Germany. After the ecumenical enthusiasm which culminated in the celebrations of the 500th anniversary of Luther's birthday in 1983 and at least two visits by Pope John Paul II, who enforced further consultations between the confessions, the contemporary climate has chilled. Especially after the protest of nearly 250 protestant theologians against the Common Declaration on Justification in 1999, the former search for community was replaced by an ecumenical approach which accentuated the differences and the confessional profile of the Christian denominations.

It might be non-compatible to the American situation in the ecumenical dialogues, which – at least to me – seem much more vibrant and intense than they are in Germany right now. However, in the experience of a "pendulum professor" who spent nearly 16 years traveling back and forth over the Atlantic, the need for understanding of the particular German situation in the US educational system is evident. In no way does this deny the necessity of the German academic world to take notice of what is going on in Northern America. We hope that this book can become another little stone in the larger tessellation of world Christianity on both sides of the Atlantic.

I would like to thank the following people for their patience and enthusiasm to make this project reality: first of all, Otto Hermann Pesch who allowed us to translate his manuscript and who supported the work of the translator through many talks and detailed explanations; secondly to Deirdre Dempsey. Her ingenuity and sensible understanding of the German language allowed both the translation into proper English and the easing of possible misunderstandings by informing both of us about current changes in American English. The work was graciously supported by Karl Cardinal Lehmann, Bishop of Mainz, to whom we would like to send the book before he retires from his see in Germany. A number of students helped with polishing and clarifying passages of the book: Paul Monson, my American TA, who had a sensitive way to deal with the strange professor from Germany; and Patrick Sperber and Christin Neugeborn, who served as TAs in Frankfurt. Last but not least, thanks are due to Dr. Andy Tallon and his team from Marquette University Press who finally made this book available in its final shape.

Frankfurt/Milwaukee
Summer of 2013
Markus Wriedt

TRANSLATOR'S PREFACE

Otto Hermann Pesch's *Das Zweite Vatikanische Konzil: Vorgeschichte – Verlauf – Ergebnisse – Nachgeschichte* has been enormously popular in Germany since its initial publication in 1992. Proof of this popularity: the 2001 edition I translated was the fifth edition! The popularity of the book is one of the reasons Karl Cardinal Lehmann supported the translation into English. I am grateful to Cardinal Lehmann, and to Professor Otto Hermann Pesch and Professor Markus Wriedt, for providing me with the opportunity to work with this text. I owe a particular debt of thanks to Professor Wriedt, who had the initial idea of a translation of the book into English; he secured the funding from Cardinal Lehmann. I would also like to thank my colleague Abraham Fisher, Ph.D., who helped me with both the proofreading of the translation and the index.

The primary audience of the original work was intended to be German-speaking Roman Catholics interested in the "take" of a well respected Roman Catholic German systematic theologian on this important event in the life of their Church. The translation enables English speakers to access this "German voice." Because we aim in this translation for a non-academic audience, we made the decision to leave the notes of the German original untranslated. They were deemed much too "German" – references were made to almost exclusively German authors and works. It did occur to us that the lack of notes might be an irritant to U.S. academics who are reading the text; they, however, will be able to avail themselves of the notes in the German original. Speaking of translations: almost all the quotations of Vatican II documents were taken from Austin Flannery, O.P., *The Basic Sixteen Documents Vatican Council II: Constitutions, Decrees, Declarations* (New York: Costello Publishing, 1996).

I have occasionally been asked why I, a member of the Judaism and Christianity in Antiquity Section of Marquette University's Department of Theology, with a degree in Northwest Semitic

Languages, agreed to the task of translating a book on the Second Vatican Council. I do a great deal of translating, but primarily of Hebrew Bible texts. I accepted the job for a number of reasons, but first and foremost was the certain conviction that my mother, Barron Dempsey, whose commitment to her faith and to her Church continue to inspire and support me, would want me to. I dedicate my work on this translation to her.

Many of us here at Marquette University have fond memories of Professor Pesch; he delivered the Père Marquette lecture, published by the Marquette University Press under the title *The Ecumenical Potential of the Second Vatican Council: 40 Years After.* Professor Pesch stayed in Milwaukee for about a week after the occasion of the Père Marquette lecture, giving additional talks and meeting with graduate students and faculty members. We in the Department of Theology were saddened to hear of his death, early in September. As one of my colleagues said, when he heard of Professor Pesch's death, "I'm just very glad he was able to serve the Church as long as he did and at such a critical time." *Requiescat in pace.*

Deirdre Dempsey
Milwaukee, Wisconsin

CHAPTER ONE

"AN INSPIRATION
LIKE A FLOWER"

THE PREHISTORY OF THE
SECOND VATICAN COUNCIL

I. AN ALMOST SPONTANEOUS IDEA

1. CHANGE IN THE CHURCH?

Roman Catholics are an extreme minority in the tradition-ally Protestant northern states of the Federal Republic of Germany: for example, Catholics are only 3% of the population in the state of Schleswig-Holstein and only 8 % in the city-state of Hamburg. Because of this minority status, these Catholics are for the most part conservative and resistant to change because of anxiety and fear with regard to their ecclesial identity. When in 1959 the Second Vatican Council was announced by Pope John XXIII, there was no doubt that some changes would be in store for the traditional monolithic Church to which these Catholics were accustomed. An anecdote from this period, apocryphal but nonetheless illuminating, is told about a conservative Catholic from this area, a farmer in the state of Niedersachsen; the punchline is: "They can decide what they want to in Rome, I'm staying Catholic." The pun characterizes – this is why it is so apt – the greatest challenge that the Council posed for a wide-spread Catholic mentality of that time – and after 50 years, still poses for many Catholics: that something in the Church might, can, and indeed *should* change, in all areas from liturgy to canon law to theology and the interpretation of binding church doctrine. The idea that *nothing* can change, unless the change emphasizes the Church's changelessness more clearly, was considered by the overwhelming majority of Catholics all over the world as exactly what is Catholic.

Our anecdote makes one thing clear: even from the place that the overwhelming majority of Catholics consider the bedrock of all changelessness, from Rome, nothing can be changed. One must if necessary remain "Catholic" without Rome and against Rome. The joke has become bitter reality in the movement of the French Archbishop Lefebvre, who died in March of 1991. Since Lefebvre, despite all efforts and the greatest possible accommodations of the Roman Curia, did not refrain from consecrating Bishops, according to canon law his movement is in "schism," "separated" from the Church of Rome, a "rival church."

2. "... INSPIRED BY A GREAT IDEA"

How, under these circumstances, could the Council have occurred at all? From publications of the last decades, publications based on the evaluation of published and unpublished sources as well as on the questioning of witnesses, we now have more precise knowledge of how Pope John XXIII's plan for the Council ripened; we also know more of the preparations that were made even before he took office, preparations in which he did *not* participate. We shall return to this at the end of this chapter. However one looks at it, the Council was an almost spontaneous idea of the Pope, and without his idea a Council would not have occurred, certainly not *this* Council. On the contrary, nothing could have been further from the men of the Roman Curia; there was not public opinion within the Church that would have supported something like this.

An *almost* spontaneous idea! If we agree with two of the Pope's backward glances, one in an address to pilgrims from Venice on May 8, 1962, the other a diary entry from September 15, 1962, then it was a *completely* spontaneous idea. According to the Pope, the idea occurred to him in a famous and much-discussed conversation held on January 20, 1959. On that day, a Tuesday, around 9 in the morning, just three months after his election, the Pope held his usual routine briefing with the Secretary of State, Cardinal Tardini.

Under Pius XII, Domenico Tardini had been, along with Giovanni Battista Montini (later Pope Paul VI), under secretary of state, with the rank of a simple prelate (*Monsignore*). The two, Tardini and Montini, did the work of "*sostituti*" ("acting representatives"), because Pius XII, himself Secretary of State under Pius XI, did not appoint anyone to this office, so that he might make all the decisions usually made by the Secretary of State. Toward the end of his papacy the Pope fell out with Montini; he promoted him, as was usual, to ArchBishop of Milan, but did not elevate him to cardinal. Upon his election, John XXIII immediately elevated the other "*sosituto*," Tardini, to cardinal and named him Secretary of State with the full responsibility of this office. His reason: "There are already too many '*sostituti*' running around me here!"

It was with Tardini, therefore, that the Pope held his routine conference that morning. As the Pope later described it, the situation of the Church in the world was discussed. In terms of members and influence, the Church had never been more powerful in the modern period than under Pius XII. The Church had become, however, a foreign body in a changed world: respected, but misunderstood and unloved. A third of humanity lived under intentionally atheistic regimes. The number of practicing Catholics in the traditionally Christian countries was at most 30%. In Italy, including Rome (2-3% practicing Catholics!), and in France regions were completely "de-Christianized," a situation that was well known from a widely read novel at that time, *Diary of a Pastor* by Georges Bernanos. In the developing countries a gulf had grown between clergy and laity – the distant background of the modern "Theology of Liberation." And even where the Church was not persecuted, a culture grew that turned away from Christianity, in science to art, in lifestyle to ethical convictions. This culture gained influence even in the Church. Catholics wanted, after two centuries of futile defense, to be allowed to be modern in thought and feeling. While, unlike the situation in the 16th or 19th century, no public opinion existed in the Church for a Council – no one considered this actually to be possible – there was an atmosphere in favor of reform, decentralization, reconciliation with a world against which the Church for a long time, wrongly, had lead blanket attacks, and an aversion to a church pressure that hitherto had dominated the entire life of Catholics.

This was discussed on that January morning. "Suddenly," as John described in 1962, "there arose in us an inspiration like a flower that blossoms in an unexpected Spring. Our soul was illumined by a great idea ... A word, solemn and binding, formed itself on our lips. Our voice expressed it for the first time – Council!" We know that the Pope in this account compressed the content of a whole series of conversations he held with his Secretary of State, with whom he met almost daily – but in this summary, the intentions and perspectives that guided the Pope in his Council plan come clearly to light: the Church should finally give a helping answer to the problems of the modern world – and stop digging itself in.

We now know that the continuation of the report, too, is not pure historical truth, but speaks more of the tactful magnanimity of the Pope: "To tell the truth, we feared that we had produced confusion, if not outrage... But the face of the Cardinal revealed a clear expression. His agreement was immediate and joyful, the first sure sign of the will of the Lord." It could hardly have been like that. On the contrary, historians have not made up their minds if Tardini did not attempt, through a sort of "service according to the letter," to delay the preparations for the Council in the expectation that the death of the Pope in the foreseeable future would finish off the plan. It is conceivable, even very possible, that Tardini immediately understood that John would not be dissuaded from his "inspiration," and as a result took flight into his well known grumpy submissiveness and hyper-correct willingness to serve. Several witnesses report that Tardini frequently spoke, rolling his eyes and groaning, of "the one above." This was a reference to the work rooms of the Pope on the fifth floor of the Vatican Palace, where the Pope once more in his irresistible way had ordered the Cardinal to do something that caused discontent. Of course the Pope heard about "the one above" comment, and explained to the Cardinal privately: "Dear Tardini, let me correct one thing: 'the one above' is the Lord God over us all. I'm only 'the one above on the fifth floor.' Please, don't confuse the hierarchy!"

II. WHAT IS A COUNCIL?

Before we get into the prehistory of the Second Vatican Council, we have to clarify what a Council actually is. This is not as obvious as it might seem and, where there is clarity, this clarity is not so problem-free as to make questions unnecessary.

1. *The Situation in Light of Canon Law*

The regulations of the *Codex Iuris Canonici* of 1917 (CIC 1917) were authoritative for the Second Vatican Council. These enshrine, in canons 222-229, what had been determined at the Council of Trent (1545-1563) about participants and process and at the First Vatican Council (1869/70) about levels of authority. The cited canons are in Book II of the CIC; the sequence of Bishop of Rome, Ecumenical Council, Cardinals, and then the Roman Curia is clearly the order of rank.

Canon law gives no definition of the nature of the Council; this can be determined on the basis of the individual regulations. The following can be said: *The Ecumenical Council is the assembly of all those who have a higher level of jurisdiction for the goal, together with and subservient to the Pope, of executing the highest teaching and lawgiving authority.* The circle of "those who have jurisdiction," those entitled to a vote, is named (canon 223): all the reigning patriarchs, primates (the old, obsolete title of the supreme Bishop of a whole country – the Archbishop of Warsaw is Primate of Poland, and the Archbishop of Salzburg still maintains the honorific of Primate of Germany), metropolitans, archbishops, bishops, abbots as well as the superiors of the so-called personal prelatures (Opus Dei, for example), the leading abbots (abbots primate) of the monastic congregations (Benedictine, Cistercian, etc.), and the superior generals of the orders subject directly to Rome rather than to the Bishops (for example, the Franciscans, Dominicans, Jesuits, Redemptorists, etc.). Theologians and experts (*periti*) have only an advisory voice – although they had the main burden of the work on the texts and their influence is therefore great, if not actually definitive.

Together with the Pope the Council exercises the highest authority over the universal Church (canon 228 § 1). The Council is not, for instance, only an advisory body to the Pope, and certainly not an assembly where members come to a mutual agreement, which then the individual members by their own authority put into action (sort of like an international political conference). The Council is – as a body, not as the sum of all Bishops – bearer of the highest and universal church authority. It serves as a warning against speaking too quickly of the "monarchical structure" of the Roman Catholic Church.

Council resolutions are definitively obligatory only if they are confirmed by the Pope and published by his order (canon 228). That is why there is no appeal from the Pope to the Ecumenical Council (canon 228 § 2). Only the Pope can convene a Council (canon 222 § 1); he or his representative presides over it. He alone establishes the topics to be treated and the order in which these topics will be treated. He can postpone, interrupt, and dissolve the Council. The participants in the Council can suggest topics to be discussed, but only if the presider approves them are they discussed (canon 226).

In a word: the Council, which is, with the Pope, the bearer of the highest ecclesial authority, stands at the same time under the Pope. There is no Council against the Pope or Council resolution against the vote of the Pope. But a Pope can disagree with the Council and there can be papal objection to Council resolutions, or at least their non-observance by the Pope. All this had an effect on the Second Vatican Council. The Pope forbad topics that the Council had wished to handle – sometimes to the joy of one and the disappointment and anger of the other. Through the Pope, or in his name, formulations were pushed through that the Council did not actually want – again to the joy of one and to the disappointment of the other. All this remains to be discussed.

The two canons that have not yet been mentioned both deal with questions of procedure. Each member of the Council is duty bound to participation – he can be represented by a "procurator" only on the grounds of a credible hindrance, and then only in the discussions; the vote of an absent member is not counted (canon 224 §§ 1-2). No participant may, without the approval of the presider, leave the Council early (canon 225). These two canons are the result of past scandals, and attempt to prevent their repetition. The first canon recalls to mind that the German members of the Council of Trent (1545-1563) did not come not to the first session for political reasons. The second canon recalls the departure of 88 bishops from the First Vatican Council before the vote on the dogma of papal primacy.

Underscoring the absolute subordination of the Council to the Pope, canon 229, the last canon dealing with the Council, stipulates that at the death of the Pope during the Council the Council is automatically terminated, unless the new Pope orders its continuation.

John XXIII died after the first session of the Council. The friends of the Council were terrified that the new Pope would not continue the Council. They breathed a sign of relief when the election of the Archbishop of Milan and Cardinal Giovanni Battista Montini as Paul VI became known. The new Pope, whom John XXIII had wanted to be his successor, would carry on.

Thus far we have considered the Council according to the canon law of the time. For further clarification a few comparisons might help.

2. For Comparison

a) At first glance we are perhaps inclined to say that a Council is something like a parliament of the universal Church. At the First Vatican Council, and then again at the Second, the methods of parliamentary negotiation had been employed: plenary and committee meetings, amendments (*modi*), numerous readings, votes, minutes by professional stenographers, for example. But a Council is completely different from a Parliament:

+ A Council does not consist of elected, but of "born" members – who owe their "birth," that is their church office, only in a very limited way to an election process (actually only the higher superiors of orders are elected, the Bishops are not).
+ A Council does not permanently guide the fate of the Church, but assembles only at intervals that often can be counted in centuries. A Council is called only for extraordinary reasons.
+ A Council has, as we have seen with our glance at canon law, no power beyond the borders that the Pope as its presider sets for it. The Pope has all authority in actual fact without a Council – although not absolutely independent of the Bishops of the entire world.
+ The Council does not elect its highest presider, even if he dies during the course of a Council; the Pope is elected by the College of Cardinals. This tradition reaches back to the time when the Pope first and foremost was the Bishop of Rome and the cardinals were the pastors of the Roman parishes. This election process is today a topic of discussion. However, the fact is, and will remain so for the foreseeable future: the assembly that according to theology and church law represents the universal Church does not elect the highest Bishop of the universal Church.

+ The most important difference between a Council and a Parliament, however, lies beyond the juridical realm. A Parliament has its authority for a fixed time from the people who make it, through elections, their representative. A Council has its authority in that the men who are gathered together were, according to the understanding of the faithful, called to their office through Christ himself. They are therefore not responsible first and foremost to the people of the Church, but to Christ, who of course, through the Holy Spirit, also speaks through the people of the Church. Without the Holy Spirit, and the pressure exerted by the Holy Spirit – theologically expressed: through the effect of the gift of grace of the Holy Spirit – a Council would never occur and a Pope would never be motivated to convene one. Soberly considered, a Council is an impediment to a Pope's official duties, since, according to canon law, he could exercise his highest authority alone, after proper consultation. This is even more the case for the administrative offices (the "congregations") of the Curia.

b) A Council cannot be compared to a full assembly of the World Council of Churches (WCC):

+ The WCC is not a church, and does not intend to be one. It is an advisory body of Churches – "the churches in ongoing consultation," as the earlier General Secretary Visser t' Hooft phrased it. Decisions are binding on the members only in so far as they agree with these decisions: in order to reach agreement, one must shape the decisions appropriately. No Church can railroad another Church.

+ In the WCC *Churches* vote, not the individuals – hence the fair but controversial quota rule, which weighs each vote according to the number of affected church members. In a Council, on the other hand, each Bishop votes for himself, as one called by Christ into his teaching and leadership position, not as a spokesman for his Church.

+ The General Secretary does not set the daily agenda; he sets on the daily agenda what the member Churches wish to consider. (This does not rule out theological and ecclesiastical influence, particularly on the part of an effective General Secretary.)

+ Any member or member church can at any time leave the
WCC or one of its General Assemblies under protest.
According to canon law a Council Father cannot depart from
the Council without permission of the Pope.

+ And of course the General Secretary is elected, if not by the
General Assembly, then by the Executive Board.

c) A Council does not function like the United Nations, even taking
into account the different areas of interest:

+ The most obvious difference is again the democratic principle
"from under to over": all offices are elected, the daily agenda is
given by the members, suppressing points on the daily agenda
is not juridically possible, except with political manipulation.

+ The delegates vote subject to directives for their countries, as
in the WCC – only not according to a quota rule, a situation
now known to be a fundamental problem for the effectiveness
of UN resolutions.

Of course departure as well as expulsion from the United Nations is possible, as membership in the United Nations is voluntary; there are no "born"
members. Even a Pope cannot exclude a residing Bishop from the council, unless he condemned him beforehand according to process on account of false
doctrine or disobedience in office. The most obvious commonality between
a Council and the United Nations, different from the WCC, is that both, in
the space of rapidly reached borders, laid down by law, exercise power and
can bind the members – at least according to the law, since in both occasions
there is room for passive resistance. Expressed in a different way: in the space
of the relevant rules the resolutions need no ratification and no acceptance by
those who are most affected.

3. The Point of a Council

A Council, therefore, is a unique event. Its uniqueness lies, according to the canon law current at that time, in its *powerless authority*.
Read without consideration of the historical context, the almost innocent naivety with which CIC 1917 strung together the following
rules, seemingly without a problem, is amazing: obligatory nature of
the resolutions only on the basis of confirmation by the Pope; highest
authority of the Council over the universal Church; no appeal from
the Pope to the Council. These rules almost irresistibly lead to a slightly cynical suspicion: perhaps, after the dogmatization of the papal

primacy in 1870, it seemed certain that a Council would never again be necessary. It may be taken as out of the question that the intelligent editors of the CIC 1917 would have allowed these tension-filled clauses to remain, if they had expected that this tension would ever again have to be endured. The new canon law of CIC 1983 subtly weakened the position of the Council vis-à-vis the Pope, and correspondingly strengthened the position of the Pope and of the Curia; one must, after the Second Vatican Council, calculate that another Council might occur. We shall return to this in the conclusion, when we speak of the effects of the Council. According to the contemporary legal position that was the basis for the Second Vatican Council, frankly spoken, the Council is the *completion* of the papal office for the goal of the *representation* of the worldwide unity of the Church. The *representation*, mind you! Because when it comes to *fact* and *reality*, the unity of the Church – we bracket off now many heatedly discussed problems – is represented and secured in the papal office. The Pope remains integrated in the Church; he does not stand outside the Church, somehow opposite the Church. The First Vatican Council neither dogmatized that nor intended it, and that is also not the sense of the formula, that the "*ex cathedra* rulings" of the Pope "from himself, not on the basis of the agreement of the Church" (*ex sese, non ex consensu ecclesiae*) are unchangeable (*irreformabiles*). One must not imply this of the First Vatican Council – not that we can go into details here. The Pope cannot act without contact with the Bishops, and there have been for a long time institutional forms of this permanent contact. The Pope could not pronounce, for example, a dogma, if the majority of Bishops said to him that this dogma did not exist in the belief of their local Churches; he cannot persevere in laws for the universal Church if the majority of the Bishops of the world make it clear to him that these laws cannot be carried out. The idea still prevalent in the Protestant world that the Pope could impose on the entire church whatever he wants is naïve. *However*: in order to exercise his office as chief Bishop of the universal Church, as guarantor and representative of the unity of the Church, and *at the same time* his integration in the universal Church, the Pope does not need to convene a Council; he can establish and maintain the necessary contact with the Bishops of the world with other and cheaper means. For the *demonstration* of this unity and this communication with the universal Church nothing is more appropriate than the Council. Without detracting from his chief authority, the integration of the papal office in the universal Church becomes visible and clear.

Another comment about the First Vatican Council: The Bishops are not, according to the teaching of the First Vatican Council, some sort of officials of the Pope, but rather leaders of their dioceses by virtue of their own right, in other words by virtue of the *immediate* authorization through Christ, as the Catholic faith understands it to be given. The German Chancellor Otto von Bismarck had – out of obvious political interest in the political discrimination against Catholics – publicly declared after the First Vatican Council that it was now clear that the Bishops were nothing other than recipients of orders from a foreign power. The German Bishops at that time explained, in a famous letter of 1875, that the Pope as Pope is "Bishop of Rome, not Bishop of some other city or diocese, not Bishop of Cologne or Breslau, etc."

The writers of the letter note that "[B]y virtue of the same divine investiture, upon which the Papacy is based, the Episcopacy also exists; it has its rights and duties by dint of the order given by God Himself. The Pope has neither the right nor the power to change this order. It is therefore a complete misunderstanding of the Vatican decisions to believe that through these 'the Episcopal jurisdiction is merged into the papal,' that the Pope has 'in principle stepped into the position of each individual Bishop,' that the Bishops are only 'tools of the Pope, his administrators without their own responsibility.'" Pope Pius IX upheld this statement in 1875.

This unity of the whole Church through the assembly and the resolutions of those who by virtue of *their own* authority lead their dioceses in binding community with the successor of Peter becomes clear and receives a particular emphasis in the Council. At the same time, the connections and historical ties of the office of the Pope are also clearly represented in a Council; without a Council, these connections could escape notice, encouraging the picture of the Church as an absolute monarchy. This is the point of the thesis represented here: according to prevailing canon law, the Council is the completion of the papal office for the goal of the representation of the structures of Church unity.

Should this thesis be understood as a lightly ironic belittling of the Council? The Council Fathers did not think so. The last section of Article 22 of the Constitution concerning the Church reads: "In so far as this College [of Bishops] is composed of many, it represents the diversity and entirety of the People of God; in so far as it is assembled under one head, the unity of the flock of Christ. In this College the Bishops, under the true preservation of the primatial precedence of their head, work in *their own authority* for the best of their faithful, indeed for the universal Church... The highest power over the universal Church, which this College possesses, is *in solemn fashion* exercised in the ecumenical Council." We are not finished with some questions raised in this section.

4. The Authority of the Council

What has been said to this point characterizes the situation according to prevailing canon law. The open question is whether it has to be this way; this question becomes pressing if the latent tension built into canon law becomes an open tension in the event that, against all expectations, a Council again assemble. The simple question is: Where does a Council get its authority from? If we knew this, then we would know what authority the Council has: could it perhaps be beyond the borders of prevailing canon law? This question points back into the history of the Councils – by which are meant councils with the claim to be "ecumenical" councils, those that want to represent and bind collective Christendom.

This question is not yet answered. The usual answer of Catholic dogmatists is: a Council has its authority (*suprema potestas in ecclesia universali*) on the basis of the fact that here in the Council the totality of the Bishops appointed by Christ make decisions – and the supremacy of the Pope is a result of the office of Peter established by Christ. Two questions remain unanswered with this explanation. First: Why don't only the individual Bishops, or a majority of them, have the highest authority, rather than the assembly of Bishops as a *body*, which indicates that the minority must submit to decisions and cannot withdraw on the basis of the appointment of the individual Bishop by Christ? A divine appointment of the Council has in any case never been maintained (and cannot be deduced from a biblical text such as Acts 15). Why then, in doubtful cases, does the Council have a legal precedence over the individual Bishops? And the other question: where does the papal supremacy over the council come from? This was in the history of the Councils anything but self-evident, above all not in the dogmatically important councils of entire Christendom, the first eight Councils up to the Fourth Council of Constantinople (869/70). These Councils all took place in the East, and their decisions were proclaimed as Imperial law of the Eastern Emperor. The agreement of the Bishop of Rome was necessary for their recognition in the West. The Western Church was either weakly represented or not represented at all at these Councils, for example at the very important Council of Constantinople in 381.

The solution to the puzzle lies in the fact that every Council is different. In Catholic Church history, the enumeration of 21 ecumenical councils (including the Second Vatican Council) is the norm, but this number depends on a document ordered by Pope Pius V in the 16th century, the *Editio Romana*. Hubert Jedin, the well-respected German Catholic Church historian who died in 1980, distinguished five types of Councils and in the process tapped into reflections of medieval theology about which Councils are to be considered "ecumenical." What are the five types?

a) The first eight Councils. Their ecumenical character is not in question, since both the Eastern and the Western Churches participated, and the Western Church has accepted them. Characteristics of these Councils were: they were *Imperial Councils*, called by the Emperor. Under imperial supervision, also occasionally under imperial pressure, the Bishops negotiated and made decisions about controversial questions. Their decisions were proclaimed as Imperial law.

b) Papal General Councils. These begin with the First Lateran Council of 1123. Their characteristics: they are convened by the Pope, there is no participation of the Eastern Church, but (non-voting) participation of secular representatives. The theological thematic was extended also to questions about the relationships between Church and secular power. They are representative of the (western!) Christendom of the *Corpus Christianum*.

c) The so-called Reform Councils, a product of conciliarism and of the Great Western Schism (1378-1417). There were only two of these: The Council of Constance (1414-1418) and the conflict-plagued undertaking of Basel-Ferrara-Florence-Rome (1431-1445). The Council of Constance was called by the king, the Council of Basel by the Pope, who also transferred it. The basic idea of the Reform Councils was: the Council should become a permanent, regularly convened institution, capable of exercising some control over the Pope. The Popes, who owed their regained power to the first of the Reform Councils, were able to fend this off. We are not able here to delve into the reasons. In any case, the Fifth Lateran Council, in the time of the young Luther (1512-1517), was once again a Papal General Council, as in the Middle Ages. An important point about the Reform Councils: They understood themselves to have their authority directly from God, and *therefore* they were authorized to stand over the Pope.

d) *The Council of Trent* (1545-1563) was, according to form, a true Papal Council – called by the Pope, if not without pressure from many sides, above all from the Emperor. It had, for the first time, something close to the form and process of a modern council. It was distinguished from the medieval councils in that, while representatives of the princes were invited, including those who had gone over to the Reformation, only questions concerning dogma and Church reform were handled. With the Council of Trent the time of the Councils that represented the *Corpus Christianum* was at an end; the fact that the Papal Bull that convened the Council also confronted the Council with the task of peacemaking, but this task was left undone, is evidence of that.

e) *The First Vatican Council* was according to form and theme equal to a Papal Council in power. Obviously no invitations were issued to the secular and religiously neutral states, but an invitation was issued to the Orthodox Churches of the East, who of course turned down the invitation. The Protestant Churches were also not invited: which ones would have been? Unlike the contemporary situation, no conversation partners such as the WCC or confessional international associations existed. The Protestant Churches were simply asked to return to "the flock of Christ." The papal connection with the Council is obvious in the Pope's (Pius IX) repeated interventions with the formulation of the drafts and his role as presider over the sessions. With the First Vatican Council the superiority of the Pope over the Council, as it is fixed by canon law, is finally in actual fact achieved. The prohibition mentioned above concerning departures should now for all time put a stop to the kind of scandal that occurred before the final vote, the demonstrative departure of 88 Bishops; this departure made evident to the whole world the lack of unanimity surrounding the issue of papal superiority.

This trip through the problems of the Council question should make this clear: the Second Vatican Council began its work under a theological and legal handicap, which bore the deep scars of Church history. Catholic theology is wise enough to declare that the question of the nature and authority of a Council can only be answered by the Church within the framework of its prevailing circumstances. This declaration takes care of non-sensical constructions – for example, the binding nature of the Council of Nicaea (325), the first ecumenical council ever in Church history, hangs on the proof that the Pope formally approved it. A question like this was simply not urgent at that time. If this is the case – that the answer to the question of the authority of a Council depends on the state of consciousness of the Church – would we not have to conclude: the present position of canon law is one that might not be the last word?

Two different things in any case are certain: given the current legal position the Council could prevail *against* the Pope, against his views and those of his Curia, only with the strength of argument, not legally. And: it was unavoidable that the inquiries of late medieval conciliarism, thought to be dead since the time of the First Vatican Council, proved to be just in hiding. With this we have arrived at the question of the prehistory of the Council.

III. THE UNCOMPLETED FIRST VATICAN COUNCIL (1869/70)

1. THE PROGRAM OF THE COUNCIL

The prehistory of the Second Vatican Council begins with a Council that was never formally ended, the First Vatican Council. More than anything else, what is known about this Council is that it dogmatized the entire primacy of jurisdiction of the Pope and, imbedded in this, the infallibility of his teaching office in questions of faith and morals on the occasion of solemn doctrinal rulings. This is at one and the same time correct and incorrect. The Council had set itself a comprehensive set of tasks, as it was solemnly opened on the 8th of December, 1869, and no one could at that time have foreseen that a good seven months later, on the 18th of July 1870, the Council would be at an end. A comprehensive program had been envisaged: since 1864, both the Curia and the Bishops were concerned about the question of what topics should be discussed at the Council. Five different commissions worked since 1867 on the drafts of resolutions for the Council discussions. After the beginning of the Council there were four deputations that executed the amendments and drew up the improved drafts – one for questions of faith, one for disciplinary and order matters, one for the Eastern Uniate Churches, and one for the missions – an indication of the broad spectrum of topics.

The announcement of the Council sharpened the contrasts among Catholic laity. On the one side "liberal Catholics," above all in France, Germany, and the Danubian Monarchy, officially named the Austro-Hungarian Empire, strove for reconciliation between the Church and the modern world. On the other side the so-called "Ultra-montanists," above all in Italy, but with strong groups also in England, France, and Germany: they allowed themselves, in their enthusiasm for the Pope, to be carried away almost to the point of blasphemy (re-workings of hymns about Christ for the Pope!). They stood unconditionally behind the so-called *Syllabus* of Pius IX, from 1864, a list of "The Errors of the Century" (*Errores saeculi*); along with what would still today be considered error are found items that we would today consider as givens, even worth defending, ranging from religious freedom to reconciliation of the Church with the modern world, from the freedom to ask reasonable questions to socialism and democracy. The "Ultra-montanists" seized this *Syllabus* as the Magna Carta for their relationship to the modern world. Since the effort to make sure that all the consulters involved in the preparations on the drafts of resolutions were the supporters of the *Syllabus* was successful, and since some Bishops expressed the wish, favorably received in Rome, that the *Syllabus* be made the basis of the Council discussions, the comprehensive program of the Council becomes sufficiently clear. Strengthening this is the fact that, without any clue as to the near future, yet with a sort of instinct, the dogmatic decisions concerning the Pope and infallibility were given priority on the agenda (which is why they passed). With this we come to that close connection that shall be meaningful for the Second Vatican Council.

2. THE RESOLUTIONS AND THE TERMINATION OF THE COUNCIL

After vigorous criticism of the first outline, and a thorough re-working, on April 24, 1870 the Dogmatic Constitution *Dei Filius* ("The Son of God"), which dealt with faith in relationship to reason, was accepted and promulgated by the Pope. The discussion of another, similarly comprehensive, constitution dealing with the Church should have followed. But in January 1870 a group of extreme members of the majority had organized a petition to the Pope, asking him to put on the agenda the dogmatic decision concerning the infallibility of the papal teaching office. In spite of vigorous interventions of the minority, the Pope complied with this wish. To the draft *De Ecclesia* ("Concerning the Church"), which had already been distributed on January 21st to the Council Fathers, he added on March 1st a *Caput addendum de Romani Pontificis infallibilitate* ("Additional Chapter concerning the Infallibility of the Roman Bishop"), which stemmed from the preparatory work of 1869.

On the 27th of April the decisive step was taken: at the renewed pressure of the "Infalliblists," the Pope decided that the section on the Pope should be removed from the entire draft of *De Ecclesia,* worked up into its own Constitution, and debated before any of the other chapters of the draft. The result is the Constitution *Pastor Aeternus,* which deals with the primacy of the Pope, that under well known and much discussed circumstances – a powerful storm rendered the reading of the document inaudible for all those who were not standing close to the podium – was passed on the 18th of July, 1870, and immediately confirmed by the presiding Pope. It was the fourth session of the Council.

We are "indebted" to this circumstance – the removal of the section on the Pope from the draft of *De Ecclesia,* the re-working of that section into its own Constitution, and its advancement on the daily agenda – for the Papal Dogma of 1870. After the session there was a general departure out of the hot Roman summer into vacation, with the expectation that the work of the Council would resume on the 11th of November, 1870. Only 100 Council Fathers remained in Rome and discussed further in the appropriate committees; another solemn, resolution-passing session never occurred. The Franco-Prussian War broke out, the Italian government used the outbreak of the war to annex the Papal States, troops of the Italian army moved into Rome, the Pope became the proverbial "prisoner in the Vatican" (the modern Vatican City, "Città del Vaticano" was established in 1929).

The connection with the Second Vatican Council now becomes clear. The first Council remained a skeleton. Unlike at the conclusion in Trent, the Council Fathers never signed the entirety of the decrees – which, in the face of papal confirmation, did not mean much. More important is the practical incompleteness: we received an isolated doctrine of the papal office because of the premature passing of a resolution, without this resolution's insertion in an integrated doctrine on the Church. This was mirrored in the collapse of the resistance from the opponents of the dogma. On the one hand they did not have to fall victim to a doomsday mood, since the "maximalists" had not succeeded in the discussions; a moderate line had, occasionally very much to the annoyance of the Pope, asserted itself. For further counterweights one awaited the continuation of the Council, when the remaining doctrine of the Church should have been discussed, above all the more exact version of the relationships between the Bishops and the Pope. In what direction this would have gone is indicated by the position of the German Bishops vis-à-vis Bismarck, which we have already mentioned.

The War between the Northern Confederation of Germany (under the leadership of Prussia) against France prevented the minority, who were for the most part in France, Germany, and Austria, from having contact with one another. The events in Rome made a resumption of the Council in November unthinkable. Already on the 20th of October – given the travel conditions of that time therefore the last possible moment – the Pope postponed the Council *sine die*, to an undetermined time.

Since then, from time to time, the question of a continuation and a formal conclusion of the First Vatican Council would arise – more and more utopian as more and more time elapsed from the original event. But for all those who were knowledgeable, the announcement of the Second Vatican Council was understood through this lens. Not, however, by the representatives of the Curia. That becomes clear with a brief look at the time between the two Councils.

IV. PAPAL CENTRAL GOVERNMENT

STYLE AND FORM OF CHURCH GOVERNANCE

It is not particularly malicious to say: The interest in a continuation of the First Vatican Council must not, could not, have been particularly strong on the side of the Roman Curia. A centralized style of governance of the Church through proclamation of doctrine, teaching discipline (condemnation of theologians with differing opinions on doctrine), and legal regulations for the entire Church had already asserted itself in the decades before the First Vatican Council, as a consequence of the recovery of the Church after the Napoleonic period. Now it had received the best conceivable dogmatic protection.

This is very easy to understand. The pivot and central point of the Vatican dogma – and to be more exact, its entire internal theological problematic, which continues to have its effect today – is the "legalizing" of the binding dogma, its building up into a legally enforceable instruction. It is often said that the First Vatican Council dogmatized the "infallibility" of the papal doctrinal decisions. This is incorrectly expressed. According to the wording of the text, the proclaimed sentences are not "infallible," but rather the authority that issues them is: the Pope in certain solemn acts of doctrinal decisions. The sentences themselves are not infallible, but, according to the text, *irreformabiles*, not capable or in need of alteration, therefore legally not open to attack. The immediate interpretation of the Vatican definition by sympathetic Catholic dogmatics, classically represented by, for example, the famous German Theologian Matthias Joseph Scheeben in his 1872 work on dogmatic theology, emphasized as an advantage what could only shock Protestant interpreters: the *ex cathedra* pronouncements of the Pope have legal force, and demand both interior and exterior *obedience*. This is crucial: if the solemn doctrinal decisions are issued in the form of law, then it cannot be improper if other teaching office positions follow in legally formulated shape – if not in the form of laws (*canones*), at least in the form of statutory orders. In any case they always have effects that can be asserted with the means of canon law or indeed by state church law means – there is not a possibility of appeal. A post-1870 execution of the teaching office that did not strictly keep to the borders of the dogma did not *need* formally to speak *ex cathedra*. It can prevent resistance simply through the normal juridical efficiency of its statements.

Rome ruled the Church between the two Councils according to this basic model. Rome did not cede anything of its own authority to the dioceses; disciplinary matters were centrally regulated – soon through the new code of Canon Law of 1917, transposed into legal norms. Doctrinal problems among theologians that were of more regional importance, for example the discussion concerning the theses of the so-called "modernists," Rome appropriated for itself, and made these problems, because of this appropriation, public for the first time in the entire Church. The nuncios – where concordats and diplomatic relations could be reached – became instruments of surveillance of the local Churches, and only Bishops with very powerful personalities defied the nuncios face to face. A practice developed that can only be characterized thus: the entire Roman Curia, each decision maker of a Roman office, participated practically in the primacy of jurisdiction of the Pope, and even in the infallibility of his teaching office.

This reveals an internal problem: The Pope cannot, in actuality, personally decide everything. But the dogma grants primacy and an infallible teaching office only to him. This of course does not exclude someone else doing the groundwork, but it does exclude independent decisions of offices, based on their own authority, *in the sphere of the primatial authority of the Pope*, although such decisions in reality are unavoidable. The result in practice: a maximalist interpretation of the Dogma of 1870 that for many Catholics leads to the observation: we would be happy if "Rome" would just stick strictly to the Dogma of 1870 and the boundaries that were drawn there – we would still have much to discuss. We shall mention just a few details concerning the main methods of Church governance that will clarify the explosive nature of the Second Vatican Council.

ENCYCLICALS AND INSTRUCTIONS

It was after the First Vatican Council that the method of a papal letter, the "encyclical," was developed into a real device of papal doctrinal pronouncement. The Pope discussed in the form of encyclicals matters that earlier would have belonged to a Council. Theological questions (for example, in connection with modernism, Church relationships, methods of Biblical interpretation, later the so-called "Nouvelle théologie"), social questions (the "Social Encyclicals" of Leo XIII and Pius XI), education questions, political questions (*Vigilanti cura*, Pius XI against the Nazis), liturgical questions, questions of piety (the Marian Encyclicals), Church music – the number of encyclicals soared. The "Instructions" are of almost the same weight, above all those from the Congregation for the Doctrine of the Faith, which at that time still was called *Sanctum Officium* – documents that always had to be personally approved by the Pope.

We could say: Encyclicals, Instructions, and similar teaching documents are not statements of the infallible teaching office, and the discussion then could, with complete justification, continue. However, Pius XII did away with this idea in the Encyclical *Humani generis*, which contained the famous "Encyclical paragraph." When the Popes take positions in Encyclicals on questions that up to that time were subject to open discussion, then these questions are, according to the intentions of these Popes, immediately withdrawn from open discussion. The Scripture passage "Who hears you, hears me" (Luke 10:16) would be relevant here, and therefore the argument that infallible doctrinal decisions are not at issue would not hold water.

A boundary was stepped over here, and again a line to the Second Vatican Council appears. Had this Encyclical paragraph been followed, there could not have been a Second Vatican Council. Resolutions were made at the Second Vatican Council that clearly exceeded what was laid down in the influential Encyclical of Pius XII. Further discussions were held, particularly on ecumenical themes, against orders.

With this we are now at the immediate prehistory of the Second Vatican Council.

V. JOHN XXIII

It is difficult here not to be detailed and clear, but we have to force ourselves. Some things about this great Pope will be handled in more detail later in the book.

PIUS XII AND JOHN XXIII

In the early morning hours of the 9th of October, 1958, Pope Pius XII died. I still remember vividly: A fellow student, who had heard the early news, came to me and said, in a reverent, subdued voice, "The Holy Father is dead!"

Nothing illuminates better how this man, for us Catholic theology students, embodied the Church at that time: the sometimes unloved, sometimes perceived as oppressive, but powerful, respected Church, which we, despite everything, were determined to serve obediently. We theology students could conceive that *non-Catholic* contemporaries were angry with the Church, hated her, mocked her in literature and art, but we could not conceive that there were *Catholics*, indeed theologians, who complained bitterly about the dictatorial ruling style of the Pope. Who would follow him, and what would the Church without a Pius XII look like?

It was a tense Conclave, without favorites. Only gradually did the majority vote become evident, for the Patriarch of Venice, the scholarly

Church Historian (his specialty was Patristic Theology) and experienced diplomat of the Curia, who had served in difficult lands such as Turkey: for Angelo Roncalli, who chose the name John XXIII.

A greater contrast to Pius XII cannot be imagined: the farmer's son from a north Italian village near Bergamo – the successor of the Roman from an old family; the heavy man, who suggested that the bearers of the "*Sedia gestatoria*" had to receive a special bonus from him – successor of the gaunt Pius; the man, who secretly snuck out of the Vatican, in order to speak with simple people in Rome – successor of a virtually mythic royal figure; the man, who of himself said: "They'll get accustomed to me just like they'd get accustomed to a simple parish priest" – successor of the man who loved solitude more than anything, from whom the gardeners ran, when he went for his walks in the Vatican garden, the man, who even in the Conclave, after the papal election, could not resist making a joke ("All Popes with the name of 'John' had short pontificates") – successor of a Pope for whom every simple address to an audience turned into a teaching office explanation with the intention of reminding all theologians of the Catholic world of their duty.

Over night the new Pope changed the face of the Church – not through doctrinal and disciplinary decisions, but through his humanity. Suddenly there were papal jokes and papal anecdotes, and not whispered behind a protective hand! (What whisky does the Pope drink? Answer: Johnny Walker.) The Pope was always worth a magazine story. The Pope unexpectedly invited his last visitor of a morning to lunch. In short: the Pope carried conviction – this Pope who, in the essentials, maintained the protocol, wore the cumbersome tiara, which his successor put aside for the first time, used "we" even in the less official addresses, simply because he thought that this was necessary and that he, against his feelings, must learn to do things this way. This Pope carried conviction, who never in his dreams thought to reform the Church in the sense of the worldwide well-known Hans Küng (who respects him so much); who made diplomatic mistakes for which no one blamed him; who allowed himself to be carried on the *Sedia gestatoria*; who in his spiritual statements, demonstrated above all in his "Spiritual Diary," expressed himself in a way that can appear to us completely distant and foreign, because it was the clerical piety of the 19th century.

This man now led the Church – and had, as noted at the beginning, the "inspiration" of the Council. It became the work to which, considered in hindsight, his entire life coursed, his life's work.

THE PARADOX OF JOHN XXIII

The figure and work of Pope John XXIII are a theological and political paradox, almost a contradiction. The tensions between his nature and his work are held together only through his unique personality, which mocks all conceivable theoretical contradictions.

The man, who according to ecclesial origin, theological education, and personal piety was completely a Catholic priest of the end of the 19th century, beginning of the 20th century in Europe, in Italy, wanted to make Catholics, as he said in his Pentecost address of 5 June 1960, "Citizens of the world," the way the entire world is meant when we honor Jesus as the Savior of the world. The man who, as a young priest, on the day after his ordination, in a "feeling of complete devotion" made a resolution, indeed "the holy vow," "to be faithful to the Seat of Holy Peter," and who as Pope did not allow the slightest doubt as to whether he knew his prerogatives of primacy and would share them with no one, convened a Council that according to his intention should function free and spontaneously and lead the Church from the structure of the centrally ruled "complete society" to *communio*, to the community of dioceses. The man who had had as a slogan of his priestly life, "to recognize and to do the will of God," who placed his papal office under the slogan *oboedientia et pax*, Obedience and Peace, and who was never troubled by a Reformation concern about "righteousness of works" because he had never read a line of Protestant theology, created the foundation for a dialogue among Churches and of an ecumenical theology, a foundation that is still of vital importance today. If it is his personality alone that allowed this paradox to exist, then this means that on the theoretical, theological, dogmatic, political level, the tension cannot be evened out. Only the larger force of a convincing and credible humanity was capable of this. What have we said with this! Is John the living Catholic counterpart for Dietrich Bonhoeffer's experience of feeling as a Christian more at home among the "religionless," who had *no* theoretical theological problems, than he did among Christians?

But we must here break off our portrait of John XXIII, and recommend those who are interested to the available biographies.

VI. THE ANNOUNCEMENT OF THE COUNCIL

PLANS FOR THE COUNCIL

As already mentioned, John XXIII, looking back, described the plan for a Council as a sudden inspiration granted to him on the day before the famous January 20th, 1959 conversation with Cardinal Tardini. The older biographical portrayals have relied on this. Today we know, from recently opened sources, that the Pope's description of a sudden inspiration condensed thinking and activities from the previous months. As his biographer, Peter Hebblethwaite, has formulated it, "the decisive moment" appeared to him as "a moment of decision." Of course the moment was decisive: The plan for a Council, ripened and even discussed with the closest confidants, now had to be discussed with his most important co-worker who had not yet been informed. Only if the Secretary of State placed himself "at the head of the movement" would it be possible to overcome the expected resistance of the Curia. Therefore the conversation of the 20th of January 1959 retains its historical importance for the Council. It was not, however, the date of the decision. We cannot say for certain that John XXIII moved in on the day of his coronation in St. Peter's with a prepared plan for a Council in his head. It is even less likely that Angelo Roncalli had brooded for a long time on a plan for a Council, worked on his promotion, and then as Pope had the chance to set the plan into motion. A Council "did not lie in the air." Quite the opposite: all the remarks about Councils in the doctrinal manuals treat the theme "Council" with the undertone of a purely theoretical possibility. Anecdotes about this or that theologian who harbored as his life's dream to be a Council theologian were circulated as examples of lack of reality.

But plans for a Council actually lay in secret compartments in the Vatican offices. Pius XI had thought about a continuation of the First Vatican Council, one that would conclude the Council, but had abandoned the project because of the difficulties. Pius XII, the Pope who can be considered the high point of a papal development built on the foundation of the First Vatican Council, a development that caused a future Council to appear superfluous, had a Council in mind from the beginning of his time in office, and had preparations underway. These preparations were known only in papal diplomatic circles and did not reach the public. The perusal of these preparations had enlightened Pius XII about the difficulties to be expected from a Council, and he did not pursue the plan.

This explains why the head of the *Sanctum Officium*, Cardinal Alfredo Ottaviani, while still in the Conclave from which John emerged as Pope, let fall the word "Council." The Archbishop of Palermo did the same a little later, in a conversation. It is understandable that exactly these two Council Fathers, who belonged to the strictly conservative group and attempted to put brakes on the Council where they could, later took the credit for having introduced Pope John to the idea of a Council. But why did they apply the brakes, if they were in favor of the Council?

The secret content of the preparations influenced two events in the pontificate of Pius XII; these two events, as we know today, were intended in a certain way as substitutes for a Council and therefore are indicative of what sort of Council it would have been. In 1950 Pius XII published the Encyclical *Humani generis*, a settling of accounts with all theological currents of the last half century; this encyclical contained the Encyclical Paragraph of which we have just spoken. Pope Pius XII proclaimed on 1 November 1950 the Dogma of the Assumption of Mary into Heaven, a great setback to the nascent ecumenical endeavors in the Church. A Council under Pius XII would have fixed the contents of *Humani generis* and then, as a crowning conclusion, proclaimed the Marian Dogma. This view of how a Council under Pius XII would have looked is supported by the fact that a third of the notes in drafts of the dogmatic topics available at the opening of the Second Vatican Council refer to *Humani generis*; the drafts bore the mark of the Roman Curia and contained sentences from the First Vatican Council and from the Anti-Modernism documents of the turn of the century. In a word: it would have been a doctrinal and defensive Council.

JOHN XXIII'S IDEA OF A COUNCIL

After taking office, Pope John had read a few of the preparations from the time of Pius XII. He knew, without long consideration, that he would *not* convene *this* Council. The details of his idea for the Council developed in the following years. In a matured form we encountered the idea first in the opening speech, to which we must return in the following chapter. It is clear on the basis of recently available sources that the resolutions that the Council passed are in no way those with which Pope John had reckoned; of course he, from everything that we know, would never have subverted them. From the beginning it is clear: "his" Council should not be pre-occupied with clearing up questions of doctrine and discipline, but should concern itself with the witness of the Church in the modern world. It should be, as he himself named it, a "pastoral" Council. The basis of the resistance to the plan of the Council becomes clear. The resistance was not necessarily a resistance to the plan of a Council, but to an idea of a Council that turned its back on the preparations already made by the men of the Curia. In any case, the question of *which* intention John pursued with the Council is more important than the biographical question of how he got the idea to hold a Council; this question is now more or less answered. We shall encounter again the question of the intentions of the Pope.

But first the question had to be dealt with: "How do I tell my child?" – that is, those who would have to carry the major part of the work of preparation, the men of the Roman Curia. In January of 1959 Pope John had made his unalterable decision. He had already mentioned his intentions to a very few confidants. One could not rely absolutely on discretion, particularly since the Pope himself had difficulties not letting his tongue run away with him. Therefore he called together the seventeen cardinals who were in Rome for a discussion to be held on the 25th of January, 1959, at the end of a Mass in the Abbey Church of St. Paul-Outside-the-Walls (San Paolo fuori le mura).

THE ANNOUNCEMENT

The choice of this particular church for the meeting did not seem out of the ordinary. St. Paul-Outside-the-Walls was, since his time as a student in Rome, one of the favorite churches of Pope John. The visit seemed like the end of the obligatory visits to the main churches in Rome, visits that every new Pope must complete.

After the Mass the Pope withdrew with the cardinals to the chapter room of the Benedictine cloister connected with the church and addressed them. A few of the cardinals had been informed of what was to happen, the others had no clue. The Pope attempted at first to make all well disposed to his idea: he paid tribute to their, anti-modern, anti-Modernist, and partly militantly anti-communist prevailing mood.

"We know that not only many friendly and enthusiastic circles, but also those that are malicious and vacillating, are looking with suspense at the new Pope." He spoke further of his double responsibility as Bishop of Rome and Shepherd of the universal Church and referred to the difficulties of a city, that "in the course of forty years has become a completely different city from the one we first became acquainted with in our youth ... A true beehive full of people, out of which an uninterrupted humming of confused voices, seeking after harmony, resounds." On the one side the Pope sees that the grace of Christ still works and produces its fruits of "spiritual increase, salvation, and holiness." On the other side he focused his gaze on those, who "misuse and endanger human freedom, reject faith in Christ, the Son of God, the Savior of the World and Founder of the Church, in that they devote themselves completely to the so-called earthly goods, under the insinuations of the one whom the Gospel names the Prince of Darkness, the Prince of this World – as Jesus Himself named him at the Last Supper – who organizes the confrontation and the battle against Truth and Good and strengthens the division between the two cities of St. Augustine and thereby always pursues his attempts to sow confusion, in order even, if that were possible, to deceive the Chosen and to bring about their destruction."

All this awakened a resolution "in the heart of the humble priest, whom the obvious chance of the divine Providence, although completely unworthy, had led to the heights of the Papacy."

And then John fixed his gaze on the seventeen cardinals present: "Venerable Brothers and Beloved Sons! Trembling with emotion, but at the same time with humble resolution, we put before you the name and the plan of a double solemn event: a Diocesan Synod of the City of Rome and an Ecumenical Council for the universal Church."

So it was out in the open, and the resistance began immediately. John responded to a Prelate of the Curia who, in the next weeks, thinking of six years of preparatory work for the First Vatican Council, objected that it would be impossible to organize a Council for 1963: "Good, then we'll open it in 1962." Which is, of course, what happened.

CHAPTER TWO

"WITH A BRAVE LEAP"

PREPARATION FOR THE COUNCIL – AGAINST ALL RESISTANCE

I. RESISTANCE: NOT ONLY IN THE ROMAN CURIA

1. OBEDIENCE ACCORDING TO ONE'S OWN JUDGMENT?

The drama of the new Pontificate had reached its high point three months after its beginning. Would the "tragic moment" now follow, the moment that foreshadows the catastrophic end of the drama? This seemed possible given the reactions of the seventeen Cardinals who, except for Tardini and a few others, were the first to hear of the Pope's plan. As John remarked later: "We could have expected that the Cardinals, as soon as they had heard our announcement, would have gathered around us, in order to express their agreement and their good wishes. Instead of this" – and here the Pope maintains a benevolent interpretation – "a pious and profound silence. Explanations followed in the next few days." And what kind of explanations!

Let us first notice the bold assumptions under the friendly cover of the Pope's speech. They correspond exactly to the pre-conciliar dogmatic situation laid down in canon law. "We could have expected immediate agreement and good wishes," said the Pope. It was clear that the Pope alone could convene a Council; according to canon law he held all the cards that would enable him to reach the result he wished, or at least to prevent any undesired result. It was also clear that the Cardinals, because of their calling and their explicit promise made at the bestowal of the purple, were duty bound to unconditional obedience to the Pope.

We know from other remarks that the Pope was fully aware of the dogmatic and legal status of his office. He said once, about the people of the Curia, "They are industrious men, but they don't govern the Church. I have that office." John could be as absolute, as intolerant of "ifs" and "buts," as his predecessor. The humane, even sometimes elegant, manner in which he got his way should not disguise this. If he did *not* get his way, it was only because he did not *want* to.

This was also the case with the Council. A "democratically" minded Pope would have had to give up the project, or at the very least would have had to dedicate much more time to it; so much time that, as many certainly hoped, the problem would have been settled by his death. The Pope was too sensitive not to have felt these speculations, and he was also enough of a realist to recognize what truth they contained. This is why he pressed forward with such alacrity, against all warnings about the six years' preparation time for the First Vatican Council. He countered such speculation and the resistance fed by it with a demand for his papal prerogative, flawlessly grounded in the First Vatican Council. In August of 1961, a good year before the opening of the Council, he expressed this with words that were ironic, mocking, and critical of the inconsistency of the opponents of the plan for a Council: they demanded obedience from others in their rebellion against the highest office of the Church; they represented themselves as working in tandem with this highest office while creating obstructions when curial obedience was demanded: "When on the 28th of October, 1958, the Cardinals of the Holy Roman Church chose me, at the age of 77, to be the leader of the entire flock of Christ, the idea spread that I would be a Pope of provisional transition. And now I am already in the fourth year of my Pontificate and I have an immense program to complete, a program that has the attention of the entire world. For my part, I consider important what was said of St. Martin: 'He did not fear death, but he did not refuse to live.'"

There is a paradox: John XXIII succeeded with the Council because he used his office without restraint and was averse to any "conciliar tendencies" toward a division of power.

This makes the following conclusion even more important: John XXIII did not have the unconditional loyalty of his co-workers when this loyalty demanded something that did not correspond to their own ideas. The criticism of the plans of the Pope, even the dismay over them, soon became loud and public. At least so public that the Pope heard of it and, when the criticism went far enough, he leaked it to the greater public.

2. VOICES OF CRITICISM

A remark from Cardinal Siri, the Archbishop of Genoa, a particularly change-averse churchman who in 1978 came very close to becoming Pope: "It will take the Church 50 years to recover from the wrong paths of John XXIII." Cardinal Spellman, the Archbishop of New York, was so shocked by the announcement of the Council on January 25th, 1959, that he said: "I don't believe that the Pope wanted to convene a Council, but he was pressed into it by people who twisted his words." What sort of picture of the new Pope is expressed by these words! And what an example of how the words of the Pope can be twisted until they conform to a certain view.

Cardinal Lercaro, the Archbishop of Bologna, who played a very important and beneficial role in the Council particularly in the area of liturgical reform, was quoted as saying: "How can he [the Pope] dare to convene a Council, after 100 years and only 3 months after his election? Pope John is hasty and impulsive. His inexperience and his lack of education led him to this step, to this paradox. An event like this will ruin his already weak health and cause the collapse of the entire structure of his alleged moral and theological virtues." These words are an example of how the criticism leveled against the plan for a Council consisted not only of practical objections but also of only barely restrained disdain for the farmboy on the Papal throne (notice the reference to the Pope's "lack of education").

Even Giovanni Battista Montini, the Archbishop of Milan, who later as Pope Paul VI would so energetically lead the Council and bring it to a close, on the evening of the day of the announcement called up his old confidant, the Orationist Father Giulio Bevilacqua: "This holy old boy doesn't seem to notice what a hornets' nest he's stirring up." Bevilacqua gave the right answer: "Don't worry, Don Battista, let it be, the Holy Spirit is still awake in the Church!"

Criticism came also in a more "elegant" form, the curial attempt to criticize without jeopardizing career advancement. An example so outrageously absurd that it has to be preserved for posterity: In the

Divinitas, the periodical of the Lateran University in Rome (where the diplomatic next generation of the Curia is educated), an article appeared in 1962 with the title "The Unity of the Faith and the Unification of the People in the Teaching of Pope John XXIII." The author was the (at that time) prelate and Professor Dino Staffa. The author names three constitutive factors of church unity: Thomism, the juridical structure concretized in the Church law book, the *Codex Iuris Canonici* (CIC), and the Latin language. The reasons given for the choice of these three factors were: the relevance of Thomism as the Church's normative theology is not "culturally conditioned" (this comment was directed against representatives of a theology emancipated from neo-Scholasticism); in the CIC Roman law is preserved as the heritage of the civilized world, and therefore the divine-legal structure of the Church is as "precise as mathematics"; Latin as the language of the Church is the resolution of the Babylonian confusion of tongues. Not one of these three factors applies to the Uniate Eastern Churches: they have no intention of committing themselves to the theology of Thomas Aquinas, they do not speak Latin in the liturgy or anywhere else, and they have their own Church law, different from the CIC; the CIC explicitly shows consideration for this Church law. If these were actually constitutive factors of the unity of the Church, any kind of Church community with the non-uniate Eastern Churches or with the Churches of the Reformation would be ruled out forever. I venture to suggest that all this could not have been overlooked by the intelligent author of the article. If he was conscious of these problems with his three constitutive factors, then the article can only be understood as an attempt at massive criticism of what the immanent Council, with the agreement of the Pope, obviously intended: the emphasis on Thomism went against the intention to get involved theologically in the challenges of the time; the emphasis on the CIC and its "mathematical precision" (something that even conservative Catholic canon lawyers dispute) was intended to torpedo the plan for its revision; the emphasis on Latin was an attack on the intention to allow the vernacular in the liturgy. This is characteristic: John XXIII suffered under criticism and disdain from his "Apparat," but he did not react with force, but with determination and confidence, rarely with even gentle pressure. Pius XII would have reacted with a couple of dismissals and demotions, and the resistance would have quickly collapsed.

John pursued his plans with crafty diplomatic chess moves that proved more than a match for any resistance. One of these chess moves was his appointments of Cardinals. These appointments are the right of the Pope, with which no one can interfere; they offered the opportunity to set an unmistakable signal. Pope John XXIII did something revolutionary. In 1586 Pope Sixtus V had decreed that the College of Cardinals should not have more than 70 members: this number had biblical associations, for example the 72 disciples of Christ, or the 72 wise men who, according to legend, translated the Old Testament from Hebrew into Greek, each producing the same translation. When John XXIII began his pontificate, the College of Cardinals contained only 52 cardinals, 12 of whom were over 80 years of age. Two weeks after his enthronement the Pope announced that on the 15th of December 1959 a *consistorium*, a gathering of all the Cardinals, would take place; at this *consistorium* he would appoint 23 new Cardinals.

Once again a holy, long-observed rule was broken. John repeated that many times and "created" (*creatura* is the official designation of someone appointed as Cardinal) altogether 55 cardinals. Paul VI continued along this line and, just as his predecessor, practiced politics with his appointments. John appointed as Cardinal the first Filipino (Cardinal Santos), the first African (Cardinal Rugambwa), as well as Bishop Döpfner of Berlin – later of Munich – who was only 45 years old when he became a Cardinal. John XXIII also appointed as Cardinal the Jesuit Augustin Bea, who was the rector of the Pontifical Biblical Institute and had been Pius XII's confessor. Bea was not a Bishop and at first, by his own wish, did not become one; John later gave into pressure and consecrated Bea as Bishop. There was no rule that only Bishops could become Cardinals, but the long custom has been that Cardinals who are not Bishops at the time of their appointments are consecrated at least as "Titular Bishops," that is bishops whose dioceses exist in name only. (Many of these dioceses once existed in the lands where Islam took the place of Christianity as the majority religion.)

This massive internationalization and expansion of the College of Cardinals was decisive for the Council, since the influence of the Cardinals – it became almost a given, that each national Church had at least one Cardinal – on the Council was naturally huge. The expansion and the internationalization made the Cardinals of the Curia into a minority. The consequences are a question of accounting.

II. OBJECTIVE –
AGAINST MANY EXPECTATIONS AND FEARS

1. A FLOOD OF EXPECTATIONS

It is now time to consider more carefully what John actually wanted with the Council. The resistance against the Council was based above all in the fact that none of the traditional grounds for the convening of a Council actually existed. There was no crisis in the area of Doctrine that would have made the solemn rejection of an error necessary. There was no need to close ranks against a threat from the outside (along the lines of the late medieval threat from the Ottoman Empire). There was no need to introduce "a reform of the head and the members," since the situation of the Church was in no way comparable to that at the time of the Reform Councils of the 15th century. Would it not be better to address whatever reforms might be needed by means of intelligent central government, in contact with the dioceses, rather than by means of a mammoth event, at which chaotic discussion could be expected? (Chaotic discussion that did, in part, occur.)

In hindsight we can see what the Council, despite all the theoretical objections, brought about: the clarification, the completion of the structure of the Church in the tension-filled relationship between episcopacy and Petrine office – as we have already described in the previous chapter. And: the Church's abruptly adult and lived consciousness of itself as a World Church – we shall speak more of this at the end of the book. But *before* the Council we had only the experiences of Church history and the canon law and dogmatic handicaps. It required theological, legal, and political fantasy to imagine a concrete objective that would be more than a gigantic show; it is not surprising that the members of the curial bureaucracy were the last who were able, or wanted, to engage in this imagining. But the worldwide episcopacy and the laity could do it! This led to the first tensions. The Pope had the igniting idea – and it remained really *his* idea; as chapter 1 showed, the most important effect of earlier preparations and all the ideas conveyed to him was his decision to convene another Council. His piety was such that he was prepared to entrust himself, against all too human cares and fears, to the guidance of the Holy Spirit, to whom he consistently credited his idea for a Council. He had no fear

of the expected conflicts; his faith led him to believe that the guidance
of the Holy Spirit would assert itself *in* these conflicts. The accusation
that he acted rashly – or, put more positively, the demand that everything from the outset had to be predictable and calculated – did not
bother him. *However* – this meant that that the Pope did not from the
very beginning have a clear idea of what the Council should and could
achieve. His biographers all maintain that at least in the first phase
of the preparatory work and partly in the year of the opening of the
Council the statements of the Pope about the objective of the Council
remain curiously vague – with consequences that will be discussed
in the next chapter. On the other hand, among theologians and laity,
in part encouraged by the Bishops, the idea of a Council released a
flood of accumulated reform expectations, which reached from reform
of the liturgy to a new process for dogmatic statements, from curial
reform to decentralization, even democratization, of the Church. This
freedom of discussion, which he was determined to guarantee, enabled
the Pope to clarify what *was not* in question. In the interplay of the
discussion in the entire Catholic world the goals the Council should
set for itself and the themes it should treat became clearer to the Pope.
More exactly: John XXIII saw how his original intuitive idea could
and should be concretized.

Two books played a particular role in this discussion, because they
attracted the interest of the Pope and the displeasure (and occasionally also the clandestine joy) of the Curia and exerted influence in the
Church. The first was a book written by the Archbishop of Paderborn
(a diocese in the northern parts of Germany) and later Cardinal
Lorenz Jaeger, with the title *Das ökumenische Konzil, Kirche und
Christentum* (This was translated by A.V. Littledale in 1961, under the
title *The Ecumenical Council, the Church and Christendom*). The other
book, Hans Küng's *Konzil und Wiedervereinigung. Erneuerung als Ruf
in die Einheit*, was translated into a number of other languages and
intensely discussed in the media. Küng, with his well known candid-
ness, went so far as indirectly to recommend an agenda for the Council
that would introduce an inner-Church reform corresponding to the
justified demands of the Reformation: recognition of the Reformation
as a *religious* event; more intensive appreciation for the meaning of
the Bible and more use of the Bible in theology and liturgy; more lay
participation and vernacular in the liturgy; an emphasis on the "common priesthood" of all baptized; the Church in dialogue with other

cultures; freeing the papacy from political connections and involvement; reform of the Roman Curia and dismantling of the "Index of
Forbidden Books." Küng's suggestions proved to be prophetic: at least
in modified form all seven demands were adopted in the documents of
the Council. As Peter Hebblethwaite remarked in his 1984 biography,
John XXIII, "Never again would a single theologian have such influence [on the Council]."

What, then, in the course of time was singled out as the binding
objective of the Council?

2. NOT A COUNCIL OF UNION

From the very beginning the Pope had coined the key word
"*Ecumenical* Council": a "Council for the universal Church" (from
the announcement address). This Church was, of course, the Roman
Catholic Church and the uniate Eastern Churches, not the whole of
Christianity. Once again the strongly traditional ground upon which
the Pope stood evinces itself. The Pope paid no attention to the discussions that had been held since medieval times inside and outside
of the Church, discussions that reached a conclusion that the term
"ecumenical" should be reserved for those Councils that represented Christianity in its entirety. The Pope understood by "ecumenical"
Council exactly what canon law understood: the Council of *the* universal Church that according to its self-understanding remained, after the splits, the true Church of Jesus Christ – the Roman Catholic
Church.

It was immediately obvious that the Second Vatican Council could
not be a Council of union in the style of the late medieval Councils
(Lyon in 1274, Ferrara-Florence in 1439-1442), at which re-unification negotiations with the Eastern Churches took place and could
be, at least for a short time, successfully concluded. The Pope was
enough of a realist to know that, other than in the medieval times
and even at Trent, the unity of *the* Church by means of the unification of *the Churches* could be only a long-term goal. Other than at the
First Vatican Council, no formal invitations to participate were sent to
the non-Roman Churches, even to the non-uniate Eastern Churches,
with which the Pope had maintained close contact since his time in
Bulgaria, Greece, and Turkey. The Pope had these non-uniate Eastern
Churches in mind when he gave the Council the goal *also* of seeking

the unity of the Church. Primarily, though, the key word "unity" meant the inner unity, the unanimity of the Roman Catholic Church itself. This was the pre-requisite and means by which the Church, opening itself up to the world, would pass on its message in a more credible manner to this world.

This does not mean that the overcoming of the division of Christianity into separated Churches was only a minor theme for John XXIII. This might have been the case for the leading men of the Curia, among whom no one was knowledgeable enough to deal with the question, but not for the Pope. When the Pope's announcement speech in St. Paul-Outside-the-Walls was finally made public in April of 1959, the world read that the Council would "mean the building up and the joy of Christians ... a further invitation to the faithful in separated communities also to follow us with good will on this search for unity and grace." What the Pope actually said on January 25, 1959, sovereignly disregarding the normal official rules about what could and could not be said, was: "... and a *friendly* and further invitation to *our brothers* in the separated *Christian Churches, to participate with us at this feast of grace and brotherliness,* for which so many souls in each corner of the world hope." The words printed here in italics are those that the anxious translators and editors weakened, so that they agreed with the canon law.

The original text was also, of course, not a formal invitation; in this original text the unity of the Church through the reversal of the Churches' split remained a theme subordinate to the main goal of new witness to the world. The ensuing public discussion of this subordinate theme in the countries traditionally more influenced by the Churches of the Reformation (for example, Germany, Switzerland, Holland, France, and the USA) brought this theme of the unity of Christianity more into the limelight and attracted more attention in Rome and from Pope John. The importance of this theme of Christian unity gained considerable significance when John XXIII appointed the rector of the Pontifical Biblical Institute, the aforementioned Jesuit priest Augustin Bea, as Cardinal and assigned him the direction of the ecumenical matters at the Council. We shall return to this topic.

The first public clarity resulted from a press conference held by Cardinal Tardini on the 30th of October 1959. He announced that the Pope had a plan to invite the separated Churches to send *official observers.* This proved to be a good solution. It did not obligate the non-Roman Churches to anything, therefore sparing them long and tortuous internal conflicts; it did not obligate the Church of Rome to anything, therefore preventing pre-Council division. Nevertheless, the status of *official* observers gave possibilities of influence to representatives of *Churches* without giving them a vote. We shall speak of this in more detail later.

3. WHAT THEN SHOULD THE GOAL OF THE COUNCIL BE?

An often-told anecdote relates the story of a visitor asking John XXIII what he expected from the Council. The Pope went to the window of his workroom, opened it, and said: "We expect that the Council will let in fresh air." What should, what might, the fresh air blow into the room?

Before Roncalli's departure from Venice to attend the Conclave, from which he would not return to Venice, he told the seminarians of his diocese: "The Church is young; she remains, as always in her history, capable of change!" This was certainly a programmatic statement! Change, according to Roncalli's statement to the seminarians, should always occur; this was no uncertain sentiment on his part.

Pius XII, originally a canon lawyer and a curial diplomat, had never done any pastoral work. It is understandable that he understood and allowed "change" only when adaptations to realities were necessary; these adaptations always had to answer to theology and canon law. His life's work was to guide the Church safely and if necessary with flexibility through the dangers of the time and, if possible, to develop new spheres of activity for the Church. John XXIII had been a professor of Church History; like Pius XII, John XXIII had served neither as curate nor as pastor. He had, however, worked for two decades in pastoral care on the administrative level; these supervisory roles provided him with rich experience, even beyond the borders of his own country. From this time comes his burning and enduring interest on a Christian answer to the "social question," which at that time, despite *Rerum Novarum*, Leo XIII's "Social Encyclical", still awaited an answer. After this Roncalli served as a curial diplomat in different, but always difficult, missions: first in the Balkans, then in Turkey, and finally in post-war France (where he annoyed the French politicians by visiting not only French garrisons but also German prisoners of war and where he, much to the displeasure of Rome, protected the so-called "worker priests" as long as he could). Finally, since 1953, he had been Archbishop of Venice, a diocese that had difficult social problems. "Change" for Roncalli was a given, something he was well-acquainted with not only from the history of the Church but also from open encounters with the faithful of different cultures.

John began his papacy with the sober conviction that the faith owes it to the world not to reject its questions and anxieties, but to accept them as though they were the own questions of Christians. He coined a term *aggiornamento*, an idea with manifold means that will always be associated with John XXIII. Does it mean "adaptation"? This is how opponents understood the term and they sounded the alarm: so loudly that friends of the Pope endeavored in lectures and articles to prove that John XXIII, in contrast to his predecessor, had not carried out the shadows of a course change. Proof is no match, however, for clear facts. If it had been about "adaptation," then opponents would have been right to sound the alarm. What was meant with *aggiornamento*?

Aggiornamento was originally a merchant's term; *aggiornare* means to update books or registers. This is part of what John XXIII meant. According to the traditional Catholic understanding, what is of human manufacture in the Church can and must be adapted to the times. As we now know from recently published contemporary evidence, the Pope from the very beginning had an *aggiornamento* of canon law in mind, the later carried out and 1983 introduced revision of the CIC. Paul VI achieved even more than John XXIII in this area of adaptation of the changeable. He laid aside the tiara, the cumbersome three-tiered crown, shortened the trains of the Cardinals, got rid of the *Sedia gestatoria*, and tightened up the organizational structure of the Curia, just to name three examples. John XXIII did a few things in this regard as well. He got rid of the stilted style ("the luminous Holy Father," "the elected one, in his inspired and lofty address," "as we from illustrious lips have learned") in the *Osservatore Romano* (*Roman Observer*, the official newspaper of the Vatican) as well as the three genuflections required of employees when they arrived for consultations with the Pope.

However, *aggiornamento* is more than this in the usage of the Pope. Above all it means the internal renewal of the Church, the renewal and revival of the faith and of the community life in the Church. Faith and Christian living should be a matter of today and not a beautiful tradition without formative power for the present and the future.

Internal renewal if it is not to get stuck in mere inculcation of what is handed down means that faith and Christian living must develop a positive relationship with the world in which they exist. Faith and Christian praxis can only become alive if people believe that they develop strength and perspective for life that is experienced *now*, life that is as it is, not how the Church would like it to be. Neither simple adaptation nor "survival strategy" but the internal urgency of the matter results in faith's turn toward the world and a positive attitude toward the questions of the time.

There is certainly no doubt that this was not first and foremost in John XXIII's thoughts. After all, every living theology and every living ecclesial body lives from the constructive debate with the challenges of the times. Furthermore, it would be a grotesque injustice to accuse the Popes who were John XXIII's predecessors of inattention to the signs of the times. The opposite is the case, at least since Leo XIII. A difference does exist, however, and to identify this is at least in the sense of a collective judgment *not* an injustice, although this might require differentiation in the details. In the era of Pius IX, X, XI, and XII, the encounter with the "world" and the "time" was first and foremost *confrontation*; with John, this encounter is *dialogue*. *Before* John the world is an opposing, indeed a hostile challenge that must be countered; the members of the Church must be immunized against the world through clear direction as to what they as Christians must do and must ignore in this world. With John the world is a questioning world, to which the Church owes a helpful answer. Before John the Church is the *Societas perfecta*, the "complete society," that has everything that it needs; this complete society has something to give to the world, but the world, and particularly the other Churches in the world, has nothing to give to it. With John, for the first time, the idea that the Church must allow itself to be questioned by the world does not border on the obscene.

At this point the narrowness of the papal conception of renewal of the Church comes to light; this narrowness created problems at the Council that were almost insurmountable. If the Church must allow itself to be questioned by the time in which it lives and works, then this also pertains with regard to its proclamation. Just as with its ways of life, the ways and modes of expression of its proclamation, of its Dogmas, *could* be not "up-to-date": not understood any more and therefore not successful in its claim to open the way to human salvation. In a very general sense the proclamation also must undergo *aggiornamento*. How is this done?

It is completely absurd to accept that the Pope wanted to put up for consideration even a tiny bit of a defined Dogma. He did not have to be Pope to rule that out – it sufficed that he was a theologian and Churchman of *his* generation, with a completely neo-Scholastic education. Theologically he was characterized by the fundamental idea that the truth of the faith can be contained in sentences, if necessary in solemnly defined sentences, which as such could never be overhauled. The idea that words that at one time properly expressed the truth of the faith might at some other time be misconstrued in such a way that no one except for a couple of Church historians understand what was originally meant by them would never have occurred to John XXIII. Nonetheless he was enough of an historian to know that a change in the formulation of the truth of the faith had happened before.

This theological generation had the same means of reconciling change with preservation of proclamation and doctrine that my generation, in its student years, had: only the vague differentiation of a fixed "kernel" from a changing "husk"; by "husk" was meant the variety of terms and ideas by which the fixed kernel of truth was displayed for the faithful. To illustrate this by means of a Protestant-Catholic conflict: since the Council of Trent it has been a fixed "kernel" of the Catholic doctrine of justification that not "faith alone" but the unity of "faith, hope, and love" justifies humanity before God. Whether faith, hope, and love are most properly to be interpreted as *habitus* or as a movement in the soul is, can, and must be discussed.

It is now clear (as some theologians realized at that time), that this differentiation of kernel and husk is completely inadequate for gaining control over the problem of preservation and change in the realm of proclamation of doctrine. What can be done if the *kernel* produces the lack of understanding? Is this so-called "kernel" ever distinct from forms of speech, that is, distinct from "husk," which then would be not so easy to differentiate from the kernel? And further: might it not be the duty of the Church to stand by its word even if the world does not understand? Aren't there words of the language of faith that no Christian can do without, because they carry the facts of the faith with them? And if yes, then where are the borders between adaptation that is appropriately supported for the sake of the faith of the people and the necessity to risk the "folly of the cross," be it convenient or inconvenient?

Here the concept of *aggiornamento* fails; even more, it leads almost inevitably to a lack of clarity because it produced different expectations and fears according to the preconceptions of those who heard it.

4. A PASTORAL COUNCIL

It is clear that Pope John could not conquer this lack of clarity by means of a precise agenda. Even if he could have done this he would not have dared, because he would have prematurely taken a stance, provoking new resistance, in a theological discussion that had just begun in the Church. However, his kind of reaction or, more precisely, the agenda that he now actually did make, indicates that he at least had an intimation about, given his own theological assumptions, the impermissible problematic. People of a different stature would not have let themselves in for the risk of a Council; possibly this concern resonates in the critical voices that we have cited. It is typical that John did not entertain *this* doubt: he reacted in a different way. He set the Council primarily a *spiritual* task: a "pastoral Council."

He created actually almost a new type of Council – there had never been a Council that did not have the task of resolving doctrinal and juridical conflicts. This was something absolutely new: a Council that had as its chief aim the bringing together of the universal Church for the purpose of discussing, from a wide range of perspectives, how the proclamation of the Christian faith might best be affected in the world. It was clear that change might be decided upon so long as it was not subject to theological objection. The Pope had his own clear opinion about questions of doctrine; he did not, however, think himself capable, even as Pope, to discern from the very beginning the exact course of the immovable borders.

On the 30th of June 1959, at the opening session of the ante-preparatory commission of the Council, the Pope formulated the Council's objectives with the following words: the Church endeavored, "true to holy principles on which she is based and to the unchangeable [!] doctrine that her divine founder had entrusted to her …, with a brave leap to strengthen again her life and her cohesion, with regard also for the conditions and demands of the day." The consequence: he guaranteed complete freedom of discussion at the Council. The Holy Spirit would take care of the clarity. If the Holy Spirit did not, then the Pope would not be able to take his place – true to the words of Pius XI: "There are three segments of a Council: that of the Devil, who tries to confuse the documents; that of people, who contribute to the confusion; and that of the Holy Spirit, who clarifies everything." This, as "realists" might say, "naïvely pious" confidence manifested itself in a few important individual measures – or rather in their omission.

For example, although he was President of the Council according to canon law, Pope John XXIII did not enter the Council hall again after the opening until the closing meeting of the first session; he followed the debates on a television screen. Insiders report that the picture was on the entire day, but John only turned the sound up when a speaker particularly interested him. Or: when the Roman diocesan synod, called by John himself, passed horrifyingly petty resolutions, completely ignoring the intentions of the Pope, John was deeply disappointed. He did not, however, question the resolutions, but actually defended them in public. The diocesan synod continued the ban on priests' visits to movie theaters, theater, opera, and race tracks; priests were forbidden from watching too much television, frequenting bars and restaurants, and driving in cars alone with a woman: if the Holy Spirit did not hinder these bans, then one must simply wait until the Holy Spirit made his presence felt more decisively.

Pope John did interfere once, when the Council encountered its first crisis on the occasion of the discussion of the draft on Divine Revelation. Characteristically, however, the Pope did not use his authority in order to reserve the decision for *himself,* but so that the *Council,* on the basis of a new outline, could discuss further. The Pope as arbitrator in an important crisis: this understanding of the Petrine office is *one* decisive element in the current "progressive" discussion of the papal office. The successor of Paul VI, incidently, was much less hesitant in this regard.

The immediate theme of this chapter has been touched upon; this theme, after review of the basic issues, can now be more concisely discussed.

III. THE EXTERNAL PREPARATION: A BATTLE WITH THE DEVIL IN THE DETAILS

1. TECHNICAL PROBLEMS

At the time of the announcement of the Council voting members numbered around 2750. How could discussion sessions be held with these kinds of numbers? Anyone who sees a photo from a plenary session of the Council is stunned; the photos beg the question of how such a plenary session could possibly function. For comparison: the Council Fathers at the First Vatican Council numbered about 800. In 1962 that meant: including accompanying personnel and advisors quarters had to be found in Rome for around 10,000 people. (Obviously not in the Vatican.) Around 100 busses had to be rented, in order to transport the Fathers to the sessions in St. Peter and then to bring them back.

The Council hall was the broadside of St. Peter's, together with the platforms. Since the paths to the speaker's pulpit are very long, which would have required the speakers to walk for a long time, microphones were set up at each block of the seating plan. According to earwitness accounts, the loudspeaker system must have been excellent. And not to forget: in a side room off the right aisle of St. Peter's a refreshment bar was set up during the Council; this bar quickly gained the nickname of "Jonah Bar," a punning allusion to the Greek and Latin text of Matthew 16:17. It has been suggested that some events of the Council might have been influenced by the proximity of this bar.

2. THE PREPATORY COMMISSIONS

On the 17th of May, 1959, about four months after the announcement of the Council, the Pope formed the *Commissio antepraeparatoria*, the "Ante-preparatory Commission," the assembly that would set the preparations for the Council in motion. Cardinal Tardini, the chair of the Commission, requested that the Bishops, the Superiors of Orders, Catholic Universities and Faculties send in suggestions, "postulates," for the discussion program of the Council. 2821 Postulates were submitted. The *antepraeparatoria*, as it soon became known, sifted through the material and then passed it on to the responsible curial offices. These could make recommendations (*proposita*) and give suggestions (*monita*). On June 5th of 1960, the evening before Pentecost, John XXIII introduced the more detailed preparations with his *Motu proprio* entitled *Superno Dei nutu*. For the "Second Vatican Council" – the first time this designation was officially used – ten "preparing commissions" would be formed. Nine were to be organizational, and according to theme entrusted to the appropriate Roman offices. They were to deal with the following themes and problem areas: questions of doctrine (the Theological Commission), Bishops and the administration of dioceses, "discipline" (way of life) of clergy and people, the practice of the sacraments, studies and schools, orders, liturgy, the Oriental Churches, missions, lay apostolate. With the exception of the lay apostolate, they all had corresponding offices in Rome. The Pope named the heads of these offices as the chairs of the corresponding preparatory commissions.

The tenth commission was the so-called Central Commission, formed on the 16th of June, 1960. The chairs of the nine preparatory commissions (identical with the heads of the Roman congregations) and the chairs of the national and/or regional Bishops' conferences belonged to this Central Commission. The number of the members of this Central Commission eventually rose to 102 members and 29 advisors – the size of one of the larger of the German state parliaments! The individual commissions were also enlarged by new members. By the end of 1961, 827 people were busy with preparations for the Council; two-thirds of these were European (a statistic that would change at the Council).

These arrangements underscore an important difference between this Council and earlier Councils: members of the preparatory commissions were not only theologians and canon lawyers, who had no vote at the Council, but about half of them were also Bishops and the superiors of orders. This was no doubt an advantage: future Council Fathers could become experts at this preparatory stage, and were better prepared for the actual Council Commissions that would be formed at the Council itself.

The other difference appeared a clear disadvantage: The connection with the offices of the Curia. This subjected the preparatory work to the strong influence of curial officials, that is, of those who did not welcome the Council and who were suspected of plotting to delay or even to prevent the Council. The start of preparatory work did not augur well for a felicitous outcome; the men of the Curia took unrestrained advantage of their dominance.

Biographers are still puzzled about what John XXIII intended with this decision. For that reason the decision between the "John-myth" and the "John-paradox," mentioned above, begins at the very latest with this decision. The myth maintains: No one wants to think the Pope capable of not foreseeing what would come (and what we shall soon describe): the almost complete collapse of the agenda prepared under the influence of the Curia. Had he committed a catastrophic mistake? Later, from all this, through a sort of "dialectical change," much good does come: therefore the myth of Pope John would like to believe that he had foreseen all of this. His decision to name the Prefects of the Roman Congregations as Chairmen of the preparatory commissions would be, then, a chess move of real craftiness.

The myth, however, must be "de-mythologized." The sources that are now available to us leave no doubt: the Pope followed the genesis of the "Schemata" with great attention and sympathy. The marginal glosses he had entered to the texts tell the story not only of a careful reading of the texts but also of the Pope's frequent satisfaction, sometimes effusively expressed. There is not a hint of a disassociation from his closest colleagues who led the preparatory work. According to his own statements he was very sure that the agenda would find overwhelming support among the World Episcopacy. This also explains why the Pope, even at the beginning of the Council, was convinced he would be able to bring the Council to a close in only one session. This is also the reason why no plans were made concerning in which order the work on the planned documents of the Council might be divided among numerous sessions – no one expected that these sessions would be necessary. If the Pope experienced *one* tragic moment relative to the Council it must have been the moment when he realized that he himself would not experience the end of the Council: the agenda with which he was so satisfied was not accepted by the overwhelming majority of the World Episcopate. We shall return to this tragic moment, and its consequences, in the next chapter. For the time being, all this brings the "John-paradox" to its most extreme point. At the end of chapter one we were forced to realize that personality was stronger than theory in John XXIII. Despite this, it is hard to accept that this experienced, much traveled, and well educated man could in all earnestness believe that that "fresh air" that he wanted to let into the

Church through the Council could possibly flow from what he had read of the work of the preparatory commissions.

The "John-paradox" has its own contradictions. John did something that his biographer Peter Hebblethwaite characterized as the most important personnel decision of the Pope: he established the "Secretariat for the Promotion of the Unity of Christians" (known as the "Christian Unity Secretariat") and named the Jesuit Augustin Bea, whom he elevated to Cardinal, as its head. Since in the other preparatory commissions neither interest nor expertise in the area of ecumenical relationships of the Church existed – hardly a surprise, since the Curia was composed almost entirely of Italians, and the only Protestant Church that existed at that time in Italy was the small Church of the Waldensians, concerned above all with distancing itself from the Church of Rome – ecumenical matters could only find a place at the Council if a completely unique institution, distinct from the other Curial offices, took over the responsibility for them. This was the task of the Christian Unity Secretariat. In terms of protocol it was subordinate to the Congregations – it was "only" a Secretariat. The Pope, however, provided it with additional competencies and refrained from linking the Secretariat to one of the other offices; such a connection would have limited the Secretariat's freedom.

The establishment of the Christian Unity Secretariat, a suggestion of Archbishop Cardinal Jaeger of Paderborn, sent a clear signal. The non-Roman Churches should be, in so far as it was practically and legally possible, conversation partners at the Council. In warm and clear words the Pope, in the *Motu proprio*, defined the sense of the Christian Unity Secretariat: "In order to show in a particular way our love and our good will toward those who bear the name of Christ but are separated from this Apostolic Seat, and in order to enable them to follow the work of the Council and willingly to find the way to achieve that unity that Jesus beseeched from his Heavenly Father, we have established this special bureau or secretariat." The appointment of Bea proved to be a truly inspired choice. Bea searched in universities and seminaries throughout the world for experts on ecumenical questions. Since not many Italians had expertise in ecumenical questions, German, English, and French, rather than Italian, were the main languages spoken at the Secretariat. To the displeasure of many in the Curia the Christian Unity Secretariat became the first gateway for the "foreigners," who up till this point had been to some extent kept out of the preparatory commissions. And not only these "foreigners." The Christian Unity Secretariat had been assigned the task of contact with the non-Catholic Churches and their representatives. The skillful and charming Bea succeeded at this task so well that soon the non-Catholics were coming in and going out of the Secretariat. We shall discuss the consequences of this later. Put succinctly, Hebblethwaite does not exaggerate when he concludes that, without Bea, John XXIII would not have gotten the Council that he wanted. Bea "educated" the Pope for ecumenism. But: what could the Pope have hoped for from contact with non-Catholic Christendom, if he was so satisfied with the agenda? The John-paradox here achieves a provisional highpoint, a highpoint that will only be surpassed by what will be described in the next chapter. At one point, though, the myth and the paradox meet: John's determination to protect freedom of speech at the Council was never, even for a minute, in doubt. He was prepared to be surprised by what he had never thought of.

3. THE "SCHEMATA"

The name "schema" has long been given to the discussion and resolution agenda drawn up for the debates in a Council. They are composed – like the draft of a law – in the form of a potential Council resolution, and the discussion revolves around amending the draft (through so-called *Modi*, petitions for amendment), correcting the draft, or rejecting the draft. Whoever draws up the first draft, the "Schema," has the upper hand: he is in the better bargaining position, since the others are in the position of re-acting to his draft. The circumstance that in the preparatory commissions the dominant representatives of the Curia held the upper bargaining hand did not augur well for a felicitous outcome, as already mentioned. While these representatives spread the opinion that the Second Vatican Council would be the best prepared Council in Church history, many were already disappointed by the Council, even before it had begun. The Council itself would effect the change; whether the Pope had calculated exactly this turn of events is, as already indicated, a source of controversy. In any case, the following happened:

On the one hand, the 2821 postulates brought such a flood of material that drowning was the only option. On the other hand, the Pope left the commissions without directives; apparently intentionally, probably however not in order to let them stew in their own juice, but because he was scrupulously worried about interfering with the freedom of the discussion. The inevitable result: the commissions worked out, altogether, 69 drafts. Had they been passed, this would have meant 69 Constitutions, Decrees, and Declarations. The Central Commission, which had the task of examining the drafts, met for the first time on the 12th of June, 1961, and then another six times. The 69 Schemata were not, because of their origins, any sort of advance to new shores; they were much more a summary of papal declarations during the last decades and a continuance of the theology and praxis that dominated in Rome. How could they have been anything but this? And Pope John counted on the quick agreement of the Council!

These very drafts worked now like an admission of defeat. Without the dominance of the Curia such an admission would never have taken place. This way, the Council was forced in the statement on the prepared drafts to reflect on where the universal Church stood and where the universal Church wanted to stand.

Despite all the secrecy some of the content of the prepared drafts leaked out in the following period. But above all: the representatives of the national Churches already sat on the examining Central Committee, and they saw what was brewing. The Central Commission had been called "a Council before the Council." No one expected a revolution. But voices from the World Episcopacy soon became unmistakably audible: all the problems caused by world development must be tackled by the Council (a communication from the French Cardinals and Archbishops from the 26th of October, 1961). The Church must become universal in the true sense of the word (Cardinal Frings of Cologne, in Genoa on the 19th of November, 1961). Decentralization is necessary (Cardinal Alfrink of Utrecht). A deeper and broader ecumenical understanding is necessary (Archbishop Jaeger of Paderborn). Nature and function of the episcopacy in harmony with the Papacy, as well as a deepened self-understanding of the Church are the tasks of the Council; this would enable the Church to grasp the requirements of the time (Cardinal Montini of Milan). All this made it clear: the Curial course would, as had already happened in the Central Commission, encounter sharp opposition at the Council. Those who claimed to represent and lead the universal Church would be forced to hear what the universal Church really thought. Therefore there is hardly a Schema worked out by the preparatory commissions that eventually became the basis for the discussion at the Council. Not one of the original 17 Schemata of the Commission for the Discipline of Clergy and Laity was passed by the Council. Of the six Schemata of the Theological Commission under Cardinal Ottaviani, head of the *Sanctum Officium* and one of the most honorable but theological unbending traditionalists at the Council, only two were accepted by the Council, and only after fundamental re-working. Nine Schemata of the Commission on Sacraments received no approval from the Council. Only the Commissions for the Liturgy, for the Orders, and for the Lay Apostolate submitted Schemata, one apiece, that formed the starting point for Council resolutions. Other drafts were knitted together – details later – and thus entered into Council texts.

In short, it was a frustrating experience for those who after all had worked honorably and intensively for years. The work was not, however, for nothing: in a dialectical sense, it was a comprehensive lesson in how things could *not* be done (any more). The trip to Rome was worthwhile for the Council Fathers, to continue *this* groundwork.

4. THE ORDER OF BUSINESS

The intensive work of 1961 made it possible for the Council to be convened earlier than expected – just barely later than the Pope from the outset had planned. On Christmas Day, 1961, the Pope issued the Constitution *Humanae Salutis*, which called the Council for the following year. The exact dates followed on the 2nd of February, 1962: Opening Day would be the 11th of October, 1962. At the same time, the Christian Unity Secretariat issued invitations to the Churches not in union with Rome to send *official* observers. They were official representatives of the Churches without the right to vote, but with the right of participation in all sessions and, even more important, with the right to read all the drafts in all the stages of discussion. Suggestions for improvements in the drafts could be submitted to the Christian Unity Secretariat; the "observers" had more or less the status of privileged advisors. The Pope made sure at the beginning of the Council that the observers got the best seats in the Council Hall, on a platform at the left of the presidium, seen from the nave, to the right of the beginning of the transept.

Non-voting experts on the different topics of the Council were also invited, appointed by the Pope (who was advised about whom to appoint). While the members of the preparatory commissions were drawn exclusively from the clergy, these experts, the so-called *Periti*, included laypeople. These experts more or less produced the texts under the authority of the members of the commission. From the second session on, *Auditores*, "auditors," were allowed in; they could participate in the sessions but could not speak. This was an opportunity to honor people who could not be made *Periti*. From the third session on, women were present among the *Auditores*.

On the 6th of August, 1962, the Pope gave a point of order to the Council; this would be changed many times during the course of the Council. The following information about this point of order is given so that readers can better picture a Council debate.

First a distinction must be drawn between "General Congregation" and "Session." The General Congregation is the assembly of all the Council Fathers for *advising* and *discussion*. Session is the solemn closing assembly with the decisive, binding vote. Altogether there were four sessions of the Second Vatican Council.

Along with the full assemblies of the Council, the work was carried out in the commissions. At the beginning of the Council, Council commissions were formed that had the job of incorporating the changes called for during the debates (*modi*), editing the text drafts, and, if necessary, drafting a completely new text; these Council commissions were drawn from and corresponded to the preparatory commissions of the Council that had been appointed by the Pope. These Council commissions were not assembled by the Pope alone, however; two thirds of the members of a Council commission were elected by the Council itself, while a third, and the chairman, were appointed by the Pope. Each Council commission had 24 members, 16 of whom were chosen by the Council.

A presidium of ten Cardinals, appointed by the Pope, had leadership of the negotiations. This later proved to be too cumbersome; before the beginning of the second session this arrangement was changed. The presidium was expanded to twelve members, but from this time on the presidium did not lead the sessions; this was done, in turns, by a group of four "moderators," including Cardinal Döpfner of Munich and Cardinal Alfrink of Utrecht. Moderators and the presidium formed from that time on the so-called presidential council. This council was responsible for the presentation of the texts to the General Congregations, after these texts had been edited in the Commissions.

An advisory session of the General Congregation proceeded as follows: the text drafts presented by the presidium or the presidential council were debated under the guidance of the moderator. One or more reporters from the commissions commented on the presented text. Then the Fathers could speak, to suggest changes, to voice reservations, or even to plead for rejection of the entire text. This took place for the most part in two steps: first a debate over the text in its entirety, then over its different sections. The vote followed, in the opposite order: first over the individual sections, then over the revised entire Schema.

Because of the enormous numbers of Fathers, those who wished to speak had to register beforehand with the presidium; this ruled out spontaneous interventions.

The time allotted to a speaker was 10 minutes; later the 10 minutes were reduced to 8. This time limit was a hard-and-fast rule even for the Curial Cardinals; at the beginning of the Council they had considered themselves to be exempt from the time limit. On one spectacular occasion at the beginning of the Council Cardinal Ottaviani, the Chairman of the Theological Commission, exceeded the time limit. The moderator, Cardinal Alfrink, reminded him that his time was up; Ottaviani, undisturbed, spoke on. When after 17 minutes Cardinal Ottaviani still was not finished speaking, Cardinal Alfrink turned off the microphone. Ottaviani continued to speak, until he noticed that no one understood him anymore. The Fathers clapped for Cardinal Alfrink, and Cardinal Ottaviani went back with a flushed face to his seat. Shortly afterwards Ottaviani left the Council Hall and did not return for two weeks.

Along with the oral interventions, the Council Fathers also had the right to formulate written requests for changes; they submitted these requests to the commissions for consideration during their editorial work. It is decisive that votes could be brought to a close only with a two-thirds majority of those Fathers who were present. The debates were to be continued as long as was required to obtain a two-thirds majority, in one or the other direction. This was intended to be a way of avoiding votes that ran the risk of passive obstruction. In connection with events that we shall examine later, this procedure soon proved impracticable. The new procedure required a two-thirds majority for the *acceptance* of a draft; a *rejection* required only a simply majority. 50 Fathers sufficed to submit a new draft to the moderator;

this tightened up the editorial work in the commissions and prevented manipulations, delaying tactics, etc. The moderator had the right to bring about the end of a debate with a simple majority, thus preventing attempts at "filibustering."

A flaw that time and time again had a disturbing effect and was never fixed: at the vote over the individual sections of a draft only Yes or No were possible (*Placet* or *Non placet*). At the vote over the entire draft a three-part vote was possible: *Placet, Non placet,* and *Placet iuxta modum* ("Yes with reservations"), which meant "Yes" with the qualification that the Council Father adhered to a request for a change (*Modus*) that had not been accepted. Because this reservation was only possible in the vote on the entire text, it was unclear which requests for change were targeted by the reservation. Had the procedure been reversed, that is, had the three-part vote been used for the individual sections, then it would have been possible to ascertain at the final vote whether the individual Council Father linked his approval or rejection of an entire text with an individual request, or whether he, despite a reservation in an individual section, did not want to deny his approval to the whole text. The result would have been clearer, had this been the case. It is a stroke of luck and a testimony to the relevance of the Council discussions, that in the final analysis all resolutions passed with an overwhelming, *qualification-less* majority. Even without the frustrating constraint of an order of business, the Council Fathers had felt compelled to agree.

IV. THE OPENING: THE HOUR OF JOHN XXIII

The opening session of the Council on the 11th of October, 1962, left a lasting impression on Council historians. 2540 voting members, in the Bishops' garb of all the rites, with mitres or the corresponding head covering, marched into St. Peter's. The Pope met the Bishops in the so-called Benediction Hall of the Vatican and went on foot with them to St. Peter's Place. He wore — and the gesture was immediately understood — not the papal tiara, but the miter: he wanted to open the Council as the Bishop of Rome and "colleague" of the brothers in Episcopal office. Only at St. Peter's Place, on the way to the Portal, did he allow himself to be carried in the *Sedia gestatoria*, so that the thousands who had assembled in St. Peter's Place could catch a glimpse of him. At the Portal of St. Peter the Pope left the chair and went by foot with the Bishops to his place, the papal throne behind the altar. His face was turned to the people when he sat, as the Eucharist had always been celebrated in St. Peter's.

The rite of the opening of a Council has been established since the Council of Vienne in 1312. The hymn *Veni Creator Spiritus* ("Come, Creator Spirit"), the celebration of the Eucharist according to the form of the Holy Spirit, that is, according to the liturgy of Pentecost, celebrated by the Deacon of the College of Cardinals, in this case by the French Curial Cardinal Tisserant, the "enthronement" of the Gospel on the so-called "Council altar," set up in front of the president's table, the recitation of the Creed, the chanting of Matthew 28:18-20 and Matthew 16:13-18 in Latin, Greek, Old Slavonic, and, this time, in Arabic.

The opening became the hour of John XXIII by means of the Pope's homily. It is a textbook example of confidence in the Holy Spirit's guidance on the path of the Council, of an unrestrained claim to the authority to impose his will and convene a Council, and for, despite a friendly tone, biting criticism on those who had either tried to prevent the Council or, when the Council was no longer preventable, tried to bend it from the beginning to conform to their own views. We know today that the Pope had completely independently worked out the Italian version of his opening speech ("... from the first to the last word from me ..."), but also that the official Latin version derived from the Italian contains, in not a few nuances, significant toning down of the original text. For the sake of historical truth we have to quote here from the official version that was actually read.

"In the daily exercise of our pastoral office, it sometimes happens that we hear certain opinions which disturb us – opinions expressed by people who, though fired with a commendable zeal for religion, are lacking in sufficient prudence and judgment in their evaluation of events. They can see nothing but calamity and disaster in the present state of the world. They say over and over that this modern age of ours, in comparison with past ages, is definitely deteriorating. One would think from their attitude that history, that great teacher of life, has taught them nothing. They seem to imagine that in the days of the earlier councils everything was as it should be so far as doctrine and morality and the Church's rightful liberty were concerned. We feel that we must disagree with these prophets of doom, who are always forecasting worse disasters, as though the end of the world were at hand."

(According to reports, at this point many of the Council Fathers involuntarily glanced over in the direction of Cardinal Ottaviani and his like-minded companions.)

"Present indications are that the human family is on the threshold of a new era. We must recognize here the hand of God, who, as the years roll by, is ever directing men's efforts, whether they realize it or not, towards the fulfillment of the inscrutable designs of his Providence, wisely arranging everything, even adverse human fortune, for the Church's good. ... If this doctrine is to make its impact on the various spheres of human activity – in private, family, and social life – then it is absolutely vital that the Church shall never for an instant lose sight of that sacred patrimony of truth inherited from the Fathers. But it is equally necessary for her to keep up to date with the changing conditions of this modern world, and of modern living, for these have opened up entirely new avenues for the Catholic apostolate. ... Nor are we here primarily to discuss certain fundamentals of Catholic doctrine, or to restate in greater detail the traditional teaching of the Fathers and of early and more recent theologians. We presume that these things are sufficiently well-known and familiar to you all. There was no need to call a Council merely to hold discussions of that nature. What is needed at the present time is a new enthusiasm, a new joy and serenity of mind in the unreserved acceptance by all of the entire Christian faith, without forfeiting the accuracy and precision in its presentation which characterized the proceedings of the Council of Trent and the First Vatican Council.... In these days which mark the beginning of this Second Vatican Council, it is even more obvious than ever before that the Lord's truth is indeed eternal. Human ideologies change. Successive generations give rise to varying errors, and these often vanish as quickly as they came, like mist before the sun. The Church has always opposed these errors, and often condemned them with the utmost severity. Today, however, Christ's Bride prefers the balm of mercy to the arm of severity. She believes that present needs are best served by explaining more fully the purport of her doctrines, rather than by publishing condemnations. ... Indeed, if we consider well the unity for which Christ prayed on behalf of his Church, it would seem to shine, as it were, with a threefold ray of supernatural, saving light. There is first of all that unity of Catholics among themselves which must always be kept steadfast and exemplary. There is also a unity of prayer and ardent longing prompting Christians separated from this Apostolic See to aspire to union with us. And finally there is a unity which consists in the esteem and respect shown for the Catholic Church by members of various non-Christian religions. ... Hence, it is true to say that the citizens of earth and heaven are united in the celebration of this Council. The role of the saints in heaven is to supervise our labors; the role of the faithful on earth, to offer concerted prayer to God; your role, to show prompt obedience to the supernatural guidance of the Holy Spirit and to do your utmost to answer the needs and expectations of every nation on earth. To do this you will need serenity of mind, a spirit of brotherly concord, moderation in your proposals, dignity in discussion, and wisdom in deliberation. God grant that your zeal and your labors may abundantly fulfill these aspirations. The eyes of the world are upon you; and all its hopes."

CHAPTER THREE

"WE ARE A COUNCIL – NOT SCHOOLCHILDREN"

The Course of the Council

I. THE EXTERNAL RESULT AT THE OUTSET

The industriousness of the preparatory commissions had produced 69 Schemata; it would have been a nightmare, had all of these been dealt with and passed by the Council – something that Pope John, in principle, expected to happen in the first session! It would have been a nightmare, then, if these drafts had not been so strongly influenced by the Curial offices and their theologians. Altogether 16 documents were passed; the number of the final documents was a result of careful editing of the texts: leaving sections out, shortening texts, focusing on crucial points, even at times expanding the drafts. When the Council was solemnly closed on the 8th of December, 1965, the Council Fathers had accomplished exactly what the Council had come to want to accomplish. Of course, those texts that were not dealt with at the Council did not simply disappear. Some were consciously left to post-conciliar regulation, not always a happy decision, since it left the matter to the competence of the officials of the Roman Curia, who had never given up their passive (and where possible, active) resistance to the Council. There were now, however, counterweights to this resistance – at least this is what the Council Fathers hoped.

The 16 documents were composed in three legal forms: Constitution, Decree, and Declaration. The order is one of weight.

"Constitution" is an old legal form of ecclesial edict, patterned after the imperial edict in the Roman Empire. In the Middle Ages a Constitution was a *disciplinary law* of a general Council, of the

Pope, or of his officials, particularly those of the Pope (*Constitutio Apostolica*); this was still the case in CIC 1917, can. 884, which references a Constitution of Pope Benedict XIV from 1741. In addition Constitution also means, since the Middle Ages, a document with which a *dogmatic* decision is formulated. The Second Council of Lyon, in 1274, formulated a *Constitutio de summa Trinitate et fide catholica.* The First Vatican Council formulated both of its dogmatic decisions about the faith and papal primacy in the form of a *Constitutio dogmatica.* The same thing happened when Pius XII, in 1950, proclaimed, by means of the *Constitutio apostolica "Munificentissimus Deus,"* the dogma of the Assumption of Mary.

We touch here on a fundamental problem of Roman Catholic reality: the range of the Constitution between law and dogma makes the transitions between proclamations of faith and law fluid. Dogmatic decisions are issued in the form of laws, following an ancient form of Roman law; disciplinary instructions for ecclesial (and individual Christian) life contain dogmatic statements that render the legal instructions unassailable. How was the word Constitution meant at the Second Vatican Council?

It is, obviously, used as the conventional means for Council statements. There are Constitutions with primarily dogmatic content (the Dogmatic Constitution on the Church and the Dogmatic Constitution on Divine Revelation), some with primarily disciplinary content (Constitution on the Sacred Liturgy), and some with both (Pastoral Constitution on the Church in the World of Today). The four Constitutions named here are the only texts from the Council in this form. If one also considers that not one of these four texts contains the *canones* that, following ancient practice, pronounced the binding teaching in the form of a rejection (*Si quis dixerit ... Si quis contradicere praesumpserit ... anathema sit,"* "If anyone says ... If anyone presumes to contradict ... let him be expelled"), then one must conclude that the concept of the Constitution was very loosely understood at the Second Vatican Council. It designates the very detailed, coherent presentation of a position taken by the Church to a particular problem; according to topic more weight is given to the doctrinal presentation, to the disciplinary order and instruction, or to the pastoral and ethical appeal. The last mentioned, the pastoral and ethical appeal, is novel and most uniquely realized in the aptly named "Pastoral Constitution," "The Church in the Modern World." This Constitution was the result

of a desire of not only Pope John but also of the "progressive" majority
of the Council to adopt a comprehensive pastoral statement, one that
would make clear that the Church considers the time to be long gone
when it encounters the world predominantly with claims, limitations,
and condemnations.

The second legal form of the conciliar documents – the majority – is
the "Decree." There are nine Decrees of the Council: the Decree on the
Instruments of Social Communication; the Decree on Ecumenism;
the Decree on Eastern Catholic Churches; the Decree on the Bishops'
Pastoral Office in the Church; the Decree on Priestly Formation; the
Decree on the Appropriate Renewal of the Religious Life; the Decree
on the Apostolate of the Laity; the Decree on the Ministry and Life of
Priests; and the Decree on the Church's Missionary Activity. Decree is
also an old legal concept; it is a technical expression for a papal edict
(for example, the so-called *Decretum Gelasianum*, "Decree of the Pope
Gelasius") or a collection of these edicts (*Decretum Gratiani*, "Decree
[Collection] of [the monk and canon lawyer] Gratianus" in the 12th
century). In canon law, Decree is first and foremost the legislative
edict or the administrative order of the Pope and the Curial offices.
However, just as with Constitution, Decree can, in the history of canon law and councils, also mean a dogmatic decision. The most famous
case of this is the "Decree on Justification" from the Council of Trent
(1547). At Trent, Decrees *de fide* and Decrees *de reformatione* were
expressly distinguished from each other (as in the case of the residen-
cy requirement for Bishops). In the language of the Second Vatican
Council, Trent's Decree on Justification would certainly have been,
given to its content and range, a Dogmatic Constitution. Decree – as
we see with the list of the nine Decrees of the Council – contains predominantly disciplinary content. The Decrees of the Council indicate
how a reality in the life of the Church should be regulated and shaped.
The dogmatic basis is briefly summarized; the instructions founded
on this dogmatic basis then follow. The Decrees are shorter than the
Constitutions.

The third form of Council resolution is the "Declaration" (*Declaratio*).
This concept is new. The Council adopted three Declarations:
the Declaration on Christian Education; the Declaration on the
Relationship of the Church to Non-Christian Religions; and the
Declaration on Religious Freedom. As the topics indicate, these
Declarations are statements on delicate and controversial questions.

They are also statements that touch on not only internal ecclesial problems but also the external relationship of the Church. The Declarations are as a rule shorter than the Decrees. These observations, together with the turbulent genesis of these Declarations, lead to this conclusion: Declarations were promulgated by the Council to address those questions that pertained to the self-understanding of the Church, and also to give instruction in matters that demanded extreme caution, in order neither to exacerbate internal ecclesial controversies nor to create unproductive misunderstandings outside of the Church.

In summary, the main statements and therefore also the thematic emphases of the Council are found in the four Constitutions. These gave the Council its unmistakable signature: the Constitution on Divine Revelation as a beacon for faith and theology in the modern world; after that, the Constitution on the Church as a representation of the understanding of the Church in the context of long prepared theological insights. The Church as "the People of God" and the addressee of God's self communication: this must have consequences for the Church's liturgies, therefore for the inner life of the Church (Constitution on the Liturgy) and for the Church's service in the world, its exterior life (Pastoral Constitution on the Church in the Modern World).

The Decrees with reforming content are arranged according to these core statements of the Council, including the special questions that were once more treated in these Decrees: the Decrees about the priestly formation and about the Church's missionary activity belong within the range of topics of the Dogmatic Constitution on Divine Revelation; the Decrees about the Eastern Catholic Churches, ecumenism, the Bishops, religious life, and priestly ministry belong within the range of topics of the Dogmatic Constitution on the Church; the Decrees concerning social communication, the lay apostolate, as well as the Declaration on Christian Education belong within the range of the Pastoral Constitution on the Church. The Declarations concerning non-Christian religions and religious freedom are, strictly understood, appendices to the Dogmatic Constitution on Divine Revelation. No Decree corresponds to the Dogmatic Constitution on the Sacred Liturgy; rules governing the implementation of this Constitution were reserved for the Bishops' conferences and post-conciliar regulation.

When one reads the texts today, whether in translation or in the Latin original, it is hard to grasp the full extent of the conflicts surrounding their genesis. At best one notices occasionally an unclear, perhaps even evasive, formulation. We shall now take a glance at the course of the Council as well as a look at a few crises and scandals. Further details about other conflicts will follow in later chapters.

II. THE COURSE OF THE COUNCIL

1. FOR AND AGAINST LATIN

We must once more take a glance back at the months immediately preceding the Council to point out three delicate problems neglected by the preparatory work; these could have cast a shadow over the external effect of the Council from the very beginning. These three problems were the question of Latin as the language of the Council, the relationship to the press, and the "observers" from the non-Catholic Churches.

In spite of some reservations, it was determined that Latin should be the language of discussion at the Council: *the language of discussion,* not only the original language of the Resolutions. It might be expected that it would have been the Bishops from the lands of the missions, above all the Bishops who were native to these lands, who would have protested this decision. But protests came from all nationalities. No wonder, since the native Bishops from the mission lands had all studied in Rome, where the lectures at the papal universities at that time were all, of course, held in Latin. They were in training. The situation was otherwise, even when the Bishops were "conservatives," with the Bishops from the USA or even those from Romance language countries (Italy and Spain, for example). They very much supported the use of Latin, but actually spoke it very poorly. According to a story that circulated, Cardinal Spellman of New York, one of the "most conservative" of the Council Fathers, once had to ask someone else to speak for him during the discussion because his Latin could not be understood by the majority of the Council Fathers.

Nonetheless, Latin as the language of discussion did not excite excessive debate. The excitement generated by another incident, however, was like the detonation of a bomb. In an unusually solemn fashion on the 22nd of February, 1962, the Pope publicly signed the Apostolic

Constitution *Veterum Sapientia* ("The Wisdom of the Elders"). This constitution was a paean of praise of Latin as *the* language of the Church. The document prescribed that in ecclesial theological faculties all lectures, except for those in Practical Theology, must be held in Latin. Hebblethwaite commented on the constitution: "It was surely the most ineffectual document ever published by Pope John. For the rest of that academic year – rarely longer – tongue-tied Anglo-Saxon professors exercised their rusty Latin on bewildered and sometimes uncomprehending students. This was all in the name of 'good Pope John' who despite his liberal image was now engaged in 'putting the clock back.'" What the English biographer reports here about the Anglo-Saxon faculties was also true for Germany. The theological faculties at the German universities, because these institutions were public, were not bound by this constitution; their students never felt the effects of the constitution, as did the German students in the diocesan seminaries and the theological colleges associated with the orders. To make it clear: I have myself heard very *good* lectures in Latin, which were not hard to understand with a decent German education in the humanities and a bit of practice with Scholastic texts. I participated in international theological conferences at which Latin was the official language, and by no means remained silent. To use Latin is certainly possible. But what was actually attempted in 1962 – so to speak overnight, and after a short period then abandoned – was a complete joke.

We now know that *Veterum Sapientia* was composed by Cardinal Antonio Bacci on behalf of Cardinal Pizzardo, head of the Congregation for Seminaries. Bacci was the Latinist of the Vatican; the Latin final editions of all Council resolutions were entrusted to him. He became internationally known for his skillfulness in inventing Latin words and expressions for modern technical terms. This sort of cooperative work with the composition of official statements is usual. In view of the predictable effects, more than one person asked himself what the document was supposed to have achieved.

It was inevitable that the rumor arose that this constitution had been forced on the Pope. Indeed, a comment attributed to the Pope made the rounds, to the effect that he himself was surprised by what he had signed. These were, however, really only rumors; the Pope himself countered them vigorously whenever he had the opportunity. The background of this constitution becomes clearer when another circumstance is noted. The Preparatory Commission that was concerned with questions of the liturgy was – as we shall speak of in the following chapters – not only industrious but also particularly efficient. It was soon an open secret that far-reaching proposals in favor of the use of the vernacular in the liturgy would be submitted to the Council. The conservatives in the Curia were greatly alarmed. The situation was intensified because of an almost providential event: On the 22nd of January the members of the Commission submitted the prepared text of the liturgy draft to the Chairman of the Commission, the old Cardinal Gaetano Cicognani (the brother of Cardinal Amleto Cicognani, an old confidant of Pope John who, after the death of Cardinal Tardini, had become Secretary of State). Somewhat anxious, but loyal to the Commission over which he presided, Gaetano Cicognani signed the liturgy schema on the 1st of February, 1962; he died four days later.

Had he not signed, the Liturgy Commission would have had to start all over. But it was now clear: the reform-minded liturgy schema was not going to be delayed again on its way to the Council hall. Since it was the last draft expected, the official convening of the Council for the 11th of October could occur. Three weeks later *Veterum Sapientia* appeared. The Pope personally treasured Latin, because it was the language of the "Ancient Fathers"; he did not, however, speak it fluently, and in the months before the beginning of the Council he practiced twice daily. The constitution is best understood as a reassuring concession to the powers of the Curia, who considered the proposals of the Liturgy Commission to be extremely dangerous. From their point of view, as it would soon be seen, they were completely right.

At this point it is impossible not to mention that the events also had an ironic side. The advocates for Latin at the Council, the Italian and many of the American Bishops (often of either Irish or Polish background) spoke miserable Latin; the supporters of the vernacular, above all the German and the French Council Fathers, spoke wonderful Latin – and during the debates about the reform of the liturgy they smugly asked the advocates of Latin, in Latin, whether Jesus would have spoken Latin. A story about the Pope's Latin has become well known, a story that the Archbishop of Cologne, Cardinal Frings, later told the clergy of Cologne. During the Council, the Pope received the Bishops of various countries, among these the German Bishops, and attempted to address them in Latin (Pope John did not speak German). He soon muddled his Latin; Cardinal Frings, the Chairman of the German Bishops' Conference, answered him in Ciceronic Latin: "Holy Father, usually you dispense us! Today we, for once, dispense you. Go ahead and speak in Italian!"

When it came to the Latin discussions at the Council, in general it worked, since the Council speeches had been prepared in writing beforehand. A carefully installed simultaneous translation system was never used. Whoever has participated in this sort of system at an international theological conference knows that it is of no use. There are just not that many trained theologians who have a mastery of the terminology of their respective disciplines *and* at the same time are brilliant translators. This is easier when it comes to political discussions.

2. COUNCIL AND PRESS

The relationship to the press was also fraught with problems. An event such as the Council naturally drew a world press – at times as many as 1000 journalists (1200 at the opening ceremony). It was clear that a press bureau was necessary, and one was established during the preparatory phase. Obviously, though, an institution that was accustomed to discussing and deciding anything of any importance behind closed doors and used the method of pointed indiscretions in order to disseminate sensitive information had no experience or practice in dealing with a free-wheeling press. The man chosen to be responsible for the press bureau was the General Secretary of the Preparatory Commissions, later appointed General Secretary of the Council, Pericle Felici; he was a wise man, but the very embodiment of a Curial official and, therefore, he had a completely broken relationship to the media. What happened in the Vatican was, according to his opinion, no one else's business, if the responsible people did not condescend to make anything public. He was also of the opinion that the Council was a purely internal matter and therefore nothing of the discussions needed to reach the outside. The public needed only to be interested when the resolutions were passed. Felici actually attempted to deal with the press with these ground rules.

On the 3rd of December, 1960, Felici held a press conference at which he announced the establishment of a Council press bureau. His initial talk address to the press follows: "It is necessary that the reporting – apart from rhetorical and journalistic stylistic flourishes, not always necessary but occasionally quite useful – be exact in the essentials, when it comes to questions of faith and morals and correspond completely with the doctrine of the Church. The gaps that are allowed in the non-Catholic press or in the news services cannot be accepted in the Catholic press. For this reason, contact with the official – or at least semi-official – information agents is required. Before someone passes along a sensational novelty, one has to determine what is actually true about this piece of news ... I hope that everyone abides by this, and controls their desire for what is surprising and sensational. Better to hang on for a minute and send out an accurate report rather than get an inaccurate report out fast ... The press bureau will, from time to time [!], announce useful and accurate information that will correspond, if possible, to your needs. I remind you, Gentlemen, of the Latin proverb: 'from friends one demands only what is honorable.' Do not push into matters that are closed to you, matters that are denied to you. Only under these conditions will we be good friends." At the end Felici urged the journalists to lead a healthy family life.

On the 21st of May, 1961, Felici was quoted as saying the following at another press conference: The press bureau was organized "according to need": "The need today is limited, and therefore the work of the press bureau is limited. The public and the journalist have to be patient. Although the Pope has often declared that it is extremely desirable for the faithful to have a lively interest in the Council, it must not be forgotten that the Council is an act of the highest teaching and governing power of the successors of the Apostles under the authority of the Pope. Everyone must look up to these men with reverential silence and pray to the Holy Spirit to illumine them." One can imagine the anger of the world press at this style. Of course good journalists were not intimidated by this sort of arrogance; on the contrary, they were stimulated to dig even deeper in their research. It is also well-known how this played out. For one thing, strict secrecy was not maintained with regard to the Italian newspapers. Reporters came close to employing the methods of secret service analysis: they compared the information (in and between the lines) in l'*Osservatore Romano*, the official newspaper of the Vatican, and filled this information out with easily established contact with Bishops and Curial prelates, who on their side had an interest in particular reports and assessments of events.

The best example is that of the secret American journalist who wrote regularly under the pseudonym Xavier Rynne for the *New Yorker*. He maintained that he availed himself of no particular insider knowledge, but relied on the sources available to the public. In 1984 an American journalist by the name of F.X. Murphy wrote: "Any journalist incapable of cracking a Vatican secret after diligently reading the Italian press, scrutinizing *l'Osservatore Romano*, and attending an embassy reception or two, should change his profession." There are almost certain clues that this Murphy is the same as that Xavier Rynne!

Thank God that the world press, incensed over Felici's attitude, very soon received support from highly placed officials. On the 30th of January, 1961, just short of two months after Felici's first press conference, Cardinal König, the Archbishop of Vienna in Austria, pointedly distanced himself from Felici: "Superficially, the Council seems to be the business of the Pope and the Bishops; in reality, it is the business of the entire Catholic Church, that is, of all the faithful. It depends in large part on you, the Catholic journalists, whether this will actually be the case .... I am thinking here above all of the journalists who write for non-Catholic publications .... It is the task of the journalists to be the public conscience of Catholics. If you have something to say about the Council, do not wait for a word from the Bishop, nor for news from Rome. Give warning, where you think you must warn; lead the way courageously, where you think you must lead; inform, whenever you have the opportunity to inform the world about the Council. If you make the Council your business, then the Council will become the business of all Christians. Talk about everything that public opinion and the faithful expect from the Council."

And finally, the Pope himself was so concerned that on the 24th of October, 1961 – the Council had not yet been formally convened, nor had a date been set – he addressed the foreign press; he stated his appreciation of the significance of public opinion and the problems of journalists and promised a further expansion of the press bureau.

Nonetheless, problems persisted, and often the only recourse left to journalists was to stay in touch with "their" Bishop and/or "their" *peritus*, from whom they might occasionally hear something. One of the greatest puzzles of the Council will remain how a man of Felici's sort, who was always on the verge of raising the ire of the world against the Council because of his dealings with the journalists, became Secretary of the Council and remained Secretary after the death of John XXIII. Presumably because he was an exceptionally capable organizer and controlled the apparat, it was simply accepted that he would exercise

an unusual amount of influence behind the scenes. From the second
period on, however, his responsibilities and influence were curtailed.

3. THE "OBSERVERS"

The third anxiety-producing question was: what would happen with
the "observers" from the non-Catholic Churches, whom the Pope had
succeeded in inviting against the resistance of the Curia?

This invitation was, surprisingly, much better received by the
Churches of the Reformation than by the Eastern Orthodox Churches.
With a great deal of diplomatic skill, but also with the occasional stirring of self-righteousness – not by John XXIII, but by high ranking members of the Curia and by the leading representatives of the
non-Roman Churches – contact was established in the years 1960-
1962. The diplomatic back-and-forth of some of this contact, which,
above all vis-à-vis the Orthodox Churches in the Eastern Block, unavoidably bordered on "high politics," is hardly comprehensible today.
We should, however, make note of it, in order to appreciate how much
new trust was successfully built up at that time, and is maintained even
to today – a significant counterweight against the very real mistrust
inside and outside of the Church about whether "Rome" is sticking to
the resolutions of the Second Vatican Council. In any case, on the 2nd
of December, 1960, Archbishop Fisher of Canterbury, the head of the
Anglican Church, paid a visit to the Pope – after some face-saving (on
both sides) maneuvers that seem odd today. As a result of this contact
the Anglicans sent three official representatives to the Council.

The Evangelical Church in Germany sent Professor Edmund Schlink
from Heidelberg; the Lutherans, the Reformed World Organization,
and the World Council of Churches sent representatives.

Only the Eastern Orthodox Churches reacted hesitantly. This had
also, if not above all, political grounds. The Patriarch of Moscow railed
against the "sirens" from the Vatican. Under these circumstances no
other Orthodox Church could go to Rome, without giving the impression of stabbing the beleaguered Russian Church in the back. We must
refrain here from describing the mostly secret, always highly difficult
activities, of necessity concealed from the rigidly anti-Communist
Curia, with which the Pope endeavored to establish a personal contact
and a basis for trust with Nikita Khrushchev, the first man at that
time in the Kremlin, without making the western powers mistrustful.

Jan Willebrands, one of the closest colleagues of Cardinal Bea and later his successor as head of the Secretariat for Promoting Christian Unity, acted in a particularly skilled manner. A little later this skill paid off with geo-political consequences: shortly after the beginning of the Council the "Cuba Crisis" occurred, bringing the world to the edge of an atomic war. It was the Pope's hot line not only to Khrushchev but also to President Kennedy that, in considerable measure, contributed to settling the crisis, so that the leaders of both superpowers could save face before their people and the world.

The fact that the Pope was in the position to protect impartially the interests and yearning of humanity for peace certainly helped in the observer question. It was possible to make it clear to Moscow that the Council would not express itself along party lines or with political condemnations – although certain powers on the Council would have gladly done this. Then the great surprise came: literally on the evening before the opening of the Council the news came in that two representatives of the Patriarch Alexios were on their way to Rome. This was the direct result of a trip of Willebrands to Moscow.

4. THE FIRST PERIOD: 11 OCTOBER – 8 DECEMBER 1962

We return now to the Council hall. No work was done, of course, on the day of the opening liturgy. The work began on the 13th of October, with the election of the Council Commissions. These corresponded, according to topics, to the Preparatory Commissions. The Pope named a third of the Commissions' members, two thirds had to be elected. This immediately caused the first altercation (still mild!), which resulted in the first work session ending after only 20 minutes. Ballots were distributed, on which 16 names were to be jotted down. But which ones? The men of the Curia had, counting on the inexperience and trust of the "newcomers," the "foreigners," who were gathered together, plotted a sophisticated move: along with the ballots, under the guise of simple information, a list was distributed of the names of those who had been members of the corresponding Preparatory Commissions – and as we know, the majority of these were the representatives of the Curial line. The plan backfired when resistance came immediately from members of the Presidium. The Cardinals Liénart (of Lille) and Frings (of Cologne) claimed the microphone, with gentle force against all the attempts to stop them from speaking, and said, very innocently, that not enough was known about possible choices for these Commissions, a little time was needed to get to know one another. For this reason, the election should be delayed for a few days, to give the Bishops enough time to discuss among themselves. Deafening applause! That was the moment when the American Bishop Robert J. Dwyer said, "We realized that we were a Council – not a class of schoolchildren that had been called together." The representatives of the Curia, however, were warned from the very first day that the Council would not allow itself to be manipulated.

In the following days the national and regional Bishops' Conferences gathered together and drew up lists of candidates. The most successful were those of the central European and French Cardinals, because they gave consideration to the experts from all parts of the world and therefore conveyed the impression of great fairness. While the Preparatory Commissions had been in great part composed of Europeans, the Council Fathers were now only about half from Europe; the Commissions that would be crucial for the work of the Council were now international.

In the course of the period the General Congregation met 36 times; there were 640 Council speeches and 33 votes. One after another the most important drafts were discussed: Liturgy, Revelation, Communication, Eastern Catholic Churches, Church. Nothing was ready for publication. But this was – despite the disappointment of many Catholics about the "disunity" at the Council – normal. Two months as a "warming up period" of the Council were really not too much. It was more important that the Council find its form, and that the Fathers learn how to control the mechanism of discussion and to see through the behind-the-scenes events. The Fathers could not be taken by surprise again after the first period.

It also became clear that priorities had to be set, reduced, and consolidated, if there was to be any hope for concrete results. This succeeded at the end of the period with the help of the Coordinating Commission, appointed on the 6th of December, 1962, to which the Munich Archbishop Julius Cardinal Döpfner belonged; the Commission had close contact with the Fathers. At the beginning of May, 1963, new drafts could be sent to the Fathers, drafts to which they themselves had contributed.

At this point we have to return to a circumstance, already mentioned, that would be fateful for the Council.

5. THE AGENDA OF THE COUNCIL

The Council was scarcely opened when it became obvious that it suffered from an incomprehensible lack of planning. The Pope had not passed along a timetable by which the many drafts would be discussed, worked on, and passed; nor had he commissioned anyone to come up with such a timetable. The Presidium proved to be not very efficient. Everyone in the Curia, however, including the Pope, believed that by Christmas of 1962 the Council would be long over. The first discussions bogged down in the topic "Liturgy," the weeks elapsed, one draft after another was turned back by the Council for fundamental revision, and the idea of a short Council lost any kind of grip on reality. But there did not seem to be any plan for the continuation. What appears in hindsight as the completely normal "warm up" phase of the Council was in reality its first and fundamental crisis, in which nothing less than the conception of the task of the Council was at stake. Unlike the men of the Curia, the foreign Council Fathers and even some of the Italian Council Fathers who were not from Rome had had from the very beginning the expectation that this would be a difficult Council, necessitating numerous periods. The nature of the crisis that developed between these two concepts of the Council, and the lack of planning with which this crisis was met, was for a long while inexplicable. Now it is capable of explanation, and we must here mention again the names of two of the most important Council Fathers.

The first is Cardinal Suenens, the Archbishop of Brussels. In 1962 he had written a pastoral letter to his diocese on the topic of the Church in the modern world. Just by accident the Pope happened to read this pastoral letter. The Pope thanked Suenens and let him know his full agreement; at the same time he asked that Suenens compose a report with his suggestions about the work, organization, and goals of the Council. Suenens answered with two memoranda: one was what the Council should *not* be, the other what the Council should be and do. The second memorandum made such an impression on John XXIII that he made its thoughts the basis of a speech on the 11th of September 1962 – with far-reaching effects into the opening address. The conceptual and organizational kernel of Suenens's proposal was that the Council should group its work around two poles held in tension: the internal life of the Church (*ad intra*) and the life of the Church in its external relationships (*ad extra*). (This would prove significant later for the work of the Pastoral Constitution, "The Church in the Modern World.") Cardinal Suenens belonged from that time on to the closest circle of friends and advisors to the Pope.

The other Council Father to mention here is Cardinal Montini of Milan. In 1983 a letter came to light through a copy given by Cardinal Suenens to the Paul VI Archive in Breschia; this copy of the letter was published in "L'Osservatore Romano on January 26, 1984. This letter, in which Cardinal Montini expressed his deep concern about the further course of the Council, had been written by Montini on the 18th of October, 1962, only a week after the opening of the Council and sent through the usual channels to the Pope. Cardinal Montini suggested that the Council concentrate on one topic, the topic "Church," in order to finally fit the First Vatican Council into a magisterial clarification of the self-understanding of the Church. Out of purely pragmatic grounds Montini did not consider it a good idea to begin the Council with the topic "Liturgy," since this meant a deviation from the purpose given to the Council and in this respect also a misleading of the public. The topic "Church" would be clarified in three ways: the Mystery of the Church, then the Mission of the Church, and finally the relationships of the Church to those that did not belong to her. In Montini's plan, the Council would require three periods. It is not difficult to recognize that this plan describes not only the topics of the texts adopted by the Council, but also the further progress of the Council itself. Three periods were envisioned because Montini still believed in October of 1962 that the topic "Church," that is, the Dogmatic Constitution on the Church, could be dealt with in the first period. In November Pope John grasped the situation and asked Montini and Suenens to speak to the Council about what they had said in private to him. Suenens did this in his very structured speech on the 4th of December. Montini followed on the 5th with the development of his suggestions for the continuation of the work of the Council, as he had articulated them in his letter in October. So the first period became a rehearsal for the actual tasks and decisions that awaited the Council in the following years.

The day of the papal tasking of Suenens and Montini must have been the most painful in the pontificate of Pope John. Asking these two cardinals to speak to the Council meant that John XXIII realized without a doubt that he would not be able to lead the Council to its conclusion. He had learned from his doctor that he only had a few more months to live. Now he could only hope that Montini would be his successor. The chosen few knew about this hope. Montini was smart enough to remain silent in the Council hall – until December 5. Pope John now characterized his relationship to the Council this way: it had been his job to bring a large, heavy ship out of the dry dock; "another will have the task to fetch it from the sea." However, at the time the Council closed the period as if nothing decisive stood before it.

On the 8th of September, 1963, the Council was supposed to re-convene. John XXIII died on the 3rd of June, marked for months by the disease from which he would die. The Council was suspended, in accordance with canon law. On the 21st of June, not even three weeks after the death of John XXIII, after only a two-day conclave and on the sixth ballot, the Archbishop of Milan, Cardinal Montini, emerged from the election as Pope Paul VI. As we remarked earlier, many Catholics in the world had been filled with anxiety, worried that the Council would not continue.

Today we know that that fear was groundless: the election fell to the wish candidate of his predecessor, who himself had accepted his successor's conception for the continuation and further agenda of the Council. Montini had been chosen as a moderate progressive – and he fulfilled these expectations, although they were not the expectations of the Curia. The day after his election he announced, in a radio broadcast, that he would continue the Council. He set the new date as the 29th of September. A whole series of statements and measures in the following weeks made his course clear – we can skip these here.

6. THE SECOND PERIOD: THE 29TH OF SEPTEMBER – THE 4TH OF DECEMBER, 1963

In the opening address the Pope explained what he as Archbishop of Milan had already put on record: the Dogmatic Constitution on the Church had to be the main focus of this session. Further goals of the Council would be the internal renewal of the Church, the promotion of Christian unity, and the question of the Church in today's world. The Pope emphasized the need for a clarification of the teaching on the episcopacy and its relationship to the Petrine office. "This will produce guidelines for us, as well, from which we shall draw teaching and practical uses in the exercise of our apostolic mission."

The topic of Church actually occupied a month; the draft was fundamentally re-worked and was accepted by vote as the basis of further discussion. The Decree on the Bishop's Pastoral Office and the Decree on Ecumenism followed, in logical succession to the Dogmatic Constitution on the Church. The Ecumenism schema still contained the sections on the Jews as well as on religious freedom. Both encountered resistance from different quarters; because of the resistance, these sections were separated from the document and only the first chapter of the decree was voted on. Then the last votes were taken on the Decree on the Instruments of Social Communication and the Dogmatic Constitution on the Sacred Liturgy. The Dogmatic Constitution on the Sacred Liturgy and the Decree on the Instruments of Social Communication were then adopted in the solemn closing session on the 4th of December, 1963, approved by the Pope, and made public. The Pope used a new confirmation formula; this formula, without detracting from the relevant canon law, was clearly in accord with the thinking of the College of Bishops in the matter of the Universal Church. In accord, therefore, with that thinking that created the most difficulties in its conflict with the forces of inertia during the debate on the Church schema. The Pope anticipated the statement of the Dogmatic Constitution on the Church (not yet adopted) that dealt with this matter. The formula, which from now on would be used for all the texts of the Council, ran: "Each and every one of the things set forth in this Dogmatic Constitution has won the consent of the Fathers of this most sacred Council. We, too, by the apostolic authority conferred on us by Christ, join with the Venerable Fathers in approving, decreeing, and establishing these things in the Holy Spirit, and we direct that what has thus been enacted in synod be published to God's glory. Rome, at St. Peter's (date). I, Paul, Bishop of the Catholic Church."

This was followed by the signatures of the Fathers.

7. THE THIRD PERIOD: THE 14TH OF SEPTEMBER – THE 21ST OF NOVEMBER, 1964

The tangible results of this period were the adoption of the Dogmatic Constitution on the Church and the Decrees on Ecumenism and on the Eastern Catholic Churches. At the same time, this period is the phase of the great crisis of the Council, even though for all appearances the Council was in high gear and moving rapidly forward. Schema after schema was submitted, discussed, and worked on according to the determined procedure: after a general debate a vote was held as to whether the schema would be accepted as the basis of further work (this was now always the case). After this it was handed over to the Commission for the inclusion of the *Modi*. Once these were included, the text was submitted again and brought, section by section, to vote. The newly introduced proposed amendments were again given to the Commission, included, and the final composition was put to general vote without new debate – along with either "Yes" or "No," a vote of "With Reservation" was also a possibility. The vote in the General Congregation had the character of a straw vote; the "official" vote took place in the final session of the period.

In the vast majority of cases, because of the intensive work during the vote in the General Congregation, the "No" votes were a vanishing minority, often under 20. The *Juxta-Modum* votes ("Yes with reservations") kept within boundaries; they were never threatening and increased into the hundreds only at particularly controversial passages. At the solemn session the "No" votes routinely sank again. The periods were arranged so that the sessions devoted to exhausting discussion alternated with routine sessions dedicated to voting on the prepared texts or sections thereof.

So – did everything run smoothly and efficiently? By no means – but we shall return to discussion of these crises as soon as we cover the fourth period.

8. THE FOURTH PERIOD: THE 14TH OF SEPTEMBER – THE 8TH OF DECEMBER, 1965

Only five texts from the projected 16 were now completed – although these five were of considerable significance. Difficult and also important texts were still waiting in the wings, however. Unlike the previous periods, the announcement of the decisions of the Council was not kept until the last, period-ending session: there were three solemn sessions during the course of this fourth period. At the first, on the 28th of October, the following were adopted: the Decree on the Bishops' Pastoral Office, the Decree on Priestly Formation, the Decree on the Appropriate Renewal of the Religious Life, the Declaration on Christian Education, and the Declaration on the Relationship of the Church to Non-Christian Religions. In the second solemn session, on the 28th of November, the Dogmatic Constitution on Divine Revelation was adopted – at this point, although this draft had been among the first to be discussed in the Fall of 1962 – and the Decree on the Apostolate of the Laity. In the third solemn session, on the 7th of December, the Pastoral Constitution on the Church in the Modern World was definitively voted on – the longest Constitution of the Council, and the most controversial. Along with this Constitution, the Decree on the Ministry and Life of Priests, the Decree on the Church's Missionary Activity, and the Declaration on Religious Freedom were also voted on. The solemn final assembly on the 8th of December, the ninth solemn session of the entire Council, passed no resolutions, but was a final liturgy of the Council.

This fourth period was calmer than the third. The clock was ticking, since this period was supposed to be the last. The bulk of the work was now done in the Commissions that polished the texts. The General Congregations were occupied above all with votes, since the large discussions had all been held in the third period. For the sake of the work of the Commissions there were numerous pauses between the General Congregations. So, step by step, the drafts were made ready for a vote, even if this occasionally meant squelching discussion that might have been helpful.

Often a topic was delegated to the Pope or to post-conciliar committees for work – often on very reasonable grounds, as for example in the case of the revision of the ecclesial legal code, but occasionally with problematic results, as in the case of the draft concerning the Sacrament of Marriage. We shall report on many of these details in later chapters.

III. SCANDALS AND CRISES

It has been said that, compared to the work of a normal parliament, the work of the Council was not only extraordinarily efficient but also exceptionally calm. The press and television had more than enough sensational material to report, however, especially in the third period. A minority – small in number but influential in terms of their control of the Apparat – of curial prelates and curial Cardinals, as well as the conservative Bishops, realized that they could not succeed – neither with the drafts that were produced under their influence nor with the discussions over the changes. As all means and tactical chess moves – for example, postponements of votes, delayed submission of drafts that had been worked over because of alleged or actual lack of time – failed, this group then took refuge behind the Pope. This was correct according to canon law, but conveyed contempt for the opinion of the overwhelming majority of the world Episcopate. In numerous cases the Pope personally intervened on behalf of the curial minority. This resulted in the impression that the Pope regularly appeared to be holding the Council in contempt – also in the media. We shall examine one such situation.

I. OMENS

A first, mild, but alarm-ringing altercation has already been mentioned: the postponement of the election of the Council Commissions in the first work session on the 13th of October, 1962, by means of which a curial attempt at manipulation was repulsed.

The second omen also occurred during the first period, and has already been touched upon: the debate on the draft of the topic "Divine Revelation" became hopelessly bogged down. The question was: should the schema presented by the Preparatory Commission as the basis of the discussion be used? After a confusing back and forth, the Presidium phrased the question unclearly and unskillfully (or, according to some opinions, particularly skillfully): should the schema be *rejected?* An overwhelming majority voted for this, but about 70 votes were lacking for the necessary two-thirds majority. The question was therefore denied – the schema had to be used. Had the question been whether the schema should be *retained*, the result would have been the opposite. It was now predictable: a crippling debate would ensue, with numerous attempts at haggling and infighting, and great embitterment would be the result. John XXIII realized this after a night of reflection, and he himself pulled the schema back and established a Coordination Commission that was charged with preparing a new schema. This move avoided a poisoning of the climate; it took, however, until the last period to get the Dogmatic Constitution on Divine Revelation ready for adoption.

The third omen – in the second period, on the 8th of November, 1963 – was Cardinal Frings's attack on the procedures of the *Sanctum Officium*, as the Congregation for the Doctrine of the Faith was known at that time. "The procedure of the *Sanctum Officium*," Frings stated, "in many cases does not correspond to our times, is damaging to the Church and offends non-Catholics. The job of those who for many years have worked in the Holy Office to protect the revealed truth is very difficult and beset with thorns. However, no one accused in matters of faith may be condemned or punished by the Holy Office without a chance for him or his Ordinary to be heard; without knowing the charges brought against him and his writings; without being given the opportunity to correct himself." Cardinal Ottaviani, the Prefect of the *Sanctum Officium*, rejected, in a trembling voice, the accusations, that could arise "only from lack of knowledge, to say nothing worse," and emphasized the care taken in the formation of judgments in his office. No one can really deny this – but it was not an answer to the complaint of the Cardinal of Cologne. Pope Paul VI gave the answer: he, at the end of the fourth period, re-structured the *Sanctum Officium*, subordinating this office to the Secretary of State (thereby divesting it of its authority as *Suprema Congregatio Sancti Officii*), and gave the office procedural rules for disciplinary processes in doctrinal matters. This still left much to be desired. For example: the accused did not have the right to choose his own *Relator pro autore*, that is, his "lawyer"; he was appointed by the Curia, like a public defender. The hearings on doctrinal conflicts that had been held up to that time did not do much to awaken confidence. However, this procedure instituted by Paul VI in many points met the objections of Cardinal Frings; this new procedure at least guaranteed that someone who has been reprimanded did not first learn of it from the newspaper.

2. THE *NOTA PRAEVIA EXPLICATIVA* TO THE DOGMATIC CONSTITUTION ON THE CHURCH

The Dogmatic Constitution on the Church was ready to be put to the vote after revision necessitated by the decisions of the second period. The first two chapters went smoothly. The much disputed third chapter on the hierarchical structure of the Church was divided into 39 separate sections; these individual sections were to be voted on with either a "Yes" or a "No." The main point of contention was the doctrine on the College of Bishops and its responsibility for the Universal Church. The curial minority was opposed, because it feared for the authority of the Pope. At the relevant votes, the "No" votes rose to around 300: the hard kernel of the opposition showed itself. It would now have been appropriate to accept gracefully the wish of the majority. They had, however, another move at their disposal: after the curial minority did not succeed in the Theological Commission with the introduction of far-reaching amendments, refuge was taken behind the Pope. On the 14th of November the Fathers received a thick book with the suggested changes for the chapters still to be dealt with, chapters 3-8, along with the responses of the Theological Commission to these suggestions. The book began with *Nota praevia explicativa* ("prefatory explanatory note") that ruled out any reduction of the papal primacy through the teaching on the College of Bishops developed in chapter 3 of the Constitution. The General Secretary Felici announced that this "preface" had also been submitted to the Theological Commission, but came from a "higher authority," which could only be the Pope. Two times, on the 16th and on the 19th of November, Felici explained that the *Nota* was not a part of the text, but was meant as an interpretive tool – which sufficed.

It was an utter scandal – legal in canon law, but caused only because a small minority, which professed to represent the Universal Church, did not wish to submit to what the Universal Church had publicly expressed as her conviction. The fact that there was no contradiction between the statements of the Constitution and the *Nota* does not change anything: this meant a clear stress in the delicately balanced relationship of the Bishops and the Pope, if the Pope *wants* to take advantage of it. Did the Pope want this?

3. "BLACK THURSDAY": THE 19TH OF NOVEMBER, 1964

Something similar to the *Nota praevia explicativa* happened on this day with the Decree on Ecumenism, immediately before its adoption by the final vote. After the 5th of October, when the revised version had been presented, there were hardly any objections, but around 2000 *Modi* to sift through and include. The final vote should have been held on the 20th of November, but the final text had still not been distributed on the 19th of November. General Secretary Felici announced that the text was "not yet ready," since, again at the bidding of the ominous "higher authority," 19 changes were still to be made. He read these out loud and, unlike the *Nota praevia*, some of these changes were at the very least a weakening of the text – we must return to this later.

What had happened behind the scenes? The Pope had sent a list with 40 text changes to the head of the Secretariat for Promoting Christian Unity. Because of lack of time Bea could submit the changes only to a few colleagues from his close circle – and could include only 19 in the text, those 19 that Felici had read out loud. Once again the text had been changed through means that were not established by the Council, and the conservative opposition had, once again, shown what they thought of the Council.

The day became "Black Thursday" because of another scandal, however. The Declaration on Religious Freedom was ready, and the final vote was foreseen for this period. It was predictable, how the vote would turn out – the only possibility for the opponents of the Declaration was to stall and gain time. A petition from about 200 Spanish and Italian Bishops, the most important opponents of the Declaration, asked for more time to study the document – that is, postponement until the next period. On the 18ᵗʰ of November Felici announced that a vote on the proposed postponement would be held on the 19ᵗʰ of November. Again it was clear, how this vote would end up – negative for the postponement. As shortly after 11 am on the 19ᵗʰ of November the vote was to take place, Cardinal Tisserant announced that the vote on the postponement had been postponed – after deliberations with other members of the Presidium.

St. Peter's was a madhouse. The Fathers, including members of the Presidium, left their seats and stood around discussing in groups. Fortunately it was the hour at which the famous "Jonah Bar" was open. The three North American Cardinals, Meyer, Ritter, and Léger, had the opportunity to formulate a petition to the Pope: "With all respect but with great urgency we ask you, that before the end of this period of the Council the Declaration on Religious Freedom be voted on, otherwise we lose the confidence of the Christian and the non-Christian world." 441 signatures were collected immediately at the Jonah Bar, and eventually the petition gathered 1000. But it did not help: the Pope only gave the assurance that he would set this Declaration as the first point of business on the agenda for the fourth period.

3. THE POPE'S MOTIVES

The Pope himself, Paul VI, was and is usually held responsible for all these restrictions on the freedom of the Council. What were his motives – was he actually legally and politically responsible?

There are sufficient indications, even before he became Pope, that Paul VI did *not* share the fears and wishes of the conservative minority. In the previously mentioned letter of the 18th of October, 1962 to John XXIII, Cardinal Montini left no doubt that he approved of the teaching on the collegiality of Bishops, provided that the decisions of the First Vatican Council on the primacy of the Pope would not be called into question. He repeated this opinion in his opening address to the second period. At a highpoint of the curial machinations Paul VI obliquely let Cardinal Ottaviani know that the Council Commissions were organs of the Council, not its judges – including the Theological Commission, of which Cardinal Ottaviani was the chairman. Many other such indications could be cited. Publicly the Pope kept a low profile and protected his colleagues, but he sought quietly to assist the direction of the Council *majority*.

One must also come to the conclusion, if one is honest, that the Pope acted as he did in order to avoid having the curial minority, with whom he had to work, embarrassed in the vote by the majority of the Council. The Pope did indeed achieve this – even the minority reconciled itself with the controversial texts and made an overwhelming majority possible at the final votes. And finally, the Pope energetically backed curial reform at the Council, created the Bishops' Council as a permanent fixture, and – not least – quickly implemented the reform of the liturgy.

After the incident with the *Nota praevia explicativa*, Cardinal Frings of Cologne had suggested leaving – as the minority at the First Vatican Council had done and despite the prohibition in canon law. Cardinal Döpfner, one of the moderators, responded: "We can't stab the Pope in the back." If this anecdote is correct, then Döpfner would have the more correct judgment of the Pope's motives.

IV. THE CONCLUSION

Scandals like those just described should not detract from the work achieved by the Council in the three years of the four periods. Whoever has worked in committee even on a *small* text and knows the process of how *Modi* are included, whoever has had overall responsibility of shepherding a text from its first version to its final, readable, logical conclusion can, despite scandal and "Black Thursday," feel only a great respect for the work of the Council that produced the kinds of texts that we now have before us – under the kinds of conditions that were unique in Church history.

So the thunderous applause was understandable, as General Secretary Felici announced in the General Congregation of the 6th of December, 1965, that this, the 168th General Congregation, would be the last of the Council. On the 7th of December, in the solemn session, there was yet another sensation: after the adoption of the last document of the Council the Pope and the representative of the Ecumenical Patriarch Athenagoras lifted the mutual excommunication that had existed between the Eastern and Western Churches since 1054. With this, the Roman Catholic Church opened communion to the Eastern Orthodox Churches – for the non-Uniate! The Eastern Orthodox Church has not ratified this and still today refuses Roman Catholics participation in the Lord's Supper.

On the 8th of December the closing liturgy of the Council took place outside at St. Peter's Plaza. In his homily, Pope Paul VI said: "Behold, this is our greeting. May it rise as a new spark of divine charity in our hearts, a spark which may enkindle the principles, doctrine and proposals which the council has organized and which, thus inflamed by charity, may really produce in the Church and in the world that renewal of thoughts, activities, conduct, moral force and hope and joy which was the very scope of the council."

Different Cardinals read messages from the Council to governments, scientists, artists, women, workers, the sick, the suffering, and the young; these messages were then handed over to a representative of each of the groups by the Pope himself. The intercessions were recited in the variety of rites and languages of Christendom. It was 1:20 pm, Middle European Time, when the Pope dismissed the Council with the words: *Ite in pacem Christi* – "Go in the peace of Christ."

CHAPTER FOUR

"LATIN FOR TOURISTS & GUEST WORKERS"

The Reform of the Liturgy

I. THE MOST OBVIOUS AND LONGEST LASTING REFORM WORK OF THE COUNCIL

In 1967, in the journal "Word and Answer," published by the Dominicans of the House of Studies in Walberberg, near Bonn, an article by Maternus Einig, the Docent for Liturgy, appeared under the title of this chapter. He summarized one of the objections against the most obvious and lasting reform work of the Council, an objection that had already been mentioned during the Council discussions by the conservative side: the unity of the Church was particularly illustrated on the level of language in every liturgy throughout the world. This slogan – "Latin for Tourists and Guest Workers" – shows how quickly such arguments, which were still earnestly debated in the 60's, can become outdated and lose significance. On the other hand, I was recently confronted, not so long ago, with just this argument: during a lecture I was asked to take a position on whether the liturgical reform of the Council was a delayed concession of the Church to the outdated nationalism of the 19th century!

There were problems not only with the Latin, however – during the preparations for the Council and afterwards. Two often-quoted anecdotes illuminate the situation in the initial phase of the reform of the liturgy. The question: "What is liturgical reform?" The answer: "When on Sunday you enter the sacristy of a church and ask, 'how do you guys do this, here?'" The other anecdote: a priest hopelessly loses his way in the loose sheets of the provisional text of the German liturgy, as he tries to find the readings for Sunday. Forgetting that the microphone is on, he mutters under his breath, audible for the entire congregation through the loudspeaker system, "Darn Council!"

The loose sheet salad at the ambo is now a thing of the past. The effects of the liturgical reform continue, although other reforms instituted by the Second Vatican Council have, in the opinion of many, been thrown into reverse gear. What can now not be reversed?

a) The vernacular in the liturgy: our children and our grandchildren experience a solemn Latin Tridentine Mass just as we experience a liturgy of the Orthodox Church, in Greek or Old Church Slavonic: impressed, but with the feeling: This is not our worship service.

b) The consciousness that the *community* is the subject of the liturgy and the liturgist is its "presider" and "leader," not the sole "celebrant" of the Mystery before a community that has a "bystander" role.

c) The corresponding new self-understanding of the priest: he faces the community. He is not just "a brother among (sisters and) brothers," or the executor of the will of the community, but he is no long "mediating" "between" God, Christ, and the community. He is the proclaimer of the Gospel, from which he lives as much as the community, and therefore he is the community's servant, advocate, but not master.

d) The "functionality" of the liturgy. In a glance back at the history of liturgy one can characterize the reform work of the Council as the re-discovery of the original Roman liturgy and the dismantling of superfluities that developed in the course of time (above all through Frankish influence). This fact, rather obvious to the specialist in liturgy, can be explained quickly. In the early Middle Ages the Roman liturgy prevailed in the regions of France, West Germany, and the Netherlands, but the native traditions had the effect that the Roman liturgy was enriched by certain of their elements. One of these elements was the private prayer of the celebrating priest, lightly spoken, on the way from the sacristy to the altar, during the approach to the altar, during a few ceremonies (for example, the altar kiss), etc. Little by little these private prayers became more firmly fixed in the liturgy until they were a prescribed part of the liturgical formula, muddling the basic structure of the liturgy. Along with this, little by little the idea spread that the Mass was a kind of dramatic portrayal of the life, and particularly of the passion, death, and resurrection, of Jesus. It was easier to explain the liturgy to the "people" in this way; this, in the interest of drama, lead to further ceremonies that did not make any sense within the ancient Roman understanding of the liturgy. The liturgical reform has pretty much done away with all of this. There are still "private prayers," that is, liturgical texts spoken in a soft voice by the priest; there are still "dramatic" elements in the liturgy. These no longer, however, disguise the transparent structure of the liturgy for the participants. The result is, at first glance, a greater soberness, less ceremony, more informality. There is also room for more spontaneity – a dagger in the heart for all friends of the liturgical "mystery play." But apart from some unnecessary iconoclasm in the first years after the Council, the idea of the liturgy as "mystery play" was always *the* great and disastrous misunderstanding of the Christian Mass. (I say this without the slightest intention of criticism of the Eastern Orthodox Church's understanding of the liturgy: the participants in the earthly liturgy are understood to be sharing in the celebration of the "mystery" of the *heavenly liturgy*.) The main causes of that misunderstanding were: the development of the clerical liturgy and the exclusion of the community from liturgical involvement since the early Middle Ages; the anti-reform hardening of just this clerical liturgy in the face of the Reformation – because with Luther the community began to sing again in the liturgy!

e) The celebration of the liturgy by the priest with his face toward the people and the placing of the altar as close as possible to the community. The celebration with the priest with his back to the people is not forbidden, but will never again be the norm.

f) The space for a greater variety of forms, whether through the greater variety of possible texts or through the greater freedom allowed the liturgical participants. In the liturgical directions it reads, for example, that the priest should "with these or similar words" (*his vel similibus verbis*) greet, invite, etc., and this means: the following text is only a suggestion, not an order.

g) Finally, the discontinuation of the liturgy as a stage for self-promotion of extra-liturgical intentions. That is perhaps a little mean, and maybe a bit iconoclastic. But it is certainly not false to suggest that the pre-conciliar liturgy, particularly in the realm of church music, offered numerous possibilities to "show off" without risk – the audience was not only certain, but also quiet. Some pastors who could afford it paid musicians of the local philharmonic orchestras, so that the church choir and the organist could be shown to the best advantage. Of course no one can see into consciences, and no one can calculate what happened for the honor of God and what happened for one's own honor. But the immediate resistance of a great part of the church musicians against the liturgical reform, the lack of willingness of choirs to put themselves at the disposal of the reform and the improvement of the community singing, does give one pause. No one disputes the artistic poverty of the first attempts of the new liturgical music after the reform of the liturgy. But this poverty was also the result of the refusal of the actual artists to help. It cannot be said that the reform of the liturgy was understood and seized as the chance for completely new church music forms *with* the community – after the model of the Lutheran church music in the post-Lutheran period. Unless I am mistaken, only in recent times has a change for the better emerged. We shall return to the details later.

Now, however, after this preview of the overall result, we must examine some details further.

II. THE LITURGICAL MOVEMENT – PREHISTORY OF THE REFORM OF THE LITURGY

1. LITURGY BEFORE THE COUNCIL

How was it before the Council? One received sufficient visual instruction at the Council itself. The opening liturgies were of course pre-conciliar liturgies in their entire splendor: one had after all the world famous "Capella Sistina." But the Eucharistic celebrations that opened the regular General Congregations were, according to eye and ear witnesses, dismal pre-conciliar "Masses": a "low" Mass, that was softly "read" by the celebrant (a Council Father) at the altar – the Council Fathers had already all "privately" celebrated Mass in their domiciles – along with this, simultaneously, there was the singing of one or two hymns by the choir. It is to be supposed (if one may bring to bear observations at German Cathedrals and their Cathedral Choirs), that the Council Fathers who were present were engaged in fulfilling their breviary duty.

Another anecdote is well attested and leaves behind, despite its joyous cause, mixed feelings. At one of these liturgies the famous Cathedral Choir from Aachen sang the "High Mass in B minor" of Johann Sebastian Bach. It was the first occasion that this work, written for the Catholic liturgy at the Dresden court church, was performed at St. Peter's. But not all the Council Fathers knew the significance of this: on account of the uncontested length of the work apparently some Council Fathers left St. Peter's after the Kyrie.

Gradually the Bishops did participate in the so-called community mass. However, it was only during the fourth period – the Dogmatic Constitution on the Sacred Liturgy was adopted at the end of the *second* period! – that the Eucharist was celebrated according to the reformed liturgy, a liturgy that Pope Paul VI energetically supported.

The reform of the liturgy was the longest and most intensively prepared project of the Council. That was the reason it could be considered first at the Council, to the joy and terror of the Commission members. "Joy" because that was a recognition of the groundwork already accomplished; "terror," because now the reform of the liturgy became the exercise yard for the "warm up" period of the Council. Just as an aside: occasionally one hears the comment that the fact that the Council began with the Dogmatic Constitution on the Sacred Liturgy is indicative of Vatican II's priorities; this is an interpretation that attempts to put the situation in the best possible light. The truth is unfortunately more prosaic. No less a figure than Cardinal Montini, the later Pope Paul VI, a great promoter of liturgical reform, expressed complete opposition in his letter of the 18th of October 1962 to the Council dealing with the Dogmatic Constitution on the Sacred Liturgy before it dealt with the Dogmatic Constitution on the Church. However – now to keep to the topic at hand.

The liturgy before the Council was the result of a liturgical reform by Pope Pius V in the year 1570. This Pope expected here, as elsewhere with the unyielding implementation of the decrees of Trent, an improvement of conditions because of centralized regulation. For the first time the variety of western liturgies ended and the Roman liturgy – in the Mass, Prayers of the Hours, and the sacraments – asserted itself into the last corner of the Roman Church. The single exception: rites that had already existed for more than 200 years were allowed to continue. Not coincidentally, the order from which Pius V came, the Dominicans, profited from this exception – up until the Second Vatican Council they had their own form of the celebration of the Mass. This was also the case with the Milan Diocese, with the tradition of the so-called Ambrosian liturgy; this led to the Archbishop of the Milan Diocese, Cardinal Montini, celebrating a Milan liturgy in the first session of the Council: now, suddenly, a multiplicity was again fashionable!

Since 1570, then, the liturgy was dictated from beginning to end; no intervention was allowed and even the distance of the extended hands at the *Dominus vobiscum* ("the Lord be with you") was regulated. Not to mention the volume at which the words of Christ at the institution narrative of the Lord's Supper could be spoken: only the ones standing closest could hear them – *propter mysterium* ("for the sake of the mystery") was the rationale.

Of course everyone knew – at the very least every priest, because of his education – that this Roman liturgy was, at one time, a liturgy with divided roles: priestly prayers, choir, congregational chant (*Ordinarium*), lector, cantor, deacon, and ministers. At the so-called "solemn High Mass" that also became completely clear – with the one exception that here the choir undertook, if necessary, along with the multi-voice chanting of the *Ordinarium* (Kyrie, Gloria, Credo, Sanctus, Agnus Dei), also the part of the congregational chant. But the "solemn High Mass," even in large parishes with numerous priests, took place only on feast days; it was not the normal Sunday liturgy (with the exception of the cloisters). In the "normal" Mass on Sunday, and certainly on the weekdays, the priest took over all the functions. This had the result that Catholics would say that the priest "read the Mass," that is, he, at the altar, literally "read" the formulas, in a soft voice, according to the liturgical regulations ("Rubrics") partly half out loud (so that the ministers could answer, if possible – the sole remaining division of roles!), partly whispering (above all the Canon with the institution narrative). The congregation "was present," but heard and understood nothing.

How did the believers occupy themselves? The only possibility was that they did something "parallel" to the actions of the priest, or were requested to do something. The possibilities were: to pray privately, together privately prayed (for example, the Rosary), or sang hymns. Before the beginning of the liturgical movement, of which we shall soon speak, the following "normal forms" of the celebration of the Mass were the result:

+ The "solemn High Mass" (*missa sollemnis*): mentioned above.
+ The "simple High Mass" (*missa cantata*): without deacon or sub deacon, with the designated prayers sung by the priest (oration, preface, the Lord's Prayer, the beginning of the Gloria and the Creed), if possible with choral singing as at a solemn High Mass. In well-equipped communities the "simple High Mass" was the normal form of the Sunday liturgy. The congregation, of course, remained passive and prayed by itself – as always.
+ The "sung Mass," in the countries where a body of song was available, as in Germany, but not in France or England: the priest "read" the Mass, the people sang church songs accompanied by the organ; these songs had been selected so that they at least somewhat fit the sections of the liturgy read at the altar (so, to the Gloria a song of praise, to the distribution of communion a Eucharist song, etc.) For a Mass 5-6 songs with numerous stanzas were needed. Only at the institution narrative (whispered by the priest in such a low voice that no one in the congregation could hear him) was the continuous singing of songs interrupted.
+ The "low Mass": the priest read the Mass, the congregation prayed – also silently. This was the normal form of the weekday Mass: from today's perspective, it was an eerie event. The weekday Mass was practically the private Mass of the parish priest with open church doors.

Behind this practice stood – also an anti-Reformation inheritance – an extreme ideology of the "sacrificial character" of the Mass and of the corresponding function of the priest as "sacrificial priest." In keeping with this, the Eucharistic Prayer ("Canon"), the text in which this ideology saw the sacrificial character of the Mass anchored was treated for a long time like a secret document: it could not be shared with the believers. I myself have had in my hands an old prayer book from the beginning of the 20th century in which the text of the Mass was printed in two languages, Latin and German, with the exception of the Canon. The editor made the point with this omission that the Canon had sacrificial power only in the mouth of the priest, and was not necessary in German translation.

2. THE LITURGICAL MOVEMENT

The Sunday liturgy is the occasion when pastors, because of the Sunday obligation, have their congregation together, at least the practicing members, more than at any other time. So the question could not be avoided – whether this frozen, dead liturgy could remain as it was; whether the benefit of a demonstration of ecclesial unity offset the wasted pastoral opportunities – because the extra-liturgical "prayers," the precursor of today's Liturgy of the Word, did not create any sort of sufficient counterweight.

Such considerations had led to attempts at renewal, since the 17th century in France and around the turn of the 18th century particularly vigorously in Germany; these attempts included the translation of liturgical texts. The native "German vespers," stronger in southwest Germany than anywhere else, is an echo of one such reform attempt: it goes back to Bishop Ignaz Heinrich von Wessenberg, who died in 1860; von Wessenberg was committed to the Enlightenment and therefore controversial, was dedicated to pastoral work and reform. On the whole, these attempts were not successful – but their theological bases intensified in the 19th century, despite neo-Scholasticism: new interest in the Church Fathers, in the study of the Bible, in the history of early Christianity, the renewal of the orders after the secularization. This all led in the 1880's to a liturgical renewal, a renewal that was particularly at home in the cloisters of the Benedictine order: Solesmes in France (Fr. Guéranger), Beuron in Germany (Anselm Schott), and from 1913 also and particularly Maria Laach (Ildefons Herwegen). In 1903 Pope Pius X took notice of these attempts at liturgical renewal, and supported them in the Universal Church: new editions of choral books, reform of the rubrics and the breviary – and at the same time a pastoral orientation. The actual breakthrough happened with the famous speech of the Benedictine Lambert Beaudin at the Catholic Day in Mecheln in 1909 ("the Mecheln event").

From there the liturgical movement encompassed church circles in Belgium, Holland, France, and in the German-speaking realm. The decisive element in this was the liturgical movement's relationship with the Catholic Youth Movement, which put into action the ideas of the liturgical movement in its liturgies and therefore advertised them – so that, not least because of the many priests who came out of the Youth Movement, a generation later the liturgical movement belonged to the common property of the church, at least in those places where value was placed on "keeping up with the times." One kept up with the times so well that in the 30's, because of a few "exaggerations," there was unrest in Rome. The German Bishops blocked that cleverly, in that they founded a "Liturgy Council" with an affiliated commission of experts, making the liturgical movement their own concern.

The image of the Church that stood behind the liturgical movement was confirmed through the 1943 encyclical *Mystici Corporis*. After the war there was finally international cooperation; in 1943 – one is astonished these days, at what was possible in the midst of the Second World War – the Pastoral Liturgy Institute was founded in Paris, in 1947 the Liturgical Institute in Trier. In 1947, Pope Pius XII published the encyclical *Mediator Dei*, which the liturgical movement understood as their *Magna Charta Libertatis*. From then on the liturgical movement was a matter for the entire Church – along with the attempts at renewal of the liturgy.

On episcopal as well as broader church levels there now followed a series of one small partial reform after the other: the reform of the Easter liturgy (it again could be celebrated on Saturday night rather than on Saturday morning) in 1951 and again in 1956; permission for the evening Mass on Sunday; loosening and finally a lifting of the regulation forbidding eating or drinking anything after midnight before the morning of reception of the Eucharist; permission for wider use of the vernacular by the other sacraments, above all by baptism, marriage, and anointing of the sick (not, yet, however, by the sacrament of penance). Only in the encyclicals concerning church music (1955) and the following instruction (1958) was the resistance of the church musicians in evidence: active participation of the congregation – yes, but in Latin, please.

3. A SUNDAY BEFORE THE COUNCIL

How, then, did the liturgy look right before the Council and in light of the success of the liturgical movement?

The "solemn High Mass" (*missa sollemnis*) remained untouched. Now it was more or less understood that the congregation sang at least the short answer to the priest's call (*Dominus vobiscum – Et cum spiritu tuo*, etc.). Teaching the congregation simple Gregorian chants also proved successful in many instances, so that it might happen that the Church choir generously put aside their singing of the Creed and chanted a Gregorian Creed with the congregation, instead.

The "low" Mass became more and more the completely private Mass of the priest, without the congregation. Also on the weekday, if it was possible, the most important accomplishment of the liturgical movement asserted itself: the "Community Mass." This is a completely (through one or more prayer leaders) translated Mass – while the priest, held to the regulations, "read" the Mass in Latin. Only the "answers" were spoken in Latin by the congregation, where they were chanted in Latin at the High Mass. A variation of the Community Mass was the *missa recitata*: here the priest spoke all the texts out loud in Latin, except for those that the rules dictated he whisper – that is, above all, the Canon; more and more this regulation was not followed. This Mass form was of course only acceptable for those who had graduated from a high school with a strong humanities program – therefore the weekly Latin test for the Catholic youth in "Gymnasium," the preparatory German high school.

The "sung Mass" in the way it has been described became evidence of a congregation that lived behind the moon. Singing obviously also occurred in the Community Mass, at the places where in the Latin High Mass singing occurred – only now in German. This sort of celebration of the Mass was called the "German High Mass." Of course, at the same time the priest "read" his prescribed Latin text. He had to do that also when the singing was in *Latin* – only the reform of the liturgy associated with the Second Vatican Council did away with this requirement.

Not only was the Mass renewed according to the intentions of the Liturgical Movement, but also other forms of liturgy – particularly Vespers and/or Compline. Since here only the priest was duty bound to the Latin, "the German Vespers" or "the German Compline" (in one form, very similar to what is found today in the Lutheran Hymnbook) soon became the property of the Youth Movement and a beloved Saturday form of liturgy in the "progressive" parishes. To avoid suspicion of lack of rigor in liturgical matters, pastors influenced by the Liturgical Movement were mindful of para-liturgical forms such as Eucharistic Adoration, the Rosary, the May devotions to Mary, Heart of Jesus Friday, Novenas (prayer cycles lasting nine days, for example before Pentecost), the Stations of the Cross ... and the leaders of the Liturgical Movement, for example Romano Guardini, wrote books about the Stations of the Cross, the Rosary, etc.

So, before the Council, a typical Sunday in a Catholic Church congregation looked like this:

7 a.m. (at the latest): "Early Mass" – usually celebrated as the "low Mass," as on a weekday, and without a homily. Attended above all by the mothers who had to afterwards make breakfast for their families.

9 a.m.: Children's Mass – milder conditions and greater freedom prevailed.

10:30 a.m.: "High Mass" – except on feast days usually "German High Mass"; the official congregational liturgy, with homily.

11:30 or even noon: "Late Mass" – mostly a "sung Mass," with homily; before the lifting of the rules against eating and drinking after midnight, often without distribution of Communion, because experience had shown that almost no one came to Communion since they all had had breakfast. The "Late Mass" was attended above all by those who slept in, to whom the entire "liturgical fuss" was burdensome and a quirk of the pastor. And those who slept in were numerous, since many people still had to work on Saturdays.

5 p.m. or 6 p.m.: Eucharistic Adoration – for about a half an hour. It closed with the "sacramental blessing," the blessing with the monstrance and the consecrated host. Since the end of the 1950's, instead of the Eucharistic Adoration an Evening Mass was celebrated. The attempt to combine the Evening Mass on Sunday with the practice of Eucharistic Adoration died a quick death – by necessity it lengthened everything, and even the pastor wanted to have a free evening on Sunday.

III. THE GENESIS OF THE
CONSTITUTION ON THE LITURGY

The development of the Dogmatic Constitution on the Sacred Liturgy, the basis for the reform of the liturgy, can be quickly described. Of the over 2800 suggestions that arrived in Rome at the request of Secretary Tardini, nearly a fourth of them dealt with some aspect of the liturgy. The responsible Preparatory Commission was, like all the others, assigned to the responsible Roman office, in this case the Congregation of Rites. The head of this Congregation, Cardinal Gaetano Cicognani, an experienced curial diplomat who, however, lacked any pastoral experience, was the chairman of the Preparatory Commission. The final roster of the commision consisted of 24 bishops and 36 consultors, including the commendable Secretary Annibale Bugnini, a Lazarist. Bugnini was so engaged in the preparation and then the implementation of the Dogmatic Constitution on the Sacred Liturgy that even his promoter Paul VI was not able to protect him from all internal curial attacks. In 1975 his enemies succeeded in having him reassigned from Rome to Tehran, as Apostolic Delegate. He was not embittered, but used the time to write a valuable, extremely informative book on the reform of the liturgy.

1. THE PREPARATIONS

German and French participants were not among the Bishops and consultors first appointed to the Preparatory Commission – in other words, Bishops and consultors from those countries with the most experience with the Liturgical Movement were not appointed. Thank God, however, that this was not possible at later appointments. During the Council, anybody who was anyone in the field of liturgy was in Rome, influencing each phase of the developing Constitution and preparing the translations as well as the measures for their implementation. It required three conferences lasting over numerous days, interrupted by the work of thirteen sub-committees assigned to different questions of detail, but the attempt to prepare the final draft was successful. On the 13th of January, 1962, nine months before the opening of the Council, the final draft of the Dogmatic Constitution on the Sacred Liturgy was ready. We have already described how the

President of the Commission, five days before his death, signed the draft. No wonder, then, that the negotiations began with this text.

However, what the Fathers on the 11th of October, 1962, at the opening of the Council, got in their hands was not the text that had been adopted by the Commission, but a text that had been revised by a work group secretly called together at the behest of the new president of the Commission. Certainly the substance of the text was not changed, but important, concretizing explanations were left out, and provisions that promoted the use of the vernacular were weakened. For example, the text of the Commission had said that the Bishops or the Bishops' Conferences of a particular language area should "determine" (*statuere*) the use of the vernacular in the liturgy; the revised text said that they could "suggest" (*proponere*). That corresponded to a preceding *nota* – not only the Dogmatic Constitution on the Church received one – that said that the Constitution wanted to put forward for a general reform of the liturgy *normas generales et altiora principia,* "general norms and overarching principles," the implementation would be left to the Holy See. It was again clear at the beginning of the Council – if it had not been made sufficiently clear by the encyclical *Veterum sapientia* and the circumstances of that encyclical's publication – that in the Curia and also in the Episcopate there was decisive resistance to the reform of the liturgy. One took cover behind the formal argument: the Council represented the entire Church, including the uniate Eastern Churches; therefore it could not make *general* decisions that affected only *one,* the Latin Rite. Therefore: only general principles. Despite this, everything went well – at the end, surprisingly well.

2. THE VOTES

Most dangerous was the suggestion that because of their detailed theological foundation the drafts had to be referred to the Theological Commission – the successor of the former Central Commission – that is, to Cardinal Ottaviani. It was clear to everyone what this would mean. In the general discussion Ottaviani had already made it clear where he stood – it was that speech at which the discussion leader Cardinal Alfrink had, after seventeen minutes, shut off the microphone. The liturgy, according to Ottaviani, is "holy ground." Were the Fathers planning a kind of "revolution"? It was that biblical allusion that the advocates of the reform countered with the already-mentioned question, whether Jesus spoke Latin. The phrase "holy ground" characterized the feelings of the anxious: the liturgy was – liturgical history notwithstanding – since Pius V *the* bulwark that protected the Roman Catholic Church from penetration by foreign influences, because it made the Church identifiable at any time and preserved concretely for the believers a consciousness of God's holiness, of the Church, of their faith and of the norms of the Christian life. Of late, the post-conciliar developments in liturgical reform indicate that these arguments should not be taken lightly. It is only questionable whether it was still sensible to want to preserve a consciousness of God's holiness in *this* way and in *these* forms.

Compared to *this* understanding of "holiness," a great deal of "profane" was taken into the liturgy. The liturgy is not so easily an object of identification as it was earlier: in England (and in the USA), the celebration of the Eucharist can hardly be distinguished from an Anglican (or Episcopalian) Eucharist (and in Germany, the Catholic celebration of the Eucharist is very similar to a high church Lutheran liturgy). Among other things the reform of the liturgy has brought us traditionalist movements, some of which agitate at the right edge of the Church (*Una voce*, "The Priestly Fraternity of St. Peter"), some of which operate outside the Church ("The Pius X Brotherhood" of the now deceased Archbishop Lefebvre). The resistance was unable to hinder the reform.

From October 22 until the 14th of November 1962 the liturgy schema was discussed – as already mentioned, as the introduction of the discussions of the Council and therefore with a high commitment: 29 speakers just on the first day and a half! To everyone's great surprise there were, at the vote on the 14th of November on the question whether the schema could count as the basis for further discussion, only 46 "No" votes – although 180 *Modi*, so a good deal of work for the Commission; this work was done very thoroughly in the intersession that led up to the beginning of the second period. In this period the *Juxta-modum* ("Yes with reservation") votes rose at the individual votes, until the two-thirds majority for acceptance fell short. Therefore a point of order controversy arose: was the affected chapter therefore rejected – or was it only to be referred back for improvement? The latter mindset asserted itself. The process was also streamlined (as later with the Dogmatic Constitution on the Church) by means of the method of the *Quaesitum* (questioning): one emphasizes the particularly controversial points, interprets them in the most accommodating way for the opponents, and then asks whether this accommodation might be acceptable; this method made the work of the Commission easier. On the 22ⁿᵈ of November in 1963, the vote was held on the entire schema – and it went through with only 19 opposing votes to 2158 yes votes. On the 4ᵗʰ of December, in the public closing session of the second period, the approval by the Pope and the solemn pronouncement followed.

IV. MAIN POINTS OF THE CONSTITUTION ON THE LITURGY

1. THE VERNACULAR IN THE LITURGY

The Dogmatic Constitution on the Sacred Liturgy has 130 articles – almost double the number of articles in the Dogmatic Constitution on the Church, although the text of the Dogmatic Constitution on the Sacred Liturgy is just about half the length as that of the Dogmatic Constitution on the Church. The Dogmatic Constitution on the Sacred Liturgy consists in great part of nothing but individual directives, while the Dogmatic Constitution on the Church provides a cohesive account. There are seven chapters in the Dogmatic Constitution on the Sacred Liturgy: General Principles, Eucharist, Other Sacraments, the Divine Office, the Liturgical Year, Sacred Music, Sacred Art and Sacred Furnishings. What are the main points? This assessment is not an excessive simplification: there is actually, when it comes to the practical directives, only one main point; that point is the far-reaching allowing of the vernacular in the liturgy. When proposed amendments of the Constitution proliferated, the occasion was always articles that concerned the lifting or loosening of the obligation for the Latin text – and the proposed amendments supported weakened formulations. Nothing had been left untried in the effort to fend off this threatening "disaster," even outside of the Council preparations. In 1960 the new *Codex* of liturgical regulations (*Codex rubricarum*) appeared, provisionally put in force without prejudice for the Council; this work was clearly intended by its promoters to make the reform of the liturgy superfluous through, for example, simplifications and a correction of the calendar for feast days. In 1961 and 1962 there followed official new editions of the Latin missal and of the breviary. In 1962 a newly composed rite for adult baptism appeared. Was the reform of the liturgy still needed?

The Council did not allow its hands to be tied by these attempts to create a *fait accompli*. It decided on the vernacular. The restrictive preface planned by the opposing side was erased. In Article 36 the Bishops' Conferences could once more "decide" (*statuere*) and not only "suggest" – the approval of the Holy See was required, but that was almost always required. And the approval of the translation of liturgical texts is once again a matter for the Bishops' Conferences – at least according to the wording of the Constitution. *What* was now allowed in the vernacular?

a) In the most sensitive question, that of the use of the vernacular in the celebration of the Mass, compromise was necessary. Therefore the relevant Article 36 contains a threefold restriction: the use of the Latin language should in principle be preserved (§ 1) – to what extent is not determined. In other words: the opponents were allowed the fiction that, as in the past, Latin remains the official liturgical language of the western Church.

The vernacular was approved in the form of a double permission: it is permissible to extend the limits of the employment of the vernacular (§ 2). In other words, it is allowed to allow the vernacular. Finally, the vernacular should be used "particularly" in the readings, directives, petitions, prayers, and chants. In other words: the Canon is taboo. I can still remember clearly: no one had ever dreamt that the Council could venture so far. I do not know whether the opponents of reform at that time believed that they had averted the worst. The supporters had apparently agreed to the formulated restrictions with a wink, and trusted in the weight of the development that had been put into motion – and they turned out to be right.

b) It was easier with the rest of the sacraments. Pope Pius XII had already done the spade work. So Article 63 stood in tension with Article 36: there is no more "allowed to allow," the vernacular is now prescribed: there *should be* more space provided for the vernacular.

c) Article 101 is more reserved: clerics should use Latin for the Divine Office. The same is true for the order priests, but the responsible superior can allow prayers in the vernacular: for the clerics for the promotion of a better execution of the Divine Office; for the communities of non-clerics, particularly women religious. There were actually women's cloisters in which the Divine Office was prayed in Latin by members of the community who did not understand a word of Latin.

2. THE THEOLOGICAL FOUNDATION

The vernacular in the liturgy is the immediate consequence of the fundamental approach of the Constitution. If this is accepted, not only is the vernacular the result, but almost all the other reform requirements as well. The fundamental approach consists of the re-discovery – that is, the confirmation of the re-discovery already made by theology – of the liturgy as *the comprehensive proclamation act of the Church*. The fundamental approach signals the end of the "mystery play" – and the end of the understanding of the sacraments as only "means of salvation." This, though, presumes the Council's understanding of Church, which we have yet to discuss – therefore we shall not, here, venture any deeper into the theological section of the Constitution on the Sacred Liturgy.

In the liturgy we find everything that makes up Christian belief: the message of God's act of salvation in Christ; the faith of the Church and the confession of that faith; the faith of the individual, publically proclaimed in the reception of the sacrament; the reminder of the consequences for one's life. For this reason, the Council can say – the highpoint of the entire Constitution on the Sacred Liturgy – that liturgy is "the summit toward which the activity of the church is directed; it is also the source from which all its power flows" (Article 10). The liturgy, then, cannot remain a matter for clergy alone – the congregation must "actively participate," *actuosa participatio*; this idea surfaces again and again in the Constitution on the Sacred Liturgy. If there is to be "active participation," then the congregation has to understand everything directly, not through a translator. And even more than this: if there is to be comprehensibility, then the ceremonies must change. Readings belong at the ambo – and if the homily interprets the reading, that is, the Gospel, it is best if one stays at the ambo. The altar must be closer to the people. In older Churches, new altars are installed at the beginning of the nave; the high altar catches the eye, but becomes unfunctional. Because the liturgy is once again an event with distributed roles – these would be limited only at the simplest weekday Mass – the priest does not have to "read," for example, what the congregation says or sings, what the lectors recite. The result:

during the Liturgy of the Word the priest does not sit or stand at the altar, but in a chair positioned behind or besides the altar – almost like on a Bishop's throne, something that helped reconcile some pastors with the liturgical reforms. And above all: it only makes sense that the pastor, that is, the "celebrant," sees his congregation at the Celebration of the Eucharist.

This is still not sufficient. If the texts of the liturgy are to be understood, then many of them cannot remain as they were, because they come out of an antiquated piety that is incomprehensible in the present day – for example texts that clearly mirror anti-body and anti-world attitudes. The Council prescribed not only the vernacular, but also the adjustment of the liturgy itself to the needs of the Church of today, particularly the needs of the "mission lands."

V. THE RESULTS – AND A JUDGMENT

1. RESULTS

We have turned, naturally enough, to the consequences of the Constitution on the Sacred Liturgy, consequences that were not visible until the end of the Council, after the first regulations governing the implementation of the liturgy reform went into effect on March 7, 1965. In fact, the text of the Constitution on the Sacred Liturgy reads, from Chapter 2 on, like a detailed instruction manual, the explosive nature of which no one notices at first. However, anyone who had enough imagination could imagine even then what would happen in the ensuing years – especially since the decisions of the Council were immediately made known through the media and the congregations were prepared or, in some cases, forewarned.

The first result: the already mentioned "loose leaf salad" at the ambo and the altar. The Liturgical Commissions of the dioceses began immediately with provisional translations and provisional new texts. Bishops enacted regulations – for example, which parts of the *Ordinarium* could be replaced by a song in German, or whether a song should be sung *after* the dismissal prayer, etc. This all happened at the beginning in a very non-uniform fashion – along with the freestyle liturgy of some chaplains and pastors, who suddenly considered it permissible to make their own personal style of piety the standard for the liturgy.

This improvisation stage has been over since around 1970 – according to the opinion of some, it ended too quickly. The end came as it had to come: imagination petered out after a time, when Sunday after Sunday one had to come up with something new. One begins to be thankful when there is an established, suitable-for-book lovers "Massbook," in which everything was laid out in an easy-to-read way. This is the case in German-speaking lands since 1974. Nonetheless, this does not mean a return to pre-Council stiffness, because the elements of spontaneity are built into the Ordinary Form of the Roman Rite. The pastor can, if he is determined to do so, add four additional, short homilies to the main homily at Sunday Mass – at the greeting, at the introduction to the prayers of the faithful, during the silent prayer after Communion, and before the dismissal – and if he wants, also at the introduction of the sign of peace. In the new Massbook are found the new texts that in the Latin new order of the liturgy were introduced from Rome as substitutes for the old texts. It is easy to forget: there is also a Latin Massbook with the reformed liturgy, the so-called "Latin prototype"!

A more important result: as expected, the vernacular did not come to a stop before the Canon (Eucharistic Prayer). Those who were charged with this weighty matter were correct: a Latin-vernacular mixed liturgy, Latin texts framed by vernacular texts, could never have felt normal. Very quickly Rome approved the Canon of the Mass in the vernacular, and with this the liturgy was completely in the vernacular. The cause of this approval was pressure from some of the Bishops' Conferences, above all from the Netherlands. But I can still remember how, in 1968, we did not believe our ears! Still in 1965 – or better, *already* in 1965! – the already-mentioned Roman Instruction on the Implementation of the Constitution on the Sacred Liturgy had extended the authorization of the vernacular far beyond the boundaries of Article 36 of the Constitution on the Sacred Liturgy. However, Rome had strictly reserved for itself the vernacular in the Canon of the Mass. In 1968, however, the vernacular was allowed for the Canon of the Mass, along with three new Eucharistic Prayers of differing lengths, which were oriented toward the formulae of the ancient Church and now along with the old Roman Eucharistic Prayer could be used, with the success, that this last, in normal praxis of a congregation, is used so good as never.

And finally: the liturgy reform brought a radical change to the biblical readings in the liturgy. Along with the New Testament reading – as an alternative or as an addition, depending on the decision of the leader of the liturgy – came an Old Testament reading, so that now, on Sundays, three readings are the norm. This happens now in a three year cycle that is arranged so that within these three years the faithful can hear almost the entire New Testament and – particularly during the weekday Masses – a large portion of the Old Testament, as well. They should also hear homilies on these texts, since the biblical homily has become the norm for Sunday Masses.

Admittedly, with the new ordering of readings a piece of ecumenical unity was surrendered, since up to this time the liturgical ordering of readings in the Roman Catholic Church and in the German Lutheran Churches had been more or less the same. In order to make greater variety possible, the Lutheran Church in Germany had – on a voluntary basis, but for the most part complied with – furnished an additional ordering of texts for sermons, texts that are read by the preacher, at the pulpit, immediately before the sermon. The ecumenical price of the new ordering of readings created by the Catholic liturgy reform seems not to be too high, in my opinion. The German Lutheran Churches must ask themselves, in light of the decreasing interest in Bible groups and of the loss of Bible knowledge even among candidates for confirmation, where the faithful will, in any sort of comprehensive way, be confronted with the text of the Bible.

And now a post-Council Sunday Celebration of the Eucharist looks not only like an Anglican Sunday liturgy, but also like a Lutheran liturgy celebrated in the liturgical high form – and occasionally Catholics who are not German have confused the different liturgies, attending a Lutheran liturgy in the belief that they were at a Catholic Mass. The Catholic liturgies are now more informal than in – completely un-Lutheran – stiff Lutheran high liturgies. Perhaps it is sometimes an advantage, after all, if after a significant delay one incorporates the concerns of Luther that could have been fulfilled in 1520.

2. A JUDGMENT

a) Our congregations have accepted, with an overwhelming majority, the liturgy reform and do not want any other liturgy. The "solemnity" does not have to suffer because of this – it is there, but no longer without the participation of the entire congregation. This demonstrates that the reform hit the nail on the head – and hit it squarely on the head in the face of the massive opposition against the liturgy reform that rose up immediately after the Council and today is to be met with only in communities that have the structure of sects. Apart from these groups, even the friends of the old liturgy do not want the old Mass, completely "read" in Latin and partially translated, back; even fewer would yearn for the return of the untranslated Latin Mass.

b) The Latin Mass remains limited to – and maintained for – those occasions in which one wants to preserve the musical treasures of the Latin liturgical tradition. The achievements of the liturgy reform are not surrendered: in any case the people sing the acclamations, if possible parts of the *Ordinarium*. A "proper" Latin Mass in a Catholic Church looks like this, today: introductory part in Latin, with corresponding hymns; then the German portion follows: readings, homily, Creed (the last either spoken in German or chanted in Latin), prayers of the faithful – the hymn sung after the reading can be in Latin. After the prayers of the faithful the Mass continues in Latin; the priest *chants*, in this instance, the Eucharistic Prayer, with the Words of Consecration, in Latin. Many congregations are in the position – but for how much longer? – to chant the Our Father in Latin along with the priest.

It has come to be the reasonable practice that a polyphonic Latin Mass does not necessarily have to be *completely* chanted. For example, the congregation can chant the *Kyrie* and the *Sanctus* according to a simple Gregorian formula, then the Choir can take over the *Gloria* and the *Agnus Dei* – the choir can sing the *Benedictus* during Communion. And since the *Proprium* provides space for a variety of hymns, the choir has plenty of opportunity to show what it can do.

c) The liturgy reform contributed considerably to the "de-clericalization" of the liturgy – despite the small Bishop's Seat for the presider. The main reason for this "de-clericalization" is that the congregation once again has their role. This is accompanied by other reforms: readings and prayers of the faithful from members of the congregation, Eucharistic ministers (both male and female), who help with the distribution of Communion (commissioned by the Bishop), female acolytes (despite continuing efforts to hinder this development), communion in the hand (allowed by Rome since 1969 and immediately introduced by the German Bishops, although of course the faithful have the choice to continue with the practice of communion in the mouth), and, finally, reception of Communion under both kinds where conditions allow – so, liturgies celebrated with smaller groups – weddings, for example; it is not uncommon to find Communion under both kinds as the norm for Sunday Mass (I have experienced this in the USA).

d) The liturgy reform has contributed to the decentralization of the Church, despite the obligation to obtain confirmation from the Roman Curia. The Bishops' Conferences were mentioned as regional authority for the first time in the Constitution on the Sacred Liturgy. Next to the concern about Latin, the concerns were the main sticking points of the resistance to the liturgy reform during and after the Council. This is clearly shown by the fact that during the Council, when votes were taken in matters pertaining to these concerns, the "with reservation" votes increased dramatically. No doubt exists: supporters of the traditional had and have a good nose for the implications of reforms. I can only agree whole-heartedly with Karl Rahner, when he says, at the end of his introduction to the Constitution on the Sacred Liturgy, that the liturgy reform brought what countless Catholics had longed for – and still, in the end, the Constitution was a completely unexpected gift.

3. AN UNSOLVED PROBLEM

The liturgy reform may have, despite everything, above all despite the unbelievable amount of work put in by those who had the job of taking care of the implementation, left a few things to be desired. The resistance, which in part took forms that caused normal perceptions of good Catholic ecclesial obedience to appear like childlike naivety, prevented one or another courageous decisions and forced compromises. A basic problem of the liturgy reform does not lie on the surface, and it is connected with the strengths of the Constitution on the Sacred Liturgy and the reforms that were implemented on the basis of this Constitution.

A critical comment heard about liturgical scholars (particularly the German ones) is: They think and act according to the principle, "Because it's so old, it's beautiful!" Indeed, the liturgy reform had restored the liturgy of the *ancient Church*, but not the completely open form of the New Testament liturgy. One must avoid at all costs this last mentioned; but the normativity of the ancient Church for the liturgy reform also has its problems. The ancient Church liturgy is in any case already a document of what is called the "re-sacerdotalization" of the ecclesial office. What is meant is the following: at the latest since the 4th century – not without reason from the time when Christianity began to be the state religion of the Roman Empire – the ecclesial office holders were again called "priests," and the worship service changed – simplified and somewhat spitefully said – from "communal celebration" to "liturgy." The New Testament had designated the ecclesial office holders by "secular" names: the Bishop (*episkopos*) is a "supervisor," literally an "inspector," the priest (*presbyter*) is an "elder," and the deacon (*diakonos*) means "waiter" or "table server."

The liturgies restored by the liturgy reform are those of the ancient Church with, put pointedly, a determined *role* for the congregation, but still not with the congregation as *subject*. The result: a liturgical creativity of the *modern* congregation is actually not provided for. Is Goethe's line relevant for the liturgy: "Woe to you, that you are a grandchild!"? For this reason, attempts to develop liturgies in completely new ways have a very hard time of it. Even the House Eucharist or the Table Eucharist is regarded with a great deal of suspicion. The claim of the Constitution on the Sacred Liturgy to adapt the liturgy to the modern world, above all in the mission lands, is now only inadequately fulfilled. Where "people's liturgy" is attempted (for example, in Latin America), it immediately is subject to all sorts of "grassroots democracy" suspicion. Attempts at a local form of the liturgy in Africa or in Asia that includes completely harmless deviations from the Roman prototype remain, after a short experimental phase, stuck or anxiously nipped in the bud. But to use the words of a prominent African theologian, Dr. Bénézet Bujo: "It is not an Africanization of Christendom, if a priest at the Celebration of the Eucharist puts on a chieftain's decoration!"

One could easily, without anxiety, show generosity and encourage creativity. The tradition of the Jewish-Christian-ancient Church liturgy is despite all clerical "enrichment" in the ancient Church of such convincing logic that every Christian liturgy, if one wanted to design it from zero, demonstrably – experiments have shown this – would arrive at the known basic pattern: Introduction, Liturgy of the

Word (Bible readings, Homily, Creed, Intercessions), Liturgy of the Eucharist (Preparation, Eucharistic Prayer, Communion), Concluding Rite. Does this basic pattern not suffice, so that then the remainder might be left to the creative fantasy of the Church under the leadership of the regional hierarchy?

VI. A COMMENT ON A CONTROVERSIAL MEASURE TAKEN BY POPE JOHN PAUL II

In 1985, Pope John Paul II, in connection with intensive efforts to reach a reconciliation with the suspended Archbishop Lefebvre, permitted priests under certain conditions to celebrate the pre-Council Mass – that is, the Mass in the form prescribed by Pius V in 1570. The suspicion that the Pope was taking back (again) a piece of the reforms of the Second Vatican Council was of course immediately voiced. What was behind this?

In 1970, with the definitive introduction of the new Mass Book, Pope Paul VI had – almost exactly to the day 400 years after the liturgy reform of his predecessor Pope Pius V – abolished the old form of the Mass that had been standardized by the Council of Trent; not only did Pope Paul VI repeal the obligation to this Tridentine Mass, but he actually forbad this form. I have always thought this unwise, since it was even then easy to see that the liturgy reform had been accepted by congregations. An instruction to the pastors would have sufficed, to the effect that they should not withhold the fruits of the liturgy reform from the congregations because of attachment to the old liturgy. One result of the ban was the strengthening of the Lefebvre movement. The 1985 measure seems to have been a completely personal decision of John Paul II. The responsible Curia officials as well as many influential Bishops apparently warned him against this move. The official document issued by the Congregation for Divine Worship and the Discipline of the Sacraments allows a window on the hesitancy: first then document declares that congregations have no problem with the ban; a little later in the document, we find a reference to problems that still exist concerning the ban.

The new permission is hedged in with conditions: the old form of the Mass can be used only with the permission of the Bishop; the concession pertains only to those priests (or groups) that have petitioned for it, it may not be imposed on anyone; it pertains only to an approved place (for example, in a particular Church, designated by the Bishop); the permission applies only to the form of the Mass Book of 1962, so to an already slightly reformed form of the *Liturgia Piana* of 1945; and the old Mass could only be celebrated in Latin, there could not be a mixing of the elements of the old liturgy and the post-Council liturgy as one saw fit. Particularly this last point is an appropriate criterion, since I do not believe that even the "conservative" pastors would like to do without *all* the achievements of the liturgy reform. But above all: the permission for the old Mass, which must be issued by a Bishop, is contingent on the petitioner's formal recognition of the orthodoxy of the liturgy reform of the Second Vatican Council. Even up to today, accusations by reform opponents that the liturgy reform contains false doctrine have not ceased.

The whole matter was a "chess move" by the Pope, a sort of test question put to the followers of Lefebvre. They had to show their true colors and indicate what they *really* wanted: did their resistance really have only to do with the Tridentine Mass or were they advocating for the rejection of the entire Council? And they did indeed show their true colors: Archbishop Lefebvre did *not* reconcile himself before his death in March of 1991. Nonetheless, the offer to his followers of return to the Church still contains an amount of accommodation that "left leaners" in the Church can only dream of.

When it comes to the liturgy reform, one could speak of the Pope distancing himself from the Council if he, for example during one of his trips abroad, celebrated the *Liturgia Piana* form of the Eucharist. Cardinal Ratzinger did this for the traditionalist Priestly Fraternity of St. Peter. According to reliable information, at that time German presses responsible for printing Catholic liturgical materials were inundated with calls about how and where one could still acquire the old Mass Books. It will take an entire generation until the liturgy reform wins the spirit and heart of the *entire* Church. But we can already say today that the liturgy reform is the most lasting work of the Council.

That is true also with respect to ecumenism. How can, for example with regard to the thorny problem of open communion, the fundamental difference between a Catholic Celebration of the Eucharist and a Lutheran Communion liturgy be made clear to Catholic Christians, when the external form is so very similar? Not only in the USA, but also in Germany, Lutheran pastors are entitled to use, during the

Service of Holy Communion, our second Eucharistic Prayer, the first
of the three new ones.

CHAPTER FIVE

THOSE WHO BELONG TO THE PEOPLE BECOME "THE PEOPLE"

The Understanding of the Church

I. IMAGES OF THE CHURCH

1. FROM THE HIERARCHY TO THE PEOPLE

"For, thank God, [to-day] a child seven years old knows what the Church is, namely, the holy believers and lambs who hear the voice of their Shepherd." (*The Smalcald Articles*, Martin Luther)

"He has, however, willed to make women and men holy and to save them, not as individuals without any bond between them, but rather to make them into a people who might acknowledge him and serve him in holiness. ... Christ instituted this new covenant, the new covenant in his blood (see 1 Cor 11:25); he called a people together made up of Jews and Gentiles which would be one, not according to the flesh, but in the Spirit, and it would be the new people of God. For those who believe in Christ, who are reborn, not from a corruptible but from an incorruptible seed, through the word of the living God (see 1 Pet 1:23), not from flesh but from water and the holy Spirit (see Jn 3:5-6), are finally established as 'a chosen race, a royal priesthood, a holy nation, a people for his possession ... who in times past were not a people, but now are the people of God' (1 Pet 2:9-10)." (Constitution on the Church, Article 9)

It is quite odd how long it took before a council of the Roman Catholic Church accepted, as an essential description of the Church, such a simple, such a biblical idea as the Church as the faithful people of God – and without speaking in the same breath of office and hierarchy! It is also odd how long it took until those belonging to the *laos theou* (cf. for example 1 Peter 2:10; Acts 18:10) – that is, the *laikoi*, the "laity" – were acknowledged as "the people of God."

Was this view of the people as made holy through spirit-given faith blocked for centuries in the Roman Catholic Church precisely because it was Luther who so decisively championed the idea of the Church as the faithful people? That Luther – unwillingly – blocked fruitful developments in the Church of Rome, in that he provoked anti-reform defensive reactions, can be ascertained elsewhere. In the context of the liturgical reform this has already been proven, and so we are not far from the truth with an assumption of an anti –reform constriction here. Luther of course had every reason to accentuate his new (and yet simply biblical) opinion of the Church. "They like it, that they are considered the Church, like Pope, Cardinals, Bishops," he wrote in 1537. This thesis was actually current: the hierarchy was the Church, while the faithful only had a share in her.

This was of course a thesis of *late medieval* theology. That the tradition spoke *for*, not *against* Luther is obvious today from every description of the history of the doctrine of the Church. We limit ourselves here to a few references that profile the situation at the eve of the Second Vatican Council. We have already indicated the biblical support in the cited texts – this will have to suffice.

2. FROM THE PATRISTIC PERIOD TO THE REFORMATION

The time of the Church Fathers before Constantine and the end of the Christian persecution, as well as the image of the Church provided by Augustine, is characterized by the variation and deepening of the biblical images. The nature of the Church was expresses in metaphors such as *mysterium* (in the sense of: revealed salvific plan of God), "People of God," "House of God," "Bride of Christ," among others. Characteristically: one spoke of the inner mystery of the Church and did not have to speak of office and hierarchy – although the last was already fully formed and functional, even including a certain particular standing of the Church of Rome, if not yet in the sense of the later (medieval and modern) papacy.

The much referenced "Constantinian change" really meant a *change* for the Church image. Heinrich Fries, German theologian and ecumenist (1911-1998) coined the term: Church as Empire. This was the result of ecclesial offices modeling themselves after Imperial Roman offices, in part assuming the functions of these offices and therefore their robes: the red color of the Bishops' official dress goes back to the red color of the robes of the imperial officials. For the first time the development of primacy of office led to a description of the nature of the Church – soon strengthened by Gelasius I's "Two Swords Theory," and since the much discussed *Dictatus Papae* of Pope Gregory VII from the year 1075 the "spiritual sword" has been firmly in the hand of the papacy. The *Ecclesia Imperatrix et Domina* (the Church as Empress and Mistress) became increasingly identified with the hierarchy. At the coronation of the Pope, Jeremiah 1:10 was applied to the Pontiff: "Behold, I have this day set you over the nations and over the kingdoms, to pluck up and to break down and to destroy and to overthrow, to build and to plant." The same for 1 Corinthians 2:15, cf. 6:3: "But he who is spiritual discerns all things, and he himself is judged by no one." Titles that had applied to the entire Church, for all office holders, were now limited to the Pope: *Papa, Sedes Apostolica, Vicarius Christi, Mater Ecclesia* – and the "Mother" Church was, at the end, the Roman Bishop's Church, that is, the Lateran Basilica – "Ship of the Church," "Ship of Peter," "Mystical Body of Christ," etc. The laity were the subjects of the hierarchy – and since that pleased no one, from the clerical side this saying seemed obvious: *Clericis laicos infestos oppido tradit antiquitas* – "Since ancient time the laity are opposed to the clerics." The French theologian and ecumenist Yves Congar (1904-1995) asked ironically: "Which ancient time? That of St. Paul?" The saying was included in a Constitution of Pope Boniface VIII (papacy: 1294-1303). It is not surprising that Luther felt it necessary to write an essay in 1522 with the title: "Again concerning the falsely named spiritual rank of the Pope and the Bishops."

Nonetheless – this is added for the sake of completeness and justice – this development of Church as Empire did not occur without any resistance. For example, in the 12th century the Abbot Joachim of Fiore taught about the coming Third Age of Salvation History, the Age of the Holy Spirit, which would dissolve the Age of Church as Empire. This teaching was, as Abbot Joachim's teaching on the Trinity, condemned by the Church at the Fourth Lateran Council in 1215. Despite this condemnation, his theories played a significant role later, with the Franciscans; a few radical Franciscan theologians identified the founder of their order with the prophetic figure sent from Heaven who, according to Abbot Joachim's teaching, would introduce the Age of the Holy Spirit. This conglomerate of theories, in part fanciful and, in the end, resulting in violence, reflects a deep dissatisfaction with the Imperial Church and the deep fundamental conviction that the Church should define herself through a spiritual mystery and not through her powerful outward appearance. The ideal of a Church of the poor, however misshapen and sometimes misused, was nonetheless never eradicated in the time of the Church as Empire. This is true also when only a few – in the late Middle Ages it became more (William of Ockham, Marsilius of Padua) – might have thought that the imperial power of the Church rested on an usurpation and actually was an offense to her nature.

The Church was spoken of as a spiritual reality by theologians who beyond a shadow of a doubt were faithful to the Church and sharply repudiated Joachim of Fiore's theses – Thomas of Aquinas, for example. In his Commentary on the Creed, which originated from sermons to the "student community" in Naples, Thomas said: "Church is the same as assembly (*congregatio*)" – Luther argued exactly this in his 1537 "Von den Konziliis und Kirchen" – "Therefore the holy Church is the same as the assembly of the faithful." This same Thomas had also – at the time of Pope Innocent IV, to whom the emperors had conclusively succumbed in their battle with the papacy – not considered it necessary to write a treatise on the Church. The ecclesiology (Doctrine of the Church), however, which can be puzzled out of his other statements, particularly those in the realm of the Doctrine of the Old and New Law and of the Sacraments, has drawn criticism of "spiritualization" (from the Catholic scholars) and of "reification" and of "Papism" (from the Lutheran side).

3. FROM THE REFORMATION UNTIL THE
EVE OF THE COUNCIL

Conciliarism, introduced in order to end the decline of the papacy and the great western Church split, was no help with the clericalization of the Church. It only shifted weight within the clerical Church, and it was the adherents of conciliarism who considered it a given that the Church is essentially identical with the hierarchy.

So it remained to Luther, driven by his interest in necessary reform, not only to connect again with early medieval and high medieval claims,

above all in his writing "To the Christian Nobility of the German
Nation on the Improvement of the Christian Position," but also to turn
to the Bible for theological answers to questions about the true nature
of the Church. The consequences on the Catholic side are known. The
institutional and papal Church was not only politically and legally (according to canon law), but also theologically established. The famous
definition of the nature of the Church coined by the theologian and
Cardinal Robert Bellarmine at the turn of the 17th century is characteristic and successful because it is easily remembered; it is directed
directly against the Reformation understanding of the Church: "The
Church is the assembly of men gathered in the profession of the same
Christian faith, and in the communion of the same sacraments, under
the reign of legitimate pastors, and especially of the one vicar of Chris
on earth, the Roman Pontiff." Here, as in the entire tradition of the
Doctrine of the Church, Acts 2:42 had an effect: "They held firm on
the teaching of the Apostles and on the community, on the breaking of
the bread and on the prayers." That means: Church is always constituted through binding profession, liturgy, and communal living. But the
sharpness in Bellarmine's definition is also unequivocal: the Church
is not only – what still sufficed for Thomas – determined through
community in profession of faith and sacrament, but everyone in the
Church must live under legitimate ministry and "particularly" under
that of the Roman Bishop. The Church is therefore defined through
its juridical constitution and her "Romanness." Both belong as a visible
form of the Church so much to its nature, that no one took umbrage
at the Cardinal's sentence: "The Church is as visible and tangible as
the assembly of the people of Rome or the Kingdom of France or the
Republic of Venice." Now "Catholic" had become a confessional term,
to which one no longer had to add "Roman."

Justice demands the statement that subsequent Catholic theology grew beyond Bellarmine's definition, above all in the Catholic
"Tübingen School" of the 19th century, with their fundamental idea
of the Church as a living organism, in which the incarnation of the
Word of God in a certain way continues in history. In the 20th century
a new theology of the Church could link itself with this fundamental
idea. Roman Guardini formulated the motto in his book, *The Church
and the Catholic and the Spirit of the Liturgy* (London 1935): "The
Church awakens in the soul." This new theology of the Church reflects
back to the idea of the Church as the Body of Christ. Its places were

the liturgical movement, the Bible movement, the (Catholic) Youth Movement. Its cult book was *The Spirit of Catholicism*, by Karl Adam, the Tübingen dogmatic theologian.

In Pope Pius XII's 1943 encyclical *Mystici Corporis*, this idea of Church as the Body of Christ received the highest confirmation through the institutional Church ministry. But this all happened under the secure roof of the Bellarmine definition – very distant from questioning the definition of the Church from the perspective of ministry. On the contrary, one gets the impression, looking back; this totally new theology was the – successful – attempt to shift the stress from a reality of the Church that could no longer be called into question to her inner mystery, so that one might endure in this reality. Pius XII in his encyclical had used the idea of the "body" in order to derive the official structure of the Church from the picture of the body. The necessity of the theological new consciousness was felt by the theologians who under the popes after the First Vatican Council, when it concerned freedom for critical questions, had nothing to smile about. Humanly and spiritually they could endure the short leash of the Magisterium, indeed the direct surveillance (through spies!) in the knowledge of a deeper mystery of the Church. How *successful* this new consciousness was, however, is indicated by the enthusiasm for Church and Pope among the Catholic laypeople, laypeople who had no idea of the conflicts of the theologians – conflicts that had cost more than one broken existence!

How little the new consciousness of the mystery of the Church asserted itself where it would have been well received is indicated by what the 1917 *Codex Iuris Canonici* said about the laity – so, about the People of God! Only *one* basic canon (682) defined their theological place in the Church: the laity have the right to receive spiritual goods and the means to salvation (the sacraments) from the clergy. All the rest are only prohibitions and duties: Laity may not wear clerical clothes, may not "usurp" the office of the preacher; they must give clergy reverence appropriate to their rank; may become members of fraternities and sometimes take part in the administration of Church property. That is about all that the *Codex* had to say about the laity. In the old *Wetzer und Welte's Kirchenlexikon* of 1882-1901, at the heading "Laity," one finds only the cross-reference "s. Clerus" ("see clergy.'")

That was the position of the "People of God" before the Council. One last indication of the position was the already quoted arrogant speech of the General Secretary of the Council, Felici, at the press conference. Felici distinguished between the "teaching" and the "listening" Church. That it came eventually to a conflict-ridden change, one whose end process could not be foreseen, is due to a process set in motion at the Council. Therefore we are going to look first at a few characteristic details of the history and the origin of the Dogmatic Constitution on the Church and the documents associated with it.

II. THE BATTLE SURROUNDING THE COUNCIL'S UNDERSTANDING OF THE CHURCH

1. THE PRELUDE TO THE CONSTITUTION ON THE SACRED LITURGY

We have already noted in the previous chapter that it had nothing to do with planning: only external and controversial circumstances led to the Constitution on the Sacred Liturgy being the first document taken under advisement. So it is even more significant that in the prepared drafts this Constitution, without prior agreement, introduced the central themes of the conciliar understanding of Church. Already in the introduction this Constitution spoke of the Church in the style of the later Dogmatic Constitution on the Church. In biblically inspired language the "Mysterium of Christ and the real nature of the true Church" were addressed: at the same time divine and human, invisible and visible, contemporary and oriented toward he completion at the end of days. Through participation in the Liturgy the faithful were built into a holy temple in the Lord, into a dwelling of God in the Spirit and should become signs among the nations. Articles 5 and 26 expressly used the later so important concept of the Church as "sacrament."

Such formulations did not exercise obvious influence on the work on the Dogmatic Constitution on the Church. But Council Fathers who carried through the theological basis of the Liturgy reform with this language would express themselves with the same meaning at the discussions – and conflicts – around the Dogmatic Constitution on the Church. After the liturgy schema was accepted as the basis of discussion it was also clear that no draft about the understanding of the Church had a chance for agreement if it, in the old style, spoke about the Church in only legal and institutional language.

2. THE FIRST DRAFT OF 1962

The Dogmatic Constitution on the Church went through three stages of work-up, of which the transition from the first to the second draft was the most decisive one. The step from the second to the final draft was mainly redactional in nature – which does not mean that bitter battles were not waged. The Preparatory Commission *De doctrina fidei et morum* ("For questions of doctrine and morals"), the predecessor of the later Theological Commission, was subordinate at that time to the *Sanctum Officium*; as a consequence this Commission was under the leadership of Cardinal Ottaviani. This Commission was responsible for the preparation of the Dogmatic Constitution on the Church. The Secretary was the Jesuit Sebastian Tromp, of the Gregorian University; he had been the main author of Pius XII's *Mystici Corporis*. As was the case with the Liturgy Commission, the main burden of the draft and editorial work belonged to the Secretary. One large difference between the two commissions: Sebastian Tromp did not represent a thrust into the future. The Commission – or rather, a sub-commission of the Commission-- presented a draft, the organization of which we need to visualize if we want to understand the later debates:

1. The nature of the Church Militant;
2. The members of the Church and the necessity of the Church for salvation;
3. The Episcopate as the highest level of the sacrament of ordination and the Priesthood;
4. The Bishops;
5. The States of Perfection;
6. The Laity;
7. The Teaching Office of the Church;
8. Authority and Obedience in the Church;
9. The relationships between Church and State and religious tolerance;
10. The necessity of preaching the Gospel to all people and in the entire world;
11. Ecumenism;
12. (As an appendix, with its arrangement still open), the Virgin Mary, Mother of God and Mother of Humanity.

The entirety filled a volume with 123 pages. With just a glance at this arrangement the following is evident:

a) It is a loose series of individual problems, joined together only according to a loose system. One can, with a little goodwill, recognize the following system: The Nature of the Church (1); People in the Church and the Distinctions in Rank (2-6); The Inner Structure of the Church (7-8); The External Relationships of the Church (9-11); Mary as a Type of the Church (12). In fact, the Sub-commission did not want to work out a complete treatise, but hoped to address each question that it considered pressing and in need of decision.

b) The draft is recognizably overloaded. Clarity would be possible if one bracketed off certain spheres of questions and made these into separate documents. This did indeed happen. Separate decrees developed – concerning Bishops (from Chapter 4), concerning members of orders (from sections of Chapter 5), concerning the Lay Apostolate (from sections of Chapter 6), concerning the mission activity of the Church (from Chapter 10), concerning Ecumenism (from Chapter 11). Sections of Chapter 9 went into the Pastoral Constitution on the Church in the Modern World and into the Declaration on Religious Freedom.

c) Something else evinced itself: precisely because all these later independent documents were originally part of the Church schema, it is clear that for the Preparatory Commission this Church schema was intended to be, and in fact became, the heart of the conciliar pronouncement. Particularly Cardinal Montini of Milan, after his election as Pope Paul VI, always gave the impression, particularly in the opening addresses of the 2nd and 3rd sessions, that this teaching was the most important of the entire Council.

d) Finally – the draft also indicated where the conflict would come: the "above to below" thinking, just assumed as a given. The Church "Militant" is not only a typical medieval concept, but it characterizes much of the Church of the late 19th and early 20th centuries – defending itself in a hostile world, declaring its legal claims and asserting itself through strength. From the Church Militant as a whole the glance shifts to those who belong to her – which is completely different from the question concerning "the People of God"! – and then to the church members in detail, beginning with the Bishops to, at the end, the laity. That is essentially the program that the First Vatican Council had undertaken but could not complete, because the Primacy question was given priority.

The further chapters of the draft indicate that the members of the Commission were aware of the developments since 1870, but were inclined to solve them on the basis of the First Vatican Council. The Modernist Controversy from the beginning of the century had not been able to hinder the "invasion" of historical critical methods in biblical interpretation; therefore one had to speak about the teaching office. The secular neutral state, still the great enemy in 1870, was by this time obvious reality, agreed to by millions of Catholics worldwide – therefore, one had to speak in new ways about Church and State as well as about religious tolerance; how that was intended in the draft was shown later by the obstinate resistance to the Declaration on Religious Freedom, particularly from parts of the Italian and Spanish Episcopate. In Spain the Catholic Church was the State Church, in Italy canon law, where it touched the social realm, was also state law (so, for example, no state divorce, no marriage before a civil magistrate, etc.). Moreover, the ecumenical must no longer be ignored. And finally, Popes Pius XI and Pius XII had already promoted the notion of the "Catholic Action," therefore the so-called "Apostolate for the Laity." From the Sub-Commission's draft it is clear that the members did not yet understand this as an expression of the life of the Church in its own right, but in a certain way as the extended arm of the institutional Church. This meant that one could not manage with the meager words of canon law on the laity. The general impression given by the draft: an admission of newly emerged problems, but a processing of these problems along the traditional lines, or better: conciliar strengthening of earlier processes, particularly those already carried out by Popes Pius XI and Pius XII. In any event, the draft yielded no fundamentally different picture of the Church. The draft aimed therefore at an expanded fulfillment of the First Vatican Council by means of the completion of what remained unfinished at the time of the First Vatican Council. The Second Vatican Council would have been nothing other than the close of the First Vatican Council.

3. BREATHTAKING CRITICISM

After his experience with the Liturgy schema, Cardinal Ottaviani sensed what would come. With the introduction of the proposal, which was debated for the first time from 1-7 December, 1962, so at the close of the first session, Cardinal Ottaviani remarked that he knew where the guns had been placed from which one would now shoot at the draft. It would be said that it was "negative, Scholastic, not pastoral, and not ecumenical." He recommended reading the text through calmly.

The Fathers did this – and the result was a Council debate of such theological sophistication never again achieved at the Council (according to some observers). The following were the main objections and suggestions for improvement:

a) The draft lacked a logical conclusion. This was a criticism leveled by, among others, Cardinal Montini, the soon-to-be pope.

b) The Church was described too infrequently in new perspectives; these new perspectives would not need to contradict the old perspectives: too little on community, too much on society. The Bishop of Strasburg, Elchinger, expressed it in biting contrasting pairs: Yesterday the Church was considered as an institution, today we experience it as community. Yesterday the Pope was the sinecure of all eyes; today one visualizes the Bishops united with the Pope. Yesterday the individual Bishops were the focus; today the focus is on the totality of the Bishops. Yesterday theology highlighted the meaning of the hierarchy; today it reveals the People of God. Yesterday, theology emphasized what separated, today it emphasizes what unites. Yesterday the theologians considered the inner life of the Church, today they look to the Church that is open to her surroundings. It was clear what the readers wanted to say – the draft belonged to yesterday.

c) The draft spoke too legalistically; it identified the mystical Body of Christ too directly with the Roman institutional Church and neglected salvation history and the eschatological dimension of the Church. That was a request that the Cologne Cardinal Frings represented, and which led to the late insertion of the 5th article of the Constitution and the elaboration of the 7th chapter on the Pilgrim Church.

d) The most noteworthy speech of the discussion, and one of the most noteworthy of the Council, was given by the Bishop of Brussels, de Smedt. He expanded the reproach of the overly legalistic language concerning the Church to a criticism of the language and mentality of the whole draft; he spoke of "seeking after fame and prestige in its indiscreet superlatives." When the Church describes her mission, she must avoid all triumphalism. She must not portray herself as determined to conquer, marching from victory to victory. She must not reduce her own life to the activity of the hierarchy, allowing herself to be carried away by clericalism. And finally – she must not make any concessions to legalism. The uniate Easterners endorsed this criticism from their own perspective, a perspective that often proved to be very beneficial during the Council. The Patriarch Maximus IV Saigh spoke of Roman exaggerations and of the undue emphasis on the doctrine of papal primacy in comparison with much more important doctrines. The Patriarch Hakim missed the presence of any broader Church traditions in the text and suggested that the text cultivate more of the language of John XXIII. The Coptic Archbishop Issac Ghattas explicitly said that the text reduced the Body of Christ to the Church Militant and the Roman Church.

These statements are important for the light they shine on the situation of the uniate Eastern Churches. The Roman Curia chalked and chalks them up to its own account, approving a liturgy for the uniate Eastern Churches as well as their own law, expressly acknowledged by the CIC. But the uniate eastern Churches had never had any lasting, "raising of consciousness" effect in the Roman Catholic Church – that is, not until the Council. They were not allowed to pursue any missionary work; from a complex of political and ecclesiastical reasons, they had never pursued this outside of their own traditional territories. Theologically they remained a peripheral phenomenon in the public consciousness of the Church – and so it is not surprising that the draft of the schema on the Church, apparently without intention, argued as if they just did not exist. It was through the Council that the Catholic public really first became aware that these uniate Churches, with their own theological importance, existed. This recognition was due in large part to remarkable Council Fathers: for example, the Patriarchs Maximus and Hakim, whose speeches were some of the highpoints of the Council.

e) One last criticism, which must have cut the authors of the draft to the quick, was also brought forward in this first round of discussions: the document lacked any mention of the humiliated Church, of the poor Church, of the suffering Church. This last point came, understandably, particularly from representatives of the Church in the Eastern Block countries.

The discussion was, according to the protocol, only a general debate, with the aim of bringing about a vote on whether the draft should be accepted as the basis of further, more detailed, discussion. The prospects did not look good. In an interview, Cardinal Ottaviani expressed himself about the numerous new perspectives and demands on the text: "Not everything that is new is true or good." He revealed how he valued the objections: as innovations, although all the speakers had emphasized that they were concerned with forgotten *ancient* truths about the Church. Bishop Musto of Aquino (the home of St. Thomas of Aquinas) excited the rage of the gathering – as a murmur of protest that interrupted his speech – when he did not shy away from speaking of "a spectrum of heresy," with regard to the criticism. It was unacceptable that such things could be said within the walls of St. Peter; these voices raised in attack against the principles of the institutional and hierarchical Church would draw the wrath of God.

It did not help. Unlike with the Liturgy schema, this draft did not obtain agreement as the basis of further discussion. A formal decision was avoided, however, in order to spare the Commission a spectacular defeat. The text was turned back for complete re-working to the Commission.

4. A NECESSARY SAVING OF FACE

What was rained down on the authors and supporters of the draft would have, under normal circumstances, caused each member of the Commission to resign, recognizing themselves to be hindrances to the further work of the Council. The mindset of the "Carabinieri of the Lord" (as Cardinal Ottaviani referred to himself), of the "staff officers of Christ" (as a Lutheran theologian put it, after conversation in the Congregation on the Faith) reacted differently, however – "grip the helm tighter" was obviously the motto. Even as it was clear that their group had no more than 300 votes at the Council, even as the "battle" was long lost, they fought bitterly about important details. They also put the Pope, as earlier described, in a tight spot, forcing him to spare them a public defeat through interventions. These interventions were seen by the public as evidence of the Pope's authoritative style and his disregard of the Council, while they were actually the opposite:

the Pope wanted to present his image of the Church, which was that of the majority of the Council, so that the defenders of the old image might reconcile with it.

When a judgment is made on a conflict, it is only fair to present the opponents in a positive light. Therefore a remark to protect the honor of the men of the Curia is necessary. Because today the thoughts of the majority of the Council seem so obvious, the question is even more pressing: why did the opponents persist in their viewpoint? It is pointless to speculate about psychological blocks or motives of lust for power. If such existed, those concerned would have to answer before God. Outsiders have no insight into this and should not, therefore, assume such motives. It could not, however, have remained hidden from intelligent men such as Ottaviani that the medieval power of the Church was over – although a letter from the Cardinal to a Catholic publishing house could at that time still result in an irksome book getting pulled from circulation, without consideration of financial loss. There is no possible doubt about the personal integrity of this conservative protagonist. Cardinal Ottaviani is described by all who knew him as an exceptionally charming man. It is also known that he, a baker's son from a large family from the poor quarter of Trastevere, in Rome, donated all of his extra income to an orphanage that he had founded and personally looked after. Why then this resistance, this anxiety before a breach in the dike, should a new image of the Church emerge? I know of only one reason, and can only suppose this: insufficient contact with pastoral reality. The administration of an orphanage does not replace this! One can easily enough imagine what happened whenever His Eminence was received at the door by the sisters of the orphanage to know that no contact with reality took place here. Anyone who knows the Church only from the perspectives of the Lateran University, the Curia, and Vatican City cannot grasp what goes on even just with Italian Catholics, not to mention French, German, American, Dutch, as well as Spanish and Polish Catholics, when they speak of "the Church." Unless, of course, such Vatican officials and curial diplomats chose to do themselves damage by opening themselves to these different experiences – Pope Paul VI had done this, as Archbishop of the Diocese of Milan and through his engagement with French theology, and in particular with Yves Congar ("may his theology succeed at the Council" – this is attributed to Pope Paul VI). Whoever does not do this will not be able to understand why, beyond all the lovely things Pius XII had already said about the Church, something further had to happen and be said. One can best experience this spirituality, which is not at all malicious, at most overly bureaucratic, by spending an afternoon in Rome visiting Roman churches: St. Peter's, S. Maria Maggiore, St. John Lateran, St. Paul-outside-the-Walls, S. Clemente, S. Maria d'Aracoeli, S. Maria sopra Minerva – with the exception of St. Paul, all churches in the inner city, reachable by foot. One does not necessarily need to be showy, but just once, for just awhile, to sit inside of stately Renaissance buildings in the midst of the turbulent Roman traffic, to divine what would occur to a "general staff officer of Christ": "… and the gates of the netherworld shall not prevail against it" (Matthew 16:18). What do a couple of Protestant-infected Catholics beyond the Alps or across the big pond matter there, with their eternal nagging and reform madness? Despite the catastrophic pastoral situation in Rome, it is unbelievably difficult, spending a bit of time in these churches, to imagine that the Church today is questioned and challenged. If the matter has a psychological side, then it is that someone who is on the ecclesial "general staff" was educated to shelve any further questions and to do his work in a faithful, objective, and experienced, also if necessary occasionally cunning, manner, day after day, 12 to 14 hours. The best evidence of this mindset is an unusual phenomenon that I can attest to from many examples known to me personally: only with Lutheran conversation partners did they occasionally reveal what tortured them and what they had to suppress daily. With Catholic partners the unity of person and official duty was seamless.

5. THE SECOND DRAFT AND THE FINAL EDITION

We return now to the Council Hall. Between the first two sessions hard work was done – this time with the help of theologians who did not necessarily agree with the Curia, but nonetheless who gained great influence, in particular, Yves Congar (France) and Karl Rahner (Germany). When the Council Fathers reconvened in autumn of 1963, a completely new draft and two notebooks with suggestions for improvement were available. The new draft now had four chapters: 1. The Mystery of the Church; 2. The Hierarchical Constitution of the Church, with Special Reference to the Episcopate; 3. The People of God, with Special Reference to the Laity; 4. The Call of the Whole

Church to Holiness. Among the suggestions for improvement was an important suggestion attributed to Cardinal Frings as well as to Cardinal Suenens. This suggestion was that all statements in the third chapter that concerned **all** the members of the Church together should be taken out of this chapter and made into its own chapter on The People of God; this chapter should be placed between chapter 1 and the chapter 2. This was something quite different than just an editorial suggestion; it was – under the innocent pretense of a small editorial change – the definitive overcoming of the clerical image of the church at the Council. According to the new order of the chapters, first The Mystery of the Church is dealt with, then its social manifestation, the Faithful as The People of God, then the chapters follow concerning the categorization of members of the Church – in the old language: concerning the ranks in the Church: Bishops (Priests, Deacons), Laity, Members of Orders. It should be noticed that the henceforth third chapter is not entitled "The Hierarchy" but "The Hierarchical Constitution of the Church, with Special Reference to the Episcopate." In comparison with the Laity and the Members of Orders, the officeholders appear not as a particular group of members in the Church but as representatives and organs of the "constitution" of the Church, *means* through which God leads his *constituted* people – in every other regard they are Christians, members of the People of God like all others. The uniqueness and the particular path of Members of Orders (now Chapter 6), was introduced through a chapter concerning "the Call of the Whole Church to Holiness" – again a clear repudiation of that portrayal of two "classes" of Christians that described the Members of Orders as better Christians in light of their membership in "The Rank of the Perfect." The entirety was concluded by a chapter on "The Eschatological Character of the Pilgrim Church" (Chapter 7) – again making the point that the Church, neither in her structures nor in her members, is something finished and self-sufficient. No, everything is underway and only by her complete union with the community of those who have died with God does the journey end. Chapter 8 concerning "The Blessed Virgin Mother of God, Mary, in the Mystery of Christ and the Church" had its own tensions not only in terms of content but also because of its placement in the Dogmatic Constitution on the Church in this position – we shall deal with this later.

There were vigorous debates, but these were focused above all on the questions surrounding the Office of the Bishop, to which we will return later. Of course, the particular situation of the orders, the eschatological structure of the Church, and finally even the chapter on Mary were occasions for bitter conflicts. But the basic structure of the draft (including the chapter on the People of God) was no longer questioned. At the end of the discussion, the draft in its edition with eight chapters was for all intents and purposes accepted. There remained, however, so many votes to go through that it could not come to a final vote and ceremonial passing in the second session; this happened then in the third session.

III. FOCAL POINTS OF THE CONCILIAR DOCTRINE OF THE CHURCH

EXCURSUS: RULES FOR THE INTERPRETATION OF ECCLESIAL TEXTS — IN PARTICULAR THOSE OF THE SECOND VATICAN COUNCIL

In the following pages we must dissect one of the most important texts of the Council; it is useful, before we begin, to indicate a few rules to be used with ecclesial texts. Of course, all readers have the right to take the texts as they are. They *must* be understandable in terms of their own words and their own contexts — otherwise they would be bad texts. However, it always happens that readers who are not practiced with such texts find this or that sentence, this or that chapter, to be simply not understandable. It can also happen that a text seems extraordinarily balanced, and the dynamite hidden in the text or even the explosion which led to its development remains unnoticed. A few rules can be used to elucidate these sorts of texts. In theological and ecclesial everyday life, it suffices if a few experts control this paragraph. With a world event like the Second Vatican Council and with the interests that a broad but theologically unschooled public has in these texts, it is necessary to make the "secret knowledge" of the experts' general knowledge, as far as that is possible.

We name this section an "excursus." By this title we want to make clear that the following will give only brief information, at first general and then with particular connection to the Second Vatican Council.

1. TRADITION AND TRADITIONS

Immediately after the end of the Council, a euphoric interpretation of the event prevailed for about half a decade; this interpretation viewed the texts of the Council as outdated as soon as they were finished and understood the Council only as an agent of an all-encompassing explosion of the Church into the future. Pope John XXIII's "fresh air" that had to enter the Church was understood as an invitation to break with tradition. This interpretation could only end in disappointment because those who mourned the pre-conciliar Church were always present, endeavoring to win back terrain; above all, though, this euphoric interpretation had to disappoint because an attitude like this was founded neither on the letter nor on the so-called "spirit" of the Council texts. The first rule is: *No Council can be interpreted fundamentally against ecclesial tradition.* It is neither realistically imaginable nor permissible for faithful Christians to think that a Council could convene in order to announce to the world that the previous history of the Church and of Christian thought and life is nothing more than a great error and a deviation from the message of the Bible. That does not mean that a Council can say nothing new, but the relationship of what the Council says to the tradition cannot be defined according to the model of rejection. To express this rule negatively: an interpretation of Council texts based on such a rejection of tradition must be false.

The impression of something new in the texts of the Second Vatican Council is undeniable, more than with most other Councils in Church history; however, this is not a break with tradition but the revivification of forgotten *old tradition*, used to counter the narrowness of some more recent traditions. It is like an upside-down world: the so-called "progressive" Council Fathers were in reality the true conservatives, because they sought to preserve the old traditions of the Church – the common eastern and western Church tradition of the first millennium – against more recent accretions of a purely western Church sort. And the so-called "conservative" Council Fathers were in reality the problematic "progressives," in that they considered the developments of the second millennium to be so unquestionable that older traditions had lost their authority. So one can concretize our first rule of interpretation with relationship to the Second Vatican Council in the following manner:

"New" ideas in the Council texts should not be considered "innovations" until proof of this; they are to be considered critical dismantling of the narrow direction of the last centuries through the revivification of old tradition; these "innovations" represents the ancient tradition of the Universal Church.

All the problems confronting the Church are, each and every one, the result of developments after the separation between the eastern and western Church in the year 1054 – from the development of the papacy to the divisions in the western Church to the failure in the face of the challenges of the Enlightenment and of the modern world. The retrieval of forms of the Church from before the turn of the millennium is indeed certainly naïve if it is considered as a panacea for all the needs of the present; it will not do to flatly declare as normative the time of the Church between the New Testament and the year 1000. But in light of the dead-end streets in which the Western Church history in the second millennium got stuck, the "conservative" retrieval of the old tradition points "progressively" in the right direction.

2. COMPROMISE

Ecclesial texts and particularly texts from a Council, by their nature are not created or made by an individual but by multitudes, always after exhausting debates. How could it be otherwise? One person composes a first draft which then, because of the debates and the subsequent *Modi* time and again is reworked until it achieves the agreement of the full assembly. The redaction work is for the most part in the hands of the composer of the first draft, of course with the support of a number of co-workers. But as much as his handwriting remains noticeable at the end, for the most part no stone of the first draft remains standing. From this inevitability arises a second rule of interpretation: *One must always assume compromise formulae with ecclesial texts.*

Because many people want to find their own demands in the finalized text, it cannot have what one might call a unified "bite," as would the text of an individual author. It will contain compromise formulae. In the most advantageous cases, the original text is enriched through further ideas and points of view which complete and broaden the original draft in valuable ways. Not seldom, however, formulations must be worked in which weaken the original text, make it less clear, and occasionally create contradictions. Because of this, interpretation is always difficult. We cannot avoid asking about the *intention*, about the "actual" purpose behind and between the lines, about what the majority of the Council Fathers originally wanted to say but then, because of various counter opinions, at the end could say only with qualifications. The question inevitably arises: what gets more weight? The original intention or the qualifications? This consideration of the compromise character of the texts becomes particularly explosive with texts of the Second Vatican Council because for the first time a type of compromise was employed that is without example in the history of the Councils. Our second rule of interpretation is drawn from this fact:

In the texts of the Second Vatican Council one must often assume the compromise of "contradictory pluralism." The expression "contradictory pluralism" comes from the German theologian Max Seckler, who discussed this compromise type in the texts of the Council in an illuminating article. Seckler's argument:

Anyone who has come across the compromise character of many texts of the Second Vatican Council and therefore assumes that these texts are patient of different interpretations will experience, time and time again, that one side grabs one quote and says "the Second Vatican Council says" while the other side maintains, "The Council did not intend that!" The distressing thing is that both sides are right. This developed from a new form of compromise in matters of doctrine used at the Council. The concept of compromise on doctrine is actually a given in conciliar history (as well as in the history of the Reformation's confessional writings). There are two types of this compromise on doctrine: a compromise in terms of content and dilatory compromise, that is, a compromise that delays the decision. The content compromise amounts to the final common declaration after detailed consultation. If possible, it is a compromise from the lowest common denominator but it is finally a logically voiced declaration, commonly supported and accessible to linguistic and logical analysis. Clear examples of this are the ancient church confessions, above all the Christological formula of the Council of Chalcedon. The dilatory compromise articulates the indecision surrounding the question and therefore then postpones a decision. Classical examples of this compromise type are offered by the Council of Trent – not in opposition to the Reformers but in opposition to the medieval schools that fought for their dogmatic ratification at the Council. For example: the Council consciously used Thomistic and Scotistic formulae (from Duns Scotus) right next to each other, sometimes in the same sentence, in order to avoid canon-izing one or the other.

At the Second Vatican Council a type of compromise occurred that, according to Max Seckler, had never been experienced at any Church assembly. It is connected with the group dynamic processes at the Council and it was made easier by the fact that the Council, against some expectations, very consciously avoided composing deci-sions in the form of binding dogma. Because dogmatic decisions are always connected with the condemnation of the opposite viewpoint, it is one of the birthmarks (some would say the congenital defects) of this Council that it did not declare any condemnations but spoke, as the current word is, "pastorally," that is, in a helpful, orienting manner.

It is nonsense to set dogmatic and pastoral language in opposition, as if pastoral language may say whatever one wants it to say with ref-erence to doctrine, and as if dogmatic language in the final analysis must not be pastoral. At the Council, nonetheless, there occurred just such a nonsensical – albeit cunningly played – opposition of "pasto-ral" and "dogmatic"; the "conservatives" originally wanted a Council bent on binding doctrine, against John XXIII's warning in his open-ing speech. The "progressives" wanted a Council bent on the pasto-ral. The conservatives realized that they had no chance at success *and therefore* switched to a "pastoral" Council –with the aim of mitigating the dogmatic declarations that the progressives pushed through. The progressives on their side stressed the pastoral side of the Council in order to push through their doctrinal requests with the votes of the conservatives. It is an unwritten law that at a Council there may not be a close vote; there should be as high a degree of unanimity as possible.

The result is not only text material that is not completely even – evenness is seldom the case with committee texts of such detail – and texts in which there are some gaps in the logic – that was unavoidable. The problem is that some texts could only be salvaged according to the principle: you take my text, I'll concede you yours. Seckler dubbed this "the compromise of reciprocal dishonesty." Objectively one must, according to Seckler, speak of the "compromise of the contradictory pluralism."

We want to illustrate this process with two significant examples. The first example: in the third chapter of the Dogmatic Constitution on the Church, where the doctrine of the collegiality of the Bishops is defined, we find more references to the primacy of the Pope than can be found in any First Vatican Council text. And in the *Nota praevia* one finds the statement, unheard until then, that the Pope can exercise his authority at any time *ad placitum*, that is, "at discretion." It is understandable that the minority, on the defensive, looked for their salvation in the amassing of references to the Pope – and that the others conceded this to them, because otherwise their interests could only have been achieved in a massive fight.

The other example: in the Decree on Ecumenism we find, with reference to the *communicatio in sacris* in Article 8: "Yet worship in common (*communicatio in sacris*) is not to be considered as a means to be used indiscriminately for the restoration of unity among Christians. There are two main principles upon which the practice of such common worship depends: first, that of the unity of the church which outght to be expressed; and second, that of the sharing in the means of grace. The expression of unity generally forbids common worship. Grace to be obtained sometimes commends it." This remark stands in the "*general*" guidelines to the practical actualization of ecumenism, is not limited to particular services, and therefore does not absolutely preclude the Communion service. Whoever refers to this, in order to argue for the possibility of common communion (or at least of "open Communion"), has the logic of the statement and its context on his side. However, whoever uses this argument will hear vehement opposition and references to another place in the Decree on Ecumenism, according to which the churches of the Reformation " ... have not preserved the proper reality of the eucharistic mystery in its fullness, especially because of the absence of the sacrament of Orders... " (Article 22). Whoever argues along these lines will take the position on Article 8 that it allows common worship only with the Eastern Orthodox Churches. (As an aside, the question is still open about whether real unity exists between the Roman Catholic Church and the Eastern Orthodox Churches in their understanding of Holy Orders and of the Eucharist.) Why is Article 8 not more concretely worded? Why does it not say clearly in Article 22, that participation in Communion in one of the Churches of the Reformation is closed to Catholics? Why is Article 22 not relevant for the Eastern Orthodox Churches, which at the very least do not recognize the office of the Pope, and therefore a *dogma*, not just a disciplinary form of life of the Church of Rome? Logical cracks! The one side hoped in the future, that its more open perspective would prevail. The other side hoped in the post-conciliar period, where one could influence the mechanisms of the Roman Curia, dictating what should prevail in the Church.

3. SOMETHING NEW AS ADDITION

A further rule of interpretation arises at this point:

If something is particularly emphasized in the Council texts, suspicion dictates that it be relativized and weakened.

We already indicated: the new – in truth, often the older tradition – had at the Council a chance only in the form of an addition to the old – in truth, the more recent tradition. Each attempt to radically strike out the more recent tradition would have been condemned to failure. That is a rule that applies to all councils, insofar that it is true for all councils that they can never be interpreted against tradition (see rule 1). In the course of the type of "contradictory pluralism" this rule becomes the means of a tactical game. There can be no doubt: the majority of the Council wanted to force back the centralizing developments of the second millennium and particularly of the 19th and early 20th centuries, under which one groaned more loudly the more distant from Rome he was, and replace them through a model of Church according to the principle of *communio*, of which we shall talk later. Well noted: replace – with inclusion of the newly understood function of the Petrine office. Of course no one could say this too loudly – although it was occasionally indeed spoken loudly in the Council Hall. One had to, for better or for worse, awaken and strengthen the impression that the new ideas about the Universal Church as a community of participant churches and about the Bishops as "colleagues" of the Pope were "only" an addition to what was already in place, an expansion of the framework, that would actually add credence to more recent tradition of the adorned Papal office. The consequence: where the new was put into force, there were always, mostly in dependent clauses and parenthetical sentences, emphatic expressions of fidelity to the old tradition.

4. KNOW THE PRE-HISTORY(IES)

We have already pointed out that if an ecclesial text is not clear, then it is a bad text. That does not mean that a clear text immediately reveals its point and thrust. "Interpretation" is often necessary, interpretation that doesn't get by with clarifying only the conventional, "established" meaning of particular concepts in ecclesial linguistic usage, known by the specialists but not by the laity. It is very important to know the often intertwined prehistory of a text. Because ecclesial texts always have a compromise character – even when this compromise does not always have to be the compromise of the "contradictory pluralism" – only with knowledge of the debates that preceded the text as well as of the often decades-long theological discussions surrounding the question can we judge the aims of statements in an ecclesial text. It can happen that a brusque repudiation lurks under apparently completely harmless conventional formulations. Examples of this are the explanations of the Congregation for the Doctrine of the Faith to questions of eschatology or women's ordination. It can also happen that apparently totally negative formulations reflect a recognition of concerns and of just theological ideas – for example, with *Mysterium Ecclesiae* (1973) and the two instructions on Liberation Theology (1984, 1986). It can also happen that the results of vigorous debates are expressed in cautious form and with smooth and balanced formulations – as by most texts of the Second Vatican Council. Too much enthusiasm in an ecclesial text should never be expected; the likelihood of polarizing rather than integrating would be too dangerous.

A most important rule for interpretation of ecclesial texts runs: *It is very important to notice what a text* does not *say.*

What is *not* said may not be presented as endorsed by the Church. It can certainly happen, indeed in most cases does happen, that an ecclesial text is open to further modification and refinement. It can happen that a certain theological thesis represented in a preceding discussion is covered through an ecclesial statement, but not simply endorsed by it.

To actualize this by a famous example (ecumenically thorny) from the time before the Council: in the Papal Bull *Munificentissimus Deus*, in the dogmatic document with which Pius XII in 1950 raised the assumption of Mary into Heaven to a dogma, the Pope consciously chose the formulation, in relation to Mary: "... after completion of her earthly life." One reads this line without thinking and assumes that the death of Mary, expressed in somewhat flowery language, is meant here. Before the dogmatization there had been a very vehement discussion among Marian "maximalists" about whether it could be accepted that Mary had actually died, since she was conceived without original sin (the dogma of 1854) and therefore was not subject to the punishment for Adam's sin, that is, death. There are the best of grounds to consider this thesis pure nonsense. Pius XII thought so, as well, but he did not at this point want to simply reject the thesis, so he chose the cited formulation. And so there are even today Marian-excited "theologians" who, without contradiction of the dogma of 1950, maintain that Mary did not die but, as with the legends of Moses and Elijah, was transported immediately into Heaven. One must insist that the text of the dogma did not expressly accept this thesis and did not want to endorse it. With the texts of the Second Vatican Council we shall have to observe what the Council does *not* say, in order to judge what, given the background of the discussion, is the point of the text.

A further generally relevant rule:

The binding sense of a text can be obtained from the vantage point of the error that the text condemns.

Almost the entire conciliar history is one big attestation for this rule. Councils were almost always convened in order to reject false doctrines that had emerged, whose spread had become a threat to church unity, and to clarify the relevant church teaching. In the course of these councils, reform matters were treated and decided. However, until the Second Vatican Council there had not been a purely reform council. If one investigates the false doctrines that were the cause of a council or of an extra-conciliar doctrinal statement, then the "No" to the false doctrine is the high point of the ecclesial text. All the argumentation in the text serves to ground this "No"; should an orientation for further theological discussion be given, this must be grounded in the text.

We again see here the special place of the texts of the Second Vatican Council. It is the first council in church history that – whatever some might have expected – was convened very consciously not for the overcoming of an error but for the renewal of the church. For this reason the rule about arriving at the sense of the text from the error that is being rejected is for the most part not applicable, or applicable only in limited circumstances. Because of course the Council did more than simply intimate what it distanced itself from – that will come up again and again into our discussion. But it did this – with one exception, the condemnation of modern warfare – not in the form of a solemn and explicit condemnation and certainly not in the form of a dogma. Therefore it is not possible simply to arrive at the binding sense of a text from the error, but only from the thrust established by the Council majority. The rule for the interpretation of the Council texts therefore is:

Only with an eye on the prehistory and on the conciliar process of discussion itself can the sense of a Council text and the degree of its binding force be ascertained.

The use of this rule is of course particularly explosive, where the described compromise type of "contradictory pluralism" holds full sway. From this comes a further rule of interpretation, this time only for the texts of the Second Vatican Council:

5. THE ENTIRE COUNCIL – IN "DIVIDED" INTERPRETATION

If what has been described is the case with the Council texts, in what direction are they then actually to be interpreted? Are the elements, formulations, and emphases of the old tradition – that is: the *more recent* tradition – the measure? Or is it the elements, formulations, and emphasis of the new – that is: the revivified old tradition? And in order to get a grip on those conflict-rich "contradictory" texts that are simply not able to be interpreted away: what is the *authentic* interpretation: the one on the basis of the restrictions or the one on the basis of the openness in the text?

It has been said that it is exactly in this tension, which may not be interpreted as self-contradiction, that the "pastoral" impulse and the energy source lie that drive the Church into the future. To me this seems an all too paradoxical harmonization. The reality is that both sides had more or less resigned themselves to accept such "tensions" in the texts, because anything else was not achievable. The pastoral orientation is not "energy rich," but unclear and half lamed. What should, for example, a pastor do, when he is supposed to take his congregational leadership from such unequal texts? No – no virtue should be made out of the poverty of such texts, poverty which humanly is only too understandable. In another respect of course the so-called "tension" is an energy source for the interpretation. The supreme rule must now be:

The entire *Council – and not only the portions of the texts that say something one always thought, anyway.*

This rule is relevant for both "camps" of Council interpreters: the "conservatives" and the "progressives." Council interpreters would make themselves and the Church ridiculous and deprive the Church of her last piece of credibility, if they were allowed with texts such as these to act according to quarry work methods: to pick out what fits into their own wishes, and letting the other things lie. Hence another rule:

   In practice a "divided" interpretation is advisable: a theological interpretation and a church-political interpretation.

   Theology must unconditionally keep and use the openness of the Council texts. What stands in the text stands there; and more importantly, it cannot be maintained that what *does not* stand there actually does. It has nothing to do with the binding force of the texts, what this or that Council Father thought with this or that sentence, or what afterthoughts they might have had, but what the sentence offers up according to the normal lexical sense and the normal theological and, if necessary, canon law use in light of the prehistory. Because that which stands now in the texts is what the overwhelming majority of the world episcopacy brought to paper as the faith consciousness and theological insight of the Universal Church. It mirrors, so to speak, the *sensus fidelium*, about which we shall speak. No one, not even the Pope himself, whose signature (or rather, that of his predecessor) stands under these formulations, can say that this or that opinion did not exist in the Church and may not exist. The "conservatives" need to remember this and to ask themselves the question: do they want to include that in their reflections and their practice or not. Otherwise, they might want to openly declare that they consider the Second Vatican Council to be without binding force. Had the Council, of course, decided completely in their way of thinking, they would not tire of reminding other thinking people of ecclesial obedience.

   Interpretation is another matter, when it is important to estimate *real possibilities* on ecclesial levels in matters of internal and external church politics. There one stands on more secure ground the more one includes what the "conservatives," who dominate as before the Roman Curia as well as the national Bishops' Conferences, thought about this or that sentence. For the sake of justice: this does not always mean the end of the debate or an immovable insistence on pre-Council positions. For example, the cooperation with respect to the Eastern Orthodox Churches, documented in the solemn lifting of the Church ban at the end of the Council, was earnestly intended – the problem was and is with the Eastern Orthodox Churches themselves. But it very *often* means the end of the discussion and I would be lying to a Lutheran co-Christian or Lutheran Church leadership if I dared to maintain that the Second Vatican Council had opened the door to common Communion – *although* I have to almost hammer the openness of the formulations of the Council to this into the faith consciousness of the faithful, so that so much "pressure from below" is present that this is never forgotten. I want to explain this division between theological interpretation and church-political realism with a few events, the effects of which are still felt today.

- Article 8 of the Decree on Ecumenism leaves the regulation of the liturgical community to the local or regional episcopal authorities or to the Holy See. But Rome immediately after the Council made all the really important decisions in this question, that is, either anticipated the episcopal decisions or denied requests.

- Hans Küng appeals to the Second Vatican Council for his views of the nature and structure of the Church, just as his opponents do, and those who have disciplined him.

- The reaction of Rome to the paper (the result of ten years of work) on the unification with the Anglican Church (1982) – this Church made almost unbelievable "concessions" to Rome in it! – was (this was one of the first official acts of Cardinal Ratzinger, as Prefect of the Congregation on Faith), with a stroke of the pen wiped from the table, with the comment that it was not in accordance with the First Vatican Council.

- Given the collegiality of the Bishops, a central idea of the Dogmatic Constitution on the Church and the following decrees, there is a particular problem with Rome's relationship to the Latin American Bishops with regard to the question of Liberation Theology. Rome in an almost brusque fashion did not leave the clarification of this question to the regional authorities and did not limit itself to the functions of protecting and helping, in the sense of Article 13 of the Constitution on the Church.

- Canon lawyers, that is, the "critical middle," are agreed that the new *Codex Iuris Canonici* of 1983, despite years-long discussion between canon lawyers and theologians, does *not* in any decisive way take up the impulses of the conciliar Church understanding.

And finally: in his much noticed interview "On the Position of the Faith," in 1984, Cardinal Ratzinger spoke of the "pernicious ideology of the Council" of some of the faithful and priests. This unfortunate formulation was meant to refer not to the Council itself, but exclusively to some interpretations of the Council. A critical Catholic newspaper remarked that Cardinal Ratzinger destroyed the work of the Second Vatican Council. That is completely false. Ratzinger turned against only those who interpret the Council incorrectly, not appreciating the Council's respect for existing practice. For the latter interpretation Ratzinger had sufficient texts on his side. This is the same Ratzinger who as theologian had placed his confidence in "the future unfolding and development" of Council compromise – and the context made it very clear that the later head of the Congregation on the Doctrine of the Faith meant an unfolding in the spirit of the majority.

And here we come to the last rule of interpretation:

6. SPIRIT AND LETTER

It is correct: when the texts are unwieldy, the temptation grows to creep around the letter of the text and to refer to a nebulous "spirit of the Council." That is problematic and not particularly helpful, so long as it is not made clear what is meant with this "spirit." The rule reads: *The "spirit of the Council" is the will of the overwhelming majority of the Council Fathers that emerges even there where, through objections and occasionally unfair tricks of a small minority, some details were watered down and weakened – and as such is it a valid rule of interpretation for the Council texts.*

Already in the description of the process of the Council we have seen, and in the course of the interpretation of the texts shall see even more, that the overwhelming majority of the Council Fathers – a majority of which political parliaments can only dream --revealed a definite intention in their phrasing. One may here actually say: the Universal Church stands behind this or that statement. The weakening of a text came about – often at the last minute, and through manipulation – only out of political grounds, or in order to make the majority larger. As a result it is out of the question to argue that these texts, the result of "watering down" efforts, are the real statement of the Council. When this happens, and when on the basis of such texts policy is made (for example, by the naming of Bishops), then an objection under appeal to the very concrete, *non*-nebulous, documented "spirit of the Council" is justified.

A. CHURCH AS "SACRAMENT"

1. "MYSTERY" OF THE CHURCH

Even the title of the first chapter, "The Mystery of the Church," became a source of strife. Many Fathers were no longer accustomed to the biblical sense of the word *mystery* – understandable, if one, as most of the Council Fathers, read the New Testament not in the Greek but in Latin or in their own mother tongue. The Latin translation (the so-called *Vulgate*, which goes back to the Patristic Father Jerome), translates, following not entirely clear rules, the Greek *mysterion* sometimes with *mysterium*, sometimes with *sacramentum*, the latter not always in a context that has anything to do with what today we call "sacraments" in the sense of Church liturgy. Where *mysterium* is used in the Latin text, this seems to be the meaning: *mysterium* is something incomprehensible, closed to the understanding. One must take into account the common concepts fostered by the neo-Scholastic theological education all the Council Fathers had experienced. According to what the Council Fathers had been taught, there was a distinction made between a *mysterium stricte dictum*—a mystery in the strict sense, that eludes human understanding because of its content (for example the Trinity) – and a *mysterium late dictum* –a mystery that is not recognizable without divine revelation, but *after* its revelation is understandable, for example God's plan of salvation for humankind. Many of the Council Fathers might have thought: The Church should be something incomprehensible? If the idea of "mystic" is associated with the word *mysterium*, then we can understand the suspicion that a concession on some theories of the "invisible Church" is made with the idea of "Church as mystery."

The suspicion can be overcome very easily. *Mystery* of the Church stands here for an understanding according to which the Church is a part of the "mystery" of God, and that means, according to the New Testament, the same as: part of the *salvific work* of God – the Greek concept *mysterion* has the same meaning as *oikonomia* (see Ephesians 3:9).

This is more than simply the clarification of terminology. It is an important setting of the course for the understanding of Church. The *mysterium* of God, that is, his work of salvation, is anchored in God's eternity, in his gracious choice, which he announced in Christ and historically implemented (see Ephesians 1:3-14; 3:3-12). If the Church is thus grounded and maintained, then one must speak first and foremost not of a visible form, of structures, offices, authority, and claims, but of God's plan of salvation announced to us. This means that the Church is not invisible – according to the words of the Apostle, an elementary sign of her visibility is the mixed community of Jews and Gentiles – but she is absolutely inadequately described just with the reference to her visibility. The Church is, as the Dogmatic Constitution on the Church says in another context, a "complex reality" (Article 8). To put the matter in this way was and is meant as a polemic against the intention of the original draft to treat "The Nature of the Church Militant" in chapter 1, because the "militant" Church is by definition the *earthly* Church. The "militant" Church is what the word says: *fighting,* therefore defending itself against enemies, fighting for her rights – in medieval times, when it was necessary, with military means.

The unfolding of the first chapter is easily understandable: after the explanation of the title (Article 1), the text speaks first of the eternal salvific will of God (Article 2), of its historical implementation in the mission and office of the Son (Article 3), and the outpouring of the Holy Spirit (Article 4). This flow of ideas closes with a significant and here significantly used quote from the patristic authority Cyprian: The Church appears as "a people made one by the unity of the Father, the Son, and the Holy Spirit."

The Church has her basis therefore in the Trinitarian mystery of God – she is, to express it in a specialized theological fashion, grounded in the "economic Trinity." The perspective is named from which her unity should be seen and judged: whether she is the people united by the Trinitarian God. The unity of the Church shares the "complex" character of the Church herself, in that she is at home both visibly and in the eternity of God. One must keep that in mind. With Articles 5-8 the view is on the historical concretization of the Church, but bound up with Jesus' Kingdom-of-God-proclamation. The fundamental tension of this is the "already now" and the "not yet" – and again the Church receives an extra-chronological, this time eschatological perspective. The Church – one should think of the distance from what

Catholic children until the 50's still learned in catechism! – is not the Kingdom of God on earth, but "longs for the completed kingdom." The Church is the initial budding forth on earth of the Kingdom of God (Article 5).

This reality of the Church appears in the Constitution in a multitude of pictures. A particularly detailed description of the Body of Christ appears in Article 7 – an essential and honest bow to the like-named encyclical of Pius XII, much quoted in this section. This all serves a particular overall goal that becomes completely clear in the second chapter on "The People of God" – we shall come to that.

Up to and including Article 7, the language used to speak of the Church is purely theological – even, one might say, abstract. First Article 8 takes up the question of where then this Church, at home both with God and on earth, is to be found. The answer is subject to no doubt: in the Church that is lead by the successor of Peter in community with the Bishops. The formula "in the Holy Roman Church" is avoided – the use of that term in the so-called Creed of the Council of Trent and in the First Vatican Council was relegated to a footnote. The location of the Church on earth is immediately analyzed, in order to emphasize the duty to the poor, the reality of persecution, the command to humility – one notices everywhere the influence of the criticism of the first draft. Whoever has the text available should read the last two sections of Article 8.

In the introductory article we find the important sentence that gives a foreshadowing of the text in its entirety: "Christ is the light of the nations and consequently this holy synod, gathered together in the holy Spirit, ardently desires to bring to all humanity that light of Christ which is resplendent on the face of the church, by proclaiming his Gospel to every creature (see Mk 16:15). Since the church, in Christ, is a sacrament – a sign and instrument, that is, of communion with God and of the unity of the entire human race – it here proposes, for the benefit of the faithful and of the entire world, to describe more clearly, and in the tradition laid down by earlier councils, its own nature and universal mission." The Church is not the "light of the nations" (*lumen gentium*) – although John XXIII had expressed himself almost exactly like this – *Christ* is. The Council wants "to bring to all humanity that light of Christ which is resplendent on the face of the church, by proclaiming his Gospel to every creature." The Church shines and illuminates not, therefore, through herself, as it were from inside out, but by proclaiming the Gospel "to every creature." This re-flection of the radiance of Christ in the proclamation of the Gospel is now formally expressed through the use of the concept of sacrament, and this is immediately further interpreted as sign and instrument for the union with God and for the unity of humankind. What does this use of the concept of sacrament mean? We must, for this, reach back a bit.

2. THE CATECHISM CONCEPT OF "SACRAMENT"

"A sacrament," as every Catholic schoolchild learned at that time, "is an outer sign instituted by Christ, through which internal grace is me-diated to us." The school theology distinguishes outer sign between "matter" and "form." Matter is the action with an element – oil, water, bread, wine – or if need be, actions without elements, such as the con-fession in Reconciliation, the laying on of hands at the Ordination, the "yes" at Holy Matrimony. The form is the spoken word, the founda-tional word of Jesus, if this has been transmitted to us.

At *first* glance, everything applies to the Church. The Church is founded by Christ – it is for our context unimportant, whether one thinks traditionally of a "foundational act" of Jesus or of a "foundation" through the mission of the witnesses to the resurrection; there is an outer sign, as matter the visible, institutional, hierarchical structure of the Church, as form the commissioning words of Jesus, which in the activity of the commissioned come to fruition like the foundational words of the sacraments, and there is mediation of "inner grace."

At *second* glance, though, something does not seem to hang to-gether. Since the beginning of the 20th century, as the proposition of the Church as "sacrament" gradually spread, the objection was made: this establishes an *eighth* sacrament, and that contradicts the teach-ing of the Council of Trent, according to which there are seven sac-raments, no more and no fewer. Now, this naïve argument could be countered with the comment that it is just all about the *interrelation* of the Church and these seven sacraments, not about an addition. The objection raises the question of whether this proposition introduces an inadmissible unclarity into the concept of sacrament. The unclarity has two sticking points: a) The one is the concept of "sign." The sac-rament is an action with a material element. The Church is, however, not an action, but the acting itself. b) The other sticking point is the concept of the mediation of grace. According to traditional doctrine, this is an immediate effect of the sacrament, when this takes place and is respectfully received. The Church is not herself mediation of grace, but opens this mediation to those who belong to her.

This leads to a need to make something more precise: measured on the catechism concept of sacrament, the Church is *not* sacrament, but is *in advance of* the sacraments. If she is sacrament, then she is "original sacrament," "root sacrament" (Otto Semmelroth), "fundamental sacrament" (Karl Rahner). In it and out of it the seven individual sacraments result. With these individual sacraments the Church shares two essential moments that the Council of Trent expressly named: to be visible form of invisible grace (*visibilis forma invisibilis gratiae*), a formulation of Augustine. This is an open formulation, but it produces a meaning: *if* grace, forgiveness, communion with God in this world is not only to be experienced invisibly, but at the same time can be and is tangible, then this is through the existence of the visible Church, through her life, her action, her proclamation. The Church's image can be the complete opposite to her message, so that people who honestly want to be Christians feel compelled to turn their backs on her – nonetheless: the Gospel had a history in this world and will continue to have one only because this Church exists. So long as the Church does not cease, this Gospel, which sometimes condemns her, will not be forgotten.

The other moment: the sacraments "contain" (*continent*) the grace that they denote. That is a not unproblematic formulation. Innocently formulated in the Middle Ages, in order to emphasize the difference between the Old Testament and the New Testament and with this the precedence of Christ, this formulation was altered in an anti-Reformation manner at Trent, and emphasized more than was beneficial the *opus operatum*, "the effected (and through itself effective) work" of the sacrament, relaxing the connection of the sacrament to the word as its "form" – upon which (at least it had always been meant this way) the effectiveness depended. We must bracket out the controversy here. For authentic Catholic sacramental doctrine the formulation did not offer any problem: however reliably the recipient encounters the grace of God in the sacrament, if he is correctly disposed to that grace and *wants* to receive the sacrament as the gift of God, the Church member encounters the offer and promise of God's grace – and this encounter precedes even the concrete reception of the sacrament.

We are, with this, shown the Church as *fundamental sacrament*. In short: the view of the Church as fundamental sacrament seems to be a *possible theological thesis*, one that does not contradict any dogma. It remains to ask whether this thesis is not only *possible* – because then it could just be a mere thought game, as many other theological theses in history and in the present actually are – but also whether this thesis is meaningful. Does it *explain* something better than earlier explanations do? Does it *serve* the faith in terms of the meaning of salvation of the Church? Does it help for a more vibrant, alive church life? That is the question of the theological and pastoral *impulse* of this thesis.

3. THE THEOLOGICAL AND PASTORAL IMPULSE

The question about the meaning of the thesis is answered for Catholics first through the Second Vatican Council – even if here it consciously does not appear in the form of dogma. Despite this, the meaning of the thesis requires an explanation.

An aside about the status of magisterial statements is necessary here. According to *traditional* Catholic understanding the structure of the argument is changed if "the Magisterium has spoken" – and that is also true if one considers the "Encyclical Paragraphs" from *Humani generis* – as mentioned above – to be an exaggeration. *Before* the comment of the Magisterium the main question is *whether* the thesis – a new theological thesis – actually is true. The work that occurs at the desk may very well not be. Often a non-binding "thought game" is the basis of a new theological thesis or theory. This main question has its advantages. One thinks of some exaggerations in Mariology – which we must come to one more time. This question about the truth of a theological thesis was able to contain a misuse of both principles, *potuit, decuit, ergo fecit* ("he [God] could do it, it was appropriate, so he did it") and *de Maria nunquam satis* ("about Mary never enough [can be said]." Because God "can" do something, and "it was appropriate," is only too easy to "prove," because there the interest of piety switches on – and who wants to condemn piety? The main question – whether it is correct-- creates the necessary sobriety.

It is different if the Magisterium has spoken. The question *whether* it is correct is dealt with. Whoever still takes a stand and considers a magisterial statement, above all one below the threshold of formal dogma, as not the last word does this nonetheless in each case in the context of the magisterial statement, even when she or he considers this statement to be false (Hans Küng in relation to the magisterial position on his understanding of Church, or Catholic women theologians in relation to the magisterial statement concerning the exclusion of women from ecclesial office). No one can ask the question *whether* it is correct as if the magisterial statement never happened. In the normal course of events the main question will be the one about the *how*, about the *sense*, and about the *meaning* of a statement. From here originates the often almost compulsive striving of Catholic theologians, to magisterially "secure" one of their original new theological theses. So the interested Mariologists pounced on every relevant word of Pius XII at that time. The Mariologists' euphoria came to an end with John XXIII, as it became clear that John expressed no more mariological interest than was typical for his generation and his Italian background. The euphoria lived again under Paul VI, and grew with John Paul II. We are again at our theme.

This thesis of the Church as "fundamental sacrament" is now "secured" through the Second Vatican Council, and indeed in the most solemn form of a dogma. The most important references outside of Article 1 of the Dogmatic Constitution on the Church are: the Constitution on the Sacred Liturgy, Article 26; the Dogmatic Constitution on the Church, Article 9 (third section), 48, 49; the Decree on the Church's Missionary Activity of the Church, Article 1 and 5; the Pastoral Constitution on the Church in the Modern World, Article 45. What were the impulses behind this thesis?

The thesis did not have an easy time of it at the Council. Any tendencies in the direction of "Church as fundamental sacrament" had been suppressed since the late Middle Ages, and particularly after the Reformation, through the emphasis on the institutional in the Church. The 19th century unease with this emphasis led, with the help of the Romantic Movement, to a consciousness of history as a theological fundamental category and in this context to the idea of a *development* of the Church as a sort of organism. With this came – as already noted – the idea of the Church as a "continuing incarnation of the divine word," and a way of speaking of the Church as sacrament. The Tübingen theologian Johann Adam Moehler was an example of this way of thinking. This tendency was slowed down (but not stopped) by the Modernist Crisis at the beginning of the twentieth century. The braking was evident after George Tyrrell, condemned as a modernist, made himself the spokesman of the thesis of Church as sacrament in his 1909 book, *Christianity at the Crossroads*. This forced Catholic theologians to use circumlocutions – the "Church, which awakens in the souls" (Romano Guardini) – focused on the idea of the Church as the Body of Christ. Still, at the Council the conservatives objected with satisfaction that the designation of the Church as "sacrament" would posthumously make concessions to the condemned Tyrrell.

But that objection could be countered with the comment that the thesis was not the possession of Tyrrell, and above all: it does not necessarily have to lead to Tyrrell's consequences. Tyrrell wanted to disconnect the seven liturgical sacraments from their initiation through Christ and present them as *foundation* of the Church. The irony of theological history is that, exactly at the same time that the conservative Council Fathers wanted to discredit the thesis with the reference to Tyrrell, Karl Rahner, in his 1962 work *Church and Sacraments*, took up the basic ideas of Tyrrell, but this time massively secured through *neoScholastic* ideas that Rahner had consistently thought out to the end.

And with this we have arrived at the actual impulse of the thesis. It is based on the fact that through biblical studies and historical research the historical foundation of *all* seven sacraments through the *historical* Jesus is questionable. In short: it was always considered – since the high Middle Ages – clear that only God himself (that is, Christ) could initiate sacraments, because only God himself can tie the donation of his grace in a binding way to obvious signs. It was also always clear that initiation acts could not be established in the texts for all seven sacraments – we cannot enter here into the whole complicated history of sacramental doctrine. In any case, in the 13th century the seven sacraments had prevailed, and under the influence of Thomas Aquinas also the thesis that none of them were first initiated by the Apostles, not to mention the early Church. The neuralgic points were, of course: how did confirmation and anointing of the sick become sacraments of the Church? And why was the washing of the feet, which in imitation of the act of Jesus at the Last Supper (John 13, 1-14) was practiced for centuries in the liturgy of Holy Thursday, **not** a sacrament, although it fulfills all the requirements of a sacrament according to the Catechism definition?

One is traditionally helped here with the so-called "prescriptive proof": since the Church in such an important matter cannot have

lead the faithful for hundreds of years in error, and since a foundation through the Church or through the Apostles is neither provable
nor can it, from practical grounds, be accepted, a foundation through
Christ must be postulated, even if this is not transmitted to us in the
Bible. Luther had, as is well known, used the same fundamental principle with a different thrust against the ecclesial tradition: since sacraments can only be founded through Christ, only those sacraments
counted that could be proved by means of the biblical texts to have
been initiated by Christ.

The Reformation position forced Catholic theology, if they wanted
to keep the number seven, to differentiate. So one distinguished in the
post-Reformation school theology between: 1. *institutio (sacramenti)
in individuo* ("institution in [all] details"); 2. *institutio in specie* ("institution according to kind"); and 3. *institutio in genere* ("institution
according to [general] form"). With the first form of institution Christ
had indicated exactly the "matter" and the "form," for example at the
institution of baptism according to Matthew 28:19, where Jesus clearly described the pouring over with water and the Trinitarian formula
as components of the sacrament. With the second form of institution
Christ, according to this theory, had determined only the fundamental character of the sacrament, leaving the further organization to
the Church – that would be the case with the sacrament of penance,
in connection with John 20:23. With the third form of institution,
Christ expressed his will that for certain situations in the Christian
life there should be a sacrament, without specifying it more narrowly –
so for example in the case of anointing of the sick or matrimony, where
Christ's will of foundation develops only out of later New Testament
texts in connection with specific acts of Jesus. The borders between
institutio in specie and *institutio in genere* are fluid. If one compares
only the content, then at least an *institutio in genere* is not to be distinguished from an institution through the Church – apart from the
express will of foundation on the part of the historical Jesus, still postulated by school theology. This is in the meantime now questionable
for the sacraments by which even according to the reforming view the
institutio in individuo was considered a certainty – above all baptism,
still controversial with Eucharist, though with the Eucharist there is
more support than with baptism.

The thesis of the Church as sacrament is rooted at exactly this place
of the problem. The Church is *altogether* the visible-invisible presence

of salvation of God brought to us by Christ. As such the Church communicates it (God's salvation) in all her dealings with the individual faithful, expressly at the decisive turning points of life where the
person in a so-to-speak specific way requires the grace of God. How
one comes to the *seven* sacraments can be learned from the works of
the Catholic theologian Karl Rahner that have already been mentioned; how one, on exactly the same basis, arrives at *two* sacraments
can be learned from the Lutheran theologians Gerhard Ebeling and
Eberhard Jüngel.

The idea of Church as sacrament appears, cleansed from any suspicion of Modernism. Rahner wants something quite different from
uncoupling the foundation of the sacraments from an institution by
Christ: the authority of Christ comes renewed to fruition in the sacramental activity of the Church, the authority he has communicated
salvifically to the Church.

This is the hard kernel of the thesis of the Church as sacrament: the
attempt at an answer to the question about the institution of the sacraments. The Council, not without fear of the suspicion of Modernism,
went back to the attempt of the Tübingen School (Moehler), to interpret the Church as the presence of Christ in his Spirit. Our thesis
was not a temporary measure at the Council, but a thesis in its own
right. It is now a general thesis concerning the nature of the *Church*.
That is seen above all with a comparison between Article 1 and Article
48. In Chapter 1 the Church is "sacrament" because she reflects the
light of Christ when she proclaims the Gospel. The reflecting sign is
at the same time an instrument of the union between God and people and between people themselves. The thesis appears here under
Christological aspect. In Article 48 (the second and third section) the
Church is categorized as a sacrament in her pneumatological and eschatological purpose: the Church is temporary, the sacraments and
their "furnishings" (*institutiones*) fading.

The balance therefore: the thesis of the Church as fundamental sacrament, originally developed for a limited and modest goal, was taken
up by the Council in an expansive way on Christological, pneumatological, and eschatological grounds. Karl Rahner composed this formula, in later years: The Church is the eschatological presence of the
victorious grace of Christ.

4. THE FUNCTION OF THE THESIS

This thesis of the Church as "sacrament" encounters vehement argument from the side of Lutheran theology. In some Lutheran circles, it is hardly possible to awaken more resentment or to bring more emotions to the boil than when one lets drop the phrase "sacramentality of the Church." It is appropriate to go into that when we consider in the next sections the statements of the Council concerning the Church as "the People of God" and as *communio*. We should set the course here by briefly examining what the *function* is of the thesis of the Church as fundamental sacrament.

The one function consists in that it gives the Church a functional purpose. Sacramentality means "sign" and "instrument," denotes therefore a sense of being strongly oriented to and for the good of something else. This "something else" is clearly stated: the unity of humanity with God and with one another. Whoever takes this thesis of the Church as sacrament seriously has, in any case, relativized the Church considerably more than with the concepts of the Body of Christ or "People of God."

At the same time a purely technocratic understanding of this instrumentality is avoided. The Church is as sign and instrument, not only an association, for the proclamation of the Gospel; if the Church were only an association, then faith would be only a matter for the individual. Here a latent danger of the Lutheran understanding of the Church is alluded to, an understanding that – as an antithesis to the excessive institutionalism of the late medieval Church – so strongly emphasizes the pure instrumentality of the external Church and the hiddenness of the "spiritual" Church that it is not possible to grasp how the "community of hearts in faith" should develop through faith, if this is only a matter for the individual and not at all capable of being institutionalized. In contrast, the thesis of the Church as sacrament maintains: "instruments" are the "saved," those marked by the visible-invisible presence of the grace of Christ through their belonging in the Church. Instrument is the Church as Church – that means as real, and as real, also visible community.

A third function and at the same time an advantage is that this designation more than all the others refers to the *visible* side of the Church, that is to say, to the "sacramental matter." It neutralizes the offense of her actual visible appearance, since she confesses to it. The

Church as visible community on earth is so inconspicuous, so small, so lightly discarded as a sacramental element. She lives in what she is from her divine dimension, and in this then the contradiction between her appearance and that which she should bring into appearance is clear.

With the phrase "sacramentality of the Church" her secret character is finally named. The word "sacrament" translates and comments on the title of *Mysterium Ecclesiae*. In short, the word keeps in view the inadequacy of a purely institutional way of looking at the Church.

Finally: it is in any case clear that there can be no worse misunderstanding of the Catholic doctrine of sacraments than that the sacraments make possible on the strength of their "objectivity" (*ex opere operato*) a path to salvation that bypasses personal faith. The sacrament, in contrast, as such comes about when it is received in faith and devotion. If the Church therefore is "sacrament," this means: one does not stand in salvific community with God when one is "objectively" a member of the Church, but when one literally "receives" the Church as a sacrament.

Of course the designation of the Church as "sacrament" has also intellectual and practical disadvantages. These have shown themselves more starkly in the time after the Council and are a reproach to Council teaching. It is more appropriate, however, to go into this in a later context.

B. CHURCH AS "PEOPLE OF GOD"

1. THE PRIESTHOOD OF ALL BAPTIZED

How "People of God" became the fundamental concept of the Church has been noted in the description of the history of the development of the Dogmatic Constitution on the Church. *What* the Council said concerning the Church as the People of God does not reveal at first glance its explosive nature. First a short overview of this, before we work out the points.

The second chapter of the Dogmatic Constitution on the Church begins in Article 9, comparable with Chapter 1, with a Trinitarian reason for and explanation of the concept "People of God": *God's* pleasure for all humanity, his will, was "to make men and women holy and to save them, not as individuals without any bond between them, but rather to make them into a people who might acknowledge him and serve him in holiness." This will of God lead to the election of Israel and finally to the calling of a people out of Jews and Gentiles. The head of this "messianic" people is *Christ*. His dignity consists in the freedom of the Children of God on the basis of the *Holy Spirit*, who lives in their hearts. His law is the new command of love, his purpose the Kingdom of God, and so this People of God is "a most certain seed of unity, hope and salvation for the whole human race." His life principle is the *Holy Spirit*, through whom this people do not cease to renew themselves, until "through the cross, it may arrive at the light that knows no setting."

Article 10 develops the characteristic of this People of God as "royal priesthood" and explains in an exciting way – for the first time in an ecclesial document – the *priesthood of all baptized*.

Because all baptized are priests who participate in the priestly office of Christ that takes place in the sacraments, a short description of the meaning of the seven Church sacraments is necessary (Article 11).

The People of God participate not only in the priestly office of Jesus, but also in his prophetic office in living witness; this leads to a short, but well-thought through definition of the relationship between the faith of the Church and the faith experiences of the faithful, as well as the ecclesial teaching office, followed by a comment on the variety of the other gifts of the Holy Spirit to the People of God. (Article 12)

Because of the universality of the call of God to *all humankind* the People of God is one, so Article 13 is the place at which the Council discusses for the first time the question of the unity of the Church. At the end of Article 13 the Council moves to a look at the people in the Church and the people outside the Church; Articles 14-16 speak first about the Catholic faithful, then the non-Catholic faithful, and finally about the non-Christians, and closes the chapter in Article 17 with a look at the mission task of the Church.

We shall stress a few important points of this conciliar description; in order to understand this description; we turn again to the prehistory, which now has almost the character of a novel, as much as theological history can.

2. "PEOPLE OF GOD" OR "BODY OF CHRIST"?

As was already shown, it was anything but self-evident that a chapter on the "People of God" would be included in the Constitution on the Church. Originally this concept was supposed to mean the members of the Church who did not belong to the hierarchy. As the titles in the first draft indicate, from the beginning the intention was to make the theme "particularly the laity," but besides the laity only members of orders would have been talked about. In a word: "People of God" should have been the name for all Christians without hierarchical ministry.

It can be assumed that the central idea of the description of the nature of the Church would have been and remained, as already with Pius XII, "the (mystical, mysterious) Body of Christ." The agenda for the "People of God" that was determined immediately at the beginning of the debate on the second draft changed the meaning of this phrase; from that point on it designated all the members of the Church, not only the non-office holders. The difficulty developed, necessarily, how one should set this fundamental idea for the Church in relationship to the already venerable image of the "Body of Christ," especially since the conservative group among the Council Fathers would have argued against the Constitution of the Church from the basis of the ideas of Pius XII in the encyclical *Mystici Corporis*. We have already touched on the result: "Body of Christ" (together with other biblical images of the Church) was treated at the end of Chapter 1, while "People of God" came to be the central idea by which "sacrament" of the Church was described in Chapter 2. Behind this development there stands more than one can imagine by a mere reading of the text, and the commentaries are not much help in piecing together the background.

We must consider first that the idea of the Church as "sacrament" seemed discredited since the condemnation of the Modernists. Another avenue besides that of the Modernists would have to be explored. The image of the Church, very much emphasized in the Bible, as the "Body of Christ" presented itself. The great breakthrough that marked Catholic theology (until the evening before the Council) occurred in 1924 with the famous and often re-printed book of the Tübingen theologian Karl Adam, *The Spirit of Catholicism*. Entire generations, particularly of Catholic intellectuals, formed their image of the Church and their Church piety from this book, which helped them endure all the stubbornness of the ecclesial institutions. A sentence, for example, such as: "Thus all dogmas of the Catholic Church bear the signature of Christ" was like an intoxicating drink, one that mediated another image of the dogma to theologians and questioning Christians other than the clatter of the neo-Scholastic theological handbooks.

The central idea by which Karl Adam sought to grasp the inner mystery of the Church was the idea "Body of Christ." Not from nothing! After all, Karl Adam came out of the tradition of the Catholic Tübingen School, which in the 19th century had formed the idea of the Church as a kind of historical organism, whose head was Christ and whose inspiring principle was the Holy Spirit.

As a direct attack on this euphoria of the "Body of Christ" idea the German Dominican Mannes Dominikus Koster, a professor of dogmatic theology, published a very temperamental and in part unrestrainedly polemical book, under the title *Ekklesiologie im Werden*. He had – as I know from personal conversation with him – written that book without any thought of publication, and only with much trouble could the interested press get the manuscript and the permission to publish from him.

This hesitation had its reasons, as became clear. Koster – who died in 1981 – was a dyed-in-the-wool Thomist. As such it was self-evident to him that one could speak of divine reality only in analogical concepts. The nature of the Church can be described only in an analogical concept, whose content remains in the tension between similarity and dissimilarity to the intended thing, as is typical for the analogical manner of speaking. But as a Thomist, Koster knew about the essential difference between a "true" analogy and a "mere" metaphor – a difference that for us today is, for good reason, not so important. Koster's thesis is: the concept "Body of Christ" is only a metaphor for the Church – just like how one can express the power of God comparatively, saying that God rises up like a lion against his enemies. The co-operation of the members in the Church is *comparatively* similar to how the members of a body co-operate under the leadership of the head – but in truth the Church is *not* a "body." What could then be a "true" analogy for the nature of the Church? Koster answered this by reaching back to the Scriptures and retrieving the concept "People of God." The Church is a *people*, in that she is an assembly of humankind.

Karl Adam felt himself, with reason, attacked and with him the many who were dependent on him for their image of Church. Then in 1943 the often-mentioned encyclical *Mystici Corporis* appeared, and although the Pope at the end expressly explained that "Body of Christ" is only a metaphor for the Church that one should not press to improper conclusions, Karl Adam felt vindicated against Koster. Almost triumphantly he wrote, in the preface of the eleventh printing of his book (1945), that his thesis was "authentically secured" through the papal encyclical – a typical example of the hope and concern of Catholic theologians that their theses might be in some form "secured" by the Magisterium of the Church.

Other Catholic dogmatic theologians saw the situation in this manner, as well. On the other hand, the theses of Koster contained so much that was worth thinking about that an entire generation of Catholic dogmatic theologians up to the end of the 1950's found it necessary to reject Koster and make the attempt to prove him wrong or to reconcile his theses with the "Body of Christ" ideas. A wonderful example of this reconciling compromise is offered by Michael Schmaus's definition of the Church: "Die Kirche [ist] derart Volk Gottes, dass sie also Leib Christi existiert." ("the Church is 'People of God' in such a way that she exists as Body of Christ"). Schmaus brings Koster and Adam together after the model of the generic concept and specific difference: "People of God" is also Israel! Through the designation "Body of Christ" the Church as "People of God" is distinguished from the People of God of the Old Covenant – we are now today encountering problems with such a differentiated delimitation.

Koster was, as the title of his small book indicates, of the opinion that ecclesiology is "becoming," because a theological decision is ripe only when it has completed the step from metaphor to actual theological analogy. This has not, according to Koster, happened with a "Body of Christ" ecclesiology. Koster was repudiated by the majority, but the impulse that further steps needed to be taken in ecclesiology was at work, as the compromise formulae indicate. In light of *this* background the decisions of the Second Vatican Council gain in stature. The Council had demonstrably *not* – at least not consciously – taken up the considerations of Koster. Yves Congar had reported on this, from his own eyewitness at the Council, in an illuminating short article in a 1971 volume dedicated to Koster. But the idea of "People of God" as a possible description of the nature of the Church stuck, and could so-to-speak spontaneously push to the foreground at the Council. One may easily imagine with what an uplifted head Mannes

Dominikus Koster strode through the corridors of the Dominican cloister Walberberg in 1964, at the proclamation of the Dogmatic Constitution on the Church.

Two other components might also be involved. The one is an insight of exegesis, that Paul's idea of the "Body of Christ" did not have that physical organ sense that has been attributed to it since the Tübingen School and, by way of Karl Adam, into the twentieth century. On the one side, particularly in the Letter to the Colassians, "Body of Christ" is closer to something like the mythological picture of a giant body, which the Church meant for Christ – comparable to the idea of "ae-ons" – and on the other side it has a sociological sense: "Body" under-stood as "corporate body." Augustine helped with this understanding, as well.

The other component might have stemmed from the conversation with Reformation theology. With "Body of Christ" can be meant ev-erything in the Church, except for one thing: that essential *opposition* between her and Christ as her Lord, therefore the *difference* between Christ and the Church. "Body of Christ" speculations always run the risk of blocking criticism of the Church – and above all, that of the structures of the Church. Don't the members follow, "according to structure," the impulses of the head? How can one criticize the mem-bers, then, without at the same time throwing into question the activ-ity of the head?

3. THE "PEOPLE OF GOD" AND THE NATIONS

What now makes the particularity of the Church into "People of God"? Article 9 begins with the universal love of God for all people at all time. The special feature of the People of God can only serve to help assert the message of this inclusive love of God for all humankind. From the start the Church in which this universal will to salvation expresses itself is *called* out of *Jews and Gentiles.* In the light of the love of God, the difference between the nations is invalidated. These eschatological ("messianic") folk have its model in the election of Israel to God's own people. The text does not go into exegetical details – for example, how Israel itself understood its election – but the relation-ship between Israel and the Church was described in a salvation-his-tory style according to the theme "incomplete – complete." The elec-tion of Israel as well as the calling of the Church from all peoples was brought together with the idea of the *covenant*: where God established a covenant with humankind, a People of God arose. Where the *new* covenant was established with humankind, there arose the *new* People of God – distinguished, in contrast to the old covenant People, in that this People of God is born not from the flesh, but from water and the Holy Spirit. All these statements were attested with New Testament citations. They are, however, not without problems, which must be taken up again in the statements over the relationship of the Church to Israel.

Because Christ is the founder of the New Covenant, he is also the head of the new People of God. We read in short sentences, provocative in their simplicity, that the dignity of the new People of God consists in the freedom of the Children of God by virtue of the Holy Spirit; his law is the command of love, and his purpose is the Kingdom of God, that here on earth would be laid down and then must unfold unto the end of time. This happened not so that the new People of God, that rests on the free election of God and not on the achievements of its members, is sufficient in itself, but so that "although it does not, in fact, include everybody, and at times may seem to be a little flock, is, however a most certain seed of unity, hope and salvation for the whole human race." Again reminiscent of the terminology of the doctrine on sacraments: as such a People it is used as an instrument for the redemption of all. In the next section it states directly that the Church has been established so "that it may be for each and everyone the visible sacrament of this saving unity." The development and nature of the Church is described: "All those, who in faith look towards Jesus, the author of salvation and the source of unity and peace, God has gathered together and established as one church, that it may be for each and everyone the visible sacrament of this saving unity." The similarity of these words to Luther's words on the Church as an assembly of those who believe in Christ – we think back to the citation at the beginning of this chapter – is tangible.

4. THE BAPTIZED AS PRIEST

Article 10 contains statements about the priesthood of the baptized that are not valued highly enough in the context of the ecumenical dialogue. By the way, the correct (and also happier) formulation is: the common priesthood of the faithful (of the baptized) and not:

the general priesthood of the faithful. After listing all the (not so frequent) relevant New Testament texts, the spiritual qualification of the baptized is described with the name "priesthood," a priesthood led by the High Priest Jesus. At the level of exegetical discussion the "priestly" tasks of the People of God are named: prayer, praise (Acts of the Apostles 2:42-47), the Christian life as "living sacrifice, holy and pleasing to God" (Romans 12:1), the Christ witness to all who ask for it (1 Peter 3:15). Actually, the New Testament avoided the word "priest" for ecclesial ministers, using it as a soteriological category for the description of the state of salvation of those who believed in Christ (only understandable in the context of a Jewish public), and indicated, almost with a flight of irony, the *life* of Christians as that of a new "priestly" activity, as though one wanted to say (as Paul in Romans 12:1ff): *if* you really want to know where our priests are, look at the Christians: their *latreia,* their "priestly worship" consists in their *life* and in the *proclamation of the Gospel.* Historical development had led to what research loves to call the "re-sacerdotalization" of the ecclesial offices, already instituted in the 4th century. It was necessary, first terminologically, to distinguish between "priests" and "priests" and to consider the question of a possible contrast between the two. The result: the common priesthood of all baptized disappeared from consciousness and eventually fell out of use in language: out of those "baptized" to "priests" came the "laity."

Since Luther re-discovered the theme of the common priesthood of all baptized – not always in a way that was completely clear – Catholic theology has, as a defensive reaction, studiously avoided the theme and left it to Lutheran theology, which soon had drawn more conclusions from it than Luther would have allowed.

Therefore even more attention is due to the sentence in Article 10 that seeks to bring the problem out in the open: "Though they differ essentially and not only in degree, the common priesthood of the faithful and the ministerial or hierarchical priesthood are none the less interrelated; each in its own way shares in the one priesthood of Christ." The commentary on the "hierarchical" priesthood contained in the adjective "ministerial" is not only a marginal comment. In the later statements about service and life of the priests the notion *sacerdos* was avoided. More important is the question, around which there is now considerable literature: what does the expression "essentially and not only in degree" mean? Is the precedence of the clergy established

here, a precedence that would directly contradict an essential critical
impetus of the Reformation?

Now, it might be that many who approved of this formulation actually believed it. However, it is worthwhile – see our excursus above,
rule 5! – to keep *exactly* in view what is in the text and what isn't. The
text maintains that the difference between the baptized and ecclesial
officeholders is *not* a distinction of rank. Difference in rank would be
a difference according to "degree" – the word *gradus*, here in the Latin
text, means "step." If no difference in essence existed between the baptized and the officeholders – who first and foremost are also baptized
– then both would be comparable with regards to a common measure, and by this measure the officeholder would stand a step higher.
In other words: a distinction "according to degree" would distinguish
the ecclesial officeholders as Christians of a higher order, because they
could only be compared by means of that which is common to both,
their baptism. This is ruled out if they are distinguished "according to
essence."

What is the "essence" of the "ministerial priesthood"? That is said
clearly in the following sentence: It is a particular *function* that the
ministerial priest performs for his fellow baptized: "The ministerial
priest, by the sacred power that he has, forms and governs the priestly
people; in the person of Christ he brings about the Eucharistic sacrifice
and offers it to God in the name of all the people." According to this,
proclamation and administration of the sacrament are the "essence" of
the ecclesial officeholder. The priest's authority empowers him for this
particular function. "Authority" is a juridical concept, not an "ontological" one – whatever might be in the minds of some Catholic and even
Lutheran Christians in this regard.

"The faithful indeed, by virtue of their royal priesthood, share in the
offering of the Eucharist," the text continues. Never before, not even in
Pius XII's encyclical on liturgy, was the active role of the faithful theologically characterized as subject in the celebration of the Eucharist.
(We have to bracket out, at this point, the ecumenical problem of the
concept of "sacrifice" in reference to the celebration of the Eucharist.)
The article ends by repeating what had already been said about what
constitutes the priesthood of the baptized: the reception of the sacraments prayer and thanksgiving, the witness of a holy life, self-denial
and active charity.

In short: contrary to first appearances and to some criticisms I have made, I am extraordinarily happy about this formulation of the difference between the priesthood of all baptized and the "ministerial priesthood"– one must just not allow oneself to be deceived through the "ontological" sound of the word "essence."

5. SENSUS FIDELIUM AND MAGISTERIUM

We jump over the short lecture on the doctrine of sacraments in Article 11. Karl Rahner has said, in the introduction to the Dogmatic Constitution on the Church in the textbook *Kleines Konzilscompendium,* that this article --if taken seriously-- must have decisive consequences for theology, religious pedagogy, and pastoral care. Indeed, the complete connection of the sacraments to the Church means the overcoming of a particular understanding of sacraments, by which they were only "individual means of salvation" in the context of a personal relationship to God. The sacraments are communal liturgies of the Church and develop in this area what one calls their "effectiveness."

On the other side, the strong ecclesial accent must seem strange to, most of all, Lutheran readers. Must then anything and everything be molded to "the Church"? However, these statements are only read correctly if they are not applied exactly to the concrete Church as we – in all denominations – daily experience her, but to the internal mystery of the Church as sacrament and People of God, as it is described so vividly in this and the preceding articles. So seen, these statements on the understanding of sacraments are the clear theological criticism of a Church whose reality lags behind the image drawn here.

If the relationship of Church and sacrament is explained by the phrase: "participation of all baptized in the priestly office of Jesus Christ," then the relationship of the Magisterium and the sense of the faith is explained by the phrase: "the participation of all baptized in the *prophetic* office of Christ." Some things occur here that do not spring immediately to the eye.

First: we encounter here the *sensus fidelium.* It is introduced as the so-called *locus theologicus,* as the court of appeals for the establishment of that which is the truth of faith. Before the Council, the *sensus fidelium* had been an explosive issue at the 1950 proclamation of the dogma on the bodily assumption of Mary into heaven. *One* of the decisive preliminary questions was: is this teaching believed in the dioceses of the Universal Church? A follow-up question was: is the fact of the centuries-old celebration (in both the East and the West) of the feast of the "Assumption of Mary" on August 15 valid as a decisive proof, when in the majority of these centuries the feast was celebrated not out of some spontaneous impulse of the faithful people, but on the strength of the prescription of the liturgical calendar? The result of the preliminary question at that time was: this doctrine is believed in the dioceses of the Universal Church, with decreasing exceptions. The comment on the *sensus fidelium* was at that time one of the reasons that Pius XII in 1950 felt justified to dogmatize this doctrine.

Now the follow up question is important: what happens if the *sensus fidelium* does not accept what had at one time been an ecclesial doctrine, possibly a binding one? Is it also then a theological court of appeal? The problem is closely tied with the much discussed question of the "reception" of a dogma, which according to the opinion of critical theologians should be the condition for its validity. In the end, does a poll decide the validity of a dogma? And then is the principle of the First Vatican Council not valid anymore, the principle that states that the solemn decisions of faith of the Papal teaching office "through itself and not because of the agreement of the Church" are unchangeable?

One can see, in what witches' kitchen of problems the Council went with this phrase *sensus fidelium*. The Council showed admirable courage. The short text from Article 12 is given here: "The whole body of the faithful who have received an anointing which comes from the holy one (see Jn 2:20 and 27) cannot be mistaken in belief. It shows this characteristic through the entire people's supernatural sense of the faith, when, 'from the bishops to the last of the faithful' (Augustine), it manifests a universal consensus in matters of faith and morals. By this sense of faith, aroused and sustained by the Spirit of truth, the people of God, guided by the sacred magisterium which it faithfully obeys, receives not the word of human beings, but truly the word of God (see 1 Th 2:13), 'the faith once for all delivered to the saints' (Jude 3). The people unfailingly adheres to this faith, penetrates it more deeply through right judgment, and applies it more fully in daily life."

It demands too much of the text if one concludes from it that the papal proclamation of doctrine is actually tethered here to the sense of the faith of the Church. The formulation is quite clear that the *sensus fidelium* of the People of God, "guided by the sacred magisterium which it faithfully obeys" only has the Word of God. On the other hand the text means an essential broadening – or better, concretization – of that which the First Vatican Council had already said and what the successors of the disappointed minority at Vatican I now wanted to establish without a doubt: that the Pope is not infallible *outside* of or *in opposition* to the Church, but is integrated in her. Not the Pope first and foremost is infallible, but *the Church* can in faith not err: the "Church," all the faithful, the "People of God." The text makes abundantly clear by means of a quote from Augustine that this *sensus fidelium* includes every member of the Church ("from the bishops to the last of the faithful").

In short: the mutual dependency, indeed if need be also the antagonism between the faithful and the teaching office is established as an ecclesiological base fact. This means that there can be no valid magisterial proclamation that does not concern itself with the faithful's sense of the faith. The last reservation about the precedence of the teaching ministry before the faithful is then groundless, if one takes seriously that the ministry in the Church is based on the calling through Christ and not as it were on the people's spiritual sovereignty. The office is the representation of the authority of Christ. The people co-operate (and could do so much more) with the selection of the *office holder*, but it does this trusting that the officeholder whom they select has been picked by Christ himself. He must be then *vis-à-vis* the (rest of the) people God's witness to faith, witness to Jesus Christ – in a borderline case, also against the opinion poll "majority opinion" of the *sensus fidelium* of Church members. Or would it be thinkable that a Pope, a Bishop, a Pastor might stop proclaiming the Resurrection of our Lord Jesus Christ from the dead, because a qualitative majority of Church members might not consider this a binding truth of faith?

C. CHURCH AS *COMMUNIO*

1. A SECRET CENTRAL IDEA OF THE COUNCIL

The idea of the Church as *Communio* – therefore as community and not only as institution, so "People of God" once again, under a new aspect – this is a central idea, perhaps *the* central idea, of the Second Vatican Council, as Professor Walter Kasper (before he was elevated to Bishop and later Cardinal) wrote in an important article on the

theme; he can summon other support for this view, people who have
said the same thing. "Communio-ecclesiology" of the Council has been
the subject of much discussion and many attempts to make it fruitful
for theology. Impediments to this idea that Church as *Communio* was
the central idea of the Council are created by the fact there are also
– above all in Chapter Three of the Constitution on the Church – extensive pieces of text in the Council documents that present another,
a "hierarchical" understanding of the Church, so that this has led to
a way of speaking of a "double" or "split" ecclesiology at the Council.
Do we have therefore with "*communio* /community" a central idea of
the Council, possibly in competition with "sacrament" and "People of
God"?

To give away the conclusion: I cannot agree with this widely disseminated thesis, so long as the talk is of a *central idea*, and precisely
an *ecclesiological* central idea. That does not mean, however, that the
concept *communio* did not have a central place in the Council texts.
But this was not so from the beginning, and moreover the place of the
communio concept was so central because it did not remain limited to
the understanding of the Church.

In order to prove this thesis and above all to direct our attention
to the unexhausted potential of the Council texts, we must look first
briefly at the texts.

2. COMMUNITY WITH GOD

Walter Kasper had taken the trouble, in the mentioned article, to
gather together all the mentions of *communio* in the Council texts.
The first surprising observation: the use of the language is not rigorously dictated. Next to the word *communio* are, with the same meaning, similar concepts such as *communitas, societas, participatio*, as well
as others. This already speaks against a "central idea," that from the
beginning on clearly steered the formation of the texts – as did the
idea of the Church as "sacrament," for example. The concept came to
the foreground much more gradually and almost without intention, in
the debates of the Council. *Communio* was a "central idea" at most for
the mentors who were concerned for it with their work on the texts.

The second and decisive observation: before the concept of community was connected to the Church, is appears in the texts of the
Council first as the perfect example of the relationship between God

and humankind, expressed theologically: as a soteriological concept. In this sense it opens the Dogmatic Constitution on the Church: the point of the Church as "sacrament" is to develop the community of humankind with God. It has the same sense when, in the second Article, the text speaks of the calling of humankind to *participation* in divine life, a participation described in other places as personal community and peace wherein the dignity of the person, the truth of his humanity, exists. This *communio* was actualized in Jesus Christ in a historically unique way; he in his incarnation is in a certain way in union with every human being. This union is continued, internally actualized and universally extended through the Holy Spirit: through him to be Church means both to live in unity with God and to live with one another in community. The important places to look to check this: Dogmatic Constitution on the Church, Articles 1-4; 48; Constitution on Revelation, Articles 1 and 2; Decree on Mission, Articles 3 and 4; and the Pastoral Constitution, Articles 19 and 22.

A second set of statements around the concept *communio* concerns the way in which the person is led into community with God: through a sharing in the word and sacrament. With this we are in better known territory. Catholics have a habit of saying that they "receive Communion," when they want to say: they receive the body (and blood) of the Lord in the celebration of the Eucharist. The concept of "community" here has grown together with that *by which* one has a share, *with which* one has community. This usage of language is attested not only in the tradition of the ancient Church, but also and above all in the meaning in the New Testament of *communio* or, in the Greek, *koinonia*. It has to do with the sharing in the goods of salvation given by God: "...in the Holy Spirit, in new life, in love, in the Gospel, above all in the Eucharist," as Kaspar formulated. The Council added only the point of view that to these "goods" in which we have a share, belong not only the sacrament, but also and equally, maybe in a certain sense first, the word – and takes up with this, however consciously and willfully, a central Reformation matter of concern. The most important places to test this: the Constitution on the Sacred Liturgy, Article 55; the Dogmatic Constitution on the Church, Articles 3, 7, 9, 11; the Decree on Ecumenism, Articles 2, 22; the Constitution on Revelation, Articles 21-26; the Decree on Missions, Article 9; the Decree on Priests, Article 4.

3. THE CHURCH AS *COMMUNIO*

Since the triune God, prototype and origin of all community, is believed and recognized only in the Church and since word and sacrament are only shared through the Church, the material consequence is unavoidable: the Church also has *communio* structure. Connecting with the Italian theologian Bruno Forte, Walter Kasper formulated: "The Church is so to speak the icon of the Trinitarian community of Father, Son, and Holy Spirit." The church community is concrete there where it gathers to hear the word of God and to celebrate the Eucharist. That means that ecclesial community is concrete in the *local church*. In this regard *communio* is actually an ecclesiological technical term, and designates the basic nature of the Universal Church as a community of local churches. The Council then explains this bluntly: the Catholic Church consists in and out of local churches (Dogmatic Constitution on the Church, Article 23).

The Council was fully aware here of what it was doing and realized that it was retrieving a basic idea of the understanding of the Church from the ancient Church, an idea that in the Orthodox Eastern Churches up to today characterizes the understanding of the Church. The Council referred numerous times expressly to this (*Nota praevia*, Article 2; Decree on Eastern Catholic Churches, Article 13; Decree on Ecumenism, Article 14f). These statements meant a break that cannot be overestimated. It ended in principle an understanding of the Church that intentionally and with knowledge of the consequences set the uniformity of a central church in the place of the community of local churches; the Universal Church was so to speak one gigantic local church. Just this understanding of Church was, beyond all other relevant causes, the most important reason for the separation of the East and West Churches in the year 1054, and just this understanding of the Church developed in a more unrestrained fashion after the separation in theory and practice of the Roman West Church of the second Christian millennium. Should this then come to an end? It is no wonder, that this return to ancient church understanding of the Church provoked resistance. This was not sheer ill will or mere conservative stubbornness; it reveals a problem that the Council did not solve, but left to its post-history – as we today know: with still completely unknown egress. The question is: how do the local churches relate to the Universal Church? What does it mean to say that the

Church "consists" out of participant churches? Or very briefly: how is *communio* related to unity? This unity wants not just to be maintained but also to be made visible. The practical sticking point is: "collegiality" of the Bishops with the holder of the Petrine office, and vice versa. The entire fight between *Communio* ecclesiology and "hierarchical" ecclesiology is then conducted as a fight around the collegiality of the Bishops with the Pope.

The unsolved problem is not hidden away, but made manifest in that concept Walter Kasper called "a typical compromise formulation," "which points to a *contretemps* between *Communio* ecclesiology and 'hierarchical' ecclesiology": in the concept of the *communio hierarchica*. With this is meant that the individual Bishop is integrated in subordination to the Pope in the College of all Bishops of the Universal Church. The material basis of this is not unproblematic. According to Article 21 of the Dogmatic Constitution on the Church the consecration of Bishops is the full form of the sacrament of ordination, in which all pastoral authority of the Bishop (*iurisdictio*) is grounded. It is now added in the same article that the offices (*munera*) communicated through the consecration of the Bishop can be "executed" only in "hierarchical community" with the head and the members of the College (compare also Article 22 and the Decree on the Bishops' Pastoral Office in the Church, Article 4). *Nota praevia* Article 2 sharpens this through the distinction between offices (*munera*) and powers (*potestates*). The offices are conferred through the consecration, but their powers can only be executed on the basis of a juridical act that assigns the corresponding tasks and the affected persons to the office holder. What is problematic about this is that the office itself is – as we remember from the reflections on Article 10 of the Dogmatic Constitution of the Church – defined according to its nature as "power." A distinction and indeed a possible separation of office and power is logically not comprehensible, unless it be that the office as the basis of the power implies a higher level of being Christian. That corresponds to the pre-conciliar (and in practice continuing) distinction between office and jurisdiction, following which a named but not yet consecrated Bishop can execute valid jurisdictional acts. But it does not correspond to the conciliar understanding of the office of Bishop. The minority Bishops achieved a small victory here, conceded to them in order to make it possible that they would agree to the Dogmatic

Constitution on the Church. We chew today on the consequential problems.

Under these conditions no completely satisfactory breakthrough could be expected from the Council, where the narrowest meaning of church *communio* was concerned with the community in the sense of the participation and responsibility of all. What would happen, if – as happened occasionally in Latin America – a priest-less base community, because of the divine right of the congregation to the celebration of Eucharist, would ask the pastoral council that a laicized and married priest in the congregation exercise his ordination power on the next Sunday? The congregation and the affected priest, if he followed the call of the congregation, would be reminded very quickly by the Bishop of the *communio hierarchica*, and no pointing out that divine law in the case of conflicts breaks and must break human law would suffice. How dramatic the same problem can be in Europe is shown by the married men ordained to the priesthood in the Czech underground Church at the time of the communist regime, without whom the Czech Church would not have had a chance of survival. Rome, although thankful for the work accomplished under great danger and the building up of the body of Christ, had and has problems with recognizing them in their office – out of fear of a new discussion of celibacy.

With regard to participation and responsibility of all members of the People of God the Council used the term *communio* very "shyly," although the ecclesiological base statements in the matter point to this – cue: "People of God" – and although occasionally at a decisive place *communio fidelium*, the community of the faithful, is spoken of (Dogmatic Constitution on the Church, Article 13; Decree on Ecumenism, Article 2; Decree on the Apostolate of the Laity, Article 19). Most of the internal hopes for the Council's idea of community were directed toward this. So then the disappointment is always particularly great, when such shared responsibility is broken or hindered from the side of the *communio hierarchica* – whereby it must of course be acknowledged, that also in matters of "shared responsibility" not all that glitters is gold. Rather than focus on a scandal, it is better here to point out that such participation and joint responsibility, and indeed *with* official support, has already found numerous institutional forms; there where they are not used for the goal of self-promotion or self assertion but in selfless service, with imagination and intelligence, these forms bear beautiful fruit.

With this we come finally to a very real balance: the paradoxically tension-filled relationship of the local Church and the Universal Church structure as well as of the official responsibility and joint responsibility of all will never be solved theoretically. It is practically solvable: through rules of cooperative work and conflict management, carried out with mutual respect as well as with faithful insight into that which establishes Church. This, that is, the community with God in Jesus Christ through the participation in word and sacrament, justifies certainly responsibility, competence, duty, and also obedience – but never control and subjection. To find such rules and to awaken the will of all to hold onto them is of course difficult. It demands from the one side renunciation of privileges not strictly grounded in the God-given essence of the office, and from the other side renunciation of a "self help" that is inappropriate for the church community, therefore the renunciation of means other than theological, church political, and pastoral work.

It has been shown: the concept of *communio* was not a "central idea" of the Second Vatican Council. But this negative decision is only the half truth. The *communio* concept, with the brazen power of logic and with the strength of a re-discovered old tradition of the description of God's act of salvation, had bled like an open wound in the understanding of Church, where its stab can never again be numbed. The tasks of the future could now be fastened on it – including the problem of ecumenism and of a new unity of the Church, of which we shall speak in the following chapter. These tasks reveal what the actual base ideas of the Council were: "sacrament" and "People of God." Sharply formulated: the idea of community was not the central idea, but the crystallization of the conciliar understanding of Church – and that means the point to which the controversies around the concepts "sacrament" and "People of God" finally could be shifted, with the consequence, that at the very latest at this point each Council Father had to show his own colors. Hence the unavoidably growing reservation, the closer the *communio* concept touched on the concrete. A small detail, to which Walter Kasper refers, illuminates the correctness of this evaluation: the 1985 Special Synod on the occasion of the 20th anniversary of the Council's close felt itself compelled, in its closing document, to reinforce the *communio* idea.

D. MARY AND THE CHURCH

1. IT DOES NOT HAPPEN WITHOUT CONFLICT

The returned first draft of the Church Constitution planned as an appendix a chapter with the title "Virgin Mary, Mother of God and Mother of Mankind," in which the arrangement remained open. It was absolutely not possible, just a few years after the dogmatic definition concerning the "bodily assumption of Mary into Heaven" to be quiet about Mary at the Council. Already before the opening of the Council, on the basis of readings of the first draft, the warning came from many sides that the Council must speak not just about the "militant" Church but must also treat the unity of the perfected in Heaven with the "triumphant" Church. The concern was with the eschatological orientation of the Church, on the basis of which the "militant" Church first and last is a "pilgrim" Church on the way to her final home, which she cannot have here. Both themes remained for a good while in the shadow of the "great" disputes concerning the concept of the Church and the collegiality of the Bishops. The revised second draft first planned, as a conclusion, the chapter on the call to holiness in the Church. It was only in the third session that the eschatological and Mariological chapter was discussed at all in detail.

The present Chapter 7 with the somewhat awkward title "The Eschatological Character of the Pilgrim Church and Her Union with the Heavenly Church" came relatively easily through the votes on the 19th and 20th of October, 1964. It was possible to satisfy the concerns of those who wanted to see the truths about "last things" and the veneration of the saints expressly mentioned. There was nonetheless a short vehement dispute in the consultations (15th and 16th of September, 1964), since a few Bishops did not want to give up on adding express statements about Hell and Purgatory in the text.

More controversial were the contents and arrangement of the current Chapter 8 on Mary. Outwardly the fight was about whether this chapter should be a component – in no way an appendix! – of the Dogmatic Constitution on the Church or if it would be better to strive for a separate document on Mariology and Marian veneration. This question was in principle decided in the second session. Prominent representatives of both points of view had campaigned on the 25th of October 1963. The passionate commitment of the supporters of a separate document did not fail to have an effect, and so it came on the 26th of October 1963 only to a narrow majority (1114 against 1074) in favor of an addition to the Dogmatic Constitution on the Church. Both sides could see that it would be difficult to achieve the necessary two-thirds majority when the content of the chapter would be discussed and voted on in the following year, but attempts to avoid a conflict in front of the entire world through a simplified process with the help of a special commission failed. Therefore one had to travel the toilsome path of the first draft again, of the *Modi*, of the detailed discussion, and of the final redaction.

The fight was so passionate because behind the externally purely redactional question stood two different conceptions of Mariology that had fought with one another for centuries. The supporters of a narrow mariological explanation argued it would be an inadmissible limitation to view the task of the Mother of Jesus with regard to redemption only in context with the Church – particularly since up to the third session it was still undecided in what way the eschatological dimension of the Church and the community of the saints should be thematicized. No, these Fathers believed, the "Marian mystery" is in the end deeply rooted in the mystery of the triune God. The supporters of an integration in the Dogmatic Constitution on the Church argued against this from the collective picture of salvation history, in which Mary represents as the first believer the "type" of the Church. Mary has her personal privileges, of which Catholic Christians on the basis of the doctrine of the Church are convinced, not for herself, but for the use of the Church. The relationship between Mary and the Church was moreover the central theme in the Mariological discussion preceding the Council. And, not last, ecumenical considerations spoke for the strict avoidance of all grandiose exaggerations.

The draft finally presented led in the discussion of the 16th of September to the 18th of September 1964 to a somewhat anti-climactic exchange. It was calmer than expected, and debated without excitement. Voices were raised, however, that accused the text draft of a "minimalist" tendency. That indeed was correct – it is just that this fact can be assessed in very different ways. Numerous Bishops from Poland, Spain, and Italy recommended as useful a solemn consecration of the world to the Blessed Virgin. They pushed to bestow on her the titles "Mother of the Church" and "Mediatrix" – which others immediately rejected: "Mother of the Church" was not a particularly traditionally rich mariological title, and the title "Mediator" was given in the New Testament only to Christ.

The intervention of the Archbishop of Cologne, Cardinal Frings, cut the Gordian knot; the Cologne Cardinal's request to speak is yet another reason why he must be reckoned as one of the decisive figures of the Council. Frings of course had in mind that in Germany and in the countries marked by the Reformation the Lutheran Churches and Lutheran theology would be particularly attentive to the Marian statements. So Frings suggested, in view of the opinions that had been expressed, that each one sacrifice something of his personal preference. One should limit oneself to marking out strongly dogmatic ground on which all could stand together. Then is one not only invincible, but Mariology could thus be fruitful spiritually and even ecumenically. So it happened, and so Chapter 8 of the Constitution on the Church received its final form.

2. THE PLAIN TEXT

The chapter now carries the title: "The Role of the Blessed Virgin Mary, Mother of God, in the Mystery of Christ and the Church." This title has a programmatic character. The "Mother of God" (*Theotokos*) of the old tradition (Council of Ephesus 431) is the virgin from Nazareth, who through her "yes" stands in the mystery of Christ and pre-figures the visible-invisible nature of the Church.

Following this program the text first describes, adhering strictly to the biblical texts, the specific task of Mary in the Christ event (Articles 55-59). The character of the relationship of Mary to the Church follows, and indeed first negatively: Mary is the *maid* of Christ, and her task is subordinated to Christ's own mediatorship. Positive: Mary is a *type* of the Church, and Mary is in her life a *model* for the Church (Articles 60-65). Finally the Council takes a position on the nature and forms of the veneration of Mary, and expressly refers to non-Catholic Christians (Articles 66-69).

Concessions had to be made to the "maximalists," in order to win their approval. We are not spared from sentences such as these, in Article 58: "Thus the Blessed Virgin advanced in her pilgrimage of faith, and faithfully persevered in her union with her Son until she stood at the cross, in keeping with the divine plan (see Jn 19:25), suffering deeply with her only-begotten Son, associating herself with his sacrifice in her mother's heart, and lovingly consenting to the immolation of this victim who was born of her." The controversial title "Mother of the Church" is avoided, but its sense is often spoken of, when the talk is of the maternal affection of Mary for the Church (for example, Article 61; Article 62 at the end). The title "Mediatrix" is taken up in Article 62, but used with the equal-ranked usual other titles, "Advocate" and "Auxiliatrix." Right at the beginning it is said that the Council did not intend to present a complete teaching on Mary – it hinders no one, therefore, to think out other theses in the field of Mariology, and to be less restrained in pious practices than the text suggests. Of course there can be no suggestion that the Council backed off even just a millimeter from the two Marian dogmas, the 1854 dogma of Immaculate Conception and 1950 dogma of the Bodily Assumption into Heaven (compare Article 56 and 59).

Nonetheless: seen as a whole and impartially read the text is of such a responsible dogmatic rationality that for all who are inclined to think about Mary according to the principle "God could do it, it was proper, therefore he did it," the text has the effect of a cold shower. The signature of the text is: a strict orientation on the sparse biblical statements and on the dogmatically binding doctrine of the Church, Christ's sole mediatorship, in no way compromised by Mary's "cooperation" in the work of redemption (compare Article 62!), the rejection of any adoration of Mary (Article 66), the warning about exaggerations that would offend non-Catholic Christians (Article 67), and still much more.

Lutheran criticism of Mariology is certainly not calmed by this text. But a glance into the controversial theological discussion teaches us not only that theological opinions and the pious feelings definitely part ways here, but the discussion also allows one to ask whether Lutheran theology on Mary does not also have resentments to conquer, resentments that stem from an unfortunate perception of the true content and actual status of Catholic Mariology and pious practices. Many Catholic Christians would not recognize themselves in many Lutheran portrayals of Catholic Mariology.

E. THE LAITY

The last section of this long chapter must begin with an apology: I do not go into the chapter on members of orders. On this topic I would have much positive to say, as well as a bit of criticism. But I simply rather arrogantly precede from the assumption that the overwhelming majority of the readers of this book are not members of orders. I also feel that I can abstain from an analysis of the statements concerning members of orders since the evaluation, continuation, and practical application of the Council statements concerning these have already been undertaken and achieved by the most competent specialists.

I close this chapter with a look at the overwhelming majority, until now predominantly the silent majority, in the People of God: the laity. Very briefly, and as an impetus to further study:

The "discoverer" of the Lay Apostolate is Pope Pius XI (1922-1939). In his view, though, the Lay Apostolate is the lengthened arm of the hierarchy. That comes out in the formulation of Article 33 of the Dogmatic Constitution on the Church: "The laity, however, are given this special vocation: to make the church present and fruitful in those places and circumstances where it is only through them that it can become the salt of the earth." That is an indirect citation from the 1931 encyclical *Quadragesimo anno* of this same Pope.

The laity are bearers of the mission of the Church in their own right, on the basis of their baptism and their confirmation – not withstanding that this mission is executed in harmony with the leadership through the ecclesial office.

The secular vocation is described as service of God in formulations that sometimes reminds one of Luther's understanding of vocation and vocational ethics – emphasized by Luther researchers as a particularly distinctive point in Luther's theology.

Nowhere else is the servant character of the hierarchy – the idea that the hierarchy serves the laity—emphasized so much. The office holders are characterized as support for the laity in the laity's fulfillment of the "true" mission of the Church in the world.

A taste of what the readers can expect:

The hierarchy cannot and should not do everything – it is its real task to coordinate the gifts in the People of God for the good of the mission of the whole Church.

The laity accomplishes the mission of the entire Christian people in the world – the hierarchy should take over secular tasks only in exceptional cases.

The laity should seek God in their vocations and sanctify the world from within, that is, through the witness of their Christian word and life.

With reference to the calling to salvation, hope, and love and to common dignity in the building up of the Kingdom of Christ there is no inequality vis-à-vis the hierarchy. The difference between laity and office holders (see Article 10!) includes solidarity, that is, in service and in cooperative work.

The laity have the office holders as brothers in Christ – one notices: it could be formulated the other way around!

The Lay Apostolate is participation in the salvific mission of the Church itself; not through instruction and demand of the hierarchy (although that in the narrow sense is possible – for example, through the ecclesial appointment of the religion instructor), but through baptism and confirmation.

And so it goes on! Whoever takes Chapter 4 of the Constitution on the Church seriously has to say: a layperson does not have to ask an office holder, whether, for example, he may speak with his work colleagues about theological questions – earlier he very definitely had to. A layperson, in order to be totally concrete and personal, does not have to ask anyone anymore whether he may make statements in a book on theological questions – earlier he would have required permission to publish.

Regulations for implementation are offered by the Decree on the Lay Apostolate. Measured by the statements of the Dogmatic Constitution on the Church, some things there may seem hesitant, pale, "balanced." But such a decree cannot, despite its practical orientation, hit the mark on all the various different situations in all countries of the Church. Where these practical instructions seem sort of outdated or unrealistic, one can only answer: in doubtful cases, the dogmatic statements of the Constitution on the Church count for more than changeable regulations for implementation.

At the beginning of this chapter we indicated the oddity, that in an old Catholic lexicon at the entry "laity" we find only the cross reference "clergy." So can we turn the tables on this perspective and close the chapter with this joke from the Council: What is a priest? Answer: a priest is a former deacon, who has received the sacrament of ordination, who occasionally rises to the rank of Bishop, but who never is elevated to the dignity of a layperson.

CHAPTER SIX

"ELEMENTS" BECOME
THE CHURCH

The Ecumenical Unity of the Church

I. THE MOST ECUMENICAL OF ALL COUNCILS

1. AN ECUMENICAL LETTER

The lines of our narrative of the Council and our efforts to understand its texts now run together and cross over each other. After the necessarily very detailed look at the Council's understanding of the Church – the most important theme of the Council – this will happen more and more frequently. Once again we must think back on something and anticipate something. We must think back on the goals of the Council, goals that became clear to Pope John XXIII, the Council Fathers, and the general public only gradually, and were only completely clear after the first session. We have already described how the unity of Christendom in one Church, at first at best a secondary theme at the Council, gained more and more importance through the activity of Cardinal Bea, appointed by the Pope as the leader of the Secretariat for Promoting Christian Unity. Now the world was, of course, in suspense about how the Council would express itself concerning the question of the ecumenical unity of the Church, first about the relationship of the Roman Church to the Eastern Orthodox Churches, then about the relationship to the Reformation Churches.

We also need to ask the question of how the ecumenical opening of the Council affected the style of the work of the Council. With the weight accorded to the ecumenical theme by the presence of the non-Catholic observers, it was impossible for the Council to work on the texts as if the Council Fathers were alone. We begin here with our "anticipation."

The most difficult "birth" of the Council was, as Chapter Ten will show in detail, the Pastoral Constitution on the Church in the Modern World (*Gaudium et Spes*). In the course of the development of this important text, at a point of apparent helplessness, something occurred that was a model for the ecumenical atmosphere at the Council. The controversial draft had been handed over to a commission that was a mixture of a sub-commission of the Apostolate of the Laity and a sub-commission of the influential Theological Commission. The president of the commission was the otherwise little known Bishop E. Guano, a member of the Commission for the Apostolate of the Laity. Lukas Vischer, one of the non-Catholic observers at the Council who was the General Secretary of the World Council of Churches' Commission on Faith and Order sent a letter to Bishop Guano. In this letter he expressed his concern about the document and set out in a detailed manner how the Commission on Faith and Order would go about producing a document on the Church in the Modern World, were such a task assigned to his Commission. He included five documents produced by the World Council of Churches (WCC); according to the letter Vischer sent, the WCC had been at work since 1956 on a similar document, with the title "Christ's Rule over the Church and over the World."

According to protocol, this letter was impudent. It bypassed the proper channels – the letter should have been sent to the Secretariat for Christian Unity – it had not been requested, and avoided direct intervention in the work of the Council only because Vischer had sent the letter not to the sub-commission directly, but to Bishop Guano, who reacted graciously. He accepted the letter for what it was, a private communication, but had photocopies made and sent to anyone who wanted to have them (and this turned out to be a good number of people). From that point on the Lutheran observers were invisible participants in the work on the Pastoral Constitution.

This event is a wonderful model of the ecumenical concern of the separated sister Churches for the work at a Roman Catholic council. The Second Vatican Council, which was an "ecumenical" council in the sense of Roman Catholic canon law but not in the Ancient Church sense of an assembly of all the bishops in Christendom, became the most ecumenical council since the separation between the Eastern and

Western Churches. Concern for the unity of Christendom in a common Church led to the document in which ecumenical unity became the theme: the Decree on Ecumenism (*Unitatis redintegratio*).

2. THE ORIGIN OF THE DECREE ON ECUMENISM

The question of the unity of the separated Churches encountered resistance from the Curia and from the conservative Council Fathers, just as the opening of the Church to the modern world, Pope John XXIII's top priority for the work of the Council, had. This first resistance evinced itself in the unbelievable tug-of-war surrounding the concept, content, preparation, discussion, and conclusion of the Pastoral Constitution, about which we shall soon talk. The second resistance evinced itself in the attempts to wrest control of certain ecumenical projects from the Secretariat for Christian Unity, in order to push ecumenism to the periphery of the Council concerns. The comparatively quick and, until the confrontation on "Black Thursday," rather problem-free work on the Decree on Ecumenism borders on a miracle, given the conditions. In fact, it did at the onset appear as if the ecumenical question might remain more on the periphery. Among the veritable flood of drafts that were produced by the ten preparatory commissions, only three drafts concerned themselves with ecumenical questions. In December the Council assigned the Secretariat for Christian Unity the task of bringing together these texts into a draft of a uniform decree. This draft contained the following topics, all of which, according to the editors, are related to one another:

- The complex of questions around the unity of the separated Churches;
- The question about the relationship of the Church to the Jews;
- In a rudimentary fashion, the question about the relationship between the Church and non-Christian religions;
- Finally, the position on religious freedom.

The combination of these topics is certainly not without intellectual appeal, but it is also based on weighty theological reasoning. When one country after another becomes more multicultural and more religiously pluralistic – with corresponding consequences for the situation of the Church – it obviously makes a good deal of sense to free the problem of inner-Christian ecumenism from its introverted narrowness and place this in its wider context, what Karl Rahner in the last years before his death (1984) frequently called "theistic ecumenism," vis-à-vis the varieties of modern atheism. External grounds – above all the political turbulence surrounding the planned Declaration on Jews – also led to extracting this from the developing Decree on Ecumenism and broadening it to a Declaration on non-Christian Religions, as well as making the position on the question of religious freedom into its own separate document. This left inner-Christian ecumenism as the focus of the Decree on Ecumenism. From this point on the work on the Decree on Ecumenism essentially ran parallel to the work on the Dogmatic Constitution on the Church, adopting the statements of this Constitution, cautiously pushing them further, and applying them theoretically and practically to the relationship of the separated Churches. In this manner the Decree on Ecumenism was one of only five documents (out of a total of sixteen) that could be solemnly promulgated in the third session in Fall of 1964, only a year before the close of the Council – the Decree on Ecumenism on the 21st of November, 1964.

A quick look at the uncomplicated structure of the Decree might be useful before we get to questions of content. In the foreword the dark background that made a Decree on Ecumenism necessary is re-visited: the history of schisms among Christians, from the Apostolic Age until present time. Our time period was also illumined by the – at the time of the Council – over one hundred years of the Ecumenical Movement, recognized as the work of the Holy Spirit. In the first part (Articles 2-4), as is usual in a Decree intended for practical use, the dogmatic basis is laid, joined with statements from the Dogmatic Constitution on the Church. A second chapter, Articles 5-12, treats the practical actualization of ecumenical matters in general; more precisely, the challenges that Catholic Christians must take to heart when they commit themselves to ecumenical dialogue. Chapter 3 undertakes the application to the separated Churches, where in the nature of things a distinction must be made between the non-uniate Eastern Churches and the Churches and ecclesial communities that directly or indirectly sprang from the Reformation. The Council wisely avoided describing the latter in any more precise a manner.

II. THE COUNCIL ON THE UNITY OF THE CHURCH?

The first thing to notice is that the Council did not speak of the unity of the Church using the classical schema presented in the Creed: one, holy, catholic, and apostolic. There is actually no separate discussion of these four descriptors; all four are treated when the context demands it: holiness in Chapter 5 of the Dogmatic Constitution on the Church, under the title "The General Call to Holiness in the Church." Catholicity is mentioned in the context of the question of the different classifications of people in the Church, so in Chapter 2 in Articles 14-17. The apostolicity of the Church appears in the context of the question on the Magisterium, in Chapter 3. Unity comes to the fore in three places in the texts of the Council: in Article 8 of the Dogmatic Constitution on the Church, in connection with the question of God's plan of salvation with the Church; in Article 13, in connection with the question of the universal mission of the Church; and finally in the Decree on Ecumenism, in connection with the question of the relationship of the Roman Catholic Church to the other Churches – the groundwork was laid for this in Article 15 of the Dogmatic Constitution on the Church. Should one understand from this arrangement, which is certainly not accidental, that the Council wanted to issue a warning against a theological narrowness *vis-à-vis* the question of unity, against understanding the question of unity only from the standpoint of relationships to the other Churches? It is impossible to answer this question; instead, we turn to a short survey of what the Council said about unity of the Church.

1. A GLANCE BACK AT THE
DOGMATIC CONSTITUTION ON THE CHURCH

As we remember, the first chapter of the Dogmatic Constitution on the Church treated God's plan of salvation and argued theologically, abstractly, and along Trinitarian-Salvation History lines. The Church is the (temporary) result of a history in which the triune God progressively communicates and reveals himself and consequently makes this history into "salvation history." In this view of the Church, unity is implied as a foregone conclusion. Article 8 begins with the phrase, "Christ, the one Mediator," a phrase that once again named the immediate basis for the unity and oneness of the Church. Even to think of a split Church or numerous Churches as a possibility would amount to a break, a split, in God's plan of salvation. Insofar as God calls people and makes the Church the sign and instrument of this call, the Church can only be one – anything else is absurd. In this context the question arises: where is this God-intended Church to be found? According to Article 8 of the Dogmatic Constitution on the Church, "This Church constituted and organized in the world as a society, subsists in the Catholic Church, which is governed by the successor of Peter and by the Bishops in communion with him." The Latin text reads: "... *subsistit in Ecclesia Catholica* ...." This phrase, obviously, required further, more exact interpretation in an ecumenical context.

The second complex of statements on the unity of the Church is found in the explanations on the People of God. This people are called together from Jews and Gentiles so "that for each and all it may be the visible sacrament of this saving unity, that unity of humankind" (Article 9). How could an un-unified Church be a sacrament and sign of unity? Since the unity of humankind is not based on biological or racial connections, but on the Spirit of unity, on the re-birth from water and the Holy Spirit, the question arises about the relationship of this people to all the nations. According to Article 13 the People of God, who belong to the various nations of the world, foster the abilities, riches, and customs of the nations, in so far as these are good. The People of God are people among, not against, the nations of the world. The People of God must spread out among all the nations, in order to be their signs and instruments of universal unity; the People of God among all the nations must be able to experience special unity beyond national boundaries, something that the Council commented on with the wonderful quote from John Chrysostom: "He that dwells in Rome knows that the people of India are his members." For the first time the ecumenical problem sounds the note that the unity of the Church does not preclude a variety of gifts, ways of life, or local Churches; it is the task of the successor of Peter to protect the uniqueness of the local Churches and of the variety of gifts in general and to use these in the service of unity. This is the first time in the Dogmatic Constitution on the Church that the leadership function of the Roman Bishop, mentioned in Article 8, comes into the foreground. From this statement the Council then proceeded to the ecumenical question of the relationship of the Church to the Catholic and the non-Catholic faithful and to non-Christians – a second theme that needs to be subjected to a close look.

2. THE DECREE ON ECUMENISM

The Decree on Ecumenism became more concrete. After a recapitulation of the doctrine of the Dogmatic Constitution on the Church (Article 2), the Council enumerated a disastrously increasing series of ever new schisms in the Church in the course of her history: first the schisms in the Church of the New Testament (1 Corinthians, Galatians, 1 John), then the more extensive hostility of the last centuries. In Article 13 of the Decree a distinction is made between the separation of the Eastern and Western Churches and the separation in the West. In the look at these Church separations the Council then worked out differentiated instructions for the appreciation of these Churches and for ecumenical encounters with them – this is the third complex of statements that must be more closely interpreted.

The result of these instructions is a hard truth that is often either overlooked are remembered incorrectly. *The Second Vatican Council did not point out any concrete path to unity of the Church; it did not even open up more territory in which to look for a path.* This hard truth is mostly misunderstood. The central question is this: did the Council imagine the overcoming of the schism, which clearly did not correspond to God's plan of salvation, the meaning of the Church, or her task among the nations, as a "return" of the separated Christians to the Roman Catholic Church, under the leadership of the successor of Peter? Had the Council actually pointed out a way to the new unity of Christendom, then such an unrealistic "return ecumenism" would have to have been completely and utterly rejected. We quote here the hardest and "most disappointing" text of the Decree:

> Nevertheless, our separated sisters and brothers, whether considered as individuals or as communities and Churches, are not blessed with that unity which Jesus Christ wished to bestow on all those to whom he has given new birth into one body, and whom he has quickened to newness of life – that unity which the holy scriptures and the ancient Tradition of the church proclaim. For it is through Christ's Catholic church alone, which is the universal help toward salvation, that the fullness of the means of salvation can be obtained. It was to the apostolic college alone, of which Peter is the head, that we believe our Lord entrusted all the blessings of the New Covenant, in order to establish on earth the one Body of Christ into which all those should be fully incorporated who belong in any way to the people of God. During its pilgrimage on earth,

this people, though still in its members liable to sin, is growing in Christ and is guided by God's gentle wisdom, according to God's hidden designs, until it shall happily arrive at the fullness of eternal glory in the heavenly Jerusalem. (Article 3, section 5)

This text – it is in the introductory chapter of the Decree – makes clear:

a) because the unity of Church based on God's plan of salvation in Christ is a creedal question, it is obviously not subject to a diplomatic compromise;

b) because this creed refers to the "Church, which is led by the successor of Peter and the Bishops in communion with him" (Dogmatic Constitution on the Church, Article 8), one cannot avoid the conclusion that the goal must be to join all Christians to this Church, under the leadership of the successor of Peter;

c) separated Christians belong to the People of God, but this is qualified with the statement, "in any way";

d) the remark on the "sin" that the Church is "liable" to "in its members" (therefore: not in its structure), can only mean the discreet request that the non-Catholic Churches not let themselves be obstructed because of this from the clear decision of conscience;

e) at a later point the Decree states: "The manner and order in which catholic belief is expressed should in no way become an obstacle to dialogue with other Christians. It is, of course, essential that doctrine be clearly presented in its entirety. Nothing is so foreign to the spirit of ecumenism as a false irenicism which harms the purity of catholic doctrine and obscures its genuine and certain meaning." (Article 11) The problem of Church unity is the recognition of the full Catholic *doctrine*. Unity with the Church of Rome doesn't come cheap.

f) One did avoid speaking of a "return," not to mention a return to the *"Roman* Catholic" Church. At the very least that would have discriminated against the uniate Eastern Churches, which are not *Roman* Catholic.

One can certainly find soft spots in all these formulations. For example, one can ask whether the Church under the leadership of the successor of Peter has to mean exactly the same Roman Catholic Church that exists now. The reference to the purity and genuineness of the Catholic doctrine could contain boomerangs, as research of the last decades has proved. It would be better, however, not to pin our hopes

on this, given what we have said about compromise formulae at the
Second Vatican Council and what we have made manifest about the
problem area of ecumenism.

Even by the most favorable interpretation it remains obvious: all the
interpretive art in the world cannot do away with the hard truth that
it would be self-deception to imagine that the Church of Rome might
appropriate, in the area of Church unity, the model of the WCC, according to which the unity of the Church is recognized to be lost; the
Churches should now sit in a circle around their middle point, Christ,
in order to seek again the unity intended by the Lord. According to
the Catholic view prevalent among the leading theologians at the
Council, there is no lost unity, only a unity broken through schism
from the one *existing* Church. This Church, existing now and in the
past, is of course the Catholic Church, led by the successor of Peter
and the Bishops in communion with him. To say anything else was
not only tactically impossible, it was not to be expected. Historically
speaking, there is no existing Church older than the Roman Church;
she is attested in the most ancient times as "Communication Central,"
as the Church with which it was a duty to be in communion, in the
context of her role as a bulwark against the Gnostic sects. *Historically*
the Roman Western Church can consider herself as the part of the
original one universal Church that is "left over." When other Churches
separated themselves from her for reasons of faith, they did this with
the Reformation and Eastern Orthodox argument that the Roman
Church did not *remain* the one true Church. Luther argued in his
immensely polemical but extraordinarily clear work "Wider Hans
Worst" (1541; "Hans Wurst" was Duke Heinrich of Braunschweig-
Lüneburg) that the papal Church was actually a "new" Church, while
the Church reformed according to Luther's Reformation theology was
nothing other than the re-established ancient Church. The Eastern
Orthodox judgment on Luther and the Reformation is characteristic:
despite his admirable protests against the papacy Luther is still a child
of the western Church, entangled in the defection of this Church from
the common tradition of the first millennium.

In this situation the question arises: can the historical continuity of
the Catholic Church with its origins be joined with a model of unity
and re-unification that doesn't mean "return," but rather "integration"?
Concretely: in one Church, if not *under,* then *with* the successor of
Peter? This Church would have to first and foremost take seriously

the historical bases for the separation, with the lasting consequence for almost unconquerable resentments. With reference to these historical reasons for the separation this Church would have to relativize herself – otherwise any hope is not only for naught, it is also cynical. The question for the Council texts vis-à-vis the unity of the Church is this: what elements of self-relativization, in contrast to the quoted hard statements, did the Council formulate, and how are they to be evaluated in light of the rules of interpretation we sketched out earlier? Here we come to the individual problems.

3. "SUBSISTIT IN ECCLESIA CATHOLICA"

This famous formulation in Article 8 of the Dogmatic Constitution on the Church contains the most important theological self-relativization of the Church of Rome and allows us to evaluate the reality of the Decree on Ecumenism. First the full citation:

"This is the unique Church of Christ which in the Creed we profess to be one, holy, catholic and apostolic which our Saviour, after his resurrection, entrusted to Peter's pastoral care (Jn 21:17), commissioning him and the other apostles to extend and rule it (see Mt 28:18, etc.), and which he raised up for all ages as the pillar and mainstay of the truth (see 1 Tim 3:15). This church, constituted and organized as a society in the present world, subsists [*subsistit*] in the Catholic Church, which is governed by the successor of Peter and by the bishops in communion with him. Nevertheless, many elements of sanctification and of truth are found outside its visible confines. Since these are gifts belonging to the church of Christ, they are forces impelling towards catholic unity." (Article 8, section 2)

We have already discussed the context of the quoted text. The section is the one place where Chapter 1 breaks through the theological-salvation history show and says concretely what the whole thing refers to; immediately in the next section the language reverts to a merely theological argumentation – if not to an abstract one.

The quoted text follows this line of thought: The Church described up to this point – in Articles 1 through 8 (section 1)– is the creedal Church. Additions that are not in the Creed are introduced: to shepherd was the task of Peter, to extend and rule with authority the task of Peter and the other apostles. The choice of words is explained by means of the Bible citations; Matthew 16:18 is not cited here. Then the sentence follows that this Church subsists (*subsistit*) "in the Catholic Church, which is governed by the successor of Peter and by the bishops in communion with him [an anticipation of collegiality!]." The first thing said with this is that Peter and the apostles should have successors; the text presents this as obvious, but is nevertheless somewhat cursorily grounded with the argument that God erected the Church led by Peter and the apostles "for all ages as the pillar and mainstay of the truth" (1 Timothy 3:15). Everything would have argued for a simple continuation: this Church *is* the Catholic Church under the leadership of the successor of Peter and of the Bishops; no one would have wondered at this. Why was it not phrased this way? The next sentence gives a clue, with its mention of "many elements of sanctification and of truth" that "gifts belonging to the church of Christ, they are forces impelling towards catholic unity." The non-Catholic separated Churches should not be discredited by an exaggerated formula.

One observes that here the talk is not yet of non-Catholic Churches and ecclesiastical communities, but of free floating "elements." They are characterized by the yoked pair "of sanctification and of truth," targeting both areas of life and doctrine. One must not ascribe a great deal of importance to the lack of the formula ""churches and ecclesiastical communities." The Council Fathers first used this formula in the Dogmatic Constitution on the Church (Article 15). Was this reserve here, in the Decree on Ecumenism, the result of politeness? One must consider what is actually said with the famous word "*subsistit*" and with the recognition of ecclesial "elements" outside of the Church under the successor of Peter.

The theory of the "elements" annoys some people and provokes criticism, particularly from the Lutheran side. In the Catholic view, however, this theory has an undeniable advantage. These "elements" exist "outside of" the Roman Catholic Church; they have worth in that they are "gifts belonging to the church of Christ" – and now the talk is *not* of the Roman Church. These elements impel toward Catholic unity but, one must conclude if the whole sentence is not nonsensical: they do not lose their value, if they *de facto* are realized somewhere that is not the Church under the successor of Peter. The criticism that by means of the theory of the "elements" non-Catholic Christians would be subtly taken into the Roman Catholic Church does not hold true. In fact, the opposite is the case: a theory emerged, in connection with Pope Pius XII's 1943 encyclical *Mystici Corporis*, that non-Catholic Christians belonged not to the "body" but to the "soul" of the Church. According to the doctrine of the Dogmatic Constitution on the Church, however, true "Churchness" exists outside of the Roman Catholic Church, and this "Churchness" keeps the *question* of catholic unity alive, but does not receive its validation only with the achievement of this unity. If words have meaning, then this means a clear self-relativization of the Church. The unity of the Church exists in a tension between a limited, in terms of range, actualization in the papal Church and equally limited "not-yet-actualization," but an inherent tendency to this, in the non-Catholic Churches. In addition, in this context the question was asked in the post-conciliar theological discussions whether the *catholicity* of the Church, in opposition to the already cited "hard" statements of the Decree on Ecumenism, could be true Catholicism, as long as the "elements of sanctification and of truth" are actualized only outside of the Church of Christ that subsists in the Church of Rome.

At this point one may, indeed must, risk a consideration. In the section that precedes our text, the Council gave an indication of the "analogy" between Church and Incarnation. We do well to quote the entire text:

"The one mediator, Christ, established and constantly sustains here on earth his holy church, the community of faith, hope and charity, as a visible structure through which he communicates truth and grace to everyone. But, the society equipped with hierarchical structures and the mystical body of Christ, the visible society and the spiritual community, the early church and the church endowed with heavenly riches, are not to be thought of as two realities. On the contrary, they form one complex reality comprising a human and a divine element. For this reason the church is compared, in no mean analogy, to the mystery of the incarnate Word. As the assumed nature, inseparably united to him, serves the divine Word as a living instrument of salvation, so, in somewhat similar fashion, does the social structure of the church serve the Spirit of Christ who vivifies it, in the building up of the body (see Eph 4:16)."

The allusion to the formulations of the Christology of the ancient Church is unmistakable. According to this Christology, the divine Logos, the "Word" in the sense of John 1, "subsists" in the divine and in the assumed human nature. This means, to use precise Christological language: the *Logos* is *one in being* with God the Father; *Jesus* is unified with God the Logos and therefore is *one* with the Father. The formula:

"Jesus is God's son" is therefore correct, while the simplified formula: "Jesus is God" is dogmatically incorrect (even if Luther used it).

The same word *subsistit*, from the Christological language of the ancient Church, is now applied to the relationship between the "creedal Church" and the concrete "Church under the leadership of the successor of Peter in communion with the Bishops." Is therefore – and this question is asked in particular by Lutheran critics – the understanding of the Church as the continuing incarnation (of the Word), of the Church as Incarnation extended into history, of the Church as *Christus prolongatus* signed, sealed, and delivered? All Catholic interpreters reject this vehemently, although they are aware that this view had important crown witnesses, above all in the "Tübinger School" of the 19th century (Johann Adam Möhler). The rejection of the Lutheran critics is correct. As with any analogy, also here, obvious for Catholic theology, the greater dissimilarity is to be observed in the similarity. There is obviously no "hypostatic union" between Christ and the Church, as the Logos is united "hypostatically" with his assumed human nature, according to the understanding of the ancient Church. There is also no corresponding unity between the Holy Spirit and the Church. The analogy consists only in that the social structure of the Church serves the Spirit of Christ in a comparable way as the human nature in Christ serves the Logos, that is, as an organ of salvation (*instrumentum salutis*). This is also true, according to our text, for the relationship of the social structure of the Church in the *sense of a divine plan of salvation* to the Holy Spirit. Therefore it really works in its boundaries, in its "dissimilarity," only when this analogy is transposed in the continuation of the text to the relationship between the "Church of Jesus Christ" according to the divine plan of salvation and the actual Church under the successor of Peter. When that "subsists" in this, this means that the actual Church is one with the creedal Church in a way comparable to how the human nature of Christ is one with the Logos: she serves her as a concrete way of appearance.

It becomes clear that the translation "subsists in" is exaggerated. The creedal Church is not "realized" or "fulfilled," but the actual Church manifests the "Church of Jesus Christ" – the assembly of the faithful in the community of salvation, the "sacrament" of humans with God and with each other, the "messianic" people of God – in a historically limited framework. If this were not the meaning of the term *subsistit*, one could honestly have said: The actual Church *is* the Church of Christ.

Appearance in an historically limited form: the Church on the one hand participates in the scandal of the Christian faith, which is that an individual, temporally limited, and unimportant human life should manifest God with universal significance for salvation, bound forever to the man Jesus of Nazareth, never to be dissipated into a general theory about God and the world. The Church of Rome can claim that she is also a sign of contradiction in the world, like her Lord; she can also say, like him: "Blessed is anyone who takes no offense at me" (Matthew 11:6). This is true, however, only under one – often ignored – condition: that the Church here takes very seriously the "greater *dissimilarity*" of the analogy. Jesus Christ is the historically limited but *pure* illustration of God in human reality. The actual Church is not from the first so much the pure illustration of the Church as of the Body of Christ; she must constantly decide what her analogical-christological limitation is and what her human-sinful limitation is.

If the Church takes over the Christological analogy as a model of the relationship between the believed and the actual Church, and defines the relationship between the Church according to God's plan of salvation and the concrete Church with the Christological concept *subsistit in*, then she can avoid a blasphemous equalization with the humanity of Jesus only if she submits herself to the measure of the distinction between Christological and sinful limitation. Only under this condition can she demand that all the elements of sanctification and of truth impelling toward the Church must finally be integrated in her.

We asked about the elements of self-relativization, which make a simple and utopian "return ecumenism" irrelevant. The interpretation given here of the famous formula *subsistit in ecclesia catholica* means a self-relativization that exceeds the most generous pragmatic self-relativizations. Our interpretation is strengthened by the fact that other statements about the unity of the Church and the re-establishment of this unity agree with it.

4. LEGITIMATE DIFFERENCES

One of these statements is the double reference to the Church's taking root in the different cultures of the nations as well as to the legitimate differences of the local Churches (Dogmatic Constitution on the Church, Article 13). This is important for the understanding of unity insofar as up to the present precisely these legitimate differences are time and time again slighted by the practical execution of the Petrine office and its organs: by premature action by Rome when the local Church could have solved the problem herself; by the system of the papal nunciature, which often functions in a watchdog capacity; by denying a diocese any say in the choice of a Bishop; by the restrictive application of the Constitution on the Sacred Liturgy. Under these conditions it becomes hard to take the much cited phrase "unity in diversity" very seriously. Even if the steps that do not agree with either the spirit or the letter of the Council happen for well considered reasons and with a good conscience, the non-Catholic Churches will form from these steps their idea of what they might expect as local Churches, should they enter into a new unity with the Church of Rome. In Article 13 we read the remark that concrete unity manifests itself in an exchange of spiritual as well as material goods. How seriously is this remark taken, since nothing stands in the way of its actualization? Article 13 of the Dogmatic Constitution on the Church is and remains a marker and a measure of ecumenically oriented criticism.

5. "HIERARCHY OF TRUTHS"

One other statement in the direction of self-relativization was added at the last minute to the Decree on Ecumenism, hardly discussed further, and then subjected to a flood of interpretive literature: in the ecumenical dialogue there is a "hierarchy of truths" (*hierarchia veritatum*) that needs to be attended to (Article 11). One thing is certain: "hierarchy" means a holy ranking. Among the "truths" that the faith formulates and confesses in the form of individual sentences, there is then a ranking of holiness, a "holy," and therefore untouchable, ranking in terms of significance, of importance for the faithful, of significance for the Christian life. If this ranking needs to be attended to in the ecumenical dialogue then this can only mean that *each* of these truths cannot be of *equal* significance for the unity of the Church. In plain text: not all these truths can, in the same way, be made into conditions for Church unity.

Now one can open the debate about what are the more important truths and what are the less important truths in this "hierarchy." The result is not so important at this point; what is important is the opening provided for a search for unity that concentrates on a common creed and seeks, from this middle ground, to weigh the subordinated doctrinal differences. This is the direction that was followed after the Council.

6. "FULLY INCORPORATED" AND "UNITED"

Articles 14-16 of the Dogmatic Constitution on the Church offer a test case of the relationship of the Catholic understanding of unity and non-Catholic Christians. The Council avoided the common expression of "Church member" or "Church membership" as a designation for people belonging to the Church. Instead of this, the Council used words like "incorporated," "united," etc. Behind this is a controversy among Catholic canon lawyers and theologians, carried out before and after the appearance of the encyclical *Mystici Corporis*. The two definitions of the concept of "Church membership" that were in conflict with one another were the following:

a) Church membership is grounded in baptism. Through baptism we receive a permanent, constitutive Church membership in the (Roman) Catholic Church. "Active" Church membership is distinguished from this; active membership is attained by those who exercise their rights and duties in the Church (the sacraments, for example) and who are not hindered in this active Church membership by some sort of block (for example, growing up in a non-Catholic Church) or by some sort of ecclesial punishment or self-exile (schism, heresy, loss of faith). This thesis leans on the formulation of canon 87 in the 1917 Code of Canon Law (*Codex Iuris Canonici*), which claims that someone becomes a person in the Church of Christ through baptism. One sees that this thesis wants to make allowances for the fundamental fact of baptism, but remains otherwise completely in the visible dimension of the Church – a distant echo of the earlier mentioned definition of Church given by Cardinal Bellarmine. The advantage of this thesis is that Church membership is unequivocal and (legally) comprehensible. This thesis was represented predominantly by canon lawyers; a strong proponent was the Munich canon lawyer Klaus Mörsdorf.

b) The opposing thesis was: there is a multi-stepped Church membership, since there are numerous ways in which persons can

enter into a relationship with the Church and stay in that relationship, positive ways as well as negative. One could, for example, be baptized but live as a sinner; one could be excluded from
the Eucharist but not be excommunicated; one could be baptized
in a non-Catholic Church, therefore live in only an "objective"
relationship, based in baptism, to membership in the Roman
Catholic Church, but in a subjectively innocent way consider his
or her own Church, not the Roman Catholic Church, to be the
one true Church of Christ. Now, one might fix terminologically
one of these steps of connection to the Church as "Church membership" – this doesn't change anything in terms of the facts of
the multi-stepped character of Church membership. Moreover, it
is theologically indicated that such a determination should not
be undertaken *only* on legally controllable factors. In any case
the baptized is a Church member in the full sense, living in the
Roman Catholic Church because of the justifying grace of God.

This thesis is backed predominately by dogmatic theologians; a
strong proponent was the dogmatic theologian Karl Rahner. The
disadvantage of this thesis is that Church membership is then no
longer absolutely ascertainable, since judging whether a life is lived
in justifying grace is impossible from the outside. Nonetheless,
this thesis has a theological and ecumenical huge advantage: it
avoids the unbearable consequence that it is completely irrelevant
for Church membership whether someone lives in the reality for
which the Church exists: in the love and grace of God. Of course
one must now distinguish among members of the Church who, as
the Council said, belong to the Church with their bodies but not
with their hearts (Articles 8 and 14). In plain text: there can be
sinners who exercise their rights in the Church. There can also be
justified Christians, who live in peace with God, who have been
excommunicated by the Church.

With the description of both of these theses about Church membership it is clear in what direction the Council moved. Without using the expression "Church membership" in its technical sense, the
Council argued along the dogmatic lines of Karl Rahner. As a result
the "ecclesiastical elements" could be listed in a completely positive
appreciation, for the non-Catholic Christians in Article 15 and the
non-Christians in Article 16 of the Dogmatic Constitution on the

Church. The Church did not lay claim to the non-Catholic Christians and the non-Christians, but she acknowledged that these have received and do receive the same gifts that the Church has and does receive. The Church does not recognize secret "members of the Church" in the non-Catholics, but gifts that she has also been given. As the Decree on Ecumenism remarks, these gifts are sometimes brought to light more by the non-Catholics than by the Catholics (compare here Articles 4, 17, 21, 23).

7. ECUMENISM OF CONVERSION

Out of the hard and inflexible statements about the conditions for Church unity and the self-relativizations commented on above, the Decree on Ecumenism draws consequences for practical ecumenical action of the Roman Catholic Church.

First this: the originally planned title of the first chapter was: "Principles of Catholic Ecumenism." This was changed to: "Catholic Principles on Ecumenism." The reason for this was that "Catholic ecumenism" does not exist, there is only ecumenism in which the Catholic Church joins, according to her principles and her self-understanding. This does not stop Protestant critics even today from speaking of a "Catholic (Roman) ecumenism" – and, unfortunately, some ecclesial office holders have thoughtlessly spoken in a similar manner. One can only answer: if there is a Catholic ecumenism, then there must be a Protestant ecumenism, because obviously each Church participates in the Ecumenical Movement according to her own principles. The most important point of the formulations of the Decree on Ecumenism is that the Roman Catholic Church consciously entered into the *existing* ecumenical movement, a movement that originated outside of the Catholic Church. The Church under the leadership of the successor of Peter and of the Bishops in communion with that successor, which serves the one and only Church of Jesus Christ as concrete existing form, undertook efforts at unity under conditions that she did not dictate. The Church committed herself, at the same time maintaining the principle of integration, to a logically "no exit" situation. Internally as well as externally one had shown to her what would remain of "dialogue," if one's own standpoint were not placed in question. The answer of the Decree on Ecumenism is *conversion*. The constantly repeated instructions of the Decree can be summed up in the following words: conversion, devotion to one's own call, reform. Other words are repeated, as well. In reference to *conversion*: self-deception, recognition of one's own sins, in particular sins against unity, consciousness of the many commonalities with other Churches, commonalities that the Decree lists with meticulousness, study in benevolent attitude. In reference to *devotion*: pure life according to the Gospel, patient service, brotherly good-heartedness, love of truth, and humility. In reference to *reform*: everything that is of human institution in the Church (and that is a great deal, even according to traditional Catholic understanding) is subject to constant reform. Even the proclamation of doctrine, which must be "carefully distinguished from the deposit of faith itself" (Article 6), must be reformed, if it creates language barriers between the Roman Catholic Church and the separated Churches (Article 11).

The concrete instructions were derived from these basic claims, for example, the duty to be knowledgeable (hence the importance laid upon educating priests in ecumenical theology), the encouragement of inter-confessional encounters and discussions, common labor, above all in the social and educational areas, etc. This is "the road to the unity of Christians" (Article 12).

Lukas Vischer, the former General Secretary of the Faith and Order Commission of the WCC, gave a talk in 1974, on the occasion of the celebration of the ten year anniversary of the proclamation of the Decree on Ecumenism. In this talk, Vischer voiced the criticism that the Decree did not move a step forward in terms of dogmatic theology, but remained at the level of large-scale directions for practical cooperative work; cooperative work that was by no means exhausted by the possibilities listed in the text. I repeated this criticism for a long time; today I have a different opinion.

The logically "no exit" situation, the insistence on the "incorporation" of all Christians and a belief in paths to unity, contains the whole point of the Council teaching on the unity of the Church. It confirms what we said at the beginning: the Council knew no possible way to Church unity for the Catholic Christian. That is a great disappointment for all who do not project their own ecumenical wishes on the Council, but who allow the Council to say what it actually said. But the Council does ask that ecumenical work be undertaken with a contrite spirit, conscious of the difference between the truth of faith and formulation of doctrine, with an awareness of the need for education in ecumenical theology; this ecumenical work should be undertaken not only with regard to the possibilities of practical and pragmatic cooperative work. That is the Council's great admonition to everyone's conscience: not to leave everything as it is now. If both the uncertainty about the way to unity and the admonition to dialogue are to remain, that can only mean: the Council trusts that ways to unity will evince themselves in this dialogue, under the guidance of the Holy Spirit, ways that now we might at best just be able to glimpse. The very devotion to the doctrine of the Church is entrusted, even delivered over, to the work of the Spirit in this dialogue.

III. THE FUTURE OF ECUMENISM?

1. UNITY IS NOT "FEASIBLE"

Our thesis at the beginning of the interpretation of the Decree on Ecumenism has been, unfortunately, confirmed: the Council shows us no immediate and easy way to a new unity of the many confessional Churches of Christendom. It could not be predicted, in 1964, on the basis of the Council texts, what the future of ecumenism might be. With the exception of one point: the Council encouraged all Christians and in particular theologians to commit themselves wholeheartedly to the ecumenical dialogue. So for a number of years theologians competent in ecumenical questions worked in the limelight – they were asked to be on official or semi-official dialogue commissions, they produced one "consensus paper" after another. At the same time the anxieties about contact on the level of the congregations melted away, and ecumenical cooperative work progressed even to attempts to create ecumenical congregational centers, something that Christians in all Churches could not have dreamt of just a decade earlier. The Council also indirectly inspired the ecumenical strivings within the WCC, particularly in the "Faith and Order" Commission, whose General Secretary, Lukas Vischer, had been an observer at the Council. One could, just for the years after the Council up to today, write a thick book with the title *History of the Ecumenical Movement*, just as there are books on the history of the ecumenical movement up to the time of the Council. We cannot go into this history here, although we shall return to some of its details in the last chapter of this book.

This history, though, did not become a triumphal march of progress. Along with the ecumenical progress that cannot be rolled back, along with the great, impressive gestures of goodwill, we find the setbacks, the official measures – not only from the side of the Roman Catholic Church – that cause one to ask whether their blocking effect is the result of careless thoughtlessness or of purposeful intent. Ecumenical theologians work today again in the shadows of ecclesial interest and with the mistrust of many Christians who seem to prefer confessional unambiguity to ecumenical openness.

In 1964, when the Decree on Ecumenism was promulgated, neither of these directions – limelight or shadow – could have been predicted. In order to be able to appreciate the widened perspectives, we return once again to the already mentioned "model of unity" of the WCC. If one looks closely, the position of the Council is not so very distant from that of this WCC model. Both, the Council and the WCC, had no real advice about how the ecumenical dialogue should move forward. Both trust in the leadership of Christ's spirit. Both demand neither from themselves nor from each other the surrender of convictions or ways of life, so long as these have not been proven to be theologically irresponsible.

There is one difference between the ecumenism of the WCC and the so-called "Catholic ecumenism," and this difference shows the weaknesses of the Geneva concept and the strengths of the Roman. For the WCC, the unity formula – the circle of Churches around Christ as the middle point, in search of unity – is a formula that defines what cannot occur. The WCC is not at all interested in being a sort of "super Church"; the organization would break apart at even the faintest suggestion that this would be its self-understanding. The WCC consciously bracketed out – at that time – the problem of the one Church, pragmatically, in order to calm all conceivable fears. Only after the time of the Council – perhaps incited by the Council? – the WCC made the visible unity of the Church into a theme for theological study. The Council on the other hand was willing to undergo a real test and did not bracket out, but demanded, that this paradoxical challenge be met and overcome. I do not see how one could have more honestly served this "unfeasible," yet hoped for, yearned for, unity. Especially then when one considers yet another paradox, a paradox that the Council very consciously had included in the texts as an open question.

2. CHURCH AND ECCLESIASTICAL COMMUNITIES

From the Catholic side, how should one name the non-Catholic Christians in their own Churches and communities? The traditional answer to this question was clear: in the language of canon law from 1917 they were "non-Catholic sects" (*sectae acatholicae*). In the rule not even this term was used, just simply "non-Catholics" (*a-catholici*). The 1943 encyclical *Mystici Corporis* defined the Church by means of her juridical, visible structure; only those who were baptized Catholic and who participated in a visible Church life could be counted as true members. Non-Catholics were not thought of as members of Churches and communities, but only as erring individuals, for whom one should pray. They should be urgently invited to (again) join themselves to the visible body of the Catholic Church; otherwise they could not be certain of salvation. Truth dictates that it be noted that the author of this encyclical, Pope Pius XII, had progressed beyond this view after the Second World War, and a highpoint of his cautious *rapprochement* with the Ecumenical Movement was his 1956 meeting in the Vatican with the Lutheran Bishop Otto Dibelius from Berlin – the photo went around the world. All this did not, of course, touch the principle; this was obvious in the face of the non-Catholic observer platform in the Council Hall.

The decision came about once again by means of a heading, that of the third section of the Decree on Ecumenism. Originally it should have been, completely in the spirit of the traditional language, "The non-Catholic Christians." The discussion focused on the reminder that the context of the section did not deal with Christians as individuals, but with the relationship of the Catholic Church to the various *communities* of non-Catholics. The representatives of the uniate Churches had already made it clear in the debates surrounding the Dogmatic Constitution on the Church that they lacked nothing that the Latin Church considered essential for the visible-invisible reality of the Church; they are Catholic, but in their Catholic reality nonetheless completely independent of the tradition of the Latin Church. Could one dare, in the face of the representatives, for example, of the Patriarchate of Moscow and Constantinople, to defend the thesis that the non-uniate orthodox Churches are *not* Churches solely on the basis of the non-recognition of the western understanding of papal primacy? It was not difficult – one needs to re-read the first section of the third chapter of the Decree on Ecumenism (Articles 14-18) – to speak of the Churches of the East, uniate or not, as "Churches." It was more difficult with those Churches that arose from the splits in the West – predominantly the Churches of the Reformation, but not only those.

A side comment at this point: because of the difficult historical situation, the effort was not made to distinguish non-Catholic Churches from one another. Not all Eastern Orthodox Churches separated from Rome and other Churches first in the year 1054; a few had already separated in the context of some of the councils of the ancient Church. Not all western non-Catholic Churches separated from Rome because of the Reformation – the Italian Waldensian Church separated in the Late Middle Ages, the Bohemian Hussite Church in the 15th century, the Old Catholic Church in the 19th century. Some other Churches separated not from Rome but from the larger Churches of the Reformation. In order to keep out of all these complicated problems, not only were the non-Catholic Churches not individually described, but their historical origins were not named. This explains the very general heading: "Churches and Ecclesial Communities separated from the Roman Apostolic See."

Why, though, this double title, "Churches and Ecclesial Communities"? Behind this title lurks the fact that it is not only the Church of Rome that has problems designating churches that have emerged in modern times as "Church," but these communities themselves reject the title and self-understanding of "Church," although they are members of the World Council of *Churches*.

Could one admit any "ecclesial" title for the Churches that emerged out of the splits in the West? One soon went beyond the limits of *Mystici Corporis*. In the place of "real membership" – clear in terms of canon law, but theologically much too unclear – the formula emerged according to which the non-Catholic Christians, particularly those from the splits of the Western Church, were spoken of as "not fully incorporated" into the Catholic Church. That corresponded to an impulse from the theologians to speak of a "graded" membership in the Church. Furthermore, the conviction of "elements of holiness and of truth" in the non-Catholic Churches and ecclesial communities was the consensus in the Council Hall. In general the mood prevailed to praise and acknowledge the Christian convictions and Christian practice in the non-Catholic communities, as far as that went. The consequence: not, as generally thought, *despite* their membership in the non-Catholic Churches and ecclesial communities, but *in them* the non-Catholic Christians find salvation (Dogmatic Constitution on the Church, Article 14; Decree on Ecumenism, Articles 20-23). There is no more talk about uncertainty about salvation because of deficient means of salvation.

What then do they lack, in order to be a Church? If one examines the texts that describe the "full" incorporation in the "Catholic Church under the successor of Peter," then the "fullness" consists always in the completeness of the *institutional* means by which the Church is *also* "sacrament" of the unity with God and one another. But what does it mean when, for example, only a very few people are reached by these institutional means of salvation and led to unity with God and with one another, while non-Catholic communities are led in great numbers to a living faith in God and his presence in Jesus Christ, to community in the Holy Spirit, although some of the institutional means "fully" present in the Catholic Church are lacking? Can one with great candor extol the advantages and the significance of salvation in the ecclesial life in the Churches and communities separated from Rome, and then decide on the basis of *institutional* "means" whether a Church exists or not?

The name of the Italian Bishop Andrea Pangrazio deserves eternal remembrance in the history of the Council, because he spoke to the conscience of the Council with these words:

> It is a good idea, to sum up the elements of Church that, through God's grace, have been preserved in these communities and produce saving effects. However, if I might be allowed a modest personal comment: such a catalogue seems to be a little too "quantitative," if I may use this expression. It appears to me that these elements have simply been jumbled together. I believe that a bond is needed to unify these diverse elements; we need to accentuate the center toward which all these elements are oriented and without which they do not make any sense. This bond and center is Christ himself, who is acknowledged by all Christians as Lord of the Church, whom all Christians of all communities will serve without hesitation, and who accomplishes miraculous events in separated communities through the presence of the Holy Spirit – not through human efforts but through the power of God's eternal mercy.

In a sentence: one can only deny the status of "Church" to the
Churches of the Reformation and the other western Churches that
emerged from Church schisms in the West, if one adheres, against
everything that is in the Dogmatic Constitution on the Church, to
a purely juridical concept of Church. The overwhelming majority of
the Church Fathers did not want this. A solution was provided by the
wise counsel of Cardinal König of Vienna. He suggested that the separated Churches of the West be spoken of as "Churches and ecclesial
communities." On the one hand, with this phrase none of the communities involved with the WCC would be excluded. On the other
hand, those communities that understood themselves as "Churches"
would find that in the language of the Council. In the opening speech
of the third session of the Council, Pope Paul VI addressed the representatives of the separated Churches with the cry: *O Ecclesiae* ("O
Churches"). Was this only politeness?

The Council very consciously left the theological question completely open, which of the separated Churches of the West actually
could claim the name "Church." This was a question that became more
and more important as soon as Rome no longer thought in terms of a
"return ecumenism," but could greet the separated Churches and ecclesial communities as "local Churches" in the future one Church, in
the sense of Article 23 of the Dogmatic Constitution on the Church.
The conservative forces did not leave any stone unturned in their attempts to prevent any ecumenical capital to be gained from the heading of the third part of the Decree on Ecumenism. But in principle
no one can escape the fact: "elements" (Dogmatic Constitution on the
Church) became *Church*.

CHAPTER SEVEN

"FREE US FROM THESE BUTTONS & SASHES, WHICH NO ONE WANTS!"

MINISTRY AND HIERARCHY ACCORDING TO THE TEXTS OF THE COUNCIL

The title of this chapter repeats the cry of a Bishop during the debates on the Decree on the Bishops' Pastoral Office in the Church. The "buttons and sashes" of the bishop's vestments go back to the insignia and robes of office of the Imperial officials of the Byzantine Empire. Photographs of Bishops from Latin America in the years of the disputes surrounding "Liberation Theology" show that these Bishops – with the exception of during the liturgy – usually went around dressed in the usual clothes of the poor and exploited workers, without buttons and sashes. Awhile ago, a priest with whom I was acquainted was named to the office of "papal house chaplain." Attached to the document that named this priest to this office was a list of the pieces of clothing that had been connected to this office that are now no longer used; the list also contained a list of clothing items that could or should be worn at particular events, for example, during liturgies celebrated by the Bishop in the Cathedral – a clear sign that, for some people in the Church, "buttons and sashes" are still important.

Here, however, our interest is not focused on clothing; we are interested in the understanding of the office that gave rise to this focus on "buttons and sashes," and on the new orientation of this understanding because of the Council. We are not able to go into great detail in this chapter, since it is immediately relevant to only a few (male) Christians in the Church. Indirectly, however, the whole Church experiences whether the conciliar statements about the ecclesial office are carried out in the life of the Church or if their achievement is hindered.

I. PREHISTORY

1. FROM A SUCCESSOR OF THE APOSTLES TO A MEMBER OF THE COLLEGE OF BISHOPS

As is known, the Council worked on the Dogmatic Constitution on the Church and on the Decree on the Pastoral Office of Bishops in the Church (what we will call, for the sake of brevity, the Decree on the Bishops) at the same time, although the Decree on the Bishops was solemnly promulgated in the fourth session, on the 28th of October, 1965. The Decree on the Bishops recapitulates relevant statements of the Dogmatic Constitution on the Church; it often contains word-for-word quotations from that document. The Decree on the Bishops also follows the theological guideposts set up by the Dogmatic Constitution on the Church. To remind ourselves of the decisive setting of the course: this course change succeeded through the placement of the chapter on "The People of God" before the remarks on the hierarchy.

In the debates surrounding the Dogmatic Constitution on the Church and also, of course, in the discussions on the Decree on the Bishops the neuralgic point was the question of the "collegiality" of the Bishops, collegiality with one another and with the successor of Peter. What does it mean, not just in theological theory but also in practice, when the "Supreme Bishop of the Catholic Church" (First Vatican Council) must consider all the Bishops in the world – around 3000 at the time of the Council – his "colleagues in office"? What does it mean when the individual Bishop does not operate as a lone warrior, with all the authority and responsibility, but has and executes his office as a member of a "college," or, as the expression is in the Council texts, a member of a "body" (*corpus*)? Traditionally, and confirmed by the Pope at the First Vatican Council: the Bishops exercise their office by "divine right," as unmediated holders of jurisdiction, not as officials of the Pope. The Bishop is "sole lawgiver in his diocese" (*unicus legislator in sua Dioecesi*), that is, his order alone gives legal strength to ecclesial instructions in the realm of his diocese and binds the faithful to ecclesial obedience. Even today this is legally the case with only slight restrictions, in spite of the growing significance of the Bishops' Conferences, of which we will speak later. It pertained – and still pertains – also in the relationship of the Bishop to any diocesan synod he calls. While the Ecumenical Council, together with the Pope, exercises the highest leadership and teaching authority in the Church, a diocesan synod is a purely advisory organ, and the Bishop – in the last few decades there have been a few object lessons – is completely free to grant or deny authority to the synod's decisions. Bishops' Conferences, which had existed in various countries for quite a while (see Article 37 of the Decree on Bishops), were consequently not decision-making bodies, but only informal advisory boards; they had only *de facto* influence, and that only through their respective presidents or chairmen.

This was and is not in debate. In debate was the question: does a Bishop become the holder of his office formally through naming executed by the Pope, that is, confirmation with subsequent consecration by two or more Bishops, or does he become Bishop through his acceptance, through the episcopal consecration, into the "Body of Bishops"? In the first instance, the episcopal consecration is an isolated event for the individual Bishop; the consecrating Bishops merely execute the Pope's elevation of the Bishop into his office. The Popes of the modern period, whenever they had the opportunity, have performed the episcopal consecrations, particularly those of Bishops of dioceses outside of Europe. This description of the elevation to the Bishop's office corresponds to a long unquestioned thesis, extending back into medieval theology, which maintains that the nature of the sacrament of ordination consists in the communication of the authority to celebrate the Eucharist and, in particular, to execute the consecration of the Eucharistic gifts. The priesthood in the Church was defined in relationship to Eucharist. The consequence of this was: since the episcopal consecration did not heighten the authority of a priest to celebrate the Eucharist, then the difference between the simple priest and the Bishop consisted only in the authority of leadership bound up with the office of Bishop, the "jurisdiction." One should not, of course, have so maltreated Luther when he, in his time, disagreed that any difference between a Bishop and a simple pastor existed, when it came to the spiritual tasks of the ecclesial office; this was at a time when it could easily happen that a Bishop was satisfied with jurisdiction without consecration. It is certainly understandable that consequently

the illegal consecration of a Bishop, without naming, that is confirmation, by the Pope, was considered one of the worst crimes in the
Church, punished by the harshest ecclesial penalties. Until today the
Church, as was seen in the case of the deceased Archbishop Marcel
Lefebvre and his supporters, considers the unapproved consecration
of a Bishop to be evidence of schism, of Church division and of the
founding of a rival Church.

Faced with the rostrum filled with the non-Catholic observers,
among whom the representatives of the Eastern Churches not in
union with Rome also sat, the traditional thesis could not remain
unquestioned. Should, for example – a utopian daydream – in a
new ecclesial community with the Orthodox Eastern Churches, the
Bishops of these Churches retroactively be named by the Pope, in an
all-inclusive legal act? Even though Rome had always considered the
consecration of the Bishops in the Eastern Churches to be valid? No,
it can only work this way: the naming of Bishops, that is, the confirmation of the election of Bishops in the Catholic Church is executed
by the Pope not as Pope, as the Bishop of the Universal Church, but
as "Patriarch of the Church of the Latin West," just as the Patriarchs
in the Eastern Churches undertake in a similar manner the naming
of Bishops in their Patriarchates. It is therefore a question of jurisdiction, of the assignment of an area in which to carry out the office. The
office itself, the office of Bishop, is transmitted through the consecration, and its "validity" cannot depend on previous procedures of jurisdiction. Another thesis developed, broadly disseminated for the first
time at the Council, that the consecration of the Bishop means the
acceptance into the "College of Bishops"; it is from this membership
that all spiritual authority flows to the consecrated. This thesis had
as background the insolvable historical problem, comparable to that
which had led to the thesis of "Church as fundamental sacrament."
Historical knowledge no longer permitted the fiction that each Bishop
descended, in the authority of his office, from an unbroken chain of
laying on of hands ("the succession of the Apostles," *successio apostolica*), from *one particular* apostle. We do not know what happened to
the majority of the Twelve after the first persecution of the Christians,
in Jerusalem (Acts 8:1; 12: 17). The reports about their deaths are
for the most part legendary – with the exception of James the Elder
(Acts 12:2); even the deaths of Peter and Paul are not quite so clear,
anymore. If the validity of the concrete office of Bishop depends on

the unbroken chain of laying on of hands, going back to a member of the original circle of Apostles, then the Bishops could only be very unsure whether they actually were "validly" consecrated, and the faithful could not be certain if they had a legitimate Bishop or not. If one bases the legitimacy of the episcopal office on membership in the College of Bishops, which *as a whole* succeeds the College of Twelve, the original College of Apostles, it then does not depend on the genealogy of the individual episcopal consecration, but on membership in the "corporate body," so, finally, on the *communio* among the old regions of the Church. Whoever in a modern region of the Church belongs to the corporate body of Bishops is a Bishop, no matter how the ancestral tree of his predecessors looks. This then results in a new consideration of "Apostolic succession," one that avoids the historical difficulties of the old thesis and creates a new basis for dialogue with non-Catholic Churches.

Nonetheless, the new idea of the acceptance into the College of Bishops as the kernel of that which happens in the episcopal consecration was a recent thesis. The "conservatives" at the Council feared, not without reason, a creeping weakening of the power of the Pope, in two respects. The first: the strong emphasis on the self-reliance of the Bishop as member of the "College" would weaken – at least theoretically, since in a practical sense, as following events showed, one did not have to worry about this – the Pope's unmediated authority of jurisdiction.

Again a joke from seminary days underscores the new position: If (at that time almost unimaginable, but now this has already taken place) the Pope celebrated the Eucharist in the Cologne Cathedral, could he then sit on the throne of the Cologne Archbishop and supplant him? The answer: No, because the Archbishop is, according to old tradition, the "bridegroom of his diocese"; should the Pope sit on his Bishop's seat, this would be the same as spiritual adultery! The second way the Pope's authority could be undermined: it was, as already shown, clear in terms of canon law, that the Ecumenical *Council*, with the Pope at the head, exercised the highest authority in the Church. The idea of collegiality implied, however, that the College of Bishops as such, even outside of the Council, together with the Pope is the holder of authority in the Church. That would be a weakening of the universal authority, the primacy, of the Roman Bishop.

2. CLEAR-SIGHTED DEBATES

So suggestions for changes rained down on this position, even at the advisory stage of the submission for the Dogmatic Constitution on the Church – at first to the benefit of the collegiality of Bishops, when we are talking about the first draft, later against collegiality, as this stood in the second draft. It was the classic case where one, in order to get through the masses of *Modi*, employed the method of the *Quaesitum* provided for by the rules of procedure. The chairman put five questions to the vote; if approved, these would be worked into the draft, so that later the content would not be discussed again, only the wording. Because of the importance of the content and also to elucidate the process, these five questions are presented here:

"The Fathers are asked to say whether they wish the draft to be drawn up in such a way that it declares:

1. That episcopal consecration forms the highest degree of the sacrament of orders;

2. That every bishop legitimately consecrated, in union with the bishops and the Pope, who is the head and principle of their unity, is a member of the whole body of bishops;

3. That the body (*corpus*) or college of bishops succeeds to the college of the apostles in the charge of preaching the gospel, in sanctifying and in governing, and that this body, in union with its head, the Pope of Rome, and never without this head (whose primacy over all pastors and faithful remains whole and intact) possesses full and supreme authority in the universal Church;

4. That this authority belongs to the college of bishops itself in union with its head by divine law (*jure divino*);

5. That the draft should deal with the opportuneness of restoring the diaconate as a special and stable degree of the sacred ministry (*officium*), as demanded by the needs of the Church in various lands.

In answering these questions, the Fathers are not asked to accept or reject any particular formulation. It is merely a matter of letting the

Theological Commission know the opinions of the assembly on this question. According to the procedure of the Council, it will be the task of the Commission to examine the various answers of the Fathers and put the amended text before the general assembly for its approval." [Herbert Vorgrimler, ed., *Commentary on the Documents of Vatican II, Volume I* (NY, NY: Herder and Herder, 1967) 115-116]

The result of the vote was announced in the 58th General Congregation, on October 30, 1963. All five questions were approved by a clear majority vote; the highest number of "no" votes were cast (33%) for the question about the restoration of the diaconate. The result of the answers to these five questions was the breakthrough. In all cases, even if a bit tight on the diaconate question, a two-thirds majority was secured. That it really was a breakthrough was shown by the fact that the next day many conservative speakers sought to portray the vote as nonbinding. But it was clear: no text of the Council was capable of attaining a majority if it did not respect this vote. A compromise was reached in the question of the diaconate – we shall return to this, later. In the question of the collegiality the majority had to swallow the *Nota praevia*, of which we have already spoken and to which we shall also return.

These comments on the prehistory have to suffice, in order now to understand what will be said about the third chapter of the Church Constitution and the decrees that pertain to ecclesial offices.

II. THE "HIERARCHICAL CONSTITUTION" OF THE CHURCH

1. "HIERARCHY"

The concept "hierarchy" is not only one of the most misunderstood theological ideas – not just in its historical origins but also in its theological content – it is also in the present day for the most part negatively loaded, above all in those areas of the world in which the Catholic Church is on the defensive vis-à-vis the Churches that came out of the Reformation. How negative this word now sounds in modern ears is indicated by the fact that it has become an insult in daily speech, even in non-theological circles. One speaks of the "hierarchy" in the hospital, in the editorial room of a newspaper, in T.V. stations, in political parties, etc. What is meant is always an impersonal, top-down authority that demands unconditional obedience, at the risk of professional disadvantage.

Everything that up to this point we have said about the events of the Council as well as about the theological content of ecclesial authority has without a doubt made it clear that there is no place where "hierarchy" functions worse than in the Catholic Church; the word "hierarchy" takes on such a negative connotation that it is used for non-ecclesial structures. Lexical corrections that point out that "hierarchy," from the Greek, does not mean "holy rule" but "holy beginning" do not help very much. We now take a look at the statements made with reference to this (still) unavoidable word, in order to figure out what these hold for the future of the Church.

2. "HIERARCHICAL" CONSTITUTION OF THE CHURCH

Everything decisive for this point is explained in the third chapter of the Constitution on the Church. If one takes the explanations in the chapter at their word, all persons in the Church belong to the "hierarchy" who have received one of the steps of the sacraments of ordination – otherwise expressed: those persons who have been called to an office that counts in the traditional sense as "divine right" – this means an office attested in Scripture, either through Jesus' instruction or through a direction of the Apostles and early Church community leaders. The hierarchy then consists of the Bishops, priests, and deacons, and this is the order in which these offices are discussed in the third chapter of the Church Constitution.

At this point an important clarification is necessary, something actually quite obvious, but which always is the cause for astonishment, above all from non-Catholic Christians. Within the gradations of the sacrament of ordination, the Pope does not take precedence before a Bishop of a small diocese in a mission area. The Pope is first and foremost Bishop of Rome, and beginning with John XXIII the Popes have, since the Council, taken this task much more seriously than in earlier times. For this reason there is not anything like "papal ordination." Theoretically, at most he must be consecrated a Bishop, if he was previously only a simple priest – although this has not occurred for a very long time. The Pope is "enthroned" or more technically expressed, installed in office. Earlier, in the time of Church as "empire," and long afterward, the Pope was "crowned" with the "tiara," the triple crown that would prove its bearer to be the highest priest, highest king, and highest leader of the world – John XXIII wore it, but his successor Paul VI exchanged it for a more modest model, which he also eventually gave up. Since this time, crowning does not occur at the installation of the Pope, which after all always had extra-liturgical character.

Under the point of view of the "hierarchy of ordination," therefore, there is no difference between the Pope and the Bishops. That the Church has a "hierarchical constitution" basically signifies not less, but also not more, than that the Church is led by the Bishops. The episcopal office includes all powers within the territory entrusted to them of the ecclesial office that – according to Catholic interpretation – was grounded in the salvific action of Jesus, given to the life of the Church from the very beginning; this office brings the threefold office of Jesus Christ himself – the priestly, prophetic, and kingly office (see the Dogmatic Constitution on the Church, Articles 10-13) – into being in history. In opposition to this understanding of the hierarchical constitution of the Church would be an interpretation according to which the ecclesial office is so patently a human institution that nothing of the office of Christ is present in it: *all* members of the Church without distinction would be "office holders of Christ," and the ecclesial office holders would have only organizational functions, more or less simply a spiritual office of manager.

It is expressly emphasized here that this, contrary to widespread misunderstanding, is not the interpretation of Reformation theology, and certainly not that of Luther. The difference between both interpretations is skin thin and, at the same time, serious. Skin thin: because only the so-to-speak "base" of the office can, according to the strictest Catholic tradition, count as "divine right," the concrete arrangement of the duties and exercise of the office is subject to human regulation under the guidance of the Gospel and its demand for the meaning of the ecclesial office; this arrangement is, moreover, the result of a changing, less than pristine, historical development. In short: the exercise of the ecclesial leadership is in large part actually, from outside, very similar to the exercise of an office that does not aspire to anything more than the safeguarding of a human job of organization and advising. Proof: a Lutheran Church president who refuses out of theological conviction to understand himself as the holder of a Bishop's office, stands in the ecclesial and extra-ecclesial public under the same "role expectations" as a Catholic Bishop who has his place in the "hierarchical constitution" of the Church.

The difference of both interpretations is, at the same time, serious. For the basic understanding of the office, open to an unforeseeable variety of forms and change, impacts without fail this form and change – on the simple ground, because the "base" of the office always appears only *in* a concrete form, and the holders of the office cannot for this reason split their praxis into "principal" and "changeable" acts of office. If I am convinced that *all* Christians are "office holders," and that my particular office function consists only in organizing and coordinating the "acts of office" of the members of the Church, then I am in the administration of my office almost unassailable in terms of theological criticism of that administration – with the exception of the case where I want to attempt to interfere directly with the inalienable "freedom of the Christian." All that one could criticize would be my bad, insensitive, lazy leadership of the organization. This corresponds in absolutely no way to a Lutheran understanding of office. But can it be argued that such self immunization against theological criticism is the great temptation to which some Lutheran Church offices seem to have fallen victim? If I am on the other hand convinced that I have really received a holy authority grounded directly in the salvific action of Christ, then each of my acts of office occurs ultimately on the basis of this authority and is out-and-out subject to theological criticism: do these acts actually correspond to the sense of the authority given by Christ? An immunization against theological criticism can also occur in this instance, in the opposite direction: because each official action ultimately occurs on the foundation of the authorization through Christ, whoever criticizes the concretization of the authorization in an individual official act criticizes the Christ-given authority. This was never the Catholic interpretation. But can it be doubted that such self immunization is the temptation that haunts the offices of some Catholic vicar generals? Moreover, the *title* "Bishop" does not clear up the matter. From the Greek origin of the word (*episkopos*), this is a "secular" title, which means "supervisor," "inspector," and has the same meaning as the office of the "superintendent" established very early in the Churches of the Reformation. And so might now and then even a "Church president" pretend to be more Bishop-like than a Catholic Bishop.

We go back to the starting point. If the "hierarchical constitution" of the Church depends on the *sacramental* hierarchy of ordination and therefore basically means the leadership of the Church through the Bishops and, in derived authority, through the co-workers of the Bishops, the priests and the deacons, then the concept "hierarchical constitution" itself changes when it is applied to the relationship of the Bishops to the Bishop of Rome, to the "Head of the College of Bishops." The Pope, however his office might be arranged, has vis-à-vis his fellow Bishops at most precedence of jurisdiction, of the aspect of the power of leadership *within* the entirety of the powers of office. With reference to 1 Corinthians 12 one is inclined to say: a leap forward in the area of the "spiritual gift" of "leadership." It is the problem of the ambiguity of the concept "hierarchy," that the emphasis has shifted from the gradation of the authority of ordination to the gradations of the authorities of jurisdiction. Along these lines, on the one hand the character of the relationship between Bishops and the Pope in the "hierarchical constitution" of the Church can be considered, indeed can become exactly the central theme, and on the other hand other holders of jurisdiction can be included for whom the question of a graduated authority of ordination does not even exist – as was proven with the earlier mentioned canon law decisions concerning the enfranchised members at the Council, while under this aspect the priests and the deacons, because they have only derived jurisdiction, fall out, so to speak, of the hierarchical constitution of the Church.

3. THE THIRD CHAPTER OF THE CONSTITUTION ON THE CHURCH

Is this all unnecessary hairsplitting? Could one accuse me that I have, under the guise of fine precision, the intent to dictate what conclusions should be drawn? Now, a critical closer examination certainly must occur. Now as ever "hierarchy," against better theological insight, means in Church use, "Pope and Bishops." Moreover, we feel the effects of the allegedly exaggerated subtlety, for example in the question of what theological and canonical value the Bishops' conferences have, or should have – more on this soon. Above all our "subtlety" will be a help in reading the third Chapter of the Constitution on the Church. It reads as an outline of a theology of the office of Bishop and as an ambitious attempt to retrieve the full contour of that ecclesial office in the sense of the early Church tradition, to describe its theological characteristics correctly, and with this to lead the way to clear corrections of the theologically and practically problematic developments of recent Church history. When one reads the text with this sort of expectation, then it becomes, even without any particular foreknowledge, effortlessly understandable. On the one hand, the office and authority of the Pope is spoken of only in the form of recapitulations and subordinate clauses, on the other hand, it is not surprising when first, and only, in Articles 28 and 29, after ten articles concerning the Episcopal office (18-27), the subject becomes the priests and deacons. And the entirety is permeated, into the individual formulations, from the basic interpretation: all the hierarchical constitution of the Church is only the means to the one goal, to unite the People of God in praise of his glory. That goal is expressed in the introduction of Article 18: "In order to ensure that the people of God would have pastors and would enjoy continual growth, Christ the Lord set up in his church a variety of offices whose aim is the good of the whole body. Ministers, invested with a sacred power, are at the service of their brothers and sisters, so that all who belong to the people of God and therefore enjoy true Christian dignity may attain to salvation through their free, combined and well-ordered efforts in pursuit of a common goal."

Then the doctrine of the First Vatican Council on the primacy of the successor of Peter is sharpened and expressly newly presented. This was of course nothing unexpected, but it happened with two noteworthy accents, one negative, in that *the* biblical "Papal speech," Matt 16:18, was not cited, and one positive, in that the language is of the "colleagues" of the Pope *before* their "head":

> This holy synod, following in the steps of the Vatican Council, with it teaches and declares that Jesus Christ, the eternal pastor, established the holy church by sending the apostles as he himself had been sent by the Father. He willed that their successors, the bishops, should be the shepherds in his church until the end of the world. *In order that the episcopate itself, however, might be one and undivided he placed blessed Peter over the other apostles, and in him he set up a lasting and visible source and foundation of the unity both of faith and of communion* (italics by the author).

The Council referred, in the footnote, to the First Vatican Council. Whoever looks this up realizes with surprise that the insights at that time were the same: an emphasis on the unity of the faithful as the goal of the institution of the Church, its primary constitution under the leadership of the Bishops as successors of the apostles and Peter and his successors as principle of the unity of the *episcopacy* – therefore not as immediate principle of the unity *of the Church, that is, of the faithful*, as it often is understood. In order to make the sense of the following statements clear, it is worthwhile to quote Article 18 to the end:

> This teaching on the institution, the permanence, the nature and the force of the sacred primacy of the Roman Pontiff and his infallible teaching office, the sacred synod proposes anew to be firmly believed by all the faithful. Further, continuing with this same undertaking, it intends to profess before all and to declare the teaching on bishops, successors of the apostles, who together with Peter's successor, the Vicar of Christ and the visible head of the whole church, govern the house of the living God.

A description of the office of Bishop in its origin from the College of Apostles follows. The text cites the usual Bible passages in a way that is responsible, in part, to the insights of modern historical-critical exegesis. Noteworthy – although measured against the customary language in Church circles perhaps not so noteworthy – is the identification of the Twelve with the "Apostles." As is well known, this identification in the New Testament occurs only in Luke and the Acts of the Apostles. But the Acts of the Apostles is exactly that New Testament writing that speaks the most of a "College," a "College" that in the College of the 2700 Bishops at the Council had founded its successor institution. Noteworthy and at the same time not noteworthy is that the New Testament *episkopos*, as the Council describes him, reminds one more of the modern office of Bishop than is warranted by the actual historical facts. Of course, the Council text does not understand itself as a historical monograph, but as a confession of faith in the historical origin of the ecclesial office and with this in the regulatory power of this origin.

The following article 21 deals with the representation of Christ through the Bishop. What is meant is that the Bishop – together with the priests, as is expressly mentioned – portrays and represents Jesus Christ for the faithful in particular and for humanity in general, with the result that whoever follows the Bishop follows Christ himself. There is no question that this representation of Christ is open to a great deal of misuse, both in understanding and exercise, and for this reason the definition of the nature of the ecclesial office through this concept is also very controversial, not only between Catholic and Lutheran theology, but also within Catholic theology. The fact that the idea is very old – "where the Bishop is, there is Christ" was said by Ignatius of Antioch, Church Father and disciple of the evangelist John – guards it from the suspicion of being just a campaign slogan for the legitimatization of historically conditioned claims to power. One the other hand, a modern Bishop is not the representative of Christ in the way his secular original model, the Roman official, was the representative of the Emperor. In order to avoid all misunderstandings and abuses, it suffices to admit the plain statements of our text through which it is expressly made clear: Christ is in this respect "not absent from the assembly of his pontiffs" in that he, through their ministry – notice the order! – administers the word of God to all people and extends the sacraments to the faithful, through which new members join the body of Christ and are led, wisely and prudently, on the pilgrim journey to eternal salvation. That the Bishops are capable of this is not because of their own efforts, but because of the gift of the Holy Spirit that is given to them in the laying on of hands during the episcopal consecration – a gift that they received expressly in order to fulfill such tasks, therefore not as their personal possession.

The most important, but easily overlooked, statement is at the end of the article:

"Episcopal consecration confers, together with the office of sanctifying, the offices also of teaching and ruling, which, however, of their very nature can be exercised only in hierarchical communion with the head and members of the college. Tradition, which is expressed especially in the liturgical rites and in the customs of both the eastern and western church, makes it abundantly clear that, through the imposition of hands and the words of consecration, the grace of the holy Spirit is given, and a sacred character is impressed in such a way that bishops, eminently and visibly, take the place of Christ himself, teacher, shepherd and priest, and act in his person."

One should pay attention to the phrase: "... together with the office of sanctifying, the offices also of teaching and ruling ...." The "office of sanctifying" means – not any different than at priestly ordination – the authority and task of the administration of the sacrament. The office of teaching and ruling is now joined to the communication of this authority: derived from it. The impasse reported at the beginning of this chapter is resolved, the problem that with *priestly ordination*, in essence, with the exception of a few reservations, the administration of the sacrament that belongs to the "office of sanctifying" is conferred, while the consecration to Bishop adds to this only the authority of jurisdiction. It would have been fitting here for the Council, which otherwise in this chapter referred readily to the Council of Trent, to openly admit that it consciously and intentionally exceeded an anti-reform stricture, for which, as we shall show, the Trent Council itself contained the prerequisites.

What was already touched on in a dependent clause in the quoted text becomes the content of the following article 22: the relationship between the "College" of Bishops and the Bishop of Rome as the successor of Peter. Again, the order of the steps of the argument is important:

a. Like Peter and the other apostles, the Bishop of Rome and the Bishops form a single college – one notices the simple *and*! From this follows a fundamental connection, also historically attested through the "very ancient discipline" of the community of all Bishops of the world with the Bishop of Rome, the calling of councils and the symbolism of the execution of the episcopal consecration through *numerous* episcopal ordinaries. In this context comes the clear answer to the question of how does one become Bishop: "A person is made a member of the episcopal body in virtue of the sacramental consecration and by hierarchical communion with the head and members of the college."

b. As would be expected, it is emphasized in the next step that the College of Bishops "has no authority, however, other than the authority which it is acknowledged to have in union with the Roman Pontiff, Peter's successor, as its head, his primatial authority over everyone, pastors or faithful, remaining intact." Although the Pope has "full, supreme and universal power over the whole church," and can exercise this power freely, so that the authority of the College of Bishops can be exercised only with the agreement of the Bishop of Rome, Article 22 declares – with reference to the First Vatican Council in the note – that the order of Bishops, as the successor to the college of the apostles, in which "the apostolic college is perpetuated," together with the Bishop of Rome "is the subject of supreme and full authority over the universal church." Why "together with"? The Council gives a noteworthy biblical reason: the same binding and loosing power that Jesus Christ bestowed on Simon Peter as the rock and key bearer of the Church (Matt 16:18-19; John 21:15ff.), he also assigned to the College of Apostles, bound to its head (Matt 18:18; 28:16-20). And then we get the best confirmation of the idea presented earlier about the meaning of a Council: "This college, in so far as it is composed of many members, is the expression of the variety and universality of the people of God; and of the unity of the flock of Christ, in so far as it is assembled under one head." Now there is only the question, how then such an "expression" of variety and unity becomes concrete, if an ecumenical council cannot take place every couple of years and, besides this, with around 3000 voting members would be a somewhat difficult instrument for Church leadership. The text takes up this question and determines:

c. In fidelity to the primacy of the Pope the members of the College of Bishops act in *their own* proper authority for the best of *their* faithful, "indeed even for the good of the whole church." The exercise of the highest collegial power over the entire Church at the ecumenical Council is a special case ("in a solemn way"); normally it would happen without a Council and remains, however, collegial exercise of authority: "There never is an ecumenical council which is not confirmed or at least accepted as such by Peter's successor. And it is the prerogative of the Roman Pontiff to convoke such council, to preside over them and to confirm them. This same collegiate power can be exercised in union with the pope by the bishops residing in different parts of the world, provided the head of the college summon them to collegiate action, or at least approve or freely accept the corporate action of the unassembled bishops, so that a truly collegiate act may result."

In other words, the exercise of ecclesial authority of office in relation to the entire Church is *always* a collegial process, by which the Pope either takes the initiative or agrees to an Episcopal initiative; he can never act in a literal sense "absolutely," completely unconnected with the Bishops. His universal primacy is always only one inside of the College of Bishops, and the duty of community is reciprocal. In spite of all the parentheses about the untouchable primal precedence, this remains as the theological description of the function of the office of Peter and is therefore the criterion for judgments on post-conciliar statements and post-conciliar practice.

The *Pope* does not always have the initiative in terms of collegial processes. Article 23 of the Dogmatic Constitution on the Church elucidates this. It treats the reciprocal relationships of the Bishops with regard to the Universal Church. The individual Bishops are "the visible source and foundation of unity" for their dioceses, as they together with the Pope represent the *diversity* of the Universal Church. What, however, is a "diocese"? It is, according to the wording of the text, a "particular church." And now two sentences follow that are puzzling in terms of their connection to one another; these sentences stand out because at least up to this point in time the tendency has been in the direction of an interpretation certainly not intended by the Council. These sentences concern the Bishops'"own particular churches, which are modeled on the universal church." If one takes this literally, first there is the Universal Church, and this then is reflected subsequently in the particular Churches – so that one then from the structure and practice of the particular Churches must be able to project the structure and practice of the Universal Church. This historically as well as practically very problematic picture could not actually have been what was meant by the Council. The next sentence reads: "It is in and from these [particular Churches] that the one and unique Catholic Church exists," with reference to a quote from Cyprian in the footnote. If words have a meaning, then there is *no* Universal Church before and outside of the particular Churches, but only one that in them and from them has its reality. This does not mean that the Universal Church is only a subsequent amalgamation and therefore an umbrella organization, but that she is perceptible, concrete, and understandable only in the reality of the local churches: theologically as the unity in faith, hope, and love that encompasses all Churches, juridically as the organized community that makes the unity of the particular Churches visible.

The text goes on to emphasize the need for collaboration of the local Churches in the promotion of the unity of faith, the proclamation of the faith to non-believers, and the exchange of material goods, particularly where this collaboration contributes, as the text says, to "the whole mystical body of Christ, and in a special way, of the poor, the suffering, and those who are undergoing persecution for the sake of justice." In the last section a simplistic thesis is contradicted: "It has come about through divine providence that, in the course of time, different churches set up in various places by the apostles and their successors joined together in a multiplicity of organically united groups." The emphasis here is on *later* unity of originally independently"established" local Churches! The text intends here the patriarchal Churches of the East, with their own discipline and their own theological and liturgical traditions, and illustrates with them "this multiplicity of local churches" that shows "all the more resplendently the catholicity of the undivided church." The article closes with the important comment that modern episcopal conferences "in like fashion" can fruitfully contribute to making collegiality a reality.

The sentence about the fashioning of the particular church "modelled on the universal church" is once again a sentence on the border of "contradictory pluralism." It can be judged as a concession to the "centralists," in order to make the strong statements about the autonomy of the local churches and the mediating function of regional collaborations between individual Bishops and the Petrine office capable of consensus. As in other cases, the remaining lack of clarity has had its consequences – to the burden of the local Churches, as will be shown when we take a look at post-conciliar history.

The following Article 24 deals with the canonical mission of the Bishops. It is expressly stated: "The canonical mission of bishops, on the other hand, can be given by legitimate customs that have not been revoked by the supreme and universal authority of the church, or by laws made or acknowledged by the same authority, or directly by Peter's successor himself." The "legitimate customs that have not been revoked" concern above all the forms of the appointment of Bishops in the uniate eastern Churches – there the Patriarch names the Bishops – the "laws made or acknowledged by the same authority" refers to an old right of election in ancient dioceses; the naming "directly by Peter's successor himself" refers to the Bishops of more recent dioceses, to whom Rome had never granted a right of election. The list of these manners of "canonical mission" is important because it becomes clear: the Catholic doctrine of the primacy of jurisdiction of the Pope does *not* mean that it is *theologically* necessary that the Pope alone chooses and names the Bishops. The recently observed tendency to avoid collaboration with the eastern Churches in the choice of their Bishops and to evade old rights of election is therefore theologically open to criticism: it is a weakening of the autonomy of the local Churches protected by the Council.

Article 25 is extremely important. The doctrine of the ecclesial teaching office is presented in somewhat thoughtless language that makes no concessions to the modern consciousness of intellectual freedom. The relevant doctrine of the First Vatican Council was newly formulated, cited in part word-for-word and emphasized. In the midst of this, however, stands that section critics see as a pointed heightening, actually the unbearable completion, of the First Vatican Council, the section in which the infallible teaching office of the Pope under certain conditions is extended to the College of Bishops: "Although individual bishops do not enjoy the prerogative of infallibility, they do, however, proclaim infallibly the doctrine of Christ when, even though dispersed throughout the world but maintaining among themselves and with Peter's successor the bond of communion, in authoritatively teaching matters to do with faith and morals, they are in agreement that a particular teaching is to be held definitively." The First Vatican Council is cited in the footnote. The comforting thought that it would be a long, long time before the Bishops of the entire world be able to reach a truly ascertainable agreement in a controversial question of faith was soon blasted away: in 1968 Paul VI's encyclical *Humanae vitae* appeared, with an appeal to the consensus of the Bishops of all centuries. This encyclical, despite criticism in the entire world, is still until today vehemently defended in Rome.

The two following Articles, 26 and 27, deal with the duties of office of the Bishop in his diocese. Three items are worth remarking on: the comment that puts into concrete terms that the Church of Christ is present in the local congregation – more exactly: in proclamation of the word, in Eucharist, and in loving solidarity – and therefore the congregation is "Church" according to New Testament use of that word. Article 27 again makes clear that the Bishops, despite their subordination to the Pope, are not to be understood "as vicars of the Roman Pontiff"; a Bishop possesses an authority unique to him, on the strength of which he governs the People of God. In a moving final section, it is impressed on the Bishops that their high office gives them no ground and no cause for triumphalist behavior – the Council Fathers, themselves all Bishops, had obviously seen ground and cause to admonish each other in this respect.

4. THE DECREE ON THE PASTORAL OFFICE OF THE BISHOPS IN THE CHURCH

We said: Everything important about the office of Bishop is contained in the third chapter of the Constitution on the Church. If one immediately reads the Decree on the Pastoral Office of the Bishops in the Church right after this Constitution, one can easily see the formal and content difference between a constitution and a decree. The dogmatic statements of the Constitution on the Church are recapitulated in the (theological) first chapter of the decree, quoted in part word-for-word. In the second and third (practical) chapters these statements are converted into a strongly formulated catalogue of the tasks of the office of the Bishop and lead finally into completely practical instructions for the revision of canon law. (It does actually deal as well with the "sashes and buttons.") I emphasize only the following points: all Bishops have, because of their consecration, the right to participate in ecumenical councils; this includes also the auxiliary bishops, who do not have their own jurisdictions (Article 4): this is a clear consequence of the new valuation in the Constitution on the Church of the relationship of authority of consecration and jurisdiction.

As representation of the entire world episcopacy a permanent "Synod of Bishops" was formed, to advise the successor of Peter in the leadership of his office — of course the sort and manner of this advising is determined by the Pope (Article 5).

The responsibility of *all* Bishops for the proclamation of the faith was urgently impressed on them — a text that is worth quoting word-for-word:

> 6. Bishops, as legitimate successors of the apostles and members of the episcopal college, should appreciate that they are closely united to each other and should be solicitous for all the churches. By divine institution and by virtue of their apostolic office, they all share joint responsibility for the church. They should be especially solicitous for those parts of the world in which the word of God has not yet been proclaimed or in which, mainly on account of the scarcity of priests, the faithful are in danger of abandoning the practice of the christian life or even of losing the faith itself. Bishops should, therefore, do their utmost to ensure that the work of evangelization and the apostolate are fully supported and promoted by the faithful. It should, moreover, be their special care that suitable priests, as well as lay and religious auxiliaries, be trained for those missions and regions where there are insufficient priests. They should arrange also, as far as it is possible, that some of their priests should go to these missions or dioceses to exercise the sacred ministry there, either permanently or for a fixed period. Furthermore, bishops should bear it in mind that in the expenditure of ecclesiastical resources they must take into account the needs not only of their own dioceses but of other individual churches, since they too form part of the

one church of Christ. Let it be their care also to give help according to their resources when other dioceses or regions are afflicted by disaster.

7. Above all, they should extend their brotherly care to those bishops who suffer calumny and hardship for the name of Christ, who are in prison or prevented from exercising their ministry. They should display an active fraternal interest in them so that their sufferings may be lessened and alleviated by the prayers and help of their brethren."

The faculty is given to the Bishops to grant dispensations, in individual cases, from general canon law, if that is necessary in the particular religious situation of the concerned party. Apart from a few reservations, the so-called quinquennial authority, which before the Council each individual Bishop had to renew every five years during a routine visit to Rome, was enacted as general law.

In sentences that left nothing to be desired in the way of clarity, the Council Fathers formulated their wishes for a reform of the Curia, in Articles 9 and 10. The most important statements are:

It is very much the desire of the Fathers of the sacred council that these departments [of the Roman Curia], which have indeed rendered excellent service to the Roman Pontiff and to the pastors of the church, should be reorganized in a manner more appropriate to the needs of our time and of different regions and rites, especially in regard to their number, their titles, their competence, their procedures and how they coordinate their activities. It is also very much their wish that the functions of papal legates be more precisely determined, keeping in mind the pastoral role proper to the bishops.

It is noteworthy that in the entire Decree, when the essential episcopal duties of office are described, the order of Proclamation of the Word – Administration of Sacraments is carefully maintained (this is clearest in Articles 11 and 12)."Bishops, in the exercise of their teaching office, are to proclaim to humanity the gospel of Christ. This is one of their principal duties" (Article 12). The Second Vatican Council cites in the footnote to this sentence two reform decrees from Trent, in which the same is said. But the Trent reform decrees remained in the shadows of the dogmatic decrees, remaining unknown and ineffective, so that their citation in the Decree on Bishops amounts to a rediscovery.

Article 13 urgently reminds Bishops that the proclamation of the gospel of Christ is not an exercise in power. The Bishops must extend themselves to people, believers and non-believers, not vice-versa. Article 14 applies these principles to the structuring of catechesis, completed in Article 16 through the advice that the insights of social science could be helpful in these endeavors.

Only Article 15, on the "duty to sanctify" – that is, according to ecclesial linguistic usage: concerning the administration of sacraments – causes one to crease the brow. You don't need to be a Bible scholar, just a Bible reader, to recognize that in the introductory sentence of this article a principle statement of the Letter to the Hebrews has been turned upside down. The duty of the High Priest to offer gifts and sacrifices for sins, which according to the biblical witness is *removed* through Jesus Christ, the new and unique High Priest, is in the first sentence of Article 15 ascribed to the Bishops, in order to hang onto at least a kernel of the image of the sacrifice of the Mass. There would have been better biblical references to use, in order to emphasize the sacramental competence of the Bishops. The all-encompassing duty of community leadership with the often emphasized sequence of Proclamation of the Word and Administration of Sacraments as the most important duties would have not only sufficed, but would also have set the right tone.

Scars of Church history become visible when in Articles 19 and 20 full freedom for Bishops from state interference in matters of appointment and leadership of office is postulated, while at the same time political authorities are asked to renounce ancient laws and privileges that allowed such interference. As we know, this is an explosive theme, since the Church, where such symbiosis between Church and State exists, might not want to deny herself the backing of the State and the State might not want to deny itself the consequent support of the Church, as has been demonstrated. And so these articles have not, where there was something to be changed, changed anything. Concretely stated: in the USA the Church considers it a boon to be completely separated from the State; in Germany, on the other hand, the Church rejoices in the fact that the State, by means of the "church tax" collected by the State (to its own benefit, too), has made the Church the richest in the world; this "church tax" also supports ecclesially bound theological faculties, for which the State can only hire such professors as the Church considers unobjectionable.

Article 21 introduces a remarkable innovation: the Bishop has a moral duty (although not a legal one) to resign on the grounds of age or obvious inability to execute the duties of office. This article is for the most part rendered: at 75 years of age, at the latest, the Bishops send in their resignations to Rome; these are accepted or not, depending whether Rome is happy or not with the theological and pastoral line of the Bishop. It can be accepted, however, that most Bishops find it liberating, ten years later than the normal employee, to be able to put aside the burden of responsibility. The rule has an exception: it does not hold for the Bishop of Rome. Pope Paul VI, who was the first Pope to accept, in great number, resignation petitions according to Article 21, remained in office until his death, well past 80 years of age. And even now the idea of a "retired Pope" seems really odd. The last resignation of a Pope occurred in 1294: Celestine V, previously a monk and hermit, a compromise candidate and a kickball for the Roman clans who were in rivalry over the Papal office, abdicated his office after only half a year, in consideration of his lack of aptitude for the job. Before he left office, he was smart enough to issue a resignation protocol for Popes and new, stronger rules for the conclave, according to which his successor Boniface VIII was elected.

Whoever reads the Bishops' Decree quickly realizes that its style remains a balance between urgent spiritual admonition and legal orders, even in the second and third chapters, which directly treats the Bishop's leadership in his diocese and in his ecclesiastical region. Legal obligations were to be established through post-conciliar regulations concerning execution; this finally happened after numerous preliminary steps by means of the Motu proprio *Ecclesiae sanctae*, of August 6, 1966, the regulations of which were included in the new ecclesial canon law book of 1983. It would take us too far afield to here go into complicated details; we must, however, still take up a point that has in more recent times generated a great deal of interest and conflict.

5. THE EPISCOPAL CONFERENCE

In three articles (36-38), the Council expressed itself in the first section of the third chapter concerning the institution of the episcopal conferences. These had been taking place for a long time, some in the previous century, mostly in Europe. According to the rule that the Bishop is the sole lawgiver in his diocese, the function of the regular, mostly yearly episcopal conferences was confined to exchange of experiences and common agreements, above all for action vis-à-vis the State and for statements of the Church in public matters. It was not legally binding, but as a backward look for example into the last 150 years of Germany's Church history shows, highly effective.

The Council made numerous decisions with regard to the episcopal conferences. It wished for a new blooming of the ancient Church tradition of provincial synods and plenary councils of entire regions. Without directly equating the conferences with these synods and councils, but in a continuation of this tradition, the Council deemed the episcopal conferences to be a proven instrument of cooperation of the Bishops (article 37). For this reason the Council raised the episcopal conferences to the level of legal decision-making assemblies, capable of issuing statutes. The Council made only the following restrictions: only the ordinaries and coadjutors hold a deliberative vote. The auxiliary Bishops exercise either a deliberative or a consultative vote, as the statutes of the conference determine. The statutes, which among other things provide for a General Secretary and for commissions for the different areas of activity of the episcopal conference (for example, Faith Commission, Ecumenical Commission, etc.), must only be "reviewed" by the Apostolic See, not confirmed. Only the amalgamations of Bishops of numerous countries to a single episcopal conference requires the agreement of the Apostolic See – as in, for example, the case of the Latin American episcopal conference.

Because of the provisions of Article 38 and the 1966 regulations, the chairman of an episcopal conference, along with the Pope and the higher superiors of religious orders, is the only holder of an office within the hierarchy of jurisdiction who is elected freely and directly; along with this, he is elected for a determined period of time.

It is to be emphasized that the episcopal conference does not make the regional synods unnecessary. Like an ecumenical council, a diocesan synod or a regional synod is a rare occurrence. The importance of the episcopal conference as a regional decision-making organ, with binding legal authority, consists precisely in its regular sessions – and in the permanent activity of the general secretary and the commissions as their executors.

Deep reservations about strengthening of the episcopal conferences had existed at the beginning. There was a fear, not completely without reason, of a weakening of the Papal central authority and of increased opposition to Rome by appeal to regional prerequisites. This worry has dissipated, since Rome, through its wide reaching influence on the filling of Bishops' seats, could ensure that the required two-thirds majority was always guaranteed to vote in the way Rome preferred. Despite this, a new theological and canon law set-to concerning the theological status and legal competence of the episcopal conferences has flared up, occasioned by a Roman design to revoke the provisions of Article 38 of the Bishops' Decree. In terms of Germany, for example there have been (up to this point unsuccessful) attempts to effect a change in the statutes of the German episcopal conference, so that the auxiliary Bishops would participate in the conference with only a consultative vote, not the deliberative vote they now have. This change in the voting status of the auxiliary bishops could change the results of, for example, the election of the chairman of the conference. In 1984, the Prefect of the Congregation for the Doctrine of the Faith, Cardinal Ratzinger, granted a public interview, "On the Situation of the Faith," in which there were very clear indications of a Roman course correction in the assessment of the episcopal conferences; Cardinal Ratzinger vigorously supported the strengthening of the individual ordinary bishops.

Now there is certainly something to be said for a strengthening of the ordinary of a diocese vis-à-vis a legally binding, decision-making episcopal conference. It can frequently occur that the majority can prevent those courageous measures that a Bishop might consider absolutely necessary for his diocese, based on his pastoral responsibility. That seems, of course, not to be the intention of the new Roman design. This is clearly intended to increase the influence of the central Church administration. Now an ideal balancing of the forces through the formal rules alone will not be possible, because people who really want to can always find ways to circumvent rules. Nonetheless the central argument in favor of the episcopal conferences, an argument that is both a theological one and a canonically practical one, cannot be refuted. If it can be assumed that the collegiality of the Bishops in community with the successor of Peter is taken seriously as a basic principle of the Constitution on the Church, then the collegial collaboration of the Bishops cannot be restricted to the rare occurrence of the Ecumenical Council, or the synods of Bishops, or contact enabled by modern methods of communication. The collegial leadership of the Church would be then a pure theological theory, in practice so unbelievable and so far from experience as, for comparative purposes, the widely held theory that the Bishop is the actual pastor of his diocese (Bishops' Decree, Articles 11 and 15). Around 3000 and more Bishops in the entire world can only in rare cases really act collegially – actually only at an ecumenical council. Under the title "collegiality," therefore, as the rule, all important questions remain at the level of central Church administration in feedback with the individual bishop, who regularly, every five years, must make his *ad limina* visit. An episcopal conference on the other hand can demonstrably act collegially – simply because of the manageable numbers, the common language, as well as the common political and cultural situation in which the episcopal conference is active. Therefore nothing speaks against, indeed everything speaks much more for, that the basic ideas of collegial leadership of the Church through the Bishops in community with the successor of Peter should be concretized through an expansive autonomy of the national or regional episcopal conferences. If out of this a modern variant on the ancient ecclesial patriarchate structure developed, this would not be a bad result – Latin America, represented through the Latin American episcopal conference, under ancient Church conditions would have been a patriarchate long ago! And it does not require any great fantasy to imagine that then, without the possibility of constant interference from distant Rome, the conflict around Liberation Theology and the disagreement associated with that conflict around the Church's interaction with the poor of Latin America might have taken, and would take, a different course.

In short: the Council's sentence, according to which the whole Church consists in and from the local churches (Church Constitution, Article 23), can only be brought to life if there are intermediate authorities between the individual Bishops and the Pope, which can compel the holder of the Petrine office to have a good look at the regional particularities of the Church in various parts of the world, and could at the same time hinder him from playing one individual Bishop against his "colleagues." Is it a coincidence that the attempts at a new assessment of the episcopal conferences began after not just individual Bishops showed up in Rome for their *ad limina* visit but, in a move prompted by Rome, entire regional episcopal conferences, confronting the Roman officials with their own individual problems?

6. PRIESTS AND DEACONS

The third chapter of the Constitution on the Church, on the hierarchical constitution of the Church, ends in Article 28 and 29 with remarks concerning priests and deacons. Because they have received the sacramental ordination of office (see also the Bishops' Decree, Article 15), they belong to the hierarchy of ordination – therefore the third chapter of the Constitution on the Church speaks of them. They do not, however, have any power of jurisdiction in their own right – therefore they are dealt with only in a sort of appendix, although they bear the actual cares and burden of all the duties that in the Bishops' Decree are described in the form of an ideal picture of the duties of office of the Bishop. What does the Council say about priests and deacons?

a. The priests are time and again called "cooperators" with the Bishop. Article 28 of the Constitution on the Church says that the ordination to the priesthood comprises a "degree" of the one sacrament of ordination, therefore entrusts the ordained with a part of the comprehensive ministerial duties of the Bishop. That is the trial test for the restoration of the full understanding of the office of Bishop by the Council. The office of the priest is no longer characterized by the authority to celebrate the Eucharist, but as the task to exercise, through delegated authority, a part of the duties of the Bishop in a part of the diocese, usually the parish. One notices here also the order of the description of the duties: Proclamation of the Word, Leadership of the Congregation, Administration of Sacraments.

b. It is noticeable that more precise descriptions of the concept "priest" are lacking. This is not noticeable when one reads the English, or French, or German text. If one looks at a word register of the Latin text, one sees: the office holder is as a rule called *presbyter*; only in exceptional cases, or where the context demands it, is he called *sacerdos*. Since the English, French, or German word "priest," "prêtre," "Priester" is derived from *presbyter*, we do not notice this subtlety when we read a vernacular text. Obviously the Council wanted to take into account the New Testament fact that there the designation of the ecclesial office holder as "priest" is intentionally avoided. Therefore neither biblical nor history of religion facts help with the description of the office of priest – it is pointless, despite better theological insight, to want to change the customary language. It is about, with regards to the episcopal office, just a "degree." What this exactly consists of is not explained.

This is probably a good thing, since the explanation would have been so difficult historically that it could not have been managed in a few sentences.

c. Incidentally, the priests are the stepchildren of the Council. For this reason we have the bittersweet joke related at the end of Chapter 5. Originally a decree on the ministry and life of the priests was not even planned. Only gradually did the insight develop, that one, after so much talk of the episcopal office, might have a good and encouraging word to say to those who accomplished the daily work in the Church of Proclamation of the Word, Pastoral Care, and Administration of Sacraments – a work, from baptism to pastoral counseling, the Sunday homily, catechism, up to funerals, which the Bishops, given how their office is organized today, are for the most part relieved of. How necessary such encouragement was is evidenced by the uncertainty of many, particularly older, priests, an uncertainty that continues up to today and, as I can attest to, often manifests itself in the bitter question: "What have we done wrong?" Further proof is the positive echo that a book like the 1988 *The Meaning of Christian Priesthood* from Gisbert Greshake has found among priests – completely uninfluenced by the theological controversy occasioned by the book.

If one looks through the description of the duties of the priest's office, it becomes apparent in the Decree on Priests that the priests in principle perform the same functions in their congregations as do the Bishops. In fact the ancient Church's cooperators of the Bishops, who took over as a special ministry within the congregation led by the Bishop, have long since become the independent and responsible leaders of their own congregations. The powers of office that they, theological speaking, have as powers derived from the episcopal office, they have to a large extent in terms of canon law as permanent powers, which the Bishop cannot simply limit according to his wish. In a word: they are, if not theologically, then practically, that which in the ancient Church the Bishop was as leader of a local church. So the question arises, whether the legal position at least of the leading pastor in relationship to the Bishop ought not to be strengthened. If the Bishop is for all intents and purposes mostly administrative chief, but with regards to the rest is as distant from the concrete pastoral situation in the congregations (unfortunately) as the Bishop of Rome is distant from the situation in a far flung diocese, then that must have effects on the position of the pastor in the life of the congregation.

d. Even more unclear theologically are the statements about the diaconate. They stand "at a lower level of the hierarchy" than the priests and have no share in priesthood (Article 29 of the Constitution on the Church). They are simply ordained to a "ministry," and it remains undecided whether it is intended more as a diaconal ministry in the sense of the ancient Church or predominantly as a job in the area of liturgical ministry. Indeed the deacon today has practically all the functions of the priest in a congregation, with the exception of the sacrament of reconciliation, the anointing of the sick, and the celebration of the Eucharist. Because of the high number of "no" votes in the *Quaesitum* dealing with the diaconate, a compromise was sought with the – unrealistic – regulation that only older, already married men, established in their careers, could be ordained to the diaconate, while young, still unmarried men had to adhere to the law of celibacy. The conservatives feared, of course, a move toward the lifting of the law of priestly celibacy. The compromise would not stop that, as it must have been clear to every realist. In the different countries and once again in the individual dioceses the rules are very different: in some places – for instance in the USA – there are only deacons who are sort of "jobbing," who during the week go back to their "secular" work, in other places deacons who are first and foremost, in terms of careers, deacons, who have undergone a training specially devised for the diaconate. In this last case the deacons assist the pastor not only on the weekend, but practically discharge all the duties of chaplains, with the exception of hearing confessions and celebrating the Eucharist. Since these both – confessions and Eucharist – involve the least work and time expenditure for a chaplain, everything else – from religious instruction to pastoral counseling, from burial and assisting marriage to the homily at the Sunday Mass – was already before the Council the right and duty of the deacon, so the married deacons are a true help for the pastors, at least where the pastor supports them as co-workers and allows them to work. Whether weekend or career, it is valid: one has either married deacons, young or old, or one has no deacons at all.

III. DEEP RESPECT FOR AN IMPOSSIBLE OFFICE

In Articles 11-21 of the Bishops' Decree the Bishops have drawn a picture of how they would *like* to be. If one pictures their daily life, if one had a glimpse into their lifestyle, then one would almost think to detect a hidden sadness in the text of the Council: we would *like* to be like this, but we *cannot* be like this.

In theological theory the Bishop is the leading pastor of his diocese. But when in practice does he have opportunity and then actually also time, to conduct an intensive pastoral counseling with a burdened and questioning person? When does he hear even one confession, anoint a sick person, or speak with someone near death? In theological theory the Bishop is the head teacher of the faithful of his diocese. But when does he have (for example) the opportunity, Sunday after Sunday to form a congregation theologically and spiritually over the long haul through the homily, to strengthen them in the faith and to make them hopeful? In theological theory, the Bishop is the head missionary of his Church. But would he be in the position to deliver expert religious instruction, so that his catechumens could learn something from him? In theological theory the Bishop is responsible that his priests and theologians pass on the faith accurately and accessibly. But is he, with all of his duties of office, still in the position to be current enough in the theological discussion to be *competent* to distinguish between courageous and fruitful new directions in the theological discourse and mere pseudo-theological soap bubbles, so that the chance for clarification for the fruitful new idea, even if this is not completely developed, is not immediately squashed? In theological theory the Bishop should make sure that all spiritual gifts that are at hand in the Church – concretely therefore: all talents, spiritual impulses, and good ideas – engage in dialogue with one another and cooperate. But in practice can anyone be so unpartisan and at the same time engaged, that he, as is necessary, promotes the one and on the other hand allows opposing criticism? In theological theory the Bishop is – at least according to the Catholic understanding, it is different for the Lutheran office of Bishop – in the general area of Church administration responsible for everything and therefore also, theologically, legally liable for everything. But can he in practice, in the midst of the immense bureaucracy of a modern diocese, manage without delegation of responsibility, with the result that it is impossible for him, finally, to oversee everything in detail and he has to simply trust that "his people" work in a way that is true to his inclinations and do not simply leave him in a lurch.

And here we touch on the most difficult problem. A large institution such as the Church – and when the Church with her message really turns to *all* people, she can not avoid becoming a large institution

– reproduces almost inevitably all the pressures of other political and social institutions. The Bishop is, in the final analysis, not in demand as a human, a Christian, or a pastor, but much more as a role player. Like a politician or a manager, he has to "protect his people," even when they have performed unsatisfactorily – because nothing gets done if the people cannot depend on the protections of their "employer." Unlike the pastor, in the Sunday homily he must pick his words very carefully, so that no false conclusions are drawn, no feelings hurt, no media avalanche let loose – because what the Bishop says is, in public perception, what "the Church" says. If the Bishop risks a courageous measure, he must be careful not to receive applause from the wrong side. Indeed – and this is the problematic case – not seldom must he, for the sake of loyalty to his fellow Bishops and loyalty to the Pope, say things about which he personally, as theologian and Christian, thinks otherwise or at least differently. He must defend what he as a private Christian could never defend; he must protect people who actually do not deserve protection. If the Bishop is skillful, if he is a political natural talent, he learns to play these different roles like a virtuoso. If he is not a natural talent then it can be very lonely for him, and he might be able to speak openly and say what he really thinks to only a few very discreet friends.

Truly, the episcopal office is an impossible office. No one who has not taken leave of his senses could possibly actually want the job: all the more reason that we owe those who hold this office deep respect. Those who hold the office cannot really defend themselves. They cannot defend themselves out of the simple grounds of ecclesial obedience; they cannot defend themselves above all because otherwise they must live with the reproach, anytime they exercise the right of criticism of the Church, of not wanting to get their hands dirty.

There is another burden, indeed impossibility, for the modern priests, particularly those in parish ministry, which commands our deep respect. More than the Bishop, the priests, deacons, and all the ecclesial co-workers are confronted with the entire nerve-racking colorfulness of modern life and must address the Gospel specifically to these circumstances. More than the Bishop, the priests and ecclesial co-workers are exposed to all the uncertainties and crises of faith that the modern world has in store. While Christians who do not hold a church office, when they have an occasion of a crisis of faith, can confidently wait and rely on their history with God, model strength of faith is expected from the holders of church office, or at least a model security vis-à-vis their doubts. What now, if a priest or a deacon loses faith, for a while or forever? What, if a married deacon or an ecclesial co-worker's marriage falls apart in a way that cannot be judged from the outside and a rigorous ecclesial discipline exacerbates the problems, instead of allowing room for Christian forgiveness in the congregation?

Priests, deacons, ecclesial co-workers have the courage to make their faith into a career without being able to guarantee that this faith will never be shaken. It is almost against all reason, it can only happen "in the hope." This is the reason for deep respect for those who, in all vulnerability, take over this office. We have all reason to take the admonition of the Apostle to heart: "Let the elders who rule well be counted worthy of double honor, especially those who labor in the word and in teaching" (1 Timothy 5:17).

CHAPTER EIGHT

"I DON'T LIKE THIS SCHEMA"

SCRIPTURE, TRADITION, MAGISTERIUM, AND THEOLOGY

I. THE MAGISTERIUM SUPERIOR TO THE BIBLE?

In July, 1965, a well known German theologian gave a lecture required for his doctoral degree at the Gregorian University, in Rome; his subject was Article 10 of the Dogmatic Constitution on Divine Revelation (*Dei Verbum*). In the second section of the lecture we find the following sentences: "This Magisterium is not superior to the word of God, but is rather its servant. It teaches only what has been handed on to it. At the divine command and with the help of the Holy Spirit, it listens to this devoutly, guards it reverently and expounds it faithfully. All that it proposes for belief as being divinely revealed it draws from this sole deposit of faith."

By "word of God," as an earlier sentence in the lecture made clear, is meant the word of God "whether in its written form or in the form of tradition." For the moment we can ignore the already obvious problem of "Scripture and Tradition." Whatever else "word of God" means, Sacred Scripture is certainly meant. Therefore, very understandably, our theologian in his lecture represented – he was, after all, in terms of time and place very close to the Council events – the thesis that the Magisterium is *inferior*, not *superior* to, Scripture. At the end of the lecture Sebastian Tromp S.J., Professor of Dogmatic Theology at the Gregorian, came to up to him and explained to him that he, the doctoral student lecturer, was not in line with Church doctrine. The reason: for Trump, Article 10 of *Dei Verbum* was not in harmony with Church doctrine with regard to the Pope's definitive authority of interpretation.

So the Pope, through his teaching office, stands *superior* to the Scripture, he does not serve it, and Scripture must be obedient to the Magisterium? If Sebastian Tromp were right, it would have been a dire, truly alarming second edition of the thesis that Sylvester Priesias put forward against Luther, a thesis Cardinal Cajetan during his interrogation of Luther in Augsburg in October of 1518 did not deny: the Scripture has its authority and power from the infallibility of the Papal teaching office. What makes this connection of 1965 with 1518 so macabre: Tromp – the editor in charge of the 1943 encyclical of Pope Pius XII, *Mystici Corporis* – was present during all the phases of preparation of *Dei Verbum*, secretary in all the commissions and sub-commissions connected with the document, and wielded considerable influence. Nevertheless, he apparently, as the objection to the German theologian shows, could have said: "I don't like this schema."

This sentiment was not, however, voiced by Sebastian Tromp, but by the (yet again) influential Cardinal Liénart from Lille (France) – as a laconic judgment on the first draft, with a completely different point. The first draft attempted to cement certain neo-Scholastic positions, completely and consciously ignoring everything that Catholic theology had learned in the meantime. So the discussion around the schema of *Dei Verbum* became, just like liturgical reform, the concept of collegiality, and religious freedom; this discussion became one of the crystallization points on which the fate of the Council depended. It cannot be imagined what the consequences would have been, had the Council decided in favor of the minority in the mold of Sebastian Tromp and the Council Fathers who were advised by him. At the very least that would have meant a new exile for Catholic exegetes, much like the one that accompanied the Modernist crisis at the beginning of the twentieth century. How the Catholic doctrine of the Church would have looked we know from Sebastian Tromp himself: he had developed a doctrine of the Church in a three-volume work in Latin, published in 1960 – it is easy to discern from this what sort of spiritual nourishment, what joy in the Church, what courage for the Church's future would have been derived from Tromp's image of the Church.

We are now at the prehistory of the Constitution, crucial for the understanding of the text.

II. THE PREHISTORY OF *DEI VERBUM*

1. AN ANTICIPATED DECISION

It is necessary to emphasize two points: first, this Constitution is the most uneven text of the Council – it contains badly concealed breaks in logic, even contradictions: it is a model for the compromise of the type of "contradictory pluralism." The text is, moreover, very short; some of the decrees are longer than this Constitution. If the text is read without the benefit of some prior knowledge, the question inevitably arises: what did the authors of the text actually want to say? Occasionally they seem to take two steps forward and then one and a half steps backwards again. What emerges – and what really, given the situation, was the best that could emerge – is that everything remains open; the discussion can therefore *continue*. Exactly that openness was what the forces of the minority – there were exactly the same numbers as with the question on collegiality – wanted to prevent.

Second, the real subject of this Constitution, dealt with through the medium of the idea of Revelation, is the relationship of theology to Magisterium, more exactly: the freedom of theological investigation. That is evident in one fundamental detail: there existed no necessity – unlike with the question of the episcopal office and the understanding of Church in general – to again take up dogmatically the theme "Revelation." It could *not* be said that the First Vatican Council, in a continuation of the Council of Trent, had not dealt with this question. The First Vatican Council had done this thoroughly in the Dogmatic Constitution *Dei Filius*. If it was considered absolutely necessary to engage this theme again, in the only *dogmatic* constitution that this Council adopted other than *Lumen Gentium*, then there must have been other reasons.

These reasons are found in the fact that the original draft anticipated the document *De fontibus revelationis* ("Concerning the Sources of Revelation"). This means, according to "Catholic talk," "Concerning Scripture and Tradition." With this title, the nature of "Revelation" is presupposed to be clear. The nature of Revelation, however, was very much a theme for discussion in the decades between the Modernist crisis and the Council. This discussion – we shall get to the details soon – was supposed to have been halted. Those who had been influenced by this discussion must have, despite the First Vatican Council, placed the concept of Revelation in the center of the conciliar teaching – only for this reason could the suppression of the discussion have been prevented.

Unbelievably difficult disputes ensued and, immediately in the first session, the first deep crisis of the Council. Only in the fifth of the altogether eight versions of *Dei Verbum* was it possible to dedicate the first chapter to the theme *De ipsa revelatione* ("Revelation Itself"), on which all the rest would be oriented.

With this the Constitution received a completely new twist, which originally not only was not planned for, but was supposed to have been avoided. In plain language: it dealt with the justification of the so-called historical critical method in Biblical interpretation. If this method was condemned, then everything could remain as it was – more precisely: then the advancing emancipation of Catholic exegesis and Catholic theology in general from the obstructive results of the Modernist crisis could be turned back, an emancipation that worried Roman theology and even Pope John XXIII, before the Council. If the method was allowed, then the question of the truth of salvation entrusted to the Church and its historical transmission arises anew – now to be moored to the concept of Revelation.

In practice that has to mean: the method could, indeed must, be used on the formulations of the proclamation of Church doctrine. Because what is right for the *norma normans* must also be permitted for the *normae normatae*. If the document of the not normed, but norming norm of faith could be investigated historically critically, then so could also the ecclesial proclamation of doctrine, derived as it is from Scripture.

It was therefore no accident, but clear sightedness on both sides, that exactly at this point the battle was so bitterly engaged. Up for debate was the function of Sacred Scripture in the Church, the function of the Magisterium in relation to Sacred Scripture, and the task of theology in relation to both. In conservative eyes, everything appeared solved, while nothing appeared solved in the eyes of those who, in spite of the anti-Modernist prohibition on thinking, emphasized that theology in the service of the proclamation must have freedom of investigation at its disposal. With this we have arrived at the prehistory of the Constitution, the problems that still require explanation, and the motives present in the elaboration of the text.

2. THE PRELUDE: THE "BIBLE MOVEMENT"

Since the beginning of the 20th century the Bible Movement, along with the Liturgical Movement and the Ecumenical Movement, had left its mark on piety in wide circles of Catholic Christianity – in particular in the Catholic Youth Movement. The Bible Movement actually contributed to a growing familiarity with the Bible. Daily Bible reading became a principal requirement of a consciously lived faith; this daily Bible reading was popularized above all through the Catholic Youth Movement. This happened, in the best sense of the word, "naively." No potential for conflict was feared, since it was of course completely clear that the Bible never should be understood against the Church, and that it did not have to be. The right to be able to read the Bible as critical of the concrete Church was occasionally claimed at the level of academic theology; before the Council this was never done openly and even in a closed circle constantly only under the protestation of unimpeachable fidelity to the *real* binding doctrine of the Church. Nonetheless: out of ecumenical grounds some word about the meaning of the Bible for the Church seemed to be recommended, and as a purely pastoral matter it would have generated no conflict, particularly since it was already anticipated in the Constitution on the Sacred Liturgy (see Articles 24, 35, 51, 92). Two motives provided the conflict.

3. "HISTORICAL-CRITICAL BIBLICAL INTERPRETATION"

The first very careful use of the historical critical method by Catholic biblical scholars was not self-evident, since the method was blocked not only by the anti-Modernist decisions of the beginning of the 20th century. The Papal Biblical Commission, founded in the wake of these anti-Modernist decisions, had adopted positions to all imaginable questions – mostly in the form, "one must not teach that ...." Pretty much everything was condemned that is taught today to Catholic students in Old and New Testament doctoral seminars. The pressure under which Catholic Bible scholars had to research and work at that time can be seen by these students, if they compare the different editions of the introduction to the New Testament (translated by Joseph Cunningham in 1958) of the German New Testament scholar Alfred Wikenhauser with the later re-working of this introduction by his Munich colleague Josef Schmid, particularly the take of these two scholars on the relationship of the synoptic gospels with one another, that is, their positions on the so-called "Two Source Theory." Irony of the history of research: today, after this theory has finally found its home in Catholic biblical studies, it has been subjected to all sorts of critical inquiries and modifications. I know from former students at the Pontifical Biblical Institute (PBI) that the Biblical Commission – which is connected to the PBI – already in the 1950's regretted each of its decisions from the 1920's.

The breakthrough against the anti-Modernist front succeeded in 1943, and through no less than Pope Pius XII himself, in his encyclical *Divino afflante Spiritu*. In a famous section of this encyclical, Pope Pius XII lifted the controls on the historical critical method – indeed, he promoted the use of the method. This occurred with a certain defensive point: for defense of the *truth* of the Bible, not for illumination of its *idiosyncracy*. The truth of the Bible is debated in its details even within the Church. The historical critical method ought to help with weakening the counter arguments. When something in the Bible, according to the papal statements, sounds untrue or contrived, this is to be explained as a result of the manner of speech, writing, and thinking of the biblical authors; it has nothing to do with untruth or "legend." The governing assumption is recognizable: truth is (historically or in some other way, for example, scientifically) *accuracy*. When "the ancient authors of the East" say something that we know, given our knowledge, to be unclear and imprecise, the historical critical method can help to transform this illogic into the precision of our accustomed logic. Thus the basic idea of the Bible can remain inviolate: the Bible is not a dogmatic textbook in the modern sense, but a book from which the doctrine of the Christian faith – also a doctrine – ought to be and can be taken.

In order to properly measure the step forward that *Dei Verbum* wanted and achieved, we should once again take a look at the 1943 text, despite its length:

> What is the literal sense of a passage is not always as obvious in the speeches and writings of the ancient authors of the East, as it is in the works of our own time. For what they wished to express is not to be determined by the rules of grammar and philology alone, nor solely by the context; the interpreter must, as it were, go back wholly in spirit to those remote centuries of the East and with the aid of history, archaeology, ethnology, and other sciences, accurately

determine what modes of writing, so to speak, the authors of that ancient period would be likely to use, and in fact did use.

For the ancient peoples of the East, in order to express their ideas, did not always employ those forms or kinds of speech which we use today; but rather those used by the men of their times and countries. What those exactly were the commentator cannot determine as it were in advance, but only after a careful examination of the ancient literature of the East. The investigation, carried out, on this point, during the past forty or fifty years with greater care and diligence than ever before, has more clearly shown what forms of expression were used in those far off times, whether in poetic description or in the formulation of laws and rules of life or in recording the facts and events of history. The same inquiry has also shown the special preeminence of the people of Israel among all the other ancient nations of the East in their mode of compiling history, both by reason of its antiquity and by reasons of the faithful record of the events; qualities which may well be attributed to the gift of divine inspiration and to the peculiar religious purpose of biblical history.

Nevertheless no one, who has a correct idea of biblical inspiration, will be surprised to find, even in the Sacred Writers, as in other ancient authors, certain fixed ways of expounding and narrating, certain definite idioms, especially of a kind peculiar to the Semitic tongues, so-called approximations, and certain hyperbolical modes of expression, nay, at times, even paradoxical, which even help to impress the ideas more deeply on the mind. For of the modes of expression which, among ancient peoples, and especially those of the East, human language used to express its thought, none is excluded from the Sacred Books, provided the way of speaking adopted in no wise contradicts the holiness and truth of God .... Not infrequently - to mention only one instance - when some persons reproachfully charge the Sacred Writers with some historical error or inaccuracy in the recording of facts, on closer examination it turns out to be nothing else than those customary modes of expression and narration peculiar to the ancients, which used to be employed in the mutual dealings of social life and which in fact were sanctioned by common usage.

When then such modes of expression are met within the sacred text, which, being meant for men, is couched in human language, justice demands that they be no more taxed with error than when they occur in the ordinary intercourse of daily life. By this knowledge and exact appreciation of the modes of speaking and writing

> in use among the ancients can be solved many difficulties, which are raised against the veracity and historical value of the Divine Scriptures, and no less efficaciously does this study contribute to a fuller and more luminous understanding of the mind of the Sacred Writer.

Supported by these sorts of statements in the encyclical, from the end of the 1940's there were many positive Roman statements on the use of the historical critical method in exegesis: the letter of the Secretary of the Biblical Commission to the Archbishop of Paris, Cardinal Suhard, of January 16th, 1948, two sections in the encyclical *Humani generis* from 1950, and above all the instruction of the Biblical Commission of April 21st, 1964, between the second and third sessions of the Council, at the high point of the fight about *Dei Verbum* and apparently with the intention of influencing the discussion.

The last-mentioned instruction was a reaction to the attack of the Roman theologian Antonino Romeo against the "new methods" in Catholic biblical studies in general and against the PBI in particular; this attack was published in the theological journal of the Lateran University, *Divinitas*. The author attempted, with an appeal to *Divino afflante Spiritu*, to halt the use of historical critical exegesis in Catholic theology. As our lengthy quote from the text indicates, this was not out-and-out absurd. The encyclical defended by means of the historical critical method the *truth* of the Bible as a source of Revelation in the completely conventional sense, while biblical scholars with the help of the very same method gained a completely new image of the Bible and a completely new understanding of what "Revelation" means. Romeo maintained that the German biblical scholars in particular spread a "northern fog," lacking the clarity of Mediterranean (Aristotelian) logic. One cannot imagine the scholarly and political feuds surrounding this essay. In his polite, still worth reading, but from today's perspective hardly "revolutionary" essay on "Exegesis and Dogmatics," Karl Rahner spoke of the "shameful and, for the dignity and reputation of Catholic scholarship, so harmful an article" authored by Romeo and remarked about "the northern fog" that "one can be a good Catholic even a few hundred kilometers distant from Rome." Rahner's hope that the German dogmatic theologians and bishops would defend themselves against such sweeping accusations was not fulfilled. Seen from the perspective of the universal Church, the instruction of the

Biblical Commission showed that relations were not what they were in 1943.

The second motive led, in terms of the conflict concerning *Dei Verbum* at the Council, to the fight surrounding the freedom of exegetical method that took place at the highest ecclesial level. This explains the bitterness. One knew: after this, whatever is decided, there is not a higher court to appeal to, in hope of revision.

4. TRADITION

The third motive was developments in the understanding of the concept of *Tradition*, the classical concept complementary to Scripture and Revelation. Once again we need to remember the 19th century. Under the influence of Romanticism, the Catholic Tübingen School conceived of Tradition as an organically developing event in which the once-and-for-all-time completed Revelation, in constantly new movement and confrontations with changing times, situations, and their spiritual challenges, adopts ever new and clearer form but, at the same time, by the power of the Holy Spirit, remains true to the non-negotiable origin. Since the same is in general valid for the Church, "tradition" is the living voice of the ever present Church. This concept amounts to a completely excessive counter-position to the Reformation's *Sola Scriptura* ("Scripture alone"). It was, albeit on the basis of a completely different understanding of Tradition, strengthened through the dogma of the "Immaculate Conception" (freedom from Original Sin, nothing else!) of Mary of 1854, a dogma with a very slight grounding in Scripture, so that it in essence therefore leans on Tradition. This is shown even more clearly, and following the model of argumentation developed in 1854, with the Marian dogma of 1950 (Mary's Assumption into Heaven), which does not refer to Scripture but "is based on the Sacred Writings" and "is completely in harmony with the other revealed truths." The Church has "expressed its own belief many times over the course of the centuries," and the teaching of the dogma "has been expounded and explained magnificently in the work, the science, and the wisdom of the theologians."

The situation for ecumenical dialogue could not have been more hopeless: here a *sola scriptura*, there a "living" Tradition, for which not just Scripture but even the historically provable extra-biblical Tradition was not a limitation. And still – so Ratzinger, correctly, in his commentary – there was an energy source for further questions. The question about "the Tradition" had shifted from a question about content ("material Tradition") to the question *about the criteria of Church doctrine.* "The tradition" in the prevailing understanding was a legitimizing criterion for Church proclamation. No Lutheran theologian, of course, could agree with this, but the fact that this question of criteria existed sufficed to connect the dialogue partners.

So the conviction gained increasing weight that the Scripture can be the *sole* concrete opponent to the Magisterium, as the sole place of real, Apostolic Tradition – because the Tradition in the now prevailing "organic," "dynamic" understanding is at the end of the day identical with the Magisterium itself. This conviction that the actual problem is not "Scripture and Tradition" but "Scripture and Magisterium" was strengthened through the sensational results of the investigation of the German theologian Josef Rupert Geiselmann from Tübingen concerning the relationship of Scripture and Tradition. Why sensational? From the time of the Council of Trent and its anti-Reformation decisions it was considered Catholic doctrine that Revelation is set down in two places, from which it can be drawn, as if from two springs: *In libris scriptis et sine scripto traditionibus* ("in written books and unwritten traditions"). Geiselmann proved on the basis of a study of the Council of Trent records: instead of the *et*, it ought to have read, originally: *partim – partim*, therefore "partly – "partly." That would indeed be the perfect "Two Source Theory," in view of Scripture and Tradition. It had its plausibility – in the end though in an anti-Reformation defensive – for the protection of innumerable Church teachings that are not so anchored word-for-word in the Scripture, for example, and above all, in doctrine on sacraments. According to Geiselmann, this writing of a simple "and," and not this "partly – partly," goes back to a few of the Trent Fathers who represented the thesis of Scripture as the sole standard. This is not as surprising as it might seem to Lutheran Christians; the criterion "Only the Scripture!" has a considerable tradition. After all, no less than Thomas Aquinas had represented the position: what is binding for faith is completely and expressly in the Scripture. When Tradition also has binding force and can make claims, this is never in the area of truths of the faith, of the *credenda,* but only in the realm of the *servanda,* that is, the ecclesial way of life. The tension of this concept, that everything actually binding in terms of faith is expressly in Scripture and can be drawn from no other source, remained undercover – as is indicated regarding certain beliefs in the doctrine on sacraments – until it became apparent through the Reformation.

Geiselmann's conclusion was: The Council of Trent did not *want* to decide this *new*, or newly raised, question. The at least one and a half centuries old classic Catholic Two Source Theory, which is presented as a given in textbooks on dogmatic theology, is an over-interpretation of the Tridentine texts. One can imagine the storm of discussion that swirled around Geiselmann's ideas, in the 60's. This discussion endures today – in favor of the openness of the question. This is a result of, not least of all, *Dei Verbum*. The history of this document's genesis is given very quickly in what follows.

5. THE GENESIS OF THE CONSTITUTION

In light of the prehistory of the document, the neuralgic points around the fight over *Dei Verbum* now become reasonable.

• The problem of the "inspiration" of the Bible, the doctrine that the Holy Scripture was written down because of the inspiration of the Holy Spirit: how is this inspiration of the Holy Spirit, and with this the divine surety for the truth of the Scripture to be understood, in light of the results of historical critical exegesis?

• The problem of the inerrancy of the Bible – if "inspiration" can no longer be thought about as simply as previously.

• The problem of the historical reliability of the Sacred Scripture, particular of the Gospels – if new ideas about "inerrancy" had to be allowed.

• The problem of the Church's interpretation of the Bible, of its forms and its binding nature.

• The question of the "sufficiency" of the Scripture, and indeed of the sufficiency of content as well as criteria – if the Church's interpretation of Scripture should not be a second "source of Revelation," in the end independent from the Scripture.

The first draft of the preparatory Theological Commission under Ottaviani, with Sebastian Tromp as secretary – the draft in which, as will be remembered, a chapter "On the Sources of Revelation" was planned – amounted to a re-hash of the Roman school theology. Of course it represented an advantage, with regards to content, of

Tradition vis-à-vis Scripture, of course it represented an idea of inspiration very close to a word-for-word inspiration through the Holy Spirit, of course it taught the inerrancy of the Scripture in the narrowest form, and simply assumed the historicity of the Gospels, in the sense of an historical report. Had this document been adopted, all attempts of Catholic theology to develop a new understanding of the concept of tradition would have been condemned, along with a large part of the endeavors of modern exegesis. The damage this would have caused Catholic theology in the following decades cannot be imagined.

It corresponds to the best conciliar tradition that councils do not have the task of deciding disputes, and do not decide disputes, between different theological schools. Many Council Fathers received exactly this impression, however, after the draft was made known to them, and soon displeasure and resistance arose. This was not lost on the members of the Preparatory Commission. They had to listen to complaints that they had broken with good conciliar custom – and the members of the Preparatory Commission defended themselves against this accusation. Looking at the matter from their perspective, they had a certain case. The members understood these school disputes to be the centuries-old "classical" disputes among "Thomism," "Scotism," "Molinism," the conflicts that arose in the late medieval period that became the norm for post-Reformation theology. These disputes enjoyed the protection of free discussion – but whatever went beyond this were not themes of these school disputes, but "innovations."

Ratzinger correctly opined that it was first at the Council and through the Council that it became generally known that the old theological schools had been removed by new school curricula, and that the "innovations" are legitimate questions and themes for the work of Catholic theology: "First in this manner was the historical-critical exegesis clearly recognized as an independent theological conversation partner in the entirety of Catholic theology."

In any case: the title of this chapter, a quote of a remark by Cardinal Liénart, refers to this particular draft of the Preparatory Commission. It was put to the vote that required two-thirds majority for a cessation of discussion, but that number was not achieved; this has already been reported on in another context. In the Commission that was charged with the re-working of the draft, representatives of both directions were present in the Presidency (Ottaviani and Bea) and in the Secretariat (Tromp and Umberto Betti); both directions were also represented among the members – they were condemned to unity.

Altogether there were eight versions of the Constitution. The "conservatives" were strongly resistant, employing delaying tactics. In the Theological Commission eventually two drafts existed, which would be represented separately in the General Congregation of the Council. The majority decided *against* the conservatives, but this did not end their resistance. As in other instances, once again Pope Paul VI had to intercede, with concessions to conciliate the conservatives.

One could not, of course, deceive them. In plain language: the final formulations – which finally, with only six "anti" votes, were accepted by the Council in the last session, that is, in the eighth solemn session on the 18th of November, 1965 – are in all the neuralgic points flexible formulations that both sides could interpret to their advantage – and did so. We'll take a look at the statements of *Dei Verbum* now.

III. WHAT EMERGED?

1. THE MOST IMPORTANT STATEMENTS OF DEI VERBUM

The following comments are best read with the text of *Dei Verbum* close at hand – so that we do not have to quote the text in full, but can limit ourselves to a few, particularly characteristic, sentences.

a. "The pattern of this revelation unfolds through deeds and words which are intrinsically connected: the words performed by God in the history of salvation show forth and confirm the doctrine and realities signified by the words; the words, for their part, proclaim the works, and bring to light the mystery they contain" (Article 2; see Article 4). This statement agrees wholeheartedly with a tendency in Catholic theology to understand the concept "revelation" as a self-communication of God, not – neo-Scholastically – in the sense of a "model of instruction," as explanation or even communication of dogmas.

b. An understanding of the "obedience of faith" (Rom 16:26; cf. 1:5; 2 Cor 10:5-6) corresponds to this understanding of revelation. This "obedience of faith" must be our response to God who reveals. By faith one freely commits oneself entirely to God, making "the full submission of intellect and will to God who reveals, and willingly assenting to the revelation given by God" (Article 5). According to the exact wording of the text, faith is *also* an "assenting" to God's revelation, but much more than this. Both the new understanding of revelation and the thus-described understanding of faith meant a victory for the Council majority; this victory was relatively easy for the minority to accept.

c. The revelation brought to completion in Christ is now the source of all saving truth and moral teaching. To be particularly noted: revelation *is* source, it doesn't *have* one or more sources (Article 7). In this same article, the "inspiration" of the Holy Spirit, that is to say, the "inspiration" of the biblical authors is placed on the same level as what the Apostles mediated as the message of salvation, in that Christ's commission to the Apostles was faithfully fulfilled by the apostles "who handed on, by oral preaching, by their example, by their dispositions, what they themselves had received — whether from the lips of Christ, from his way of life and his works, or by coming to know it through the prompting of the holy Spirit." The metaphor of "mirror," however, takes the place of the concept of "source" of revelation: "This sacred tradition, then, and the sacred scripture of both Testaments, are like a mirror, in which the church, during its pilgrim journey here on earth, contemplates God, from who it receives everything, until such time as it is brought to see him face to face as he really is." This is recognizably a concession to the ideas of the minority, but easily accepted by the majority.

d. The apostolic preaching is "expressed in a special way in the inspired books" (Article 8). I do not know why this is so cautiously stated, since the Scripture "comprises," according to the text, "everything that serves to make the people of God live their lives in holiness and increase their faith" — a victory for the majority in the direction of "sufficiency" of Scripture, but the compromise in the wording is easily discernible.

e. There is real progress in the tradition, but only in *understanding*, through contemplation, study, insight, and spiritual experience (Article 8). Again a victory for the majority, through which, almost in contradiction to Article 7, it is emphasized: there cannot be, in the course of the"living tradition," new content of the faith.

f. "By means of the same tradition, the full canon of the sacred books is known to the church" (Article 8). The sole "independent" act of the tradition consists therefore in the witness to the canon of the Scripture. No one would contest this, and it is a sort of weapon for every Catholic theologian against a fundamentalist understanding, removed from history, of *Sola scriptura*.

g. Unity of and distinction between Scripture and Tradition are discussed in Articles 9 and 10, with phrasing rife with compromise: "sacred tradition and sacred scripture, then, are bound closely together, and communicate one with the other." Sacred Scripture is "the utterance of God," "tradition transmits in its entirety the word of God." Scripture and tradition "make up a single sacred deposit of the word of God, which is entrusted to the church." The task of giving an authentic interpretation of the word of God "whether in its written form or in the form of tradition, has been entrusted to the living teaching office of the church alone." However, this sentence then follows: "This magisterium is not superior to the word of God, but is rather its servant." And, finally, at the end, a phrase that bundles this all together, cutting off all discussion of criteria of distinction: "It is clear, therefore, that in the supremely wise arrangement of God, sacred tradition, sacred scripture and the magisterium of the Church are so connected and associated that one of them cannot stand without the others. Working together, each in its own way under the action of the one holy Spirit, they all contribute effectively to the salvation of souls." In the course of the struggle over the final form of the text, an addition, supported by Paul VI, was affixed to Article 9: "Thus it is that the church does not draw its certainty about all revealed truths from the holy scriptures alone. Hence, both scripture and tradition must be accepted and honored with equal devotion and reverence." It is understandable that this addition, which comes very close to the traditional "Two Source Theory," was important for the minority: there is no legitimate interpretation of Scripture without consideration of the tradition. This addition was acceptable to the majority because it established an advantage for tradition only in terms of criteria, not in terms of content. But: Scripture *alone* really does not give *sufficient* certainty about what has been revealed? And if Scripture does give sufficient certainty – the text allows this interpretation – why the advantage to the tradition? Can one be more certain than certain?

Except that the keyword is missing, in the wording of Article 10 the infallibility of the Church in *credendo*, of the Magisterium *in docendo* – that is, of the entire People of God in faith and of those called to official teaching in their proclamation of doctrine – is established: the theology-of-revelation basis of what in the Dogmatic Constitution on the Church's Article 12 is said about the sense of faith of the faithful.

h. In wording that took into account the feelings of the minority, in Articles 11 and 12 the historical-critical method is not only allowed, it is required. Attention to the literary character of the biblical books is no longer, as in *Divino afflante Spiritu*, understood defensively, but completely positively, because the word of God is accessible only through human words and human authors, who speak and write as members of their time and culture. This is why the inerrancy of the Bible can only be expressed in a Solomonic fashion: "Since, therefore, all that the inspired authors, or sacred writers, affirm should be rearded as affirmed by the holy Spirit, we must acknowledge that the books of scripture, firmly, faithfully and without error, teach that truth which God, for the sake of our salvation, wished to see confided to the sacred scriptures" (Article 11).

i. Similarly open wording is encountered in Articles 18 and 19, with regard to the question of the apostolic origin and the historical reliability of the Bible. As with the theme "inerrancy," the historical reliability of the Gospels is limited to that which "Jesus, the Son of God, while he lived among men and women really did and taught for their eternal salvation." Moreover, the biblical authors, "in writing the four Gospels, selected certain of the many elements which had been handed on, either orally or in written form; others they synthesized or explained with an eye to the situation of the churches. They retained the preaching style, but always in such a fashion that they have told us the authentic truth about Jesus" (Article 19). There is scarcely a Bible scholar who would want to contradict this summarizing statement.

2. THE FREEDOM OF THEOLOGY

We do not need to waste any more words on the unsatisfactory compromise character of *Dei Verbum* with regards to its theological and ecclesiological problems; these problems caused hurt and still cause hurt. The compromise wording amounted to providing the "pre-established harmony" between Scripture, Tradition, and Magisterium with a halo. The suspicion that suggests itself from outward appearance is groundless: that the Magisterium stands opposite to the rest of the Church and, against 2 Corinthians 1:24, strives to be lord over the faith of the Church. On the other hand, out of consideration of the minority, there was a deliberate avoidance of citation of a criterion by which it could really be tested whether the Magisterium actually fulfilled and fulfills this "harmony" – in other words: a possible conflict can only be left to the free play of powers in the hope of the effective guidance of the Holy Spirit. One can say with complete justification that that would be completely appropriate, and from its own nature theology has no other "weapon" except for argument, in the situation of a conflict with the Magisterium. But arguments must also have criteria, and to search for this contradicts, strictly speaking, the concept presented in *Dei Verbum*. Truly, one might still say: "I don't like this schema."

And yet, at the beginning, *Dei Verbum* generated positive commentary and hope for the future. Let us take a look at Josef Ratzinger's illuminating summary:

> A decisive piece of the history of the Council had, with this [the adoption of the Constitution on Revelation], found a conciliatory end. The text, solemnly proclaimed by the Pope on this day, carries of course the traces of its laborious history; it is the expression of varied compromises. But the basic compromise that carries the text is more than a compromise, it is a synthesis of great significance: the text binds loyalty to the tradition of the Church together with the 'yes' to science, and opens for faith the way into today's world. It does not abandon Trent or Vatican I, but nor does it mummify what was, because it knows that loyalty in spiritual matters can only be realized through ongoing appropriation. If we look at the entirety of what was achieved, one may safely say that the trials and tribulations of a struggle that lasted four years were not in vain.

Ratzinger was at that time 38 years old and Professor of Dogmatic Theology in Bonn; he was a theological advisor to Cardinal Frings. After the Council Ratzinger – after positions as Professor in Tübingen and Regensburg and Archbishop in Munich – was the Prefect for the Congregation on the Doctrine of the Faith in Rome, and one has to ask oneself if the Ratzinger of 1993 would still maintain this opinion. It seems unlikely. But that can remain open, since at least as a judgment on *Dei Verbum* Ratzinger's position even then may have been much too optimistic.

His German Tübingen colleague, Max Seckler, a few years after the close of the Council, had taken on the frustrating task of investigating how the task of theology was described in the relevant statements of Pope Pius XII and Pope Paul VI – no such statements, interestingly enough, exist from Pope John XXIII – and whether there are any differences. The result of this investigation, collected by Seckler with chilly objectivity and hence even more depressing, can be summarized as follows:

a. The Revelation, the *depositum fidei* ("deposit of faith"), is entrusted for explanation *only* to the Magisterium, above all to the Pope as the successor of Peter and the representative of Christ.

b. It is not only teachings on faith and morals in a narrow understanding that belong to the Magisterium, but all areas of knowledge and action that intersect with the realm of faith or even just touch on it, from medicine to political questions to the artistic character of music.

c. In this world the voice of the Pope and the voice of Christ are identical, on the strength of the particular help of the Holy Spirit.

d. From this follows an encompassing right of inquisition, taxation, and supervision – reaching to surveillance of theology.

e. The Magisterium is in its area of subject the internal norm of theological work, formally and in terms of content, and indeed the nearest and general norm of the truth.

f. Theology then can only be practiced by means of "delegation." The office, especially the Pope, "delegates" its teaching function to theologians, these never teach on the strength of their own right or their own theological insight. They provide assistance for the actual teachers, that is, teacher, of the Church, and their task is to prove *how* – not *that* – the proclamation of the Magisterium in exactly the sense that it is issued is contained in the sources of revelation. It is not even allowed that a theologian might privately hold an opinion different from what is expressed by the Magisterium, unless the Magisterium had not yet expressed itself on the subject. Seckler remarked in his conclusions that with this concept the theory had caught up with the praxis. He was right. It remains only to emphasize that this concept, devised on the basis of the First Vatican Council, not corrected by the Second Vatican Council, theoretically as well as practically can assert itself up to the limit of the feasible and extends like a red flag through all the post-conciliar Magisterium documents, particularly those that are most controversial in the public. From this position "Rome" up to today has not deviated. Pope John Paul II, during his first visit to Germany in 1980, did indeed make remarks about the freedom of theological research that caused people to sit up and take notice and stirred astonishment. But the theologians were well advised not to build too high houses on this. The 1990 "Instruction of the Congregation for the Doctrine of the Faith on the Ecclesial Vocation of the Theologian" did indeed avoid the idea of "delegation," shows noticeable feelings for the distress of a theologian in a conflict with the Magisterium, and repeats also, at least with regard to the past, the "concession" formulated in the context of the conflict concerning Hans Küng: ecclesial doctrinal formulae carry traces of the time of their development, and therefore are not helpful in the same way for every time period. But in the "hard kernel" – that there is no actual working cooperation, if necessary quarrelsome cooperation, of Magisterium and theology, but only here the official proclamation of doctrine and there theology, duty bound to internal and external obedience even vis-à-vis the not formally dogmatized official doctrine of the Church. Strictly speaking, not even the painstaking compromise of *Dei Verbum* is retained.

So the balance remains: the greatest service of *Dei Verbum* is that it kept open the question of Scripture and Tradition and their relationship to Magisterium in all the decisive questions – that is, it did not decide – exactly like at Trent. In view of the – in distinction from Trent – idea, represented only by the minority, but supported by ecclesial theory and praxis, of a "pre-established harmony" of Scripture, Tradition, and Magisterium, controlled through nothing, this was the most that could be achieved: to have texts that one might cite, when one is of a different opinion than "Rome" or other "doctrinal offices." The right to this must be constantly fought for and – as the "Cologne Declaration" of January, 1989, signed by hundreds of theologians from around the world, shows – the risk is that the struggle for this right is branded as an attack on the authority of the Magisterium.

This is not without logic. Because the representatives of the ecclesial understanding of theology were of course clear sighted enough to see: the historical critical method *could* not remain solely with exegesis, but also would be used in the investigation and appreciation of the dogmatic tradition. Then the "harmony" claimed in *Dei Verbum* would be at stake – with uncertain outcome. How "protestant" ought Catholic theology to become was the very clear sighted, yet skeptical question. Prominent and unknown theologians have received the consequences of this clear sightedness.

CHAPTER NINE

"PERFIDI JUDAEI"?

CHURCH, ISRAEL, AND
NON-CHRISTIAN RELIGIONS

I. A GOOD FRIDAY BEFORE THE COUNCIL

Good Friday, 1962: a Cardinal celebrated, in the presence of Pope John XXIII, the Good Friday liturgy. Was it carelessness or was it a conscious obstruction? In any case, the Cardinal prayed the Good Friday Prayer for the Jews according to the old liturgical form: *Oremus et pro perfidis Judaeis* – "Let us pray also for the faithless Jews: … Almighty and eternal God, who dost not exclude from thy mercy even Jewish faithlessness: hear our prayers …." John interrupted the Cardinal: "Say that again, but according to the new form!"

Already on March 27th, 1959, on the first Good Friday of his pontificate, John had caused these painful words to be obliterated from the liturgical text, and on the 5th of July, 1959, the Congregation of Rites (today: Congregation for Divine Worship and the Discipline of the Sacraments) issued an order that this change was valid not only in the churches in Rome, but for the universal Church. Today the text reads: "Let us pray for the Jewish people, the first to hear the word of God, that they may continue to grow in the love of his name and in faithfulness to his covenant. Almighty and eternal God, long ago you gave your promise to Abraham and his posterity. Listen to your Church as we pray that the people you first made your own may arrive at the fullness of redemption. We ask this through Jesus our Lord. Amen."

These sentences and the picture presented of Israel, the People of God, are a clear consequence of the Council, today no longer criticized by anyone. This new formula made it possible that today Jewish and Christian theologians can dispute about Jesus exegetically and theologically without suspicion or resentment. And this, according to the history of the Council, is the result of the personal initiative of John XXIII.

II. THE PREHISTORY OF THE DECLARATION ON THE RELATIONSHIP OF THE CHURCH TO NON-CHRISTIAN RELIGIONS

1. JOHN XXIII AND THE JEWS

In the same year, 1959, a change was made in the text from the "Prayer of Consecration of the Human Race to the Sacred Heart of Jesus." This prayer came from Pope Leo XIII, and under Pope Pius XI the following sentences were included: "Look finally full of mercy on the children of the people *who formerly were the chosen*. May the blood that once was called down upon them flow over them as a bath of salvation and of life." John had this sentence removed. Moreover, "formerly" is an incorrect translation for the Latin *tamdiu*; even the correct translation, "so long," contradicts Rom 11:29, according to which God's gifts and God's call are irrevocable. The understanding of Matt 27:25 in the traditional sense as a self-cursing of the entire people, to which the prayer alludes, is weakened today by exegesis: either this text is not historical, but mirrors the beginning anti-Jewish polemic in the New Testament – the Gospel of Matthew is written after 70, with a backward view to the destruction of Jerusalem – or the text is, historically possible, to be understood in the sense that the Zealots, cheated of their hopes, abandoned Jesus.

As is well known, John XXIII was, before his elevation to Patriarch of Venice, in the diplomatic service of the Curia. During the time of the Nazis Roncalli was working in Bulgaria and in Turkey. Not only did he receive information there about the Third Reich's persecutions of the Jews, these persecutions were carried out in front of his eyes by the Nazis and their sympathizers. Roncalli helped with the utmost commitment, and personally – he never left such matters to a secretary. He saved thousands, and hindered deportations out of Slovakia, Hungary, and Bulgaria. Jews have never forgotten that.

So Jews also had hopes for the Council; initiatives from the Jewish world coincided, time-wise, with those of the Pope. But the prehistory makes it seem more likely that a Declaration on the Jews was the intention of the Pope from the beginning. The groundwork was laid, and then came the Jewish initiatives. In any event: on the 18th of September, 1960, the Pope issued the assignment orally to Cardinal Bea, to prepare a Declaration on the Jews with the Secretariat for Christian Unity. He did not establish a separate commission for this, in order not to add to the number of commissions, of which there were already enough, and because he had particular trust in Bea's abilities in this delicate area. With this the history of the text began.

2. INITIATIVES IN THE FOREFRONT

On the 13th of September, 1960, the French Jewish historian Jules Isaac visited the Pope – with a letter of introduction from the Archbishop of Aix-en-Provence. The visitor asked, without beating around the bush, for an appropriate action of the Council. "May I have hope?" John: "You have reason to have more than hope." The Pope added, ominously, that the matter required study from the responsible parties. "What you see here is not an absolute monarchy."

Already on the 24th of April, 1960 – so before Isaac's visit – the Roman Biblical Institute, led by the Jesuits, made a corresponding application to the Preparatory Central Commission.

Around the same time the Institute for Judaeo-Christian Studies at Seton Hall University in New Jersey composed a petition and sent it on June 24th, 1960, to Cardinal Bea.

At a conference from the 28th to the 31st of August, a working group passed a memorandum. In this group the experts and lawyers of the Christian-Jewish collaboration in Europe were gathered together, above all from Germany, Holland, and France, but also with representatives from Israel and the USA. This memorandum was also sent, a few weeks after the conference, to the Secretariat for Christian Unity. As a draft for a declaration it was too bulky and for this reason did not have much of an immediate effect, but the final text of the Council agrees completely with its perspectives.

3. THE CENTRAL CONCERNS

All of these initiatives pursued two central concerns: first, a political one, the condemnation of anti-Semitism, along with an admission of the Church's guilt with respect to anti-Semitism's Christian roots; second, a theological concern, that is, a positive doctrinal statement to the effect that the Church must never forget its roots in Israel. The eleventh chapter of the Letter to the Romans must finally be taken seriously, and all the opposing statements, formulations, and practices in instruction, liturgy, theology, and matters of Church politics must be corrected. In detail, these doctrinal statements should point out:

- the *lasting* election of Israel;
- the guilt of *all* sinners for the death of Jesus;
- the urgent necessity of rejecting the charge of *deicide*, not only for Jews at the time of Jesus but also for Jews of the post-Christ periods;
- the eschatological unification of Israel with the Church in faith in Jesus according to Rom 11:26-29 as the hope of the Church;
- finally, the roots of the Church in the people of Israel: Jesus, Mary, the Apostles, and the witnesses to the Resurrection, so the founding generation of the Church, were all Jews, and they are the pillars and bases of the Church.

One can and should say all this without trying to wiggle out of the fundamental Christological difference that Christians believe Jesus to be the Messiah who has come, while Jews still wait for the coming Messiah.

III. THE PASSION OF THE TEXT

1. FROM THE ASSIGNMENT TO THE FIRST DRAFT

Up to this point there has been no discussion of what is joined with the chapter on the Jews in the "Declaration on the Relationship of the Church to Non-Christian Religions" (*Nostra Aetate*): the other non-Christian religions. That these other religions are considered in the same text with the Jews is connected with the above-mentioned history of the text. In the end, the result could not have been better, at least in terms of Church politics, which must not discount further theological questions. The scandalous history of the Declaration on the Jews in the end not only led to the inclusion of the other religions in the text, in opposition to all the preparatory drafts, but it also brought even more attention to the section of the Declaration that deals with the Jews, against the endeavors of the opponents of the text, and in the end secured the text the status of an independent document, which had not been planned originally. *Nostra Aetate* is consequently a real achievement of the Council – as is actually also *Dei Verbum*, which also had a strong Old Testament central focus. All this is now to be related in detail.

On the 14ᵗʰ and 15ᵗʰ of November the members and consulters of the Secretariat for Christian Unity met for the first time on this matter. Cardinal Bea reported on the oral assignment from the Pope. A Sub-Commission was formed for the *Quaestiones de Judaeis* ("Questions concerning the Jews"). Members were: the Abbott Leo Rudloff (Jerusalem), Gregory Baum from the Secretariat for Christian Unity, and Prelate Johannes Oesterreicher, the Director of the Institute at Seton Hall University – the principal author of the text in all stages of its redaction. The work began in February, 1961.

A prelude to the first scandal: a journalist could not resist the temptation of publishing as an interview a private conversation she had had with Cardinal Bea. This is how the Arab nations learned for the first time something of the plan of the Secretariat for Christian Unity; this led to interventions. It was feared that an interest and a particular friendship of Christians/Catholics vis-à-vis the Jews would lead to an interest and a particular friendship vis-à-vis the state of Israel and therefore would lead to the international revaluation of Israel to the detriment of the Arabs – it needs to be taken into consideration that we were in the year 1961 and the Arab world was still hoping that the state of Israel would not be able to establish itself on firm footing. The Vatican reacted uncertainly, and made attempts to calm the situation, but it was never said clearly enough: the Declaration is important for the Church, and political pressure cannot be allowed to exert influence. Actually the opposite: for a while it seemed doubtful that a theological statement about the Jews would actually come about, but that appropriate statements would simply be "distributed" among other documents.

Nonetheless the work proceeded. Oesterreicher produced a study that caused a detailed discussion in the Secretariat and was finally developed into a first draft in December, 1961. This text is so short; I would like to quote it in full:

> The Church, the Bride of Christ, acknowledges with a heart full of gratitude that, according to God's mysterious saving design, the beginnings of her faith and election go as far back as to the Israel of the Patriarchs and Prophets. Thus she acknowledges that

all Christian believers, children of Abraham by faith (see Gal 3:7), are included in his call. Similarly, her salvation is prefigured in the deliverance of the Chosen People out of Egypt, as in a sacramental sign (Liturgy of the Easter Vigil). And the Church, a new creation in Christ (see Eph 2:15), can never forget that she is the spiritual continuation of the people with whom, in His mercy and gracious condescension, God made the Old Covenant.

The Church, in fact, believes that Christ, who "is our peace," embraces Jews and Gentiles with one and the same love and that He made the two one (see Eph 2:14). She rejoices that the union of these two "in one body" (Eph 2:16) proclaims the whole world's reconciliation in Christ. Even though the greater part of the Jewish people has remained separated from Christ, it would be an injustice to call this people accursed, since they are greatly beloved for the sake of the Fathers and the promises made to them (see Rom 11:28). The Church loves this people. From them sprang Christ the Lord, who reigns in glory in heaven; from them sprang the Virgin Mary, mother of all Christians; from them came the Apostles, the pillars and bulwark of the Church (1 Tim 3:15).

Furthermore, the Church believes in the union of the Jewish people with herself as an integral part of Christian hope. With unshaken faith and deep longing the Church awaits union with this people. At the time of Christ's coming, "a remnant chosen by grace" (Rom 11:5), the very first fruits of the Church, accepted the Eternal Word. The Church believes, however, with the Apostle that at the appointed time, the fullness of the children of Abraham according to the flesh will embrace him who is salvation (see Rom 11:12, 26). Their acceptance will be life from the dead (see Rom 11:15).

As the Church, like a mother, condemns most severely injustices committed against innocent people everywhere, so she raises her voice in loud protest against all wrongs done to Jews, whether in the past or in our time. Whoever despises or persecutes this people does injury to the Catholic Church.

Just a year before the opening of the Council all systems seemed "go" for a frictionless debate at the Council. In the summer of 1962, something happened that threatened the whole process.

2. THE SO-CALLED WARDI AFFAIR

On the 12th of June, 1962, the Jewish World Congress scored in their own goal – it can scarcely be described in any other way. Doctor

Nahum Goldman, the president of the Congress, announced that the Congress would send Dr. Chaim Wardi, an official in the Israeli Ministry for Religious Affairs, as the representative of the World Congress "to Rome." Wardi was extremely well qualified for the assignment in Rome: he was an expert in Christianity, had been an observer at the Congress of the World Council of Churches in New Delhi, in 1961, and was responsible, in the Ministry, for the Christians in Israel. But:

> • An official representative of the Jewish World Congress to Rome, without previous agreement with the partner in the public crosshairs – the rationalizing explanation, that the World Congress, according to its tradition, considered representatives in the most important capital cities to be important, did not help. The Vatican felt itself diplomatically snubbed, since obviously Wardi was supposed to "observe" at the Council. But no religious community had named observers for the Council without having been invited to do so beforehand.

> • Above all, though: an official of the state of Israel at the Council – that is the confirmation of all the Arab suspicions that the Council would produce a pro-Israel declaration, in the political sense.

The newspaper reports on the matter were unclear and unhelpful – and no one corrected them. For a time the Arab leaders presupposed that the affair was a pre-arranged game between the Vatican and Israel. Again there were diplomatic attacks. Result: the Central Commission took the Declaration off the agenda of the Council, for an undetermined time. However, the public opinion in the entire world – this is the good result of this and other affairs – had become so sensitive that it was impossible to bury the theme quietly. On the evening before the opening of the Council, the Head Rabbi of Rome spoke an admonishing word. Bishops of the Council like Méndez from Arceo in Mexico urged that the theme not be circumvented. Cardinal Bea composed an urgent memorandum to the Pope.

Pope John XXIII reacted positively in a letter to the Council. Bea undertook the necessary steps with the Coordinating Commission of the newly opened Council. And so the first change resulted: the Declaration on the Jews would now become part of the Decree on Ecumenism – as the 4th chapter of this Decree, introduced with a short mention of non-Christian religions, under which the Jewish faith would occupy a special place for the Church. That was, as the developments showed, nothing short of providential. First, though, there was further turbulence.

3. FROM THE DECREE ON ECUMENISM
TO THE DECLARATION

It is a fascinating idea, to extend the perspective of ecumenism to Judaism. In the time following the decision to include the Declaration on the Jews in the Decree on Ecumenism, there was a lively theological discussion at the Council and on the periphery of the Council, a discussion in which the people from the Secretariat for Christian Unity strongly supported this idea. On the other hand, the planned insertion of the Declaration on the Jews into the Decree on Ecumenism opened up fronts of resistance.

As we have already mentioned, each draft was the subject of a general discussion on whether or not the schema should be accepted as the basis for the discussion. The representatives of the Arab Christians, among whom was included Patriarch Maximos IV, otherwise so important as a voice of the Eastern Church, used this protocol in order, already in this general debate on the Ecumenism schema, to polemicize against the fourth chapter, the Declaration on the Jews. The members of the Secretariat for Christian Unity could not defend themselves, since it was a general discussion, not yet focused on the individual chapters. The – objectively seen – most cunning political argument made in this debate was: the Church had, in the time of the persecution of the Jews by the Nazis, made its views sufficiently clear; nothing more needed to be said. On other occasions issues that would render the situation of the Church in other countries more difficult had been avoided, why not here? The Islamic governments in the Arab lands should not be unnecessarily challenged. Arab politics yielded results, and some of the Council Fathers might have thought: if consideration is given to eastern block countries, then that consideration is also appropriate for countries in the Islamic world.

There was also a theological argument against the insertion of a Declaration on the Jews into the Ecumenism Decree, an argument that was difficult to dismiss – again, presented by Patriarch Maximos: "Ecumenism is the striving toward the re-unification of the whole

Christian family, that is, the reconciliation of all who are baptized in Christ. It is a matter, therefore, of intimate family concern; if this is so, then non-Christians do not belong." The likewise valid, but completely opposite argument followed later: either a statement about all non-Christian religions or no statement at all – the first option happened.

To make it short: the matter ended at the second session with, once again, postponement; the Council Secretariat once again resorted to stalling tactics. Despite urgent petitions to carry out a general vote over the – still – fourth chapter of the Ecumenism Decree as an accepted basis for discussion, and although Cardinal Bea had the opportunity to plead his case, neither discussion nor vote was allowed.

Only later did the reason for this stalling become known, a reason known to very few in the Fall of 1963: from January 4th to January 6th, 1964, Pope Paul VI undertook his spectacular pilgrimage to Israel. At that time, the Old City of Jerusalem was still sovereign territory of the King of Jordan. One can still see, from old television footage, how the Pope moved from the Old City into the Israeli New City, and was received at the gate by the Israeli president. Given this diplomatically risky trip it is understandable why no one wanted to endanger the trip in one or the other direction a few weeks earlier, with a vote on the Declaration on the Jews at the Council.

The Pope's trip to Israel made a huge impression – but it was also accompanied by vehement Arab polemic against Israel, including in Jordanian broadcasts. The Pope could express himself as diplomatically as possible – it was always too little or too much. The blockade effect for the revised version – the third draft – soon evinced itself: the Declaration on the Jews would not be the fourth chapter of the Decree on Ecumenism, but just an appendix to that decree. Along with this, a number of weakenings of wording, omissions of offensive formulations, etc., were pushed through. But as many times before, these weakenings became the incentive to new, intensive debate and work. We arrive now at the actual and decisive debate, which took place in Fall of 1964.

There was good reason for this debate to take occur: the text of the third version had been widely publicized, and while again the consequences were misunderstandings and suspicious misrepresentations, real weaknesses in the text were also brought to light. Overly emphatic formulations of the hope for the eschatological unity of the

Church with Israel were heard by Jews as demands for conversion and as proselytizing. The great debate was opened by an explanation of the German Bishops, in which, among other things, the following was stated: "We German bishops welcome the Decree particularly, because we are conscious of the heavy injustice that was committed against the Jews in the name of our people." The debate brought the breakthrough. It became clear: the overwhelming majority of the Council, particularly the most important leaders, was in favor of the Declaration on the Jews with regards to the content. There were only a few opposing voices, which we will here ignore.

The overwhelming agreement of the Council led to far-reaching corrections – or better, in view of the previous weakening, corrections of corrections – of the third version, which must have been welcomed by the version's authors. The debate continued despite the "October crisis." The Arab opponents of the Declaration at the Council – above all, Maximos – made the untenable assumption that the Declaration and its approval through the majority of the Council were the results of the propaganda machine of the Jews. Moreover, according to Maximos, the strong endorsement of the Declaration from the American bishops in particular had to do with their good business relationships with American Jews. To say it plainly: the majority of the Council was "bought." Maximos later regretted his statements. Nonetheless, in a communiqué, he distanced himself from the Declaration with the following reason: "So long as the Jewish people remain distant from Christ, the Savior, there is on the forehead of the Jewish people, as the prophets of the Old Testament have prophesied, a mark of shame. This mark is not, however, the same as a personal crime." The Patriarch was not in the position to give a citation from the prophetic books of the Old Testament to this effect: there is none.

At the same time the political pressure continued – and also the pressure from the other theological opponents. The Secretary of State, Cardinal Cicognani, who obviously was particularly beset by all this political pressure, committed to a critical step. On the 9th of October, 1964, a plenary session of the Secretariat for Christian Unity was held. Cardinal Bea read out two letters from Cardinal Felici, the Secretary of the Council, again "in higher instruction" – this time not from the Pope but, one must suppose, from Cicognani. The first letter contained the information that the Declaration on *Religious Freedom* must once more be examined by a mixed commission – up to that point it had been planned as the fifth chapter of the Decree on Ecumenism, but now it was to become the second appendix of the Decree! The *Declaration on the Jews* had to be examined by a six-man committee, which had not yet been formed.

The main goal of Cardinal Cicognani's initiative was obviously to wrest the responsibility for both Declarations away from the Secretariat for Christian Unity. In the case of the Declaration on Religious Freedom, the mixed commission contained a majority of opponents – one notices: we are in the sphere of "Black Thursday," the day on which the conflicts around the Declaration on Religious Freedom played such a significant role. In the case of the Declaration on the Jews, the new committee was to consist of three members of the Secretariat for Christian Unity and three members of the Theological Commission.

The whole thing was once more an attempt to circumvent the Council protocol and thus the Council majority – and in this case, not on the authority of the Pope. The shot, however, backfired: Cardinal Bea protested immediately and appealed to the Pope. The Pope explained there had been a conversation about a mixed commission, but nothing had been decided. Cicognani's letter, then, was a definite attempt to stage a *coup*. As this became known, important Bishops gathered around Cardinal Frings and sent a petition to the Pope (*Magno cum dolore*, "with great distress"), in which they complained about the damage to the rules and regulations of the Council. This helped. Paul VI seems to have understood that his authority was also at risk, if one could so unscrupulously juggle with the "higher authority." In addition, vis-à-vis the Declaration on the Jews, it was helpful that along with the suggestion to form a six member commission – rejecting this was not so easy – there was another suggestion, tied to the first, to shorten the Declaration on the Jews to a single paragraph and to incorporate it into the Dogmatic Constitution on the Church. Pope Paul VI could not, after his Israel trip, allow this. He appears to have assured Bea that the Declaration would not be shortened. Besides: where would the "Jewish paragraph" be placed, in the almost finished Dogmatic Constitution on the Church? So the Theological Commission refused to deal with the Declaration on the Jews – and this was its salvation.

4. EXPANSION TO THE DECLARATION ON RELIGIONS

Already in 1963 and then again in 1964, particularly the Council Fathers from the Third World had asked that the new consciousness about the Jews be extended to all non-Christians. The Secretariat for Christian Unity hesitated at first, because of lack of expertise in the area, but after the great debate appointed working groups that were to make suggestions. Stimulus came also from the outside – from the Institute of Judaeo-Christian Studies at Seton Hall University. The driving force for this was, as with the *Declaration on the Jews*, once more the Pope, Paul VI. In his addresses and in his encyclical *Ecclesiam suam*, from August 6th, 1964, the theme of the search for God in all religions occurs time and again. This problem was extremely urgent in view of the Pope's trip to Bombay, for the Eucharistic Congress, planned for after the third session, in December of 1964. There the Pope would make a speech in front of representatives of non-Christian religions, here particularly of Hinduism. In this speech we find the following:

> Yours is a land of ancient culture, the cradle of great religions, the home of a nation that has sought God with a relentless desire, in deep meditation and silence, and in hymns of fervent prayer. Rarely has this longing for God been expressed with words so full of the spirit of Advent as in the words written in your sacred books many centuries before Christ: "From the unreal lead me to the real; from darkness lead me to light; from death lead me to immortality" (*Br.* 1, 3, 28). This is a prayer which belongs also to our time.

Such sentences were used in the Declaration, not yet voted on but at the time of the Pope's speech in its fourth version. With this recognition of religious experience in all religions the draft entered its decisive stage – but not yet out of danger!

In brief: the draft got caught in the maelstrom of "Black Thursday," when the Declaration on Religious Liberty was not allowed to be debated and the Pope did not acquiesce to urgent petitions for the adoption of the document in the third session. The vote on the Declaration on Non-Christian Religions started out, in terms of protocol, positively – but with noticeably weak participation (fewer than 2000 Council Fathers). The world press rejoiced, although it was just the vote in the General Congregation, not the decisive vote in the solemn session, with subsequent implementation. But at the same time the "holy war" against the Declaration began: broadcast polemics in the Arab world, demonstrations of Orthodox Christians with the intent to exploit the troubled position of the Catholics for the advantage of the non-uniate Eastern Churches, inflammatory writings of the sort not thought possible anymore, reports about persecutions of Christian minorities in the Middle East. The few calm and objective Arab voices were hardly heard. There was again an advisory session in the Secretariat for Christian Unity. Again the urge to weaken the text grew stronger, even to remove it from the agenda. From Spring to Fall of 1965, one discouraging report followed the other. Conservative backbenchers got publicity for themselves by opposing the Declaration – and were described in the world press as representative of the mood of the Council. Even the Pope appeared in an unfavorable light, because of some unfortunate phrases in a homily on Passion Sunday. In the voting phase the Council Fathers received suggestions for a negative vote from *Coetus Episcoporum Internationalis*, a group of ultra-conservative bishops who often did this sort of thing.

On the 14th and 15th of October, 1965, the last vote took place in the General Congregation, on the 28th of October was the solemn vote in the session, which was connected to the promulgation. The result: 2221 yes votes, 88 no votes, and 3 invalid votes.

IV. THE CONTENT OF THE DECLARATION

1. THE CHURCH AND NON-CHRISTIAN RELIGIONS

We said: given the situation, the Declaration could not have been better, objectively and in terms of content, than it became in the course of the scandal-ridden prehistory. The Declaration on the Jews is embedded in a new type of declaration on the relationship of the Church to *all* non-Christian religions. That allows opportunity, immediately in the first article of the text, to put on record the Church's changed perception of these. Earlier the Church had only turned to the individual members of a religion in so far as they were the target group of a mission. Now the Church defined expressly its relationship to non-Christian religions as a whole. Earlier the Church had defined this relationship to the "pagans" in view of Jesus' "great commission" (Matt 28:18-20). Now as the motive for the Declaration the task of the Church was specifically cited as "fostering unity and love among individuals, and even among nations." The usual apologetic "missionary" way to characterize the relation has not been chosen.

Along the lines of the Pope's address in Bombay, in the second article an important recognition of the experience of God in all religions is articulated, a recognition that in no way denies the self-understanding of the Church and nevertheless avoids any behavior amounting to an "entitlement." Again it is important to notice what is *not* said. The old opinion that the Church has to exert itself to make everyone a Church member is not taken up. Catholics were admonished to seek dialogue and cooperation with the adherents of other religions, to recognize, protect, and promote their spiritual and moral good and cultural worth, and *in this way* to give witness to their own faith. The statements of this article must be read in light of the statements of the Dogmatic Constitution on the Church (Article 16), the Decree on Missions (Article 7), and the Pastoral Constitution on the Church in the Modern World (Article 22), where in each case it is emphasized that people who have not been reached by the message of Christianity, even atheists, can achieve salvation in ways known to God himself. One cannot support such an optimism of salvation and then disqualify the non-Christian religions as being distant from God. The Church, if it thinks like this, must find consequences of the salvation that it proclaims in other religions; in other words: the Church must recognize that people live out their concrete relationship with God also in other religions. The Church's task, then, is to proclaim Jesus Christ unceasingly, in whom, according to the words of the text, "people find the fullness of their religious life" and "in whom God reconciled all things to himself."

The Council did not indicate concrete ways for the recommended dialogue. And that is because of, seen from the perspective of today, an absolutely astonishing reason: there were no experts in this field. Until the time of the Council, advocates for "interreligious dialogue" were solitary voices in the wilderness. There were in the Church, moreover, very few authorities on individual non-Christian religions, and the majority of these authorities had devoted themselves to this dialogue on biographical grounds: conversion to Christianity, living in a non-Christian country. So it happens that – and this is noticeable just by a look at the table of contents – the editors of the commentated edition of the texts of the Council in the supplementary volumes of the German dictionary *Lexikon für Theologie und Kirche* could not find a commentator for the *entire* short text of *Nostra Aetate*, but were forced to look for individual commentators for various religions. This changed, of course, after the Council. *Nostra Aetate* gave real impetus to the endeavor of the theological study of world religions, and today we have a great number of experts who recognized at that time their opportunity to break new theological ground.

How meager the expert help was at the time of the composition of *Nostra Aetate* is particularly noticeable when one reads the few vague remarks made about Buddhism and Hinduism. Confucianism and Taoism are not even mentioned – certainly not because of the justified question of whether these are religions in the customary sense of the word or more systems for living wisely, but above all because they were "religions" of China, a completely sealed-off country at that time.

The third article, on Islam, is on somewhat surer footing, and the particular respect paid to Islam is a result of the fact that the Quran was written with a knowledge of both the Old and the New Testament, and Islam therefore, is often referred to in the scholarly world as one of the three "Abrahamic" religions.

As is evident, much remained to be accomplished after this text, and a great deal was tackled in the post-conciliar period. In the post-conciliar period some euphoric hopes came back down to earth. Not just because of the fundamentalist movements in the other religions, but also independent from this, interreligious dialogue is anything but easy. Objections, suspicion, danger is always at hand. So the "prayer for peace" of the Pope in Assisi on the 26th of October, 1986 was not *with* the representatives of all religions, but a *simultaneous* prayer of all religions, proposed by the Pope. On the one hand a clear consequence of *Nostra Aetate*, but, as the loud echo out of the whole world showed, also a real test.

2. CHURCH AND JUDAISM

We would not have had even this modest initial spark for the entry of the Church into interreligious dialogue if the political and theological complications surrounding the Declaration on the Jews had not necessitated a look at the world religions. One can start to ponder the peculiar ways of God with his Church, if one imagines how here once again and in part in a macabre way the most beautiful "universalist" perspectives of the Old Testament have helped Christendom to achieve a step forward: the history of the Church's guilt vis-à-vis the Jews, the wish for change and apology, connected with the theological insight that the relationship between Church and Judaism required a radical change of thought, opened the eyes of the Church to the world of other religions because of external and for the most part extra-theological circumstances of the Church. So of course the fourth article, which describes the relationship of the Church to the Jews, is the heart of the entire Declaration. It is best if one reads the article in an edition of the Council texts in comparison with the above quoted first draft. Then everything is easily understood, in light of the prehistory. One soon recognizes: all the important points from the first draft, all the listed requests, which were connected with the commitment for the Declaration, are taken up in the text, in part word-for-word repeated, partially even more urgently formulated. There are even important expansions. For example, the charge of "deicide" is expressly rejected. Theologians and preachers are instructed to do away with legends – for example, those of "ritual murder" of Christian children, as were often used to persecute the Jews in the Middle Ages – and with pseudo-theological arguments against the Jews when interpreting the Old Testament. How long it took in some places of the Church, also in Germany, until the Christians themselves or the ecclesial authority actually started this cleaning up work in earnest! The condemnation of anti-Semitism is articulated more clearly than in the first draft. All this is at the end, in all desirable clarity, grounded in that Christ, according to the proclamation of the Church, died for the sake of the sins of *all*, which radically rules out discrimination of particular people or groups of people, on whatever grounds.

The Declaration ends in the fifth article with the fundamental comment that the Christian faith in God, who had created humankind according to his own image, does not allow us to refuse to act in a brotherly way toward certain others. "Therefore there is no basis for any theory or practice which would introduce discrimination between individuals or people with respect to their human dignity or the rights that flow from it. Therefore, the church reproves, as foreign to the mind of Christ, any discrimination against people or any harassment of them on the basis of their race, color, condition in life or religion."

3. CHURCH AND RELIGIOUS LIBERTY

During the entire work on *Nostra Aetate*, the Declaration on Religious Liberty was also getting worked on, sometimes in direct contact. It begins with the phrase that occurs at the end of *Nostra Aetate*: "the dignity of the human person" (*Dignitatis Humanae*). The Declaration on Religious Liberty is considerably longer than *Nostra Aetate* because it deals with not only the external relationship of the Church, but at the same time must comprise a position on the relationship between Church and societal freedom, Church and freedom of conscience and finally Church and State.

Here we cannot deal with this declaration in detail, and we do not have to. Whoever reads the text today has the impression that one is reading self-evident truths. This is the case, and was the case at that time in many countries, above all in Europe and America. But it happened in many places, above all in the so-called traditional Catholic lands, that the Church, gnashing its teeth, bowed to the inevitable, but did not theoretically give up its claims and sought to assert itself practically as far as possible. On the "conservative" side of the Council Fathers the conviction continued as before: only the truth, not error, has a right to exist. Since now the Catholic Church – not on its own, but through the guidance of the Holy Spirit – possesses the full and infallible truth, there cannot be any right to error. Where then State and society is Catholic, the Church can demand that the State prevent the activity of non-Catholic and certainly non-Christian expression of opinion and mission and declare the Catholic Church as the State religion and act accordingly. Where the Catholics are the minority in a society and in a State, they may and must demand that the State, on the basis of natural law, guarantee the dissemination of Catholic doctrine.

It is understandable that this model of thinking provoked vehement fights. A rejection of this model meant no less than a farewell to the complete symbiosis of Church and State as it still existed at that time in certain countries (Spain, Italy, among others). No bishop from the United States, in the situation of complete separation of Church and State, could tolerate this model, however.

That under these conditions one as clearly as possible, but with consideration for the representatives of the "silent Church," turned, also as cautiously as necessary, against any State coercion (Article 4), caused of course few difficulties. More important is the fact that the old model of thinking was banished with the thoughtful beginning of the entire Declaration: neither truth nor error are bearers of rights, persons are. Because of their freedom, persons should not be coerced to faith, either through external or through internal manipulation – which is exactly the teaching of the tradition. The Declaration begins very consciously in the first section with a "General Principle of Religious Freedom," and in the second section makes the statements on "Religious Freedom in the Light of Revelation." In other words: in consideration of the public worth of its own teaching the Church disassociated itself from a desire to occupy a privileged status in comparison to other religions and world views. Faith can only be a conviction accepted in freedom. If one reads the texts of revelation in the light of this non-negotiable insight, then it is easy to see that these support the ideas of "religious freedom" and not of any authoritative model of thought. Of course one has at the same time the best basis with which to fight against the intolerance of other groups or state organs. But such tactical considerations are not the motivation of the Declaration – the motivation of the Declaration is the insight into that which its first few words mention: "the dignity of the human person."

What about the question of truth? What about the duty of the "free" conscience, to orient itself? In no place does the Declaration say that one can encounter the question of truth with indifference. The effect of the Declaration, if it is taken seriously, is much more to open up new space for free argumentation for the question of truth. Exactly this thread was taken up by the post-conciliar discussion.

CHAPTER TEN

"NOAH'S ARK"

THE CHURCH IN THE MODERN WORLD

I. A CONFLICT OF GOALS

To make this clear from the outset: "Noah's Ark" is not the Church, with the result that "the Modern World" would be the flood! The "Ark" is the pastoral constitution "On the Church in the Modern World"; it begins with the words *Gaudium et spes*, "joy and hope," the title by which even those with no knowledge of Latin refer to the constitution. Criticism rained down, as the editorial work on this constitution was in high gear between the second and third sessions and the result was sent to the Fathers in the summer of 1964. One critic coined the phrase "Noah's Ark," complaining that all the themes that could not find a place elsewhere were included in this constitution. But why were they not allowed to disappear in the flood? The answer is found in the context of the disagreements surrounding the goals of the Council, disagreements that characterized the Council from the very beginning.

We must hearken back to the problems mentioned earlier that dogged the setting of goals for the Council, and to the public discussion around these goals. When John XXIII announced the Council, he did so as a sign of unity. He meant the unity of Christians – *Catholic* Christians – for the aim of a witness to the world. Unity therefore was for all practical purposes assigned to the witness to the world. When he was a diplomat in the countries of Eastern Europe, Roncalli had internalized the significance of Christian unity beyond the borders of the Catholic Church. When he was Patriarch of Venice he was confronted with the concrete questions and needs of the modern (industrial) world. This resulted in the two baselines of Roncalli's thought:

unity and world – and in the sense: unity for the sake of the world. The goal was the opening to the modern world, and unity was the means and the source of strength. We already saw, with our presentation of the statements of the Council concerning the unity of the Church, how that was thoroughly misunderstood. On the one side, there was the pressure that the unity of the separated Christians had to be an independent aim of the Council. Symptomatic of this view were two books of Hans Küng from the early 1960's, *The Council, Reform and Reunion* and *The Living Church: Reflections on the Second Vatican Council.* The emphasis here is clearly on an internal opening of the Church to *Christian ecumenism* and to the other cultures to which the faith must be mediated. The internal Church reforms, for the Pope the means of the witness of the Church to the world, are here for all practical purposes assigned to the goal of ecumenism. In the second of the named books Küng let slip a revealing title for a chapter: "What do Christians expect from the Council?"; the theme "Church in These Times" in the same book concerned reforms of the Petrine office.

On the other side, the theme of "the Church in the World" could not be avoided – indeed, Church in a world that had radically changed in the years following the Second World War. The impetus to push this theme into the foreground came above all from France – the "Catholic" country in which the Church already at that time was in opposition to the most self-assured neo-paganism; the impetus came also from Latin America, particularly from Brazil.

What, therefore, should the main thread of the Council be? Furthermore, *both* tendencies bumped into the conservative opposition, as portrayed in diverse ways in the preceding chapters. Only the initiative of John XXIII to set up the Secretariat for Christian Unity under Cardinal Bea, guaranteed the questions of Christian ecumenism an institutional place at the Council – we have already reported about the conflicts associated with this. On the other hand it was, since the Council itself could not be prevented, the declared intention of the conservative Council Fathers to prevent an opening to the world, and to limit it to purely internal Church themes, themes that were believed to be under control, as the prepared schemas indicate. In other words: despite all the good suggestions in the discussion after the announcement of the Council and despite all the experiences of the regional Churches with the intent of the Pope, the danger of passive resistance against the Council appeared to have concretized in the effort to neutralize the Pope's understanding of the purpose of the Council. Had this effort succeeded, the Council could not have seemed more ridiculous: it would have been one of the largest (and most expensive) absurdities of Church history – a gigantic unnecessary superfluidity, whose meager content the Curia and the Pope could have set in motion on their own.

II. THE TIME BEFORE THE COUNCIL

1. THE SO-CALLED TEXT I

It is worthwhile to take a brief look at the texts of the preparatory time. The Preparatory Commissions produced 69 "schemata." Of these, only one (with the number 7) had as its theme "social order"; this was a schema of the Theological Commission, worked out under the point of view of Cardinal Ottaviani. Besides this, the Commission for the Lay Apostolate had composed a text concerning "The Social Action of Christians." To put it more accurately: sub-commissions of both of these preparatory commissions composed the texts, since these commissions had other documents to prepare. The chairman of the sub-commission of the Commission for the Lay Apostolate was Bishop (later Cardinal) Hengsbach from Essen – he was entrusted with this task until the end of the Council. Chairman of the sub-commission of the Theological Commission was the Italian Bishop Pavan, who had been very involved in the composition of John XXIII's 1963 encyclical *Pacem in terris*; he was also a member of Hengsbach's sub-commission. The signs for cooperation of the two sub-commissions were not unpropitious, and that had good consequences for the history of the text.

The Theological Commission produced its text on the social order in a way that was reminiscent of the original schema on Revelation: in a completely neo-Scholastic fashion, as a collection of previous Catholic social teaching as laid down by, above all, Popes Leo XIII, Pius XI, and Pius XII. The first four chapters took up the following themes:

- the foundation of the Christian moral order (objective character of the Christian moral order; its absolute validity; God as its guardian – therefore opposed to "situational ethics");

- the conscience (duty to orientation to the objective moral order, the error of conscience, which changes nothing on the objective moral order);
- the errors of subjectivism and of ethical relativism;
- the sins (with attacks against false psychological theories, which want to call every sin committed under compulsion "venial").

Only the fifth chapter struck a different note, in that it dealt with the "natural and supernatural worth of the human person" and so hit on for the first time the theme of the human as an image of God, a theme that is such an important one later in the text of this Constitution. The background: the idea of the human as "the image of God" was introduced under the standpoint of the dominion of humans over the world. This is the theme in which the relationship of the Church to science, technology, and art is spoken of – and in which the later text speaks simply of "culture." Outlines for this already existed in the 1931 encyclical *Quadragesimo anno* of Pope Pius XI. The central theme of the human as the image of God in *Gaudium et spes* can be chalked up to the desire of the conservative majority in the Preparatory Committees to force the encyclicals of the last Popes on the now unavoidable Council. But "through God's providence and in spite of the stupidity of man" something good can sometimes emerge even from sinister intentions.

The draft of the Lay Apostolate sub-commission took a different route. This draft avoided for the most part any theological discussions – it assumes that these are cleared up through the (intended) Dogmatic Constitution on the Church and concerns itself more descriptively with the activity of the Christian in his or her social environment. That moves into the realm of "natural" truths – and is more positive in the consideration of human endeavor.

A three-fold tension was, therefore, pre-programmed into the text:

a. Should the text deduce theologically or should it describe concretely? If the text speaks theologically, it will and must keep itself in the realm of general theological truths. How then can it be a document on the Church in the world *today*? This sort of document cannot be produced with a theoretical theology. However, if the document speaks in concrete, descriptive terms, then readers can recognize themselves in the document – but the "concretenesses" could very easily change. Above all, though: what does the Church have to say *definitively* about these concretenesses? Should the Church enter into discussions of sociology and political science? In short, the first tension that the document had to overcome lay in the question: how can one speak concretely but still remain true to the Gospel, which remains the same despite the change of concretenesses?

b. The second tension is connected with the first: should the text speak the language of faith, or should it shift to a level on which both Christians and non-Christians stand? If one speaks in the language of faith, then one risks being misunderstood by the non-Christians. A chapter on the power of the Spirit to create new humans fell victim to this consideration, as also did a statement on the re-arrangement of the world through the liturgy and another on the "humanism of the Sermon on the Mount." Some theologians had to have been pained by this, since there had been not a few complaints that the schema was "too western European," and now exactly those themes were sacrificed that would have been close to the Eastern Church tradition. But if one entered a common level of language with non-Christians then, on the grounds of Church tradition, a "natural law" argumentation was foremost at hand – which is what is found in Text 1. But on this basis any ecumenical consensus concerning this text would have been impossible. What then could be an appropriate language, one in which Christians and non-Christians could understand one another? The final text, in my opinion, solved this problem in a brilliant fashion: one begins with a specific, understandable description of the situation and illuminates its difficulties. Then one attempts a Christian answer to this in the most unjargon language possible, letting the power of the answer to convince depend on the substance of its content.

c. The most delicate problem now appears: what kind of claim to definitiveness can such a text raise? Until the very end the title "Pastoral Constitution" was vehemently contested, and actually it is a contradiction. A "constitution" is the binding definition of a doctrine, or a binding disciplinary instruction. "Pastoral," however, includes answers to concrete realities, application of the general to the particular; "pastoral" statements are in principle susceptible to change, because the concrete and particular can so quickly change. There can actually not be a "Pastoral Constitution," if the concepts are supposed to remain precise. The suggestion was made time and again to call a first section "Conciliar Constitution," and to append to this section a second section with "instructions" (not "norms," since these are definitive), to be

known as *Adnexa* ("appendices.") But the further along the preparations of the text went, the more unlikely this two-part suggestion appeared. The – planned and then executed – second section contained
numerous "normative" elements: one needs only think of the instructions on marriage and family as well as those on war and peace. At the
same time, the first section was full of concretely descriptive sections.
It was eventually realized that, in order to de-escalate the question
of "compulsory nature," the descriptive passages on the situation in
the modern world needed to be connected to the first main section of
the final document as *Expositio introductoria* ("Introduction," Articles
4-10).

In order to get out of the quandary, another, more radical suggestion
was made: instead of a constitution, one should say everything that
one wanted to say in the form of a "declaration." This was rejected,
since it would have weakened the authority of this text, or these texts,
too much.

So it was therefore a trip between Scylla and Charybdis. Nothing
else could have been expected: exactly because of all these difficulties
suggestions were made, and the danger actually did exist, that the
schema could be deleted from the agenda. If however the enterprise
of a "pastoral constitution" actually succeeded, then it was only because the Fathers took the chance of doing something completely new,
something fully unknown from earlier councils: *to express themselves
only in provisional form.* The critical objection was immediately raised:
an ecumenical council cannot allow such a thing! The counter to this
was: Indeed it can, if it is expressly stated as such! This is therefore
what happened. The following remark to the title "The Church in the
Modern World" was added, before the beginning of the text:

> Although it consists of two parts, the Pastoral Constitution "The
> Church in the World Today" constitutes an organic unity. The
> Constitution is called "pastoral" because, while resting on doctrinal
> principles, it sets out the relation of the church to the world and to
> the people of today. In Part I, therefore, the pastoral emphasis is
> not overlooked, nor is the doctrinal emphasis overlooked in Part II.
> In Part I the church develops its teaching on humanity, the world
> it inhabits, and its relationship to women and men. Part II treats
> at length of various aspects of life and human society today and in
> particular with those questions and problems which seem to have
> a greater urgency in our day. The result is that in Part II the subject

matter which is viewed in the light of doctrinal principles consists of elements, some of which are permanent and some of which are contingent. The Constitution is to be interpreted according to the general norms of theological interpretation, while taking into account, especially in Part II, the changing circumstances which the subject matter, by its very nature, involves.

In the conclusion to Article 91 this introductory remark, phrased differently, was repeated as a part of the text:

Faced with the wide variety of situations and forms of human culture in the world, this conciliar program is deliberately general on many points; indeed, while the teaching presented is that already accepted in the church, it will have to be pursued further and amplified because it often deals with matters which are subject to continual development. Still, we have based our proposals on the word of God and the spirit of the Gospel. Hence we entertain the hope that many of our suggestions will succeed in effectively assisting all people, especially after they have been adapted to different nations and mentalities and put into practice by the faithful under the direction of their pastors.

Until this clear position was arrived at, a position that from this distance seems so obvious and sympathetic, the text experienced a history that outdoes any of the other texts in terms of chaos and disorder. Before we can talk about this, though, we have to take a look at some other basic problems that were burdensome from the beginning. They are not too surprising, since one was attempting something quite new with this constitution – but they still seem a bit surprising, after all these decades.

2. DIALOGUE WITHOUT PARTNER?

The most obvious problem connected with what has just been said is: how ought one to speak with "the world"? The normal course would be to draw representatives of the world into dialogue – to ask for advice from the women and men who earn their living in this world and deal with it, that is, the "laity." Here the next opportunity to torpedo the project presented itself. The Council, so the objection ran, is an assembly of *Bishops*. According to ancient tradition, "conciliar events" are those at which Bishops consult, possibly supported by theologians, but not by anyone else.

So from very early on the participation of the laity was discussed, but the answer at first was a complete ban. The Dominican Father Ciappi, the so-called "Master of the Sacred Palace," the official theological advisor of the Pope, reported in 1962, at a conference looking back at the work done in preparation for the Council: exclusively Bishops, superiors of orders, officials of the Roman Curia, and representatives of Catholic universities participated in the preparatory work on the Council. Laity, at least openly and officially, had played no role – and this was indeed correct. This understanding of the Council produced an internal dilemma during the first phase of the work on *Gaudium et Spes*: how can one recognize the "world" as a fully valid partner in the dialogue and at the same time not invite the "world" – as a dialogue partner – to the Council?

Not only did numerous lay organizations exist in the Church, organizations whose advice could have been put to good use, but in the time preceding the Council these organizations had held conferences and published reports. So, for example, in 1960 a conference of international Catholic organizations was held; some of the representatives at this conference were lay representatives later in the committees of the Council. On the 13th and 14th of May, 1961, the *Informations Catholiques Internationales* organized two study days with the theme: "The Church, the Council, and the Others." In a pamphlet describing this conference one reads: "A look at the world. What is the modern world, what are its hopes and its anxieties, where are people headed, and for what purpose, what do they expect of the Church?" That sounds like a questionnaire for the Pastoral Constitution! However: already on the 23rd of January, 1962, John XXIII – who was capable of reacting in a very restrictive manner in terms of canon law, when the substance of the matter had to do with something he without question believed simply had to be a certain way – let it be said: all the work and the studies on questions of the Council done by priests or laity – so, from non-Council Fathers, without exception, even if they were theologians – were of purely private character. This is, of course, correct. Spoken in such a pointed manner, however, it was like a cold shower, which immediately could be used against the project of a Pastoral Constitution.

It was Pope Paul VI who loosed the Gordian knot and ordered the summoning of laity with advisory function in the Preparatory Committees. On the 24th of April, 1964 [!], for the first time laity got

a look at the developing document. They involved themselves immediately, and a little bit later women also joined; these women remained
particularly involved with work on the Pastoral Constitution. At a
point when a depressed mood overcame the work – at the controversial discussions over the section on marriage and family – once again
the suggestion was sounded: remove it from the agenda! The content
was "not yet ripe." The lay members in the advisory committees immediately defended themselves, with success: the Council would cause
incalculable disappointment if it broke off the work on this document.

3. PAPAL INITIATIVES

At the beginning of the Council, then, the situation was characterized by a kind of "prepared unpreparedness" for the task. It was not
lost on Pope John XXIII that his theme of "unity and world" was in
danger. In his Pentecost homily on the 5th of June, 1961, he had given
the very clear indication: each believer, in so far as he is "Catholic," is
a citizen of the entire world, just as Christ is the beloved savior of the
entire world. In the formal announcement of the Council on the 25th
of December, 1961 in the constitution *Humanae salutis*, the phrase
"signs of the time," later so suspect, first occurred; these were signs that
could be and should be read. Pope John XXIII's famous speech of the
11th of September, 1962, shortly before the opening of the Council, is
decisive. Here John distinguished between the vitality of the Church
ad intra and the vitality of the Church *ad extra*, the Church in itself
and the Church in relation to the world's problems. The Church needs
to be involved in what concerns the latter: basic equality of all people in the execution of their rights and duties; defense of the sacred-
ness of marriage; social responsibility; the underdeveloped countries,
to whom the Church must show itself to be the Church of all, and
especially of the poor; societal abuses; right to religious freedom;
peace among peoples. In short: the speech contained a catalogue of
the themes that were actually dealt with later in *Gaudium et Spes*. We
know the pre-history of this speech; it is intertwined with the pastoral
letter of Cardinal Suenens from Brussels, whose ideas, together with
those of Cardinal Montini, were so important for the continuation
and the further planning of the Council.

Yet another initiative is worth mentioning: Helder Camara, at that
time the auxiliary Bishop of Rio de Janeiro, took advantage of every

opportunity he had in Rome to speak with visitors about the already dramatic problems of the Third World, problems that were just then becoming apparent to the official ecclesial consciousness. Camara was quoted as saying: "Should we then use up our entire time discussing internal problems of the Church, while two thirds of mankind dies of hunger? What do we have to say to the problem of underdevelopment? Will the Council give voice to its concern about the great problems of mankind? Ought Pope John remain alone in this fight?" In a conference in the Domus Mariae in Rome he reduced the problem to a formula: "Is the greatest problem of Latin America the shortage of priests? No! Underdevelopment." As Secretary of the Latin American Episcopal Conference Camara initiated contacts with the other Episcopal conferences and also established a connection with Cardinal Suenens. On the 1st of December, 1962, he organized a gathering, held in the Belgian College in Rome, of 50 Bishops from different continents. Here the battle plans were drawn up.

4. THE BREAKTHROUGH

Three days later Cardinal Suenens stood at the pulpit in the Council Hall and presented, as had been arranged with the Pope, his basic idea: all the texts should be grouped around the two poles, *ad intra-ad extra.* The Council Fathers applauded this. It was their move; in the opening address to the Council the Pope had once again taken up the theme. This was even more significant since the Pope had himself composed this address ("no one stuck his nose into it"). Further: eight days after the opening of the Council, on the 20th of October, 1962, the Council approved a "message to the world": "As we undertake our work, therefore, we want to emphasize whatever concerns the dignity of the human person, whatever contributes to a genuine community of peoples." The authors of this "message" were the two French Dominican theologians, Marie-Dominique Chenu and Yves Congar. Not without good reason! They were (among others) not only the theological promoters of "worker priests," but in general of the endeavors surrounding a new relationship of the Church to the modern world, as was characteristic for French theology since the 1920's. John XXIII, when he was *nuntius* in Paris, had not been able to prevent the disciplining of these endeavors, the literal banning of their theological advocates. Now came, at least for two of them, their "hour."

There was now no going back. The two papal encyclicals, the 1963 *Pacem in terris* from John XXIII and the 1964 *Ecclesiam suam* of Paul VI at first had an obstructing effect, but then stimulated the discussion. The encyclicals had an obstructive effect because the impression arose: why should we continue? Isn't everything now said? They worked as a stimulus because they delivered a model for the style of the pastoral constitution – particularly *Pacem in terris* – above all, though: because now there could be no doubt whatsoever of the interest of *both* Popes in this theme.

III. KNOTTY PROBLEMS OF THE TEXTUAL HISTORY

It is pointless to chronologically detail the history of the text and to go into the differences among the individual editions. Instead of a chronological longitudinal section we shall undertake a cross section. We must remember: after the reduction and combination of the 69 schemata from the preparatory period, at the end of the first session there were "only" 17 schemata. The future pastoral constitution was the 17th – the last of the schemata. "Schema XIII" – the "famous Schema XIII" (Sebastian Tromp), the "Schema without a name" ("pastoral constitution" was controversial up to the very end) – was arrived at only by a rearrangement of the drafts, in July of 1964. Very soon the joke surfaced: in Italy the number 13 is a lucky number, in Germany an unlucky one!

1. MANY COOKS DO NOT SPOIL THE BROTH

The new organization of the work of the Council had the result that now a complete orchestra, so to speak, of commissions felt themselves responsible for Schema 17/13:

a) The Coordinating Commission – responsible for the planning of the debates.

b) The Mixed Commission. At first there had been a demand for a commission specifically for the work on the pastoral constitution; this did not happen. After the end of the (first) session the Bishops were gone, so an election of members of the commission was impossible. A suggestion made by Cardinal Suenens was followed: the Theological Commission and the Commission for the Lay Apostolate should form a "mixed commission" for the work and editing of the pastoral constitution – this was the already mentioned mixed commission under the leadership of Bishop Guano. This commission delegated to a few experts the task of re-working the submitted drafts.

c) The Mixed Commission appointed a central sub-commission, which was entrusted with the final redaction of the entire text.

d) "Sub-sub-commissions" were also engaged in the work of the pastoral constitution, that is, a sub-commission of the Theological Commission and a sub-commission for the "Signs of the Times."

e) Along with all these there were also editorial committees and on session days occasionally small groups, often only for a single section.

Leading figures – and with this also leading sufferers in the history of the text – were Gérard Philips of Belgium, the most important man as theologian, Latinist, and on account of his good contacts to the influential people on whom the fate of the text depended. The other obsessed detail man, along with Philips, was the Frenchman Pierre Haubtmann. Finally: Charles Moeller, from Belgium. The names of the three men most responsible for the text guaranteed that this document could not possibly develop in any direction except that of French theology of the pre-Council period. This was quite positive, since then the later criticism from the non-French, particularly German, theologians could gain clear contours, something that also helped the final text.

The work, particularly in the final phase, often lasted far into the night. Whatever had to be delivered in the early morning to the Vatican press often was not ready until around 2:30 a.m.!

2. THE VERSIONS OF THE TEXT

The sixth version of the text was the one that was finally adopted. We have already spoken of Text 1; Text 2 attempted to include as much as possible from Text 1. It was feared at first that the Council would be short; later, the fear was that the third session would be the last. One felt constantly pressured by time constraints.

In the course of the work, Text 2 experienced five new editions. Text "a" was produced in Mecheln, the Belgian home of the most important editors – this text had no influence. Text "b" was produced in February of 1964 in Zurich – and was more significant. Text 3 came out of Zurich in April of 1964. This text was particularly significant, because on the one hand the laity was brought into the discussions and on the other hand contacts with the World Council of Churches began to have an effect.

After Text 3 there was no returning to a time before the departure from natural law argumentation, before the determination to use language familiar from the Bible, before the idea of the Reign of Christ as a complementary idea to humanity as the "image of God." This Text 3 was discussed at the third session, in the Fall of 1964; we shall talk about this shortly.

The result of the discussion flowed into Text 4, produced in February of 1964 in Ariccia in the mountains south of Rome – within sight of the papal summer residence Castel Gandolfo. The draft was delivered to the Fathers and according to expectation all the critique was received before the fourth session. The incorporation of this critique led to Text 5, which was then presented to the Council in session.

The renewed conciliar debate resulted finally in Text 6, which was solemnly adopted and published on the 7th of December, 1965, a day before the official end of the Council.

The decisive work phase – not difficult to guess – was the step from Text 3 to Text 4, the incorporation of the votes that had been reported at the first consultation of the Council during the third session concerning the version. Afterwards there were still many controversial details, but the outline was established.

3. AN INITIATIVE FROM THE
WORLD COUNCIL OF CHURCHES

We mentioned the contact with the World Council of Churches in Geneva that existed since the meeting in Zurich in April of 1964. It is necessary to add a bit more to this. The external event that ushered in this contact and its effects on the developing pastoral constitution is already known to us: the letter of the General Secretary of the Commission on Faith and Order, Lukas Vischer – who held this office until 1982. In this letter, which Vischer, circumventing all the

usual proper channels with an appealing impudence, sent to Bishop
Guano, he described how the Commission on Faith and Order would
approach a "schema on the modern world," if such a schema were demanded from his commission. The letter reported that in 1956 the
World Council of Churches had commissioned a study with the
title: "The Reign of Christ over the Church and over the World."
Vischer also submitted five documents: 1. a text with a position of
the Commission on Faith and Order on the question of disarmament;
2. the section of the report of the second full assembly of the World
Council of Churches in Evanston (1954) that concerned the Christian
hope in the modern world; 3. the report from Evanston on the relationships among the nations; 4. the report on the developing countries; 5. the report on the question of religious freedom. In his letter
Vischer criticized the concept of natural law – the central concept and
the model for argumentation of all the previous drafts, as everyone
knew – and placed the action of the Christian in relationship with
the resurrection of Jesus. The declaration of belief in the resurrection
is the uniting bond among Christians, and the difference between
Christians and non-Christians is based on this, as well. The letter
closed with a few wishes: practical cooperation with the Catholics, for
example in the question of refugees; an emphasis on "responsible par-
enthood," put plainly: family planning – obviously a discreet reminder
of the Lambeth Conference of 1927, which Pius XI answered in 1931
with the marriage encyclical *Casti connubii*; and finally with the wish
for a chapter on religious freedom. Among the recipients of the copies
that Bishop Guano had made and distributed privately was Cardinal
Suenens, together with John XXIII from the very beginning the promoter of the idea of a pastoral constitution.

The date of this letter, the 18th of April, 1963, is the beginning of
an ecumenical cooperation that, according to the judgment of Charles
Moeller, could have been even more intensive but still left sufficient
traces in the constitution. They are clearly *reformed*, not Lutheran,
traces – the phrase "Reign of Christ," as well as the emphasis on the
resurrection of Jesus from the dead, as the common Christian basis,
made this clear. Lukas Vischer belonged to the Reformed tradition.
But also Lutherans could only welcome what was actually achieved
– the almost complete (in the first section actually complete) repres-
sion of the natural law argument. This was already underway in the

discussion at the first session – but it was the ecumenical intervention that made this tendency irrevocable.

Vischer's letter did not have any influence on the production of Text 2 and Text "a" – both versions were just getting finished up at the time of the letter. The influence began with Text "b" of February, 1964. Immediately before the consultations in Zurich (from the 1st to the 3rd of February) Bishop Guano, Charles Moeller, and the German theologian Bernhard Häring held a long conversation with Vischer, made notes of his criticisms of the draft about to be discussed in Zurich and brought these criticisms into their discussions. In Text 3 (Zurich, April 1964), the influence of this conversation with Vischer was clearly recognizable. The *Easter* aspect of the "Reign of Christ" that persisted from this time on can be attributed to Vischer. But before the Easter of the Constitution there were also still a few Good Fridays in store; the contribution of the World Council of Churches was no magic wand, with which not only the internal ecclesial problems but also the problems caused by the relationship between Church and world could be quickly and easily untangled.

4. KNOTTY PROBLEMS

a. First of these problems was the connection with the Dogmatic Constitution on the Church, which developed at the same time as the Pastoral Constitution; the latter was at one time intended to be the concretization of the former. How can one establish the *connection between the dogmatic statements and the concrete – and therefore provisional – statements?* Both cannot just stand next to one another; on the other hand, the concrete directives relative to the modern world cannot simply be formulated as conclusions from the dogmatic statements, because then they would, albeit in an attenuated manner, share in the claim of the dogmatic statements to dogmatic binding character. If this shouldn't be the case, then how could they be put into relationship with the dogmatic statements?

b. The turn to the world on the basis of scientific analyses encountered a fundamental suspicion: did the promoters of the Pastoral Constitution want to *theologically elevate something like a worldly optimism in progress?* This suspicion fastened above all onto the strong influence of French theology on the developing document.

The German Bishops were more restrictive, and the German Council theologians, while appropriately represented in the committees, were not the leading authors and were very mistrustful. It must not be forgotten: it was a time of change from the pontificate of Pius XII to John XXIII, when optimism that the Church not only must but could reconcile itself with the modern world took root, above all in French theology and from there in the Church in general. Catch words were: "worker priests," whose ban John XXIII, as *nuntius* in Paris, had to sit back and watch, powerless, and whom he now allowed; "Action Catholique," in France the ambitious attempt to live the missionary Church in a secular society; the specific style of French pastoral care that, if need be at the cost of the territorially organized parish pastoral care, sent theologians and priests into the different "scenes"; the dialogue between theology and Marxism, which as is known started in France and from there spread to Germany and, where it was possible, to eastern Europe; the dialogue between theology and natural science, in Germany above all organized in the so-called "Paulus-Gesellschaft." All this took place with the background of the memory, that the sentence that the Church had to reconcile itself to the modern world had been formally rejected in the infamous *Syllabus* of Pius IX (1864) as well as in the *Syllabus* of Pope Pius X (1907) – in the last instance, on the express ground that this amounted to liberal Protestantism. The threat of being suspected of a much too uncritical euphoria vis-à-vis the "modern world" loomed large. Whoever considered the new "world" optimism to have good reason could escape this suspicion only if he expressly referenced the ambiguity of this "modern world," its disastrous dimension, without surrendering with this the desire to overcome old mistrust and old anxiety. In the end, this succeeded in such a convincing way – with some exceptions – that the still occasional accusation of an exaggerated optimism about progress that conforms itself to the spirit of the times is without support.

c.   A further knotty problem was the question: *what should one take up in the details?* The witticism about "Noah's Ark" has already been mentioned. If the modern world was to be the topic of conversation, as expected, suggestions about positions to be taken came from all corners of the world. In the course of the history of the text a few were slapped on top of it, while others, such as the problem of religious freedom, became their own text. In the end, in essence the points remained those that John XXIII had mentioned in his opening address, to which Cardinal Suenens had returned. This catalogue of themes consolidated itself pretty much without conflict, since they were "classical" themes of Catholic social teaching: marriage and family, economics, war and peace, the state, international order. Only the one chapter is original, the one that brings together different concerns of a scientific and artistic sort under the concept "culture."

d. The *question of the style* was particularly difficult. Even in the vernacular translations, the different tone of the wording is obvious to every reader of the Constitution. This is not only the avoidance of neo-Scholastic language – that is the case for the most part in the other documents, as well. It is also not only the sound of familiar modern, easily understood scientific accounts, because this is restricted to the descriptive section. What is most impressive is that the theological statements are stylistically in seamless harmony, which would scarcely be the case if one made the experiment of introducing a piece of the Constitution on the Church into the Pastoral Constitution.

The style must therefore have something to do with the content of the Pastoral Constitution. It is a result of the fact that one wanted originally to address expressly the non-Christians and later also the members of the Church, in so far as they work with the non-Christians in common circumstances and constitute with them "the world." Therefore not only theological academic language was excluded, but also any sort of "insider" jargon, except for the bare minimum that one needed in order to speak from the point of view of faith. In the discussions around the composition of the text, at one point the unusual suggestion was made to avoid word-for-word citations from the Bible, since the non-Christians would not be familiar with the biblical texts. This kind of rigor did not occur, but the suggestion indicates the desire to really make oneself comprehensible to a world that is not familiar with church "jargon." Not only those who do not understand this jargon *any more*, but still have some association with it, as in neo-pagan Europe, are considered, but also those who have never had command of the jargon. One can just imagine if a Hindu Council would produce a "Constitution on Hinduism in the Modern World" directed to us.

302 Pesch THE PREHISTORY OF THE SECOND VATICAN COUNCIL

The style is not just a result of a missionary method. The main reason for the "new tone" is the self-restraint of the Church vis-à-vis the world in secular matters, concerning which the Church up to that point always took the attitude of those who "know certainly" and who "have something to contribute." More details on this will follow. Only: *when* one restrains himself, then automatically the style becomes more modest, humbler, more tentative, less pathetic. Since those who produced the text had practiced this attitude for a long time it is understandable why this new tone was so easily achieved. Wherever statements in the old style were introduced into the text because of the pressure of the interventions, it sounds different, above all in context.

The authors and the Council Fathers supporting them in the meantime had a great example in the encyclical *Pacem in terris*, from John XXIII. The Pope knew in Spring of 1963 that his days were numbered. The encyclical was his heart's desire – he had summoned up all of his strength, in order to bring out *this* encyclical before his death. And it is written completely in this "new" style – with a temporary paralysis of the authors of the Pastoral Constitution as a consequence. Even the style indicates how John succeeded, literally, in tricking his opponents at the Council: with the unique mixture of conservative trust in the efficacy of his office, clarity of expression, and Italian craftiness unique to John XXIII. He could calculate for himself that with this encyclical supporting them, the majority at the Council could lap the minority with the reference to the authority of the Pope. Not for nothing was *Pacem in terris* so often cited in the Pastoral Constitution. It was also of course made extraordinarily easier that at the high point of the conflicts John's successor Paul VI entered the fray, indirectly, with the encyclical *Ecclesium suam*. This evidence that the new Pope stood behind the Pastoral Constitution rendered any resistance futile. With this we are at the next point in the history of the text:

5. THE TWO PLENARY DEBATES

In the third session (Fall, 1964) Text 3, the second text from Zurich, was presented and discussed. The passionate discussion circled above all around four important points; thanks to the high quality of the votes the text was considerably improved:

1. *Theme of atheism:* This theme was missed. The debate led to the three detailed articles on this.

2. *Why does the Church even speak of earthly matters?* In the general debate about the schema Cardinal Meyer, the Archbishop of Chicago, had already given the guiding answer: "The community of redemption forms the link between the Church and the world. God offers his glory to the whole man, body and soul, and to the whole created world. The Son has a cosmic mission because, as St. Paul says, it has pleased the Father to reconcile all things in his Son. This work is only completed at the end of time by the resurrection of the body and the mysterious transformation of the world. There will be, Scriptures tell us, a new heaven and a new earth. This transformation actually begins with men's work in the world. That work is consequently not merely something profane. Similarly, the course of the world's history is not purely contingent but corresponds to a redemptive plan on the part of God." [V. Yzermans, *American Participation in the Second Vatican Council* (New York: Sheed & Ward, 1967) 213]

3. About the two other problem areas, *Person and Family; Culture, Development, Peace, and Atomic Weapons*, there were of course conflicts. The openness of the discussion was noteworthy, carried out with great frankness, particularly in light of a position fully declared by preceding Papal encyclicals.

There was in this discussion still a quick, tricky reaction that deserves to be noted. A few Bishops said, half confused, half understanding, that the "Appendix" (as the second part of the Pastoral Constitution is still known) contained, on a series of points, more precise and better worked out statements than did the "Conciliar Constitution" (the first part). The advocates of the text immediately used this opportunity and achieved the inclusion of the "Appendix" in the text of the "Conciliar Constitution." With this move they basically saved the Pastoral Constitution – from now on, despite problems that arose, the project of a unified constitution with two parts, but *without* appendices, was never again abandoned. Based on the discussion Text 4, as was already noted, was supplied, then on the basis of the votes, provided in writing, of the Bishops, Text 5, submitted in the fourth session. Again there was a vigorous discussion. This time the German spokesmen led the criticism. It proved to be helpful that Bishop Elchinger of Strasburg organized, before the beginning of the debate on the 17th of September, 1965, a meeting of predominantly German and French spokesmen of the debate. The expected criticism was discussed and a process for dealing with this criticism was agreed upon, so that the debate could move along quickly. The main criticism revealed that even despite all this excellent cooperative work differences in mentality and in cultural contexts existed, differences that affected attitudes toward the themes.

The criticism focused for the most part on the first part. In it, according to the criticism, human history is given short shrift; the statements are "too static." The fact that sin can be understood only with reference to faith is not sufficiently explained. The text is inadequate in its treatment of the theology of the cross and the eschatological tension between this and the coming world. The text lacked critical key words like: naturalism, optimism, simplification of some problems. The particular meaning and contribution of faith to humanity's encounter with the world was not made sufficiently clear; the task of the Church through the hierarchical Magisterium and the task of the Church through the faithful were not sufficiently distinguished – in general, not enough was said about where the boundary between binding norms and temporary instructions lies. Along with this, the ecumenical aspect was too weak. The style of the text did not give enough consideration to non-believers. And finally – the text should take the responsibility for its own incompleteness: it must be clearly stated what the Church presented as "binding statement," and what the Church recommended in the sense of an instruction (according to Karl Rahner, during the gathering already mentioned).

One sees that the work, already the object of much strenuous labor and thought, could not have been questioned in a more radical way. But that did not create any wounds. The French participants – above all Jean Daniélou, Yves Congar, and Gérard Philips – took the criticism seriously, and in the final text one can observe point for point the effects of the criticism and their attention to it. It came to a decisive agreement: one wanted to ensure that the text would be accepted, and one wanted to improve it, as well. Therefore in the ten sub-commissions that were soon elected for the improvement of the text, representatives of the "opposition" to Text 4 sat – put plainly: primarily German Bishops and theologians. Charles Moeller describes the happy outcome in his commentary:

> The result of this decision was that the text was once again changed
> quite considerably – for example Chapter III of Part I was rewritten

almost completely – but that the version put to the vote by the fathers before its promulgation represented the consensus of the two main tendencies which had stood confronted since the beginning of work on Schema 13: one a concrete outlook marked by a certain fundamental optimism, the other a dialectical, paradoxical attitude insisting on the polyvalency of the world in which the Church lives.

This little-known episode has been described in detail because of its importance. In fact it was decisive because it meant that all revisions during the last two stages were made on the general lines that a balance must be struck between the opposing tendencies of the two ways of envisaging the problem. At the same time the observer delegates were to express their criticisms; two sessions on 21 and 28 November were devoted to this.

As a consequence, the final text doubtless lost a little of its homogeneity, its continuous forward movement, in favour of a presentation which multiplied contrasts. But it gained in wealth of content and complexity. In short, it acquired a more dialectical character, which the Malines Schema (Interim Text A) had possessed but which had practically disappeared from later versions." [Herbert Vorgrimler, ed., *Commentary on the Documents of Vatican II, Volume V* (NY, NY: Herder and Herder, 1969) 60-61]

Now the phase of the night work began in earnest. Because it gives a concrete insight into the work of the Council, which had met in the meantime, I would like to make a few comments. General and individual debates over Text 5 – just a reminder: the text that was newly edited on the basis of suggestions from the third session – lasted from the 21st of September to the 8th of October, 1965. The result was oral and written notations (*Modi*) of around 500 single-spaced pages! The processing was organized in the following manner: the speeches were all grouped in sections on slips of paper – there were about 3000! They were classified in the following order: general comments to the schema – comments to a chapter – to an article – to a line – to a word. This process had already proven successful with the work on the Constitutions on the Church and on Revelation. A team of twelve people, *periti* and honorary helpers (who were often the most active) produced the 3000 slips of paper by working day and night; they were photocopied and provided to the presidents of the ten sub-commissions – pretty much a sub-commission for every chapter. Already on the 17th of October – the debate was ended on the 8th of October – the first six sub-commissions were finished with the work, on the 20th of

October, the four others finished. From the 20th to the 30th of October the full assembly of the Mixed Commission busied itself with the improved text (now Text 6), in fifteen sessions. Again there were suggestions for improvement, which had to be added into the text that was already lying ready in the Vatican press, St. Martha [!]. On the 12th and 13th of November the improved text (151 pages) could be delivered to the Council Fathers. The debates and the votes began on the 15th of November. The Fathers were forced to put in night work, too – one had to read, along with everything else one had to do, 151 pages in two days, and make notes for improvements! The entire process led to a small miracle: the text became shorter, 93 articles rather than the original 106.

The "no" votes never reached a third of the total, the number that would have meant, according to the protocol, rejection. The schema was, therefore, finally "through." Nonetheless, there were altogether 20,000 *Modi* (in words: twenty thousand). Many were identical, but the attempt at least had to be made to look at them all. The vote over the suggestions for inclusion (two volumes, one with 256 pages, the other with 155) took place from the 4th to the 6th of December. Particular discussions were caused by the title "Pastoral Constitution." A counter suggestion was *Declaratio pastoralis*. The arguments for and against were as before. The title "Pastoral Constitution" was saved because of the innumerable counter proposals and the respective arguments. "Pastoral Constitution" appeared finally as the most exact title, precisely because of its paradox. As Moeller comments, "The title *Constitutio pastoralis* was therefore retained for the whole, it being sufficient to note the analogical application of that title to its various parts. No further attempt was therefore made to revive *in extremis* the all too famous and fatal division into 'conciliar constitution' and 'appendix chapters'; heaven alone knows what authority the latter would have enjoyed."

In the 168th General Congregation – the last of the Council – the complete text was voted on: 2111 "yes" votes, 251 "no" votes, and 11 that were invalid. The heavy lifters in the history of this text richly deserved the champagne at the "Bar Jonah" – I don't know if they drank it, but they certainly deserved it. Their names are written in the book of Church history.

On the 7th of December, 1965, the 9th solemn assembly, with the conclusive vote, took place: 2309 "yes" votes, only 75 "no" votes, and seven invalid votes.

> Through five phases in which it had died, and five phases of resurrection, the dogmatic part of the text had overcome an incredible number of obstacles. These had arisen from the fact that the text was completely new, contained such a mass of different problems and involved so many members of the Mixed Commission. Only the appendix chapters had victoriously won the day, i.e. preserved their fundamental tendency and a substantial part of their formulation. After a period of obscuration which lasted for two texts (Malines and Zurich), when they were demoted from one moment to the next to the rank of 'private texts', they emerged again. Then they were coupled like a row of carriages to the dogmatic train which was on the point of moving forward, and at every station their order was rearranged. One wonders whether it was not in fact precisely these chapters that contributed to salvaging the main text, which became less pretentious, more concrete and simple, while they were raised into the half-light of an important doctrinal statement and sometimes, as with marriage and culture, even into the clear light of revelation. [Herbert Vorgrimler, ed., *Commentary on the Documents of Vatican II, Volume V* (NY, NY: Herder and Herder, 1969) 70-71]]

IV. CENTRAL POINTS OF THE PASTORAL CONSTITUTION—EXAMPLES:

I have laid out the history of the text in such a detailed way because this history is almost more important than the end product itself. The opening of the Church to the world was completed in the process of the work on a text about the opening of the Church to the world. To re-work a slogan used of mass media: "The medium is the message," one could say: "The process itself is the result." The production of the text *is* the opening, it does not represent an already achieved opening. Therefore, similarly as with the Declaration on the Jews, the text, read against the background of its history, is immediately understandable. I shall explore just a few examples in some of the statements of the Constitution, and close with a few remarks of appreciation.

1. THE CONSTRUCTION OF THE CONSTITUTION

The Constitution – the longest text of the Council – has three parts, of which the first part – as mentioned, in order to stress the provisionary character of the statements and because the Church in the strictest sense is not responsible *for this* – is not designated as a separate "part," but only as "introduction." Its theme: the condition of humanity in the modern world. Then what is now designated the first part follows: the Church and the Human Vocation (four chapters), then the second part: important individual questions, in five chapters with the themes Marriage and the Family, Culture, Economy, Political Society (Church and State), International Community. Every chapter in each part is constructed according to the following pattern: description of the situation – emphasis on the ambiguity of the situation in the sense of achievement and danger (here above all the effects of the criticism of the German theologians is evident) – the word of faith as light in the situation and the orientation for its overcoming (in the first part), the tasks and possibilities of the Church in the area under consideration (in the second part). Of particular meaning are the three introductory and concluding articles, which clearly stake out the value of the Constitution, positively and negatively:

> Solidarity of the Church with the Whole Human Family: The joys and hopes, the grief and anguish of the people of our time, especially of those who are poor or afflicted, are the joys and hopes, the grief and anguish of the followers of Christ as well. Nothing that is genuinely human fails to find an echo in their hearts. For theirs is a community of people united in Christ and guided by the holy Spirit in their pilgrimage towards the Father's kingdom, bearers of a message of salvation for all of humanity. That is why they cherish a feeling of deep solidarity with the human race and its history (Article 1).

In Article 2 the Council addresses not exclusively Christians but all people in the world: "Now that the Second Vatican Council has studied the mystery of the church more deeply, it addresses not only the daughters and sons of the church and all who call upon the name of Christ, but the whole of humanity as well, and it wishes to set down how it understands the presence and function of the church in the world of today."

Article 3: In the ambiguous modern world, where we encounter both cause to admire human achievements as well as anxiety in light of the developments in the world, "the council, as witness and guide to the faith of all of God's people, gathered together by Christ, can find no more eloquent expression of this people's solidarity, respect and love for the whole human family, of which it forms part, than to enter into dialogue with it about these various problems ... The church is not motivated by earthly ambition but is interested in one thing only – to carry on the work of Christ under the guidance of the holy Spirit, who came into the world to bear witness to the truth, to save and not to judge, to serve and not to be served."

Article 91 refers to the provisional nature of the statements of the Constitution, in so far as it gives concrete judgments and instructions; the text has already been quoted.

Article 92 again underscores the solidarity of the Church with all humanity and the unity of Christians as a visible sign of this solidarity.

Article 93 admonishes all Christians to serve the edification and fulfillment of the world: "Mindful of the words of the Lord:'By this all will know that you are my disciples, if you have love for one another' (Jn. 13:35), Christians can yearn for nothing more ardently than to serve the people of this age successfully with increasing generosity. Holding loyally to the Gospel, enriched by its resources, and joining forces with all who love and practice justice, they have shouldered a weighty task here on earth and they must render an account of it to him who will judge all people on the last day. Not everyone who says, 'Lord, Lord' will enter the kingdom of heaven, but those who do the will of the Father and who courageously set to work. It is the Father's will that we should recognize Christ our brother in the persons of all men and women and should love them with an active love, in word and in deed, thus bearing witness to the truth; and it is his will that we should share with others the mystery of his heavenly love. In this way people all over the world will awaken to a lively hope, the gift of the holy Spirit, that they will one day be admitted to the haven of surpassing peace and happiness in their homeland radiant with the glory of the Lord."

2. ATHEISM

The section on atheism was added (Articles 19-21) at the end of the first chapter on the human vocation because of interventions in the

Council's consultations. The theme was particularly strenuously argued from "right" and "left." The one side wanted to simply condemn atheism and dogmatize the possibility of proving the existence of God—as a continuation and conclusion of the statements of the First Vatican Council and of the results of the Modernist controversy. On the other side there was the tendency to conduct the conflict offensively and constructively, and indeed particularly with atheism in the form of Marxism. Both tendencies did not achieve their goals, but the result of the criticism was then one of the most impressive passages of the entire Constitution.

a) In the first place, a very nuanced view of atheism was formulated. Those "apologetic" moments for atheists were named openly, above all the "considerable contribution" of the faithful to the rise of atheism as a critical reaction to religions. Among the scientific-philosophical forms of atheism discussed are clearly, without naming names, the so-called "atheism of freedom" in the sense of Jean-Paul Sartre as well as the atheism of Marxism.

b) Atheism was condemned in Article 21 as a theory "in conflict with reason and with common human experience," a theory that "cast[s] humanity down from the noble state to which it is born." Only those atheists who remained with atheism despite the claims of their consciences were concretely condemned. In any case the Church had to examine, more than previously, the grounds for the denial of God.

c) Three important statements are made about atheism and atheists in Article 21: the human cannot escape the fact that he remains a mystery to himself, and that only God is capable of completely and deeply answering the human's questioning – above all in the decisive situations in his life. Further: the remedy for atheism is an explanation of the doctrine that is appropriate for the situation, and a full and complete life of Christians and of the Church. And finally: believers and non-believers must work together for the construction of this world. For this, on the one hand an honest dialogue is necessary, on the other hand, the Church must have the freedom to operate, and must not be limited in the name of atheism. Karl Rahner and Herbert Vorgrimler evaluated this section, correctly, as a dignified answer to the atheists, without apologetics and anxiety, but also without the crusading attitude that some of the Council Fathers wanted to see in this section.

3. MARRIAGE AND FAMILY

The chapter on Marriage and Family opened the second part of the Constitution, therefore the part with the practical considerations of the problems of the present and their solutions. Celibate fixation on the problems of sexual ethics? The press had suspected something like this at the time. But in the thought process of the Constitution the insertion here is logical. That in this chapter the aspects of sexual *ethic* stand in the foreground has to do with the fact that the other aspects of Marriage and Family are treated in other conciliar texts: for example, Dogmatic Constitution on Church articles 11; 35; 41; Pastoral Constitution Articles 12; 61; 67; 87; the Decree on the Lay Apostolate Articles 10; 29. Along with this, the Council, because of pre-conciliar discussions, was under extraordinary pressure – the discussions around the proposal as well as the flood of memoranda on this theme indicate this. Under these conditions I would like to point out the following, to help in the appreciation of the final text:

a) Against bitter resistance of the "conservatives," the text backed off clearly from the purely juridical perspective of a "contract," as was a matter of course in the post-Tridentine theology of marriage and in marriage law because of anti-reforming limitations. Instead of this the explanation stood under the perspective of "covenant":

> The intimate partnership of life and the love which constitutes the married state has been established by the creator and endowed by him with its own proper laws; it is rooted in the contract of its partners, that is, in their irrevocable personal consent. It is an institution confirmed by divine law and receiving its stability, in the eyes of society also, from the human act by which the partners mutually surrender themselves to each other; for the good of the partners, of the children, and of society this sacred bond no longer depends on human decision alone. For God he is the author of marriage ... (Article 48).

Finally the personal aspect of marriage is most significant for ecclesiastical teaching on marriage. This was not surrendered in the post-conciliar theology of marriage and, although with some weakening, became the basis of the new marriage law as represented in the revised version of CIC in 1983. In this covenant the couple transmits God's love to each other and to their children; they cooperate in transmitting to humanity the love of God and, as the text nicely puts it, "are, in a certain way, its interpreters" (Article 50). With the traditional language of theology the text speaks of the "goods of marriage," and names in the context of the chapter conjugal love and fertility. This is also traditional. Only now *expressly* no order is assumed, *practically* however the love between man and woman is given primacy – and the old third "good of marriage," "the remedy against desire" (*remedium concupiscentiae*) is not even mentioned, although it is referenced specifically in a note to Article 48, along with the relevant texts from Augustine and Thomas Aquinas that also stressed this third "good of marriage."

b) In Article 49, which treats conjugal love, the moral honor of the consummation of marriage is underscored. That seems to innumerable Catholics today a matter of course – at that time, however, it was important given the anxiety of many (and not only older) Catholics, above all as a correction of an earlier condemnation of sexuality. This had to do with the long term effect of the Augustinian idea that erotic desire as such was the result of original sin. If this is the case, then even in marriage sexual activity would be a confirmation of the original sin of the original parents. For this reason in the Middle Ages the thesis was represented that even in marriage erotic love required an excuse. Thomas Aquinas broke with this teaching, according to which marriage is a sort of "legalized sexual offence." It is now on the one hand clear why the "remedy against desire" could be understood as a "good of marriage" and why one the other hand a Council that claims to have something helpful to say in the matter of marriage and family today could not possibly repeat this old doctrine. Only: where in the text do we find the apology by the Church for all the anxiety of conscience that the Church hammered into Christians for centuries?

c) In the most sensitive question of the possible separation of the marriage act and procreation of children, the Council proceeded in half step. It is important: the interior orientation toward children according to the Council text befits marriage and married love as such, not the individual marriage act. This reflects the adoption of a thesis that had gotten the Catholic moral theologians into trouble with the Magisterium since the 1920's. But the Council text is clear, if one, from the background of this conflict, notices what it *does not* say: "Marriage and married love are by nature ordered to the procreation and education of children. Indeed children are the supreme gift of marriage and greatly contribute to the well-being of the parents themselves ...."

Without intending to underestimate the other ends of marriage, it must be said that true married love and the family life which flows from it have this end in view: that the spouses would cooperate generously with the love of the Creator and Savior, who through them will in due time increase and enrich his family" (Article 50).

And just before this we read: "By its very nature the institution of marriage and married love are ordered to the procreation and education of the offspring and it is in them that it finds its crowning glory. Thus the man and the woman, who 'are no longer two but one' (Mt 19:6), help and serve each other by their marriage partnership; they become conscious of their unity and experience it more deeply from day to day. The intimate union of marriage, as a mutual giving of two persons, and the good of the children demand total fidelity from the spouses and require an unbreakable unity between them" (Article 48).

The conclusion to the just cited text presents a clear plea for family planning, developed with regard to relevant ethical viewpoints. The parents and the parents alone are responsible. The implementations read at first glance as very restrictive, above all the notice about the competence of the Magisterium. But this actually has to do with something very obvious: marriage should not be "an egoism of two," supported by a Christian theology of marriage.

d) It remains disappointing – above all in view of the following period – that the text circumvents the question of the *methods* of family planning, with a remark about the work of a Papal commission (note 14 in Article 51). Only abortion is directly condemned. Otherwise in Article 47 the talk is only, in summary fashion, of "unlawful contraceptive practices." That is very vague – a compromise formulation. Originally one wanted to say "unlawful techniques," but then one would have also condemned the "techniques" that were, in terms of moral theology, without reservations. This contains a bitter irony. In the vehement discussion after the Council surrounding the Church's prohibition on so-called "artificial" contraception, one of the arguments of the critics of the Papal teaching is the demand that the opposition prove how the aid of medical and other "artificial" methods of regulation of conception are "technique," while figuring out and avoiding periods of fertility, possible only because of refined technical equipment, is not. If human nature is capable of steering "the course of nature" even in the realm of sexuality, this cannot absolutely be so to speak "of divine law," then the *sort* of technical methods can justify no ethical distinction. To those, who wanted to say "unlawful *techniques*," it is here therefore obviously not so completely clear what they were talking about.

But as mentioned, the Council refrained here from a more detailed statement – had to refrain, because the Pope had reserved the question for further investigation. It is all the more important that Article 51 (at the beginning), regarded full chastity as a danger for the conjugal bond and commitment: "The council realizes that certain situations in modern life often prevent married people from living their married life harmoniously and that they can sometimes find themselves in a position where the number of children cannot be increased, at least for the time being; in cases like these it is quite difficult to preserve the practice of faithful love and the complete intimacy of their lives. But where the intimacy of married life is broken, it often happens that faithfulness is imperiled and the good of the children suffers: then the education of the children as well as the courage to accept more children are both endangered."

Despite the lack of exact statements about methods of family planning, the Council named a few criteria for the form of the marriage act that left room for further discussion in the Church: there can be no contradiction between God's creative will for the continuity of life and true conjugal love; the marital act must conform to true human dignity; the sexual gift of humanity outshines in a wonderful way the correspondence to the lower forms of life; criterion cannot only be good intention, but the nature of the human person and his or her acts themselves.

4. CHURCH AND STATE

The third chapter on the questions of economy would be worthy of more thorough consideration. I omit this, since for our understanding it contains what is most obvious. They are, however, worthy of attention, given the background of an ecclesial social teaching that considered private ownership, also of means of production, more or less as the indisputable cornerstone. In the text of the Council the primacy of work and its importance as a part of human meaning is unmistakable. The encyclical *Mater et magistra* of John XXIII had its effect here – an encyclical that found its continuation with John Paul II's encyclicals *Laborem exercens* and *Centesimus annus* – to the anger of all conservative economists and politicians. But the famous letter on the economy, which took the American Bishops many years to produce, shows – also to the anger of all conservative economic politicians – that this third chapter of the Constitution belongs, along with the reform of the liturgy, to the most lasting work of the Council. Given "tactical" considerations nothing else should have been expected: a Curia that agitates against Liberation Theology and seeks to shut out its episcopal and theological spokesmen, must snatch from this Liberation Theology the theme of poverty and economic injustice.

We turn then to the 4th chapter on "The Political Community." It contains very interesting details in regards to the relationship of Church and State.

a) Government must be directed toward the common good of the citizens (Article 74, third paragraph), the common good "understood in the dynamic sense of the term" (Article 74, third paragraph). Therefore the sense of the common good can change.

b) The right to resistance is expressly secured, if political power is misused: "When citizens are being oppressed by a public authority which oversteps its competence, they should not refuse whatever is objectively demanded of them by the common good; but it is legitimate for them to defend their own rights and those of their fellow citizens against abuses of this authority within the limits of the natural law and the law of the Gospel" (Article 74, fourth paragraph). It is noteworthy: this remark follows on an express emphasis on the moral duty of obedience to a legitimate political authority. And it also is noteworthy: resistance is based on a reference to natural law "and the Gospel." How both are related to one another is not mentioned. One deals with either the doctrine of the "Reign of Christ" or Luther's "Two Kingdom Doctrine"; with both one can at most justify resistance for the benefit of *the other*, never for one's own benefit. The Council wanted to allow that, however. The coy "and the Gospel" reminds us of the ecumenical problem, which is covered over here.

c) What is most astonishing is the clear and unambiguous praise of democracy: "It is fully [!] in accord with human nature that politico-juridical structures be devised which will increasingly and without discrimination provide all citizens with effective opportunities to play a free, active part in the establishment of the juridical foundations of the political community, in the administration of public affairs, in determining the aims and terms of reference of public bodies, and in the election of political leaders" (Article 75, beginning). Not only can John XXIII's encyclical *Pacem in terris* be quoted in the note, but also two radio speeches of Pius XII, at Christmas 1942 and 1944. The Pope of the Second World War, which not least was also a war between the two dictatorial systems of National Socialism and Soviet Communism, could not overlook the advantages of a democratic political system. The text of the Council is a repudiation of the Catholic view of the state of the 19th century, which could think of the state, like the Church, only in a hierarchical structure, keeping on good terms with the sovereign. The Council also strengthened the idea that Christians could represent different political opinions. "They [the Christians] should recognize the legitimacy of differing points of view on the organization of worldly affairs and should show respect for the individual citizens and groups who defend their opinions by legitimate means" (Article 75, fifth paragraph). Herbert Vorgrimler believes that this is "a clear rejection of the still wide-spread, power-politics oriented 'monolithic' unanimity of Catholics in political questions, a unanimity presented as universal." From the opposite direction, but aimed at the same target, comes the remark that in a pluralistic society a distinction has to be made between what Christians do in their own name and what they, together with their Bishops, do in the name of the Church. Vorgrimler comments on this: "Since the Church cannot prevent any organization from using the word 'Christian,' this sentence is the only possible form that the Church can use to ask a pluralistic society to distinguish between what is and is not Christian."

d) There is an crystal clear decision that an amicable separation of Church and State according to the Anglo-Saxon pattern should not be rejected. This is strengthened by the reference that the Church does not place its hope on privileges from the political authority and also rejects the exercise of certain legitimate rights, "whenever it becomes clear that their use will compromise the sincerity of its witness" (Article 76, sixth paragraph). Are also concordat (treaties between the Vatican and State Governments) rights invariably meant with this? The post-conciliar development did not stand firm on this. There are new concordats merrily made – at least in Europe and particularly in Germany, with the result that the state granted privileges and the Church yoked its hopes to this – above all the right to a say in the matter of education (from the installation of professors of theology in the state universities to the installation of teachers of religious instruction).

e) The Council text sees the most decisive issue in relationship to the state in the fact that the Church "is at once the sign and the safe-guard of the transcendental dimension of the human person" (Article 76, second paragraph). Clearly put: the human does not belong to the state. The Church claims the office of watchman. And with right! The Church "watches over" the state and the politicians not like a sort of constitutional court, but it "watches over" humans through admonition and critical word, when the political system tries to push into the untouchable realm of their human rights. And this can of course happen not only through dictatorial power. It is even more important to make sure that the reasonable and fertile cooperation between Churches – more clearly, between ecclesial authorities – and the state finds its borders at the independence and freedom of the mutual critical word, even if it costs privileges that make life easier.

5. WAR AND PEACE

The fifth chapter on War and Peace forms the last chapter of the questions treated here. We begin with some striking quotations:

"Peace is not merely the absence of war; nor can it be reduced solely to the maintenance of a balance of power between enemies; nor is it brought about by dictatorship. Instead, it is rightly and appropriately called an enterprise of justice (Jes. 32, 17)" (Article 78.1).

"Even though recent wars have wrought physical and moral havoc on our world, the devastation of battle still goes on day by day in some part of the world. Indeed, now that every kind of weapon produced by modern science is used in war, the fierce character of warfare threatens to lead the combatants to a savagery far surpassing that of the past" (Article 79.1).

"But it is one thing to undertake military action for the just defense of the people, and something else again to seek the subjugation of other nations. Nor, by the same token, does the mere fact that war has unhappily begun mean that all is fair between the warring parties" (Article 79.4).

"For acts of war involving these weapons can inflict massive and indiscriminate destruction, thus going far beyond the bounds of legitimate defense. Indeed, if the kind of instruments which can now be found in the armories of the great nations were to be employed to their fullest, an almost total and altogether reciprocal slaughter of each side by the other would follow, not to mention the widespread devastation that would take place in the world and the deadly after effects that would be spawned by the use of weapons of this kind" (Article 80.1).

"But we should not let false hope deceive us. For unless enmities and hatred are put away and firm, honest agreements concerning world peace are reached in the future, humanity, which already is in the middle of a grave crisis, even though it is endowed with remarkable knowledge, will perhaps be brought to that dismal hour in which it will experience no peace other than the dreadful peace of death. But, while we say this, the Church of Christ, present in the midst of the anxiety of this age, does not cease to hope most firmly. She intends to propose to our age over and over again, in season and out of season, this apostolic message: 'Behold, now is the acceptable time for a change of heart; behold! Now is the day of salvation'" (Article 82 – last paragraph).

Such sentences, despite their urgency, seem to us almost obvious, even occasionally a bit too indecisive. This feeling – even among Catholics – is more an effect of the Council. There is no better magisterial text on the question of peace than this first section of the fifth chapter in the second part of the Pastoral Constitution, for Catholics who do not consider war under any circumstances to be a means of politics. In order to grasp that, one must keep the starting position in view. This is characterized by three components: *a) the theory of the just (defensive) war*. In the decade before the Council this theory, after centuries of re-organization, each time reacting to the ever-changing conditions and forms of war, followed something of the following form:

• Just – which means as the last means (*ultima ratio*) of political action for safeguarding injured rights – is exclusively a war of defense against military attack. Attacks are ruled out if they are intended to lead to the restoration of injured rights.

• The conditions of a defensive war that is justified in this way are: it has to be declared and led by the civil authority (monopoly of violence by the state, directed externally, no private wars, for example with mercenaries); only the troops may be involved in battle, the civilian population must not be drawn in; the war, that is its success, must be calculable; the right that requires protection may not be destroyed through the events of the war.

• As the most extreme case of necessary defense the use of atomic weapons is permitted (on the technical level *of that time*), in the case that a war that is underway – always understanding a defensive war with this – could be ended more quickly. The macabre example of this is the use of atomic bombs against Hiroshima and Nagasaki in August of 1945, a use that was a flagrant violation of the rule that the civilian population must be protected. The American leadership – as far as the public was informed at that time! – was faced with the yes-or-no question, whether to end the war immediately, in this manner (as happened), or to continue with the war for an unforeseeably long time, and accept the death of 180,000 more American soldiers.

On the basis of this theory the German Bishops, in 1956, announced in a pastoral letter that conscientious objection to such a "just" war is not ethically allowed for Catholics.

b) Immediately after the opening of the Council, in October of 1962, the Cuba crisis brought the world to the edge of an atomic war, which not least through the helpful intervention of John XXIII was avoided in the last minute by the leaders of both superpowers. To remember: American aerial reconnaissance had undeniable photos of Soviet ships transporting rockets for installation on Cuba. Kennedy telephoned Khrushchev and threatened to drop atomic bombs on Moscow – the B-52 bombers with the atomic weapons were permanently in the air, during the Cold War. Khrushchev, who had obviously incorrectly judged Kennedy during their first meeting in Vienna, came to his senses in the last minute, gave the command that the ships should return, and allowed him to be celebrated as the savior of peace in the Soviet public. No wonder, that a series of American Bishops were not willing to accept an ecclesial condemnation of the doctrine of deterrence, in light of this "success."

c) In 1963 John XXIII's encyclical *Pacem in terris* appeared. This appeal for peace from the terminally ill Pope broke with the "Just War Theory." From this background now not only the discussions but also the statements of the chapter are understandable. What should we notice from our reading?

After an introduction that outlines the theme and details the earnestness of the situation (Article 77), Article 78 gives a description of peace on a theological basis, in really prophetic speech, as a continuous task, constantly requiring new dedication. Already in this article, those details that reject the use of violence and limit themselves to the means of defense that is also available to the weaker are recognized and praised before all others. The single limitation is that no injury of rights of others or of society ensues – that is, the carrying out of the rejection of violence must not in the end become violent, but has its limits in that which is possible in a neutral state.

With Article 79 begins the explanation of the details; the reversal is indicated by the fact that the first paragraph does not have the title "On the Conditions of the Just War" but "Avoidance of War."

First the entire inhumanity of modern warfare is described. The Council stresses the validity of the natural law of peoples and its universal principles. The principle "an order is an order" is not valid, and the text reads "we cannot commend too highly" those who have openly resisted such commands. The necessity to keep international conventions is sharply underscored (a nod to the Red Cross would have been a nice gesture).

Finally a legal securing of conscientious objection against military service on grounds of conscience is demanded, with the requirement that the objectors take up some other sort of service for the community. One should know that here in the next-to-last draft of the text conscientious objectors were given recognition "either on account of their witness for the Christian meekness or on account of sincere abhorrence of violence." In the final stress of the consultations a few Bishops achieved the elimination of this basis.

Finally after all these clarifications the Council speaks – since war is of course not all at once eliminated from the world – of the *right*, not of the *duty*, to defense from an attack. The text that we quoted above draws the borders very narrowly, so narrowly, that in view of the facts they seem illusionary. In this context we find a very abstract sounding sentence on the legitimacy of the vocation of the soldier – very even in tone, neither warmer nor cooler than the sentence on the conscientious objectors: "All those who enter the military service in loyalty to their country should look upon themselves as the custodians of the security and freedom of their people; and when they carry out their duty properly, they are contributing to the maintenance of peace" (Article

79, the end). The following Article 80 contains the only partial victory of the opponents. Here is "total warfare" described, determined through "scientific weapons." This is the literal translation of the Latin word for the description of nuclear weapons. The designation "scientific weapons" is the result of the "language war" that had its effect in relation to the discussions around Latin as the language of the Council. On the one side were the modern Latinists, who could imagine a Latin borrowing *arma nuclearea*. On the other side stood the "purists," under the leadership of Cardinal Bacci, who were of the opinion that even modern concepts must be somehow expressed through the medium of classical Latin vocabulary. Thus atomic weapons became *arma scientifica*. The issue had overtaken the war on words: because as a consequence of our text the concept "scientific weapons" *now* includes also all "conventional" weapons, insofar that they destroy indiscriminately soldiers, civilians, and cultural goods—so, napalm, defoliation, and destruction of entire harvests – the deliberately produced oil slick on the sea was not yet discovered.

The earlier version said more than the current text, which contains the line that the dangers of a war with such weapons "compel us to undertake an evaluation of war with an entirely new attitude" (Article 80, second paragraph). Originally here in the Pastoral Constitution a sentence from *Pacem in terris* was supposed to have been included, a sentence that commented that, given the possession of nuclear weapons, the concept of war as an appropriate method for the restoration of rights is senseless; even the possession of "scientific" weapons was supposed to have been condemned in the Pastoral Constitution – as previously the extermination of minorities and entire ethnic groups. Here, however, the Bishops and Cardinals who were aligned with the New York Archbishop Cardinal Spellman succeeded in their attempt to place the universal Church on the side of the west in the Cold War. The quote from the encyclical of John XXIII was taken out – in a note however, which is part of the Pastoral Constitution, it is quoted word-for-word.

Articles 81 and 82 take up the weapons race and the possibilities of creating an international authority that might actually be in the position to proscribe war. In this context it should be noted that no less a figure than Cardinal Ottaviani is to be thanked for the remarks in the next-to-last paragraph, to the effect that the promotion of peace requires above all a new education of young people and a new spirit of public opinion, and that those responsible for the formation of public opinion have a heavy responsibility. The last wars, according to Herbert Vorgrimler, were not begun by the young. A young person formed with a will for peace is the only chance to avoid future wars.

It would not be hard to figure out what recent wars, and what current armed conflicts, could still legitimately take place, according to the statements of the Council. Pope John Paul II, who has been criticized from inside and outside of the Church because of his theological positions and because of the manner in which he has executed his office, has taken the Council more earnestly, in this area, than almost any other Church leader in the world. He has never deviated from his position that the First Gulf War, in the way that it was fought – despite the massive reasons that caused it – cannot be justified ethically. According to the report of a Rome correspondent from one of the important German weeklies, already on the 11th of January, 1991, in the course of a Vatican diplomatic reception, the Pope had damned the threatening Gulf War as a "tragic adventure" and a sign of "the decline of humanity"; he added that "a peace achieved through weapons is only preparation for more use of violence." Without success the Pope warned President George H.W. Bush in telegrams of attacks "that create even worse injustice," without success he challenged Saddam Hussein to "divinely inspired" concessions. On the 17th of January he condemned the outbreak of the Gulf War as "a hard defeat for human rights" – based on the reasoning of the Council – because war is not a means to the solution of international problems, "it has never been this, and never will be this." Today, the Pope said on the 11th of January, 1991, given the modern means of total destruction, "the absolute rejection of war" is called for. No other Pope had ever spoken about a current war. Not all Church leaders followed him with audible agreement. Nonetheless, ten American Bishops called the war "immoral," and the presiders of the German, French, and Swiss Bishops' Conferences saw in this war a "sign of failure."

And the current wars in eastern and southern Europe? Everyone who reads the newspapers carefully knows how difficult the *political* diagnosis is. The powerlessness of a purely ethical argument is clear, day after day. However, there is one thing that no one should use as an argument of excuse: that the ethical formation of judgment is very difficult. To say this, one would need not to have bothered with the Council texts; an entire slate of criteria for a "just" defensive war is neglected. If one considered seriously, rigorously considered them, the result would be bitter insights and a dramatic re-orientation. The statements of the Council on the rejection of war as a political means are quite obviously at the very start of becoming an effective contribution to the "education of the human race."

V. A BRIEF APPRECIATION

We have already determined: the process is the result. In the working out of the Pastoral Constitution the "opening to the world" was *executed*. One cannot put a value on an "openness" as such – one can only put a value on what it filled out or, to put it otherwise: for what it was put to use.

In this regard one must admit – even if with this I might contradict certain critical judgments: the Pastoral Constitution is the "most successful" document of the Council. Simply because in its process there were interventions, chess moves, even intrigues – but oddly not, as in other occasions, so that in decisive places clear manipulations of the text, against the process, took place, which would bring the clearness of its statements into twilight. With the Pastoral Constitution the Council essentially succeeded in actually bringing out in words what it wanted to convey.

A further element of valuation begins with the observation that, seen in its entirety, in the relevant debates the Pastoral Constitution was comparatively less quoted than the other documents of the Council. This seems to have something to do with the judgment: "The process is the result." Where one consciously formulates in a revisable sort of way, the need for revision begins immediately after the close of the text – to the extent that the conditions change, these conditions about which the text in its provisional form wants to give advice. The most important valuation lies in the fact, that gradually, obviously occasioned by the Pastoral Constitution, the style of ecclesial pronouncements changed, at least when it has to do with ecclesial positions to actual problems. And even though one might want to criticize him: the form of expression of Pope John Paul II is also here formative: the earlier "pontifical style" of papal encyclicals is today a memory of an improbable past, no matter how one might feel about the style of John Paul II's apostolic encyclical letters. His successor follows these footprints.

Moreover – the Pastoral Constitution excited lively discussion about all its themes; the last attempts at hesitation, which still have a distant echo in the text, have become obsolete. That is true for the theological conflict with atheism as well as in regards to the questions surrounding marriage and family under the conditions of the modern world, over the best possible relationship of Church and State and, not least, the question of how to secure peace. The "opening" achieved by the Pastoral Constitution is effected in that the relevant discussions are taken up impartially and in a businesslike manner, without the need that one constantly legitimates oneself through the quotation of texts of the Council. Nothing better could come out of this, and with this we want to proceed to a closing appreciation of the entire Council.

Nonetheless: Within that what seems to be overcome today: The Constitution has foreseen in a prophetic manner most of our actual political, social and economic problems, with at the moment the only exception of bio-ethical problems of which the Fathers could not be aware in their own situation and time.

CHAPTER ELEVEN

"THE THIRD EPOCH OF CHURCH HISTORY"

THE LASTING IMPORTANCE OF VATICAN II

In the second chapter, in the description of the opposition to the Council, we quoted the negative speech of the Italian Cardinal Siri: "The Church will require fifty years to recover from the wrong ways of John XXIII." If one were a cynic, one could say, with a glance at the post-conciliar development: The recovery has made very good progress in the more than forty-five years since the end of the Council. To speak of a lasting significance of the Council – that is a bit like the conversation that is held about a heart attack from which one is recovering; spoken of temporarily, but then not at all.

There is another evaluation, an evaluation that Karl Rahner, in the last years before his death in 1984 repeatedly recited. The lasting importance of the Second Vatican Council is that the Church for the first time here, and in a way that cannot be negated, portrayed itself as a world Church and acted as such. I share this last interpretation, the theological and practical consequences of which are not yet thought out to the end, and would like to explain it a bit more at the end of our history of the Council. For this we begin with a targeted backward glance.

I. A BACKWARD GLANCE IN SOMBER HOPE

1. THREE VOICES

After the close of the Council, in December of 1965, Karl Rahner returned with the Archbishop of Munich, Julius Cardinal Döpfner

– with whom he had formed a deep friendship – to Munich, and Rahner held, in an overcrowded large room, a lecture on the theme: "The Council – a New Beginning." The feeling that one stood before an epochal departure of the Church into a new future was uncanny: for those who had borne the burden of the work and also were aware of all the resistance, and also for us young theologians (I had just gotten my Ph.D. and had begun my first job as university lecturer for Dogmatic and Ecumenical Theology). At that time Karl Rahner was already worried that it would "take a long time until the Church that was given a Second Vatican Council as a gift from God would become the Church of the Second Vatican Council."

The "Church of the Second Vatican Council"? Let us hear about this from a completely different voice, 25 years later, the witness of an unknown Catholic that is particularly indicative because this witness simply expresses what its author feels. In 1990 a community of nuns of the "Daughters of Mary of the Precious Blood," which had its cloister in the Black Forest in southern Germany, affiliated itself with the movement of Lefebvre, the Archbishop suspended by Rome. This caused a great deal of controversy in the Archdiocese of Freiburg im Breisgau, so much so that the Archbishop of Freiburg, Oskar Saier, took a position in a pastoral letter. A letter to the editor appeared in the regional newspaper, a letter that addressed itself to the Archbishop's pastoral letter:

> The pastoral letter from Archbishop Oskar Saier of Freiburg ... would have been better directed against the originators of the blasphemous and overly-informal celebrations of the Eucharist who misuse their office and dignity of the Catholic Church for the spreading of their false teaching of Modernism. The Catholic nuns mentioned have sought refuge with Archbishop Lefebvre and the Priestly Fraternity of St. Pius X, like many other Catholics, after the unfaithful office holders wanted, with force and threats, to dissuade them from the traditional Catholic faith. With this refuge-seeking they have not abandoned the faith, rather they have secured their Catholic faith, a faith that in large part has been taken apart in the official Church through the reforms. Through the Priestly Fraternity of St. Pius X, the traditional Catholic faith and the old Mass is taught, celebrated, and experienced as before the Reformation of the Second Vatican Council. The pastors of the Catholic Church would be well advised if they did not take a stand against the entreaties that come out of internal distress of the

traditional faithful and did not make reference to obedience, commands, and reforms. Faith is more than obedience.

The well-crafted joke about the German farmer with which we opened our history of the Council is therefore bitter truth. One must allow the last sentence of the letter to the editor to melt on the tongue: the writer feels himself under the imposition, in ecclesial obedience to accept changes and reforms that cause him "internal distress." He would certainly not be too tired to preach obedience vis-à-vis the Church to supporters of reform, without consideration of *their* "internal distress," had the Council reached opposite conclusions – the conclusions, that is, that the Preparatory Commissions had produced for the Council as proposals. Not only some Bishops and curial officials, but also many "traditional" Catholic faithful cannot be spared the question of "obedience according to discretion," however much claim they might have to tact and sensitivity from those who do not share their anxieties. What is most paradoxical about the remarks of our letter writer, however, is the concluding sentence. The parting shot that faith is more than obedience is directed against a council that – conclusively and with a rejection of "traditional" models of behavior – made just this clear: faith is more than obedience vis-à-vis the Church. That our letter writer could publish this sentence, and the entire letter, without positioning himself immediately on the margins of the Church – this was due to the Council that he accused of a falling away from the true Catholic faith.

But let us listen, as an introduction to our glance backwards, to a completely different voice, that of a journalist who is not closely aligned to the Church, but who evaluates and reports in a fair and insightful manner, one whom we have already quoted once already. In a report on the Latin America trip of John Paul II at the occasion of the anniversary of Columbus's exploration of the West-Indies, he wrote:

> Today … a Pope is accused, in Latin America as in Europe, of allowing his Church to lag behind the Council that was the first in history that hurled an anathema at nothing and no one. The reproach fails to appreciate the change brought about by the Council, the effects of which are less noticed now only because they are so much taken for granted. The Yes to religious freedom, the Yes to respect of those of other faiths and those of no faith, the Yes to ecumenical dialogue, to the liturgy in the vernacular, to the valuing of the laity, the Yes to the Bishops having a say in Rome – admittedly

without co-determination. What has not been overcome: The tension between papal central authority and the local Church, Roman doctrine and pastoral praxis, exclusive claims to truth and tolerance. The conflict between the Church of the Pope and a secularized world has in fact unavoidably intensified. Signposts totter – even if a Pope has a firm hand on the wheel.

Three voices, a three-time echo of the Council from different times. Which voice should be trusted, in order to evaluate the position of the Roman Catholic Church in the world? A glance backwards must distinguish between lasting consequences, unchangeable even by voices of sadness and "internal distress," and those consequences whose ambivalence blocks their future effectiveness, because it *could*.

2. LASTING RESULTS

The most lasting result we have already presented in its own chapter: the liturgical reform. Even the letter writer from the Black Forest could not entertain any illusions: it is just not possible that the Latin liturgy might once again become the liturgy of all Catholics in the entire world. For Latin was and remained the language of the liturgy of the western Church, because and so long as Latin was the intellectual and scientific language of the west after the decline of the Roman Empire – and because and so long as the liturgy remained a clerical liturgy: that was, at the latest, finished by the time of the Reformation. The preservation of Latin then became simply an anti-Reformation anachronism. Despite the anti-Reformers unambiguous fixing of the ecclesial office in its traditional shape, after the Reformation the Catholic liturgy, however hesitantly, had begun to discover the congregation. A clear sign of this is: no more Gothic cathedrals were built with many naves and a multitude of side-chapels; the Baroque churches were built as grand halls for the congregation, which gathered together under ceilings depicting opened heavens.

But anti-attitudes invest, as is known, considerable energy into holding on to what is past. Whoever wants to re-introduce Latin today as the normal language of the liturgy is the same, in a comparison made by Karl Rahner, as those Muslims who demand that the Quran be recited only in Arabic anywhere in the world.

The new self-understanding of the Church as "the People of God" is also unchangeable, with everything contained by this – above all the theologically dominant role of "the laity" as the "Members of the People," whom the office holders have the responsibility to "serve." A distinction between the "teaching" and the "listening" Church is not, according to the Council texts, possible any more, since the office holders have their authority as "listening"; they are to preserve only that which they hear in common with the people. Their leadership happens through the official open proclamation of what is heard. It is unthinkable that this newly awakened consciousness, *to be* the Church and not only to participate in Church, would once again sink back into the dumb unconsciousness of mere "sheep" that need to be "pastured." Certainly one's own history can be forgotten – and that occurs every once in a while in unenlightened forms of departure. However, since this departure happened *consciously*, it cannot now be undone. This consciousness can be, and must be, broadened; it cannot be dismantled.

The opening of the Church to the world, the express address of the Church to those who do not belong to it, accomplished above all in the Pastoral Constitution on the Church in the Modern World, can no longer be shut out. In practice one can violate much of this. One can anxiously and pettily once more turn all attention to "keeping the lambs together," immunizing them against the world to which the Council had opened itself. But one cannot ever again say: we have *no* message for the world, a message that can also be understood by those who do not belong to the faith or who have some other faith. One cannot undo once it has been said: the Church is sign and universal sacrament of the unity of *humanity* with God and one another, independent from all missionary success. If one wanted to undo it, so must one in all earnestness maintain: the Church is *not* sign and sacrament of the unity of humanity, but only the assembly of those who have been saved from the world abandoned to itself. There is no middle way. With the Pastoral Constitution on the Church in the Modern World, the Church gave the world once and for all an instrument of "social control" against the Church. The world can and should ask the question: what about the help that you offered us because of the message? And the world will make use of this social control, as has already been the case – if necessary, by the merciless means of mass media.

One will likewise never again be able to say: in the non-Christian religions there is *no* seeking for God and *no* life according to a conscience guided, even there, by God, but only a rejection of the true God. One will never again be able to say: the faith of Israel is *not* the lasting ground of the faith of the Church, or freedom of religion is *not* a basic human right that flows out of the dignity of the person. One will *not* be able to say, the non-Catholic Churches are not Churches in which "elements of salvation and truth" are found that belong to the Church of Jesus Christ – so that the members of these Churches *through* this and not in spite of it live in the grace of God. If one wanted to attempt the opposite of this, one would only strengthen: we are a European form, understood in other cultural circles, correctly, only as an import, therefore in a self-imposed ghetto and with this in the most favorable circumstance an ideological representation of Euro-American late culture, but no force for the future of the world and of humanity.

Certainly such a retreat might be theoretically considered; the trumpet for such a retreat might even, in practice, be sounded. There are historical experiences that show that hopeful departures in the Church can be stopped. But is it a coincidence that what comes to mind in this context are the conflicts surrounding 15th century conciliarism? This conciliarism was in fact destroyed in the second half of the 15th century, in favor of a newly empowered Papacy that intervened in the conflicts. One thing of course could not be stopped: the memory of the great western schism (1378-1415), a schism popes and anti-popes could not bring to a close; this lack of closure had the result that the question of a counterweight against papal claims of absolute authority were only shelved, not answered, and in acute situations once again came to the fore – finally at the Council and through the Council. No, departures in the Church that amount to more freedom, more missionary presence of the Church as a whole, more infusion of the saving power of the message and less of the power of the institution, could and can be covered over only for certain amounts of time, eclipsed by all too human interests, but not driven from the consciousness – unless the Church is willing to suffer the cost of reducing itself to a historical remnant from the past, only for a brief time more to be considered as a "power player," as many enemies of the Church today hope and predict.

3. AMBIVALENT RESULTS

More than once we have pointed out that several Council texts, through the stubbornness of the opposition – and not infrequently because of the protocol-breaching and therefore unfair resistance of conservative groups – could not be formulated with the clarity that would have allowed only *one* interpretation of the Council. Some texts are – and indeed consciously, if also reluctantly – ambivalent, and allow the representatives of different, even opposing, interests to call texts of the Council "theirs." To be noted: this does not mean that one does not know which option the massive majority of the Council would have opted for – the opposition amounted to at most around 300 Council Fathers from about 2700. Whoever then makes reference to the "spirit" of the Council against more restrictive interpretations, in truth refers not to an demon, but to the responsibly formed conviction of the majority of the Council. It is striking that those who even up to present day have not reconciled with the Council never make reference to the "spirit" of the Council, but always to "their" texts. These are also there – and so we bump up against the ambivalence:

• at the question of the Church as the universal sacrament of salvation, the People of God and *Communio* on one side, and the hierarchical institution on the other side;

• at the theme of the collegiality of the Bishops with the Pope, contradicted by statements meant to give prominence to the supremacy of the Pope;

• at the contradictory statements of the Decree on Ecumenism vis-à-vis a community in worship service;

• at the question of the unity in doctrine; of the tension between the entire teaching that must be presented, and the "hierarchy of truths" that should be considered in ecumenical dialogue;

• at the doctrine on the sense of the faith of the faithful in relationship to the Magisterium of the Pope and the community of Bishops;

• at the statements on the meaning of the Sacred Scripture; whether the doctrine of the Church does now have precedence over the Scripture in the process of the authentic interpretation through the Tradition, or whether the Tradition and therefore the doctrine of the Church remains *under* the Scripture as the highest norm of ecclesiastical life;

• at the opening to the world: how a Council actually can enter into dialogue with the world that, up to that time, had no voice at the Council, because of theological and canon law reasons;

• and at many other questions, which we in our cruise through the most important texts of the Council have not even touched.

We have portrayed how the spokesmen of the thoughts oriented toward the future at that time bet that the future would make *their* interests codified in the texts dominant, and would push aside the remnants of old thinking. They underestimated numerous factors: the influence and the administrative instruments of an entrenched Curia that governed the bureaucracy; large conservative groups in Catholic Christianity, interested in preserving a static, non-changing Church in a quickly changing world; the now limited will for reform, these years after the Council, of many Bishops on the "back benches" of the Council, even though they eagerly voted with *Placet*; the shock effect of the developments that set in after the Council as if, because of the long piled up hopes of reform, "the great freedom" for all and everyone in the Church had broken out; the claims laid to the Council by questionable theologies of "secularization" and "the death of God" – by which originally reform-friendly Bishops became anxious conservatives – and much more. To comment briefly on the last mentioned developments: one certainly cannot rejoice over everything that might have come into existence after the Council, but really had only superficial connections with the Council's intentions. Of course it has indirectly to do with the Council, since such bubbling-over re-orientations could never have been so expressed in the *Catholic* Church *without* the Council, for example under Pope Pius XII. To this extent – and only to this extent – there is a certain correctness, when one blames the Council that it could not prevent that, in the name of the Council and in profound ignorance of its texts, things could be attempted in the Church that have nothing to do with the Council. An understanding of the Eucharist as a purely communal celebration of the community meal is the last thing that the Constitution on the Liturgy would want to support. Also after the Council Jesus is not an atheist, the Church is not "democratic" in the sense that "all power emanates from the people," the priest is not only the speaker of the community, and the teaching office of the Pope and the Bishops has not changed hands to the theologians and the moderators of talk shows. It does not deserve consent, but perhaps some sort of understanding, if for many some hope was soon dashed, the nervous found all their worries substantiated, those who were full of hope became anxious, and an "optimistic" trust in the future of the Church could not be maintained on the basis of a human evaluation of the situation, but only by belief in the working of the Holy Spirit – often only as "hope against all hope" (Romans 4:18). Since 1970 the defenders of the Council have begun to speak of "restoration." Before we investigate this a little more closely, it is important to first weigh the lasting significance.

II. THE LASTING SIGNIFICANCE OF THE SECOND VATICAN COUNCIL

1. A THEOLOGICAL/BASE INTERPRETATION

We began with the thesis of Karl Rahner that in the Council the Church first understood itself as a world church and acted accordingly. Taken literally such a thesis sounds a bit triumphalistic – "world church" causes one to think of "world power." What is meant, however, is the exact opposite. The thesis aims at the self-liquidation of the Church as a *European* institution, which could export itself only as such in the "mission fields."

The facts of the case have what seems at first the almost banal background that the Church, in the time between the two Vatican Councils, had indeed become a far-reaching world church. At the First Vatican Council the churches outside of Europe and America were referred to as "mission fields," therefore represented through European-American "mission Bishops." "Mission Bishops" were ordinaries, having authority for a diocese – therefore they are not just "titular Bishops," like auxiliary Bishops and the top officials of the Roman Curia who are consecrated as Bishops. The established dioceses in the mission areas remained in a special status for a long time. Concretely: they were subordinated to the particular jurisdiction, that is, to the care and supervision, of the Roman "Congregation for the Propagation of the Faith," until they could run their own affairs completely on their own power, above all until they could put in place a sufficient number of native clergy. At the Second Vatican Council the Bishops of the now independent Churches in Africa, Asia, and Latin America appeared – greatly strengthened since Pius XI, and particularly in the time after World War II, as a result of the de-colonization. Of course they remained, in terms of numbers, in the minority, and often they were all too European, that is to say, educated in Rome. But the tendency was already irrevocable – and to remind you, the first Cardinals from these former colonies, elevated by John XXIII, were also there. The new canon law of 1983 had took this new situation into account and repealed the special jurisdiction of the Congregation for the Propagation of the Faith, which now is also called "Congregation for the Evangelization of Peoples." This Congregation is now responsible for its own area, just as the other Congregations are, and not more; the "Mission dioceses" are independent local churches like all the other dioceses of the Church.

To the fact of the strengthened presence of the young churches corresponded – and indeed even independently from this strengthened presence – the tendency from the very beginning to make the Council the end point of a European-North American form of Christianity, in any case to break the practically exclusive claim of the European and North American Church. We recognize the signs of this tendency: the vernacular in the liturgy, the critique, which began right away, of the neo-Scholastic theology of the prepared schemata, the particular readiness to listen to the voices of the eastern churches, the sensibilities for the Third World. This all justifies the judgment that has been already presented: the Church became conscious of itself as a world church at the Council, and attempted to express itself consciously as such in teaching and disciplinary directives.

2. A BASIC THEOLOGICAL TASK

The basic theological task that the Council gave itself, or better: the task the Church considered itself given and which it accepted as given, the Church could not bring to completion. Therefore Rahner also added that the Council tackled this task very "bashfully." This task, according to Rahner, is nothing less than the *crossing over of the Church into the third epoch of her history*—and in that respect this basic interpretation is theological, not only historical. One must – again according to Rahner – distinguish between three different theologically important epochs of the Church. The first was very short, but still, considered theologically, an epoch: that of the Jewish Christianity – the Church in the context of the faith of Israel. The second epoch, introduced through Paul, was the crossing over into the gentile Christianity of the western (middle Mediterranean) cultural *milieu*. We know today how many changes that brought with it, for faith, teaching, and form of the Church—and the discussion is not yet exhausted on the question of how the faith of the Jew Jesus and Paul's belief in Christ are one and the same.

Today the Church stands before the crossover from the western cultural circle into worldwide humanity. Therefore the basic theological task is: how can one communicate literally the Christian faith, change it in its form of expression and appearance, so that it can put down roots in non-western cultures without being misunderstood as a western import? There is no need for evidence about how much we were and still are at the very beginning. It also does not require any long winded announcements that here the devil is in the details and the matter is in no way settled by statements of self-hate and self-liquidation of western Christianity and the treasure of its historical experience. It has much more to do with a gigantic task of translation, which in the final analysis has to be achieved by the other cultures, if they open themselves to the Christian faith. But the Church must *allow* this to happen – and it made a beginning of this at the Second Vatican Council. That is the Council's lasting significance, even when we in the west would like to be of the opinion that for *us* the Council did not bring anything new, but only the ecclesial recognition of what had been reflected and already underway for decades in theology and in Church reform movements – a judgment of course that, in the face of the many creative processes at the Council, is extremely exaggerated.

Opening to the secular world and to cultures outside of Europe; to leave in them faith to their own formative power – what has happened from this new start of the Second Vatican Council?

III. THE TIME AFTER THE COUNCIL

1. "RESTORATION"?

The word "restoration" as a characteristic of the time after the Council – more exactly, the time from about 1970 – has become firmly entrenched in the vocabulary of contemporary church critics, both the faddish and the serious. No one can argue that there are not serious leads for this. Despite the reforms of the Curia demanded by the Council and introduced after the Council by Pope Paul VI – and the Pope knew, from his many years of activity in the Curia, where he had to begin there – and despite the establishment of regularly convening Synods of Bishops, which had the purpose of supporting communication between the Curia and the world Church, "Rome" basically kept on going as before. Let's compile *a few* facts and problem areas where "Rome" is puzzling even to completely loyal Catholics, vis-à-vis what the Curia thinks of the Council and its compulsory points.

a) In the questions that the Council did not dare to discuss because of pressure, and which had to be left over to the Pope for further revision, there was immediately great disappointment. The encyclical *Humanae vitae* from 1968 ended all hope that the Church could find its way on the basis of well-considered grounds to a different position in the question of the *methods* of birth control – and this only has to do with the methods, not with the principle. The disappointed hopes are not alleviated by all that is good and worthy of consideration that is otherwise said in the encyclical about marriage. The subsequent, ever- more sharpened teaching of this encyclical by Paul VI as well as John Paul II also causes hopes to disappear that this might have to do with a regrettable backlash, which could possibly be corrected in time. Since now Catholics throughout the world do not follow the encyclical unanimously, the bizarre situation has developed that the representatives of the Magisterium stand in opposition to the scientifically grounded conviction and the practice of great portions of the Catholic world, the world that the Council, the representatives of the world Church, knew was on its side when it made the decision to admit new questions and knowledge (the Pastoral Constitution on the Church in the Modern World). Since now this Catholic world, contradicting Rome, considers the decision of this question to be a subordinate problem and is inclined to contest the competence of the Magisterium on this issue, and since those who do oppose the birth control teaching of *Humanae vitae* do not even worry that this opposition might mean that they no longer belong to the Church, it is almost logical that the defenders of the doctrine of *Humanae vitae* exaggerate in a countermove, portraying this opposition as revolution against the divinity of God himself, as an attack on his holiness and therefore as a central question of faith. The outlook for success of this "strategy" is slight, and it is not hard to figure out the high costs this fight will finally have: costs on the reputation and trustworthiness of the Magisterium – and no one who considers the voice of the Magisterium to be an absolutely necessary counterweight and arbitrator-like authority in the free discussion among the People of God can be happy about this.

The other reverberating disappointment preceded this, the 1967 encyclical of Paul VI on celibacy. This encyclical also showed that the suggestions of highly qualified experts during and after the Council were for naught. Actually the opposite – the question of celibacy, which even according to "conservative" conviction is only a question of judgment concerning the form of church life, not a binding dogmatic statement – is a model example how all cogent arguments from theology, sociology, and pastoral experience are on the table and nevertheless, because of a claim of authority, do not lead to an change of ecclesial regulations. It is known that John XXIII never had the intention to abolish the requirement of priestly celibacy. But, and this is also pure John XXIII, he had, to the amazement and in some places the ire of many, begun to release priests from the duty of celibacy and thus make it possible for them to have a church wedding, if they wished that out of grounds of conscience and were prepared to relinquish their office. His successor Paul VI continued this practice, although in a more and more limited fashion. John Paul II had this process stopped and only continued with it when canon law demanded it: if someone could prove that he had received ordination under coercion; one pretends to be completely "modern" and extends the concept of coercion also to psychological coercion. This does not improve the matter; it only makes it worse, since now a conflicted priest has a chance of "laicization" if he is willing, practically speaking, to characterize himself as a neurotic. No wonder that upright characters among the conflict-burdened priests refuse this. In the official theological bases for celibacy – from the encyclical of Paul VI to the numerous apostolic letters of John Paul II on priestly office and formation and his Holy Thursday letters to the priests – those concerned do not find their issues addressed. In the meantime the foreseeable, even then, "desertification" of the congregations in which the Sunday Celebration of the Eucharist in the absence of a priest is less and less taken for granted, has increased dramatically – even more elsewhere than in Europe. The groans go – of course, only rarely openly – right through the episcopate; but it does not help. It also does not help that in the year 1985, from the 76 priests whom the Pope had ordained on the occasion of his first Latin America visit in 1979, 35 had left the priesthood and married. To be clear: I am certainly not of the opinion that a lifting of the obligatory celibacy for diocesan priests would correct at one fell swoop all the problems with the office of priest. Quite the contrary – it is perfectly possible that new problems would arise from this. But *some* problems, and indeed very elementary and pressing ones – I am thinking first and foremost of the distressing fates of impacted women and children – would be solvable, and a great number of conflicts, almost inexplicable to a reasonable person, would solve themselves.

b) Developments that were initiated under the protective cover of the liturgical reform were soon censured by Rome, so for examples the efforts surrounding the so-called "general absolution" as – well-grounded, in light of the history of absolution – another form of the sacrament of reconciliation and as an alternative to individual confession. Similarly, and despite all sorts of good reasons, any form of Eucharistic communion with the churches of the Reformation was blocked – and more than the so-called "open communion" was not supported. In spite of the changes since 1970 to the canon law regulations for mixed marriages that make allowances for the conscience of those concerned, changes now to be found in the 1983 Code of Canon Law, there is in not anything like an "ecumenical marriage ceremony." Only within dioceses or regions are there approved wedding ceremony formulae for either Lutheran or Catholic weddings with the co-operation of an official of the sister church. This usually does not matter to those concerned, since they do not understand the canon law or the theological nuances behind this. Actually, an "ecumenical wedding" is also a contradiction in terms, so long as the Catholic Church holds onto the understanding that the marriage is *legally* concluded first in and through the church wedding, while according to Lutheran understanding the wedding is only the blessing of an already concluded marriage. The Catholic understanding is the problem, because this understanding is not required either by the binding dogmatic points of the Council of Trent nor does it seem sensible on the basis of current Catholic theology of marriage. We do not want to be unjust: it is an exceptional achievement that pastoral points of view have here managed, with a great deal of fantasy, to find a responsible solution, in which, if sensibly carried out, all concerned can find unalloyed joy. Only: it revolves around a solution that is agreed on and tolerated by all parties – and no minister is required by the church to comply with the desire for an "ecumenical wedding" of a mixed marriage bridal pair.

With the appearance of the new missal in 1974 the liturgical reform was considered "concluded." From this time Rome watched out that the liturgy, with the exception of the vernacular, remains standardized

– even in the African bush, where in 1985 a Tanzanian liturgy, closely connected to the people and thoroughly "worthy," was forbidden because of a few deviations from the Roman prototype. The responsibility of the regional authority – the Bishops' conference – created as part of the program of the Constitution on the Liturgy does not seem to exist for Rome in the area of liturgical questions. It is therefore no wonder, that Rome and in its trail the Bishops' Conferences let an ecumenical chance of the first order pass them by: the recognition of the so-called "Lima liturgy," which was conceived and celebrated in conjunction with the conference of the Commission on Faith and Order of the World Council of Churches in 1982; since that time it has been practiced, also in the non-Catholic world, as a particularly solemn form of the Lord's Supper. No one who examines the text can miss the fact that this is a liturgy that in form and content completely corresponds to the post-conciliar celebration of the Eucharist in the Catholic Church. Its uniqueness consists above all in the musical and textual elements out of all the places where in the post-conciliar liturgy variations are permitted and welcomed. I do not see what theologically and liturgically should have hindered the approval of this liturgy as an additional liturgical formula, that is, to leave the approval to the regional authorities. Should the occasion arise, one could have made a few slight changes, changes that would not have touched the uniqueness of this liturgy but at the same time would have preserved certain Catholic essentials – for example, one could have, if one had had qualms, demanded the official form of the Words of Institution. Is it possible that the hidden anxiety got in the way of allowing the Lima liturgy – in conjunction with the important "Lima Declaration" concerning baptism, Eucharist, and office – could be understood as an opening to Eucharistic community? That could have been easily cleared up – and also a purely Catholic celebration of the Lima liturgy could have been an important sign for ecumenical hope from the side of the Catholic Church.

c) The freedom of theology, of its research and its questioning – established in the Constitution on Revelation – remains a hope, today once again enveloped with fear, fear not least because of the age-old practice of spying by Roman officials. Even the use of the historical-critical methods in exegesis – the limits of which all reasonable scholars are aware of – is once again dangerous, since the first instruction of the Congregation for the Doctrine of the Faith concerning some aspects of liberation theology, the "mistakes" of which are attributed to Rudolph Bultmann. The worries of the authors of the instruction are understandable, the description of the facts sometimes grotesque, above all the alleged internal connection of historical-critical exegesis and the alleged "Marxist" roots of liberation theology, but the denunciation of Bultmann, through whose influence also Catholic exegetes learned to use the historical-critical methods, is alarming, all the more because the former Prefect for the Congregation for the Doctrine of the Faith, Joseph Cardinal Ratzinger, has become the spokesman of a in part justified, but in part also caricaturing general attack on historical-critical exegesis. We do not even mention here the disregard of the words of the Council that, for the goal of a deeper insight into Revelation, theology must always be prepared to interpret anew the teaching of the faith.

The extent of unease among theologians became palpable when in 1990 the Congregation for the Doctrine of the Faith published its "Instruction on the Ecclesial Vocation of the Theologian," which suggested an oath of fidelity from all high ecclesial officeholders and all who teach in an ecclesial setting. It must be remarked that the instruction takes great care to describe and to dignify a theologian's conflict of conscience between intellectual integrity and obligation to church teaching. In the end, however, the Instruction demands that this conflict, if it cannot be resolved by simple submission to the ecclesial precept, must be endured in the personal conscience, in no instance may it be carried out in public, and certainly not – this was the most pressing point – in the mass media. This is the case not only for the binding dogma but also for the so-called "authentic" teaching of the Church, for which infallibility has not been claimed. If one follows this to its end, then the logical conclusion is that also the non-defined official teaching of the Church cannot be changed, since this would require open, if not actually public, discussion. But in many respects the non-defined official teaching of the Church has changed in a lasting manner, in many areas. It is not unusual that what is represented at a particular time as current "authentic" teaching of the Church is exactly what a vehemently contested opposition had already said, 50 years before. And not even defined dogma remains spared from revisions, which are more than simply new interpretations – at the Council that happened more than one time, as we have seen. Nonetheless the oath is demanded. What other sense – 25 years after the dismantling of the "anti-modernist oath" – can it have, except to have in hand an instrument for discipline that in the extreme case can cause a decades-long blockage of theology, as did the anti-modernist decisions of the early 20th century? In short: the freedom of theology exists – and this damages the reputation of the Church – only because of the *extra-ecclesial* protection of guarantees. There would never have been a "Küng case" in Italy on an ecclesial theological faculty; his chair would have been long gone before he could have written his book on infallibility.

d) The collegiality of the Bishops with the Pope and the demand of the Council for more decentralization in the Church, therefore for more respect for the uniqueness of the local churches, have not yet had much in the way of positive results. The intentional naming of conservative Bishops guarantees a conservative two-thirds majority in the Bishops' Conferences, so that no unwelcome innovations can be expected from there. Bishops' Synods in Rome are up to this point discussion in the presence of the Pope – who however never participates in the discussion and only afterwards publishes what he considers appropriate on the basis of the discussion he has heard. Even when in such post-synod papal writings sincere efforts at incorporating the variety of proposals that arise at a synod are made, that does not change the fact that these Bishops' Synods are not what the Council actually had in mind. They are more an almost humiliating caricature of what Pope Paul VI wanted, as he resolved their institution with the Council: the demonstration of the responsibility the world episcopacy has for the Church. What is the use of the most sincere and productive processes of opinion building at these Bishops' Synods, if they do not also have a binding effect on the Pope, which then would cause the Pope to at least join the discussion!

The new code of canon law also subtly devalued the Ecumenical Council vis-à-vis the Pope, and therefore eliminated the old, "naïve" thesis of the 1917 *Codex Iuris Canonici*, according to which the Council exercises the highest authority in the Church along with the Pope. It has to do, at a superficial read, only with the nuances, and in no way a direct contradiction of the statements of the Council. But two clear differences between the 1983 code and the 1917 code become obvious with a closer reading: the Ecumenical Council no longer exercises together with the Pope the highest leadership authority – now in canon 336 in place of the Council we find "the College of Bishops." In the following canon 337 the Ecumenical Council is one of three possibilities for the College of Bishops' exercise of power with and under the Pope; other forms of collegial action, whether taken up by the Bishops with the agreement of the Pope or introduced by the Pope himself, appear to have equal status with the Ecumenical Council. The text of the code of canon law itself then suggests to the Pope to attempt first the other, simpler, less cumbersome forms of practicing collegiality before he calls a council, which in the view of the code has no theological advantage over other forms. In contrast, the authority of primacy of the Pope is repeated, of course, without any weakening, and legally prescribed. When one remembers that in the 1980 draft of the code the Council was not even mentioned, then the assumption that the subtle devaluation of the Council was intentional can hardly be dismissed as imagination.

Given such precepts, the Bishops' Synods have occupied themselves with comparatively fewer important problems, and these have dealt mostly with internal church matters – the most recent topics, for example, have included the teaching on marriage (of course in the trajectory of *Humanae vitae*), reconciliation in the Church, priestly formation. There, where the heart of the Council beats – precedence of the entire people of God in the description of the nature of the Church, unity in diversity, opening to the world, dialogue and humility—there the Bishops' Synods have not made progress – that is, could not make progress. Anything approaching a pastoral strategy of the universal Church, as Karl Rahner demanded in the context of his interpretation of the Council, is missing. The slogan of the "New Evangelization of Europe" was not known to Rahner, who died in 1984, and it is certainly not what he had in mind. Pastoral care is something different from "evangelization"; the latter consists, at least up to now, for the most part of ecclesial and institutional demands, above all of ecclesial-institutional demands that, unless guided by ecumenical sensitivity, do little except cause bad blood.

It goes along with this sort of evangelization that no one has given up – as far as possible – setting great store by government privileges, a renunciation the Council had demanded. On the contrary, where the states allowed it, concordats (treaties between the Roman see and secular state governments) have been drawn up, and not infrequently the state has made itself the henchman of ecclesial interests, even purely ecclesial interests, to the cost of non-Christian taxpayers.

In the same way the Council's demand that the Roman Curia understand itself and implement itself as a *help*, not as a watchman, vis-à-vis the Bishops remains a pious wish. Immediately after the Council Pope Paul VI introduced, in accordance with Articles 9 and 10 of the Declaration on Bishops, a curial reform, which led to more friction-free teamwork. But that served the Curia – and did not function in the same manner after Pope Paul VI. In relationship to the Bishops, however, the curial reform only improved the possibilities and efficiency of the central regime. As "the Instruction on the Ecclesial Vocation of the Theologian" effectively ended any hope for license for free speech in the Church, so also most recently the writing of the Congregation for the Doctrine of the Faith on the Church as *communio*, with regard to the relationship of the universal Church to the particular churches. Even what only amounted to a soft braking by the Council against an escalating understanding and thoughtless practice of papal authority was loosened up. In objection to supposed or here and there even actual "separatist" tendencies, the hierarchical structure of the Church is not commented on using the ideas of the community of particular churches, in and from which according to article 23 of the Dogmatic Constitution on the Church the universal Church "exists," not illumined in its actual sense and therefore also limited; an impassable boundary is drawn for the idea of the Church as *communio* by the brazen comment that the community of particular churches forms the universal Church only "with and under Peter" (*cum Petro et sub Petro*). Clearly put: any critique on the present understanding and the present practice of papal primacy is critique of the nature of the Church itself. Were this true, then the entire Second Vatican Council would only be material for satire. Because then the emphasis, greater than anything up to that point, on papal primacy that was expressed in the preface to the Dogmatic Constitution on the Church, demanded against protocol of the Council, would be the actual understanding of the Church of the Second Vatican Council; this would have proclaimed an ecclesiology, a "Doctrine of the Church," that would eclipse even that of the First Vatican Council. To top it all off the Congregation for the Doctrine of the Faith also believes all ecumenical attempts for new unity of the Church aim "objectively" to bring about such a unity of Christendom "with and under Peter." The reaction of ecumenists is easy to guess and now also on record.

e) And just in general, the ecumenical dialogue! Since around 1970 it stagnates on the completely official line of protocol politeness. It is noticeable that the mutual reserve inevitably has increased: the Lutheran Church (as well as the Eastern Orthodox) has become more and more cautious, as they observe that the Roman Catholic Church intentionally returned to the old habits – this Church then becomes more reserved, as they complain of the increasing hardening of the positions of the non-Catholic Churches. How is this possible, when since this same time one "consensus paper" after another has appeared, worldwide or regionally, produced between the Catholic Church and the World Council of Churches or the Catholic Church and the Lutheran Church or one of the other churches of the Reformation? Should one come to the conclusion: exactly because theologians became serious about ecumenical opening in the Church, did those in the official ecclesial offices become more cautious, so that no unconsidered step might be regretted later? Three facts speak for themselves:

The first fact: immediately after the Council – with indications of this already during the Council – a series of at least indirect, and in part direct, anti-ecumenical measures on the part of Rome, which have not come to an end – beginning with the new instruction on indulgences, not particularly sensitive to the churches of the Reformation in terms of content and timing, published as it was on the 1st of January, 1967, the year that marked the 450th anniversary of the publication of Luther's theses on indulgences, up to the Vatican position on the ordination of the first female Lutheran Bishop, in Hamburg on the 30th of August, 1992, which the Papal spokesman immediately disparaged as an additional hindrance for ecumenical dialogue. We don't want to narrate here a story of scandal of the post-conciliar ecumenical dialogue – but it would be unbelievably easy to do so.

The second fact: since the series of anti-ecumenical actions were obvious only to a small group of knowledgeable observers of the ecumenical scene, the resignation in the broader church public came a good decade later. One can say: until the year 1980 (the Jubilee Year of the Augsburg Confession of 1530) the ecumenical interest of the church public – Lutheran as well as Roman Catholic – continued comparatively unbroken, although all the ecumenical documents of these years remained without results on the level of the institutions (so, for example, the so-called Malta Document of 1971, or the document "The Lord's Supper," or the declarations of the Pope on the

Augsburg Confession, the important results of the U.S. Lutheran-Catholic Dialogue, etc.). After that the interest fell starkly off. That impacted not only the important declarations of Lima, but also the official remarks concerning the "Luther Year" 1983 (clearly more cautious than those of 1980), and the document concerning the 16th century condemnations of doctrine and the meaning of these condemnations today. If for decades the cleverest minds in theology and in the Church consider consensus and new community among Churches a possibility, but nothing happens on the official levels, necessarily the Church interest in ecumenical dialogue limits itself to an ever smaller group of stalwarts, who do not give up hoping against hope.

The third fact: for about a decade it is noticeable that the non-Catholic Churches have lost patience with "Rome" and, after a new church unity is shattered upon the stubborn position of Rome, they do in their own communities what they could have done for a long time on the basis of their own conviction but delayed doing, among other reasons, because of consideration of the dialogue with Rome: Lutheran Churches conclude agreements for church unity with Methodist Churches, the Anglicans began ordaining women, the Lutheran world has numerous female Bishops.

It looks, at the moment, a bit grim for a new community of Churches. There are a number of detail questions that one could constructively engage without pre-judging unresolved theological questions, if one wanted to. But that did not happen even once: from stronger cooperation in the commissions of the World Council of Churches – a formal membership is at this time not desirable since it would, because of the quota rule, endanger the World Council of Churches – the Roman Catholic Church would be able, together with the Orthodox, to outvote the churches of the Reformation – to the pastoral care for marriage partners of different confessions. And why does the Pope not produce an encyclical on contemporary problems along with Geneva – as the Lutheran and Catholic Bishops' Conferences in Germany have produced memoranda? In the background is the refusal to dignify, with the Council, the Churches of the Reformation as "Churches and ecclesial communities," and to recognize the office in these Churches, because it is the office of a *church* that one recognizes as such. If the current internal politics of the Catholic Church are added to this – the naming of Bishops, the denial of the *nihil obstat* to theology professors, against the vote of their faculties and the responsible Bishops – then possibly one, even as a Catholic, might advise the Lutheran church administration: Wait and see how things develop! Respect for "the Freedom of the Christian" is not particularly popular in the Church of Rome.

f) And in order not to allow this to pass unmentioned: The theme "women in the Church," much less any of the inquiries of "feminist theology," were simply not questions of the Council – recognizable not least by the conventional "inclusive," that is, masculine, language when men and women were meant at the same time. This lack of interest at the Council made it even easier, then, for Rome and the conservative part of the Catholic Christianity to completely block this theme. The Congregation on the Doctrine of the Faith in a declaration (and Pope John Paul II in different addresses) has expressly, and with the most questionable arguments, blocked any thoughts of women's ordination. A few German Bishops expressed interest in a stronger support for women pastoral assistants. Whether consciously or unconsciously: this has a pronounced restrictive effect; it blocks, first of all, any tendency toward the lifting of the obligatory celibacy requirement. The male pastoral assistants – this was shown in the history of the origin of this new Church office in Germany since the end of the 60's – are without fail the "reserve army" of future married priests. The exclusion of women from the office would amount to such an open discrimination against women, however, that one, in order to avoid this, could not make the male pastoral assistants into priests – therefore, as desired, can again cement the obligatory celibacy rule.

Short and sweet – and in order not to shrink from a clear judgment: seldom in Church history has such a minority at a Council – as already mentioned, 300 to 500 Fathers, from 2700 – been treated so carefully, so sensitively, and at the expense of the public "image" of the Pope, when it comes to the contradictory, or at least ambiguous, formulations of the council texts. Seldom has this minority more shamelessly exploited these ambiguities of their own making, in order to bypass the clear majority will of the representatives of the universal Church. If this required any evidence, it would be provided by Rome's treatment of the proposals of the Würzburg General Synod of Dioceses in the Federal Republic of Germany, proposals that went through the thick filter of the German Bishops' Conference and were consequently quite modest – that is, Rome's denial of the proposals through purposeful neglect. The principle, born from faith and hope, of the 17th century Pietist Philipp Jakob Spener: "Wait for better times!" could be cynically changed into: "Wait for *worse* times!" A sober look at the realities brings one to the following conclusion: an opening to variety, the liquefaction of the centralized bureaucratic leadership style of the Roman Curia – and of the "Roman" Curia outside of Italy – can only be expected if *worse* times come for them, times in which they simply cannot accomplish what they want to accomplish. Therefore – and this is the most depressing result of the post-conciliar development – the *Bishops* are almost completely missing as a partner in an open discussion of controversial questions in the Church; they are so under the pressure to be loyal that they must defend all and everything that Rome orders, even including the official refusal of female Eucharistic ministers. And those who know, from private contacts, that some Bishops think otherwise and groan (and occasionally curse) under the burden of negotiating between the local Church and the central Church administration: they do not report the details in public, in order not to make their task even more difficult for themselves. The situation is similar now with professors of Theology on Catholic faculties: until they get a call, they must guard their tongues (the reason why it is again very difficult to hold chairs in Dogmatic or Moral Theology). And if they are in office, they must qualify what they say, speak in a "balanced" way, in order not to lose the teaching authority. Are we moving again to the old line: "Catholics are false"?

2. ONLY "RESTORATION"?

Where there is so much shadow, there also has to be light. Not everything that happened after the Council was "roll back"; we can speak only very briefly about this.

a) The Constitution on the Liturgy is almost completely overtaken and left behind by the brave steps that have been taken by Rome, or with Rome's active support. One needs only to be reminded of the *complete* vernacular liturgy, not envisaged by the Council, and – despite the "end" of the reform – of the much broadened availability of new (and improved older) liturgical texts, which brought alive the best from the great harvest of the liturgical tradition. Before this, all the still unfulfilled wishes pale in comparison.

b) In the restrictive declaration *Mysterium Ecclesiae* of 1973—from the Roman view clearly a condemnation of the ecclesiological theses of

Hans Küng and of many who think like him, for example, in the team of the international periodical *Concilium*—one finds, for the first time in an official ecclesial document, the declaration that dogmatic formulations also have an historical character and therefore do not, in every time period to an equal measure, adequately bring to expression what is the truth of the faith. Just for this statement one must give credit to the declaration as a milestone. And it is very significant that the already mentioned instruction of the Congregation on the Doctrine of the Faith, "On the Ecclesial Vocation of the Theologian," despite its oppressive tendencies, approved and repeated this statement.

c) Although the new law code of the Church, the *Codex Iuris Canonici* of 1983, is a catastrophe in the opinion of critical canon lawyers who have not forgotten their theology, the essential improvements should not be overlooked. It is a good thing that the number of the canons vis-à-vis the 1917 CIC is reduced by a third: a small step in the direction of an "edict free Church," where that is possible. The punishments were also in many cases limited. Above all there are now only a few instances of *excommunicatio latae sententiae*, that is, excommunication, exclusion from the Church community, that occurs automatically through the committing of the punishable act—a proceeding that not only deprived this most severe of all church penalties of any transparency, but then made this into a routine proceeding, with forms of the request for absolution as a result. There are also far reaching improvements in marriage law, even when its problematic system remains. So, for example, everyone who leaves the Catholic Church in a public act and/or goes over to another Christian church is not, as previously, bound to the ecclesial marriage ceremony formula – the previous legal rule, according to the principle "once a Catholic, always a Catholic," made some absurd and cynical misuse possible.

d) Not *everything* has come to a standstill in the ecumenical dialogue. The meeting between Philip Potter, the General Secretary of the World Council of Churches, and Pope John Paul II, when the latter visited Geneva in 1984 was clear enough: Potter greeted "the Bishop of Rome," and the Pope countered this, friendly but clear, with what his office as "Bishop of Rome" is, according to Catholic self-understanding. But – there has never been a Pope who has had such accepting things to say about Luther and the Reformation as John Paul II. In the disappointing statements about the Luther Year 1983 it became clear that the much more open speeches for the Augsburg

Jubilee and during his first German visit, in 1980, did not originate
with the Pope. It always all depended, and depends, on such occasions
on who prepared the draft of the text of the speech. But he, the Pope,
spoke these speeches—and in part also later repeated them. One cannot go back from these words, and anyone who tries to do so will be
insistently reminded of them. For the first time in history one can cite
papal speeches in the defense of ecumenical dialogue, to give ecumenists courage to face the future. At the time that this chapter is written,
the most suspenseful question is how the Church will react to the document "The Condemnations: Do They Still Divide?," a document that
was caused indirectly by the Pope. Other highly placed committees of
the Lutheran Church have in the meantime made statements, for the
most part in nuanced, positive fashion. One will be able to recognize,
in the way that the Churches receive this document and transform
it into ecclesial reality or do not risk this reception, whether the old
suspicion that only power interests and incapacity for movement hindered the Churches on their brave steps toward one another was, in
fact, correct. But even in the event of a failure of these attempts the
document will go on record about what appeared possible vis-à-vis
church unity to reasonable and expert theologians, free from any suspicion of disloyalty to their churches, at the end of the 20th century.

e) In one point the post-conciliar Church did indeed continue and
strengthen the statements of the Council: in the complexity of questions of social justice and peace. As we remember, almost the only express condemnations of the Council belonged to *this* point, that is,
with respect to the abuse of human dignity through unjust political
and economic structures, abortion, and armament with "scientific
weapons" and the total war made possible because of these weapons.
The controversy, not yet ended, surrounding Liberation Theology and
its influence on the Church in Latin America should not blind us to
the fact that this has only to do with the path to righteousness and
the possible ecclesial conditions for this – keyword: "base communities" versus "hierarchical structure of the Church." There can be no
more doubt that the Church has placed itself on the side of the poor
and defenseless. A glance at the Church in the (old and new) Federal
Republic of Germany should not deceive us: if it is correct – it is a
question of political judgment – that the Church here still stands on
the side of the powerful, that only is evidence that it is one of the slow-
est ships in the convoy of the universal Church.

IV. REMAINING TASKS FROM THE
IMPULSES OF THE COUNCIL

In one of his last articles before his death in 1984, Karl Rahner asked a question about forgotten initiatives of the Second Vatican Council. The Council as a treasure trove of new discoveries! After the short description of the post-conciliar epoch that we have attempted, this should not be wondered at. Rahner had in mind tasks that theology had not yet tackled, as well as reforms that had not yet been completely achieved. Rahner himself emphasized that he was only naming *a few* of these tasks. But these are good examples, so I, too, will name them here.

1. ANSWER TO ATHEISM

The theological answer about the meaning of atheism is still to appear. The Council condemned atheism as *doctrine*, in a rather brusque way ("… in conflict with reason and with common human experience, and which cast humanity down from the noble state to which it was born"). But the Council also made it clear that even a theoretically conscious atheism does not necessarily shut one out from the grace of God, if those who claim to be atheists live according to their consciences. Fifty years ago it was a common and undoubted thesis of Catholic theology – an inheritance of the First Vatican Council – that an atheist could temporarily, but not in the long run, remain an atheist *without guilt*. Are we therefore, Rahner asked, in the meantime surrounded by a host of villains? Who answers this question with a negative must then consider the consequences: an atheist lives in the grace of God, without which he cannot achieve salvation. The Council, with its words about "ways known only to God," provides here not a solution, but something to stimulate thought. Behind this stands the problem that engaged Karl Rahner for decades: the relationship between a world history apparently distant from God and the special salvation history of Israel and the Church. If then it is not the case in good (or should we say bad?) Augustinian fashion that with very few exceptions Hell is supposed to be the consequence of world history, then theology must give an account *how* the Church ought to be "sign and sacrament" of the salvation of a humanity that in large part cannot or will not read this sign.

2. ENCULTURATION OF THE LITURGY

It cannot suffice for the "universal Church" to translate the liturgy into the vernacular, but otherwise to preserve the Latin liturgy, that is: the liturgy of the western Church, a liturgical form oriented in the main on the pattern of the liturgy of the ancient Church. Were it to remain so, then a decisive point of the suspicion against Christianity – that it is a western import – is not without foundation. Who though has had insights about this, up to this point, or has supported such insights?

3. COLLEGIALITY OF THE BISHOPS

The collegiality of the Bishops with the Pope functions imperfectly not only on the practical level: the task of explaining theoretically-theologically how the two subjects of the highest authority in the Church can co-exist without destroying the unity of the Church has not been undertaken. It makes no difference whether the Ecumenical Council is considered the second subject or, because of the Council's subtle devaluation, the College of Bishops. Theoretically, such a double holding of the highest authority in the Church is not unthinkable. But it must be explained how it can be that the Pope, when he acts alone for the entire Church, acts as the head of the College of Bishops. Only then could it lose its restrictive overlay; that is, that the Bishops can never collectively act *without* their head, whether at a council or otherwise. How can one legally, but first and foremost morally, make absolutely sure that the Pope acts *as* head of the College of Bishops and not against it?

4. REVISABLE SPEECH

The forms and conditions have not been sufficiently thought through – those forms and conditions that are necessary so that the Church in the future can do what it so courageously did for the first time at the Council: to speak in a temporary, provisional form, consciously, admitting this fact. In practice this problem might not be so difficult. The holders of the teaching authority have at their disposal a broad palette of legally formulated means of statement of different weight. Consequences must be understood, however. A basically revisable form of ecclesial magisterial statements and positions about actual problems has results for the form of loyalty that Catholic Christians would owe such statements from the Magisterium. If one thought about this, then the entire relationship between the People of God (the laity) and the hierarchy would come into play, and the idea of the People of God would become concrete at a central and sensitive place. It is hard to predict these results. But the task has been set by the Council and – in the meantime almost forgotten! Or to be more honest: the most recent relevant statements of the Magisterium ("Instruction on the Ecclesial Vocation of the Theologian," the *Mandatum*, ever new emphases on *Humanae vitae*), with their demand for internal and external obedience even with regard to the non-defined statements of the Magisterium do everything to try to suppress the ideas of such a differentiated loyalty.

In short: the remaining task from the impulse of the Second Vatican Council consists in this – to prioritize the question how the Church can concretize her role as world Church, the role assumed at the Council. That is to be considered both theologically and practically. And with this we come to a closing reflection

V. A THIRD VATICAN COUNCIL?

From time to time the call for a Third Vatican Council becomes loud. Most recently an Italian newspaper asked Cardinal Ratzinger whether a Third Vatican Council was possible in the near future; Cardinal Ratzinger answered in the negative.

I also think that there will not be a Third Vatican Council anytime in the near future. Not for the reason that Cardinal Ratzinger gave in the interview I just mentioned. He feared that a powerful conservative majority at a Council would attempt to revoke some of the results of the Second Vatican Council. In the event this is not a particularly subtle defensive argument – one shows the supporters of a new Council the "instruments of torture," as a precaution – I do not consider this reason as a warning against a new Council. It is much more probable that exactly what happened at the Second Vatican Council would happen again: the conservative Council fathers would attempt, on the way to the preparation of the drafts, of the contributions to the debates, and if necessary again with intrigues, to push through their agenda, and the overwhelming majority of world episcopacy would not allow this and, on the basis of the experiences from 1962 to 1965, not allow themselves to be manipulated as they were at that time. I see a much more banal, but more realistic reason, that speaks against the hope of a new Council: so long as survivors of the Second Vatican Council are still with us, who can keep alive the memory of the agonizing work of these years – not only Council fathers, but contemporaries who were involved directly or indirectly – one would simply give up on such an all-consuming event. Occasionally the call for a Third Vatican Council is tied up with the utopian idea of making this Council a Council of the entire Christendom – this would multiply the difficulties.

So the announcement of an extraordinary Synod of Bishops for the year 1985 was even more surprising; at this Synod, after 20 years, the balance of post-conciliar development in a changed world was supposed to be taken. According to the information that I have, it was a spontaneous idea of the Pope, two days before his Latin America trip. In this regard, it was very much like John XXIII and the Council.

The idea of a balance sheet without the enormous bureaucracy of a Council was completely reasonable. If the intention was or had been, as indications were in a few statements, bound up with a focus on the negative results of the Council and in consideration of this focus to turn back the Council, that intention could have succeeded as little as the manipulation of the Council itself. The representatives of the universal Church in Rome had to hear again what the universal Church actually thinks and what they, as before, did not want to hear. The result then brought all the pre-Synod criticism to naught. The concluding text of the Special Synod – edited by Walter Kasper, at that time Bishop of Rottenburg-Stuttgart – overcame all fears that the ecclesial office *wanted* the Council rolled back. The Special Synod showed not less than this: the Council created a consciousness that is now long lasting. One cannot make the mature People of God immature again, unless at the price of a total loss of trust in ecclesial authority.

Our look into the negative sides of the post-conciliar period might not transport us to a place of euphoric optimism. As things are today, it could be that the Church begins its third millennium of history completely polarized by the once again strengthened conservative, even ultra-conservative, forces. But even this would show the irreversible significance of the Second Vatican Council, in caricature. In earlier times, those who contradicted would have been cut out or forced out of the Church. To judge by appearances, a monolithic Church would do what its Pope and his representatives told it to do. Today the friends of conciliar renewal fight the good fight in the Church and hope in the Holy Spirit. One can remain bravely in the Church, although one possibly experiences only disappointments with it. One can, in the Church, again even dream of another Church.

VI. A DREAM OF THE CHURCH

A line of prominent contemporaries, theologians and non-theologians, have in the last years publicly made known their "dream of the Church." I am not prominent, but I also dream of the Church. I allow myself, to dream once again this dream, at the close of our narrative of the Council.

I dream of a Church that says clearly that it exists for the sake of the Gospel and the faith of humanity.

I dream of a Church that neither in theory nor in practice believes it must help along the power of the Gospel over hearts with "measures."

I dream of a Church that in its self-understanding and in its image holds together the best elements of the Catholic, Lutheran, Reformed, and Orthodox understanding of Church in fruitful tension.

I dream of a Church that resists bureaucratization, in so far as the practical necessities allow for that, and that deals with people in a different manner than the state apparatus tends to.

I dream of a Church in which no one needs to have "threshold anxiety" when he enters the pastor's office.

I dream of a Church in which one cannot "become something" except a witness to the Gospel.

I dream of a Church that in its communal life credibly holds up to modern society and its supposed practical constraints the counterpart of an entirely different sort of co-existence.

I dream of a Church that endures conflicts, resolving them differently than is done in "the world," and in which no one can use the question of the correct interpretation of the Gospel to personally get one's way.

I dream of a Church in which no one has any anxiety about the Gospel and faith if they are not exactly the same in all places in the world as it is in one particular place.

I dream of a Church that understands its "sacramentality," the victorious presence of the grace of God in it, as the liberating freedom to pray, every day, with regard to persons and with regard to structures: "Forgive us our sins!"

I dream of a Church that knows its true worth, that therefore makes clear in both doctrine and life that it itself is not the heavenly Jerusalem, but is destined to disappear when the Kingdom of God comes, that it is now here only to prepare the way for the earthly Church and to point the way to community with God and with one another.

Forty-Five years after the Council, awakening out of such a dream is always difficult, and getting more difficult. But – without dreams, no models. And without models, no way into the third epoch of the history of the Church.

BIBLIOGRAPHIE AUS DEN LESEEMPFEHLUNGEN UND ANMERKUNGEN VON OTTO HERMANN PESCHS DAS ZWEITE VATIKANISCHE KONZIL

Vorgeschichte – Verlauf – Ergebnisse – Nachgeschichte, Würzburg 2001

Acerbi, Antonio, Due ecclesiologie. Ecclesiologia giurdicia ed ecclesiologia de communione nella »Lumen gentium« (Collana interconfessionale per la promozione della ricerca teologica 4), Bologna 1975.

Acta Synodalia Sacrosanti Concilii Oecumenici Vaticani II, Vol. II, Periodus Secunda, Pars IV, Congregationes Generales LIX-LXIV, Rom (Typis Polyglottis Vaticanis) 1972, 616-618 (Congegatio Generalis LXIII, 8. Novembris 1963).

Adam, Karl, Das Wesen des Katholizismus, Düsseldorf [13]1957.

Alberigo, Giuseppe / Wittstadt, Klaus (Hgg.), Ein Blick zurück – nach vorn: Johannes XXIII. Spiritualität – Theologie – Wirken, Würzburg 1993.

Alberigo, Giuseppe, Ekklesiologie im Werden. Bemerkungen zum »Pastoralkonzil« und zu den Beobachtern des II. Vatikanums, in: ÖR 40 (1991), 109-128.

Alberigo, Giuseppe (Hg.), Geschichte der Konzilien. Vom Nicaenum bis zum Vaticanum II, Düsseldorf 1993.

Alberigo, Giuseppe / Wittstadt, Klaus (Hgg.), Geschichte des Zweiten Vatikanischen Konzils 1959-1965. Bd. 1: Die Katholische Kirche auf dem Weg in ein neues Zeitalter. Die Ankündigung und Vorbereitung des Zweiten Vatikanischen Konzils (Januar 1959 – Oktober 1962), Mainz – Leuven 1997; Bd. 2: Das Konzil auf dem Weg zu sich selbst. Erste Sitzungsperiode und Intersessio. Oktober 1962 – September 1963, Mainz – Leuven 2000; Bd. 3: Das mündige Konzil. Zweite Sitzungsperiode und Intersessio September 1963 – September 1964, Mainz – Leuven 2001.
> *Alberigo, Giuseppe / Komonchak, Joseph A. (ed.),* History of Vatican II, Maryknoll, N.Y. 1995-2006. V. 1: Announcing and preparing Vatican Council II; V. 2: The formation of the Council's identity,

first period and intersession, October 1962-September 1963; V. 3: The mature Council, second period and intersession, September 1963-September 1964; V. 4: Church as communion, third period and intersession, September 1964-September 1965; V. 5: The Council and the transition, the fourth session and the end of the Council, September 1965-December 1965.

Alberigo, Giuseppe, Johannes XXIII. Leben und Wirken des Konzilpapstes, Mainz 2000 (italienisch: Bologna 2000).

Alberigo, Giuseppe / Congar, Yves / Pottmeyer, Josef Hermann (Hgg.), Kirche im Wandel. Eine kritische Zwischenbilanz nach dem Zweiten Vatikanum, Düsseldorf 1982.

Albus, Michael / Zulehner, Paul M. (Hgg.), Nur der Geist macht lebendig. Zur Lage der Kirche in Deutschland nach 20 Jahren Konzil und 10 Jahren [Würzburg] Synode, Mainz 1985.

Anderson, H. George / Stafford, Francis / Burgess, Joseph A. (Hgg.), The One Mediator, the Saints and Mary. Lutherans and Catholics in Dialogue VIII, Minneapolis 1992.

Angenendt, Arnold, Liturgik und Historik. Gab es eine organische Liturgie-Entwicklung? (Quaestiones Disputatae 189), Freiburg i. Br. 2001.

Antiochien, Ignatius von, Brief an die Gemeinde von Smyrna 8,10 / An die Epheser 5,1 / An die Magnesier 7 / An die Philadelphier 4, in: MySal IV / 1 (1972), 371 Anm. 14; 479.
(ebs. Die sieben Ingatius-Briefe, in: Die apostolischen Väter, eingeleitet, hg., übertr. u. erl. von Joseph A. Fischer (Schriften des Urchristentums), 10.Aufl., Darmstadt 1993, 109-225.; Die apostolischen Väter. Griechisch-deutsche Parallelausgabe, auf der Grundlage der Ausg. Von Franz Xaver Funk, Karls Bihlmeyer und Molly Whittaker. Mit Übers. von M. Dibelius und D.-A. Koch, neu übers. und hg. v. Andreas Lindemann und Henning Paulsen, Tübingen 1992.

Aquin, Thomas von, In Symbolum Apostolorum, scilicet »Credo in Deum« expositio, Art. 9: ed. Marietti, Opuscula Theologia II, Turin 1954, Nr. 972; deutsch in: Thomas-Fibel. Des hl. Thomas von Aquin Erläuterungen zum Apostolischen Glaubensbekenntnis, zum Vaterunser und zu den Zehn Geboten. Übersetzt von H. Schulte, J. Pieper, H. Raskop (1936), Neubearb. von Josef Pieper, München 1979.

Aquin, Thomas von, Summa Theologiae, II-II 10, 8, (deutsch in: DThA Bd. 15, Graz 1950, 211-125).

Aquin, Thomas von, Summa Theologiae, III 83, 5, bes. ad 3, ad 5 und ad 8, (deutsch in: DThA Bd. 30, Salzburg-Leipzig [jetzt: Graz] 1938, 358-371).
➤ *Aquin, Thomas,* Summa theologiae: Latin text and English translation, introductions, notes, appendices and glossaries / St Thomas Aquinas, ed. by *Gilby, Thomas,* Cambridge [et.al.] 2006.

Arendt, Hans-Peter, Bußsakrament und Einzelberichte. Die tridentinischen Lehraussagen über das Sündenbekenntnis und ihre Verbindlichkeit für die Reform des Bußsakramentes, Freiburg i. Br. 1981.

Arenhoevell, Diego, Die Bedeutung der Heiligen Schrift, WuA 10 (1969), 116-121; 146-148; 173-179: 11 (1970), 14-16; 3944: 97-90.

Arinze, Francis, Begegnung mit Menschen anderen Glaubens. Den interreligiösen Dialog verstehen und gestalten, München-Zürich 1999.
➤ *Arinze, Francis,* Meeting of believers: the risks and rewards of interreligious dialogue, Huntington 1998.

Aubert, Roger, Modernismus, HKG IV/2 (1973), 435-500.

Aubert, Roger, Vaticanum I (Geschichte der ökumenischen Konzilien, Bd. XII), Mainz 1965 (dt. Übers. v. Bergner, Karlhermann).

Auer, Johann, Die Sakramente der Kirche (*Johann Auer / Joseph Ratzinger,* Kleine Katholische Dogmatik VII), Regensburg 1972.

Augustinus, De Praedestinatione Sanctorum 14,27: PL 44, 980.
➤ Augustine, Saint Bishop of Hippo, De praedestinatione sanctorum, ed. by Centre Traditio Litterarum Occidentalium 2010.

Auterio, Antonio (Hg.), Herausforderung Aggiornamento. Zur Rezeption des Zweiten Vatikanischen Konzils, Altenberge 2000.

Bacci, Antonio, Lexicon eorum vocabulorum, quae difficilius Latine redduntur, Rom ³1955.

Barth, Hans-Martin, Einander Priester sein. Allgemeines Priestertum in ökumenischer Perspektive, Göttingen 1990.

Bauch, Andreas / Gläßer, Alfred / Seybold, Michael (Hgg.), Zehn Jahre Vaticanum II, Regensburg 1976.

Baur, Jörg, Einig in Sachen Rechtfertigung?: zur Prüfung des Rechtfertigungskapitels der Studie des Ökumenischen Arbeitskreises Evangelischer und Katholischer Theologen, »Lehrverurteilungen, kirchentrennend?«, Tübingen 1989.

Baum, Gregory, Die ekklesiale Wirklichkeit der anderen Kirchen, Concilien I (1965), 291-303.
> ➤ *Baum, Gregory / Peters, Edward H.* (ed.), De Ecclesia. The Constitution on the Church of Vaticanum Council II, proclaimed by Pope Paul VI, November 21, 1964, London 1965.

Baumann, Urs, Die Ehe – ein Sakrament?, Zürich 1988.

Bayer, Oswald, Die Ehe zwischen Evangelium und Gesetz, ZEE 25 (1981), 164-180.

Bayer, Oswald, Die Reformatorische Wende in Luthers Theologie, ZThK 66, 115-150.

Bayer, Oswald, Promissio. Geschichte der reformatorischen Wende in Luthers Theologie, Göttingen 1971.

Becker, Hansjakob / Hilberath, Bernd Jochen / Willers, Ulrich (Hgg.), Gottesdienst – Kirche – Gesellschaft. Interdisziplinäre und ökumenische Standortbestimmung nach 25 Jahren Liturgiereform (Pietas Liturgica Bd. 5), St. Ottilien 1991.

Beestermöller, Gerhard, Thomas von Aquin und der gerechte Krieg, Köln 1991.

Beier, Peter, Brief an Kardinal Ratzinger vom 25. November 1992, in: MdKI 44 (1993), 36f.

Beinert, Wolfgang (Hg.), Glaube als Zustimmung, Freiburg i. Br. 1991.

Beinert, Wolfgang (Hg.), Maria heute ehren, Freiburg i. Br. ³1980.

Beinert, Wolfgang, Maria/ Mariologie, in: NHthG III, ²1991, 306-336.

Beinert, Wolfgang, Rezeption. Bedeutung für Leben und Lehre der Kirche, Cath 44 (1990), 91-118.

Berger, Teresa / Geldbach, Erich (Hgg.), Bis an die Enden der Erde. Ökumenische Erfahrungen mit der Bibel, 1992.

Berliner Bischofskonferenz / Deutsche Bischofskonferenz / Österreichische Bischofskonferenz (Hgg.), »Die Last der Geschichte annehmen«. Worte der Bischöfe zum Verhältnis von Christen und Juden aus Anlaß des 50. Jahrestages der Novemberpogrome 1938, Bonn, 20. Oktober 1988.

Bernards, Matthäus, Zur Lehre von der Kirche als Sakrament, MThZ 20 (1969), 29-54.

Bernhardt, R., Der Absolutheitsanspruch des Christentums. Von der Aufklärung bis zur pluralistischen Religionstheologie, Gütersloh 1990.

Bernhardt, R., Horizontüberschreitung. Die Pluralistische Theologie der Religionen, Gütersloh 1991.

Bertsch, Ludwig (Hg.), Der neue Meßritus in Zaire, Freiburg i. Br. 1993.

Bertsch, Ludwig, u.a. (Hgg.): Gemeinsame Synode der Bistümer in der Bundesrepublik Deutschland. Offizielle Gesamtausgabe, I: Beschlüsse der Vollversammlung [mit Einleitungen], Freiburg i. Br. 1976; II: Ergänzungsband: Arbeitspapiere der Sachkommissionen, 1977.

Beumer, Johannes, Die mündliche Überlieferung als Glaubensquelle (HDG 1/4), Freiburg i. Br. 1962.

Beyer, Beate und Jörg, Konfessionsverbindende Ehe. Impulse für Paare und Seelsorger, Mainz 1991.

Biemer, Günter / Casper, Bernhard / Müller, Joseph (Hgg.), Gemeinsam Kirche sein. Theorie und Praxis der Communio (Festschrift für Erzbischof Dr. Oskar Saier), Freiburg i. Br. 1992.

Biemer, Günter / Ehrlich, Ernst Ludwig (Hgg.), Lernprozeß Christen Juden, 4 Bde., Düsseldorf-Freiburg 1980 / 1981 / 1984.

Biemer, Günter, u.a., Freiburger Leitlinien zum Lernprozess Christen Juden. Theologische [und didaktische] Grundlegung, in: *ders. / Ehrlich, Ernst Ludwig* (Hgg.), Lernprozeß Christen Juden, Bd. 2, Düsseldorf 1981.

Birmelé, André / Meyer, Harding (Hgg.), Grundkonsens – Grunddifferenz. Studie des Straßburger Instituts für Ökumenische Forschung. Ergebnisse und Dokumente, Frankfurt am Main/ Paderborn 1992.

Bitter, Gottfried / Miller, Gabriele (Hgg.), Konturen heutiger Theologie. Werkstattberichte, München 1976.

Blank, Josef, u.a., Was hindert uns? Das gemeinsame Herrenmahl der Christen, Regensburg 1979.

Böckle, Franz / Holenstein, Carl (Hgg.), Die Enzyklika in der Diskussion. Eine orientierende Dokumentation zu »Humanae vitae«, Zürich 1968.
Böckle, Franz, Humana vitae als Prüfstein des wahren Glaubens? Zur kirchenpolitischen Dimension moraltheologischer Fragen, in: StdZ 208 (1990), 3-16.

Boff, Leonardo, Die Kirche als Sakrament im Horizont der Welterfahrung, Paderborn 1972.

Brosseder, Johannes, Abendmahlsgemeinschaft als Weg zur Kirchengemeinschaft?, in: *Neuner, Peter / Wollinger, Franz* (Hgg.), Auf Wegen der Versöhnung. Beiträge zum ökumenischen Gespräch, Frankfurt 1982, 220-230.

Brosseder, Johannes, Das evangelische Echo auf die Liturgiekonstitution, in: *Becker, Hansjakob/ Hilberath, Bernd Jochen / Willers, Ulrich* (Hgg.), Gottesdienst – Kirche – Gesellschaft. Interdisziplinäre und ökumenische Standortbestimmungen nach 25 Jahren Liturgiereform (Pietas Liturgica Bd. 5), St. Ottilien 1991, 129-135.

Brosseder, Johannes / Ignestam, Evah (Hgg.), Die Ambivalenz der Moderne, Stockholm 2000.
➢ *Brosseder, Johannes / Ignestam, Evah* (ed.), The ambivalence of modernity/ Modernitetens ambivalens, Tro & tanke (1999: 7-8), Uppsala 1999.

Brosseder, Johannes / Link, Hans Georg (Hgg.), Gemeinschaft der Kirchen. Traum oder Wirklichkeit?, 1993.

Brosseder, Johannes, Konsens im Rechtfertigungsglauben ohne Konsens im Kirchenverständnis? Zur Bedeutung des Rechtfertigungsstreit heute, in: *Häring, Hermann / Kuschel, Karl-Josef* (Hgg.), Hans Küng. Neue Horizonte des Glaubens und Denkens. Ein Arbeitsbuch, München 1993, 344-363.
➢ *Häring, Hermann / Kuschel, Karl-Josef* (ed.), Hans Küng: New Horizons for Faith and Thought, New York 1993.

Brosseder, Johannes, Ökumenische Katholizität, ÖR 41 (1992), 24-39.

Brosseder, Johannes, Reformatorischer Rechtfertigungsglaube und seine Kraft im ökumenischen Gespräch der Gegenwart. Ausgewählte Beiträge zur ökumenischen Theologie aus drei Jahrzehnten, Frankfurt am Main 1999.

Brosseder, Johannes, Verdoppelt das Bemühen! Die Einstellung Papst Johannes Pauls II. zur ökumenischen Arbeit, ÖR 31 (1984), 60-68.

Brown, Peter, Die Keuschheit der Engel, München 1991.
  ➢ *Brown, Peter*, The Body and Society. Men, Woman and Sexual Renunciation in Early Christianity, New York 1988.

Brown, R.E., Maria im Neuen Testament. Eine ökumenische Untersuchung, Stuttgart 1981.

Brück, Michael von / Werbick, Jürgen (Hgg.), Der einzige Weg zum Heil? Die Herausforderung des christlichen Absolutheitsanspruchs durch pluralistische Religionstheologien, Freiburg i. Br. 1993.

Brück, Regina und Michael von, Die Geisteswelt des tibetischen Buddhismus, Freiburg i. Br. 1987.

Bühlmann, Walbert, Weltkirche. Neue Dimensionen – Modell für das Jahr 2001. Mit einem Nachwort von Karl Rahner, Graz 1984.

Bugnini, Annibale, Die Liturgie-Reform. 1948–1975. Zeugnis und Testament. Deutsche Ausgabe hg. v. Wagner, Johannes / Raas, François, Freiburg i. Br. 1988 (ital. La riforma liturgia, Rom 1983).

Bundesverband der Katholischen Arbeitnehmer-Bewegung (KAB) Deutschlands (Hg.), Texte zur katholischen Soziallehre. Die sozialen Rundschreiben der Päpste und andere kirchliche Dokumente, Köln ³1976; darin: Papst Paul VI., Populorum progressio (»Fortschritt der Völker«), 1967.

Butler, C. / Lang, Hugo, Das Vatikanische Konzil. Seine Geschichte von innen geschildert in Bischof Ullathornes Briefen (1933), München ²1961.

Chrysostomos, Johannes, In Iohannem Homilia 65: PG 59, 361.

Concilium, Das ökumenische Konzil: Seine Bedeutung für die Verfassung der Kirche. Internationale Zeitschrift für Theologie (Deutsche Ausgabe), hg. v. Wilfred, Felix, u.a., Madras/ Chennai.
  ➢ *Concilium*, International Journal for Theology, ed. by Wilfred, Felix, et. al., Madras / Cennai.
    11 (1975), H. 10 [Ökumenismus – Kirchliche Erneuerung und Petrusamt am Ende des 20. Jahrhunderts], Beiträge von Hervé-M. Legrand und R. La Valle
    14 (1978), H. 3 [Dogmatik – Offenbarung und Erfahrung]
  ➢ 113. (1978) / 3 [Dogma – Revelation and Experience [Editorial]]

19 (1983), H. 2 [Liturgie als schöpferische Tradition]
➤ 162. (1938) / 2 [Liturgy – Liturgy: A Creative Tradition]
19 (1983), H. 8/9 [Kirchenordnung – Das ökumenische Konzil: Seine Bedeutung für die Verfassung der Kirche]
➤ 167. (1983) / 7 [Ecclesial Institutions – The Ecumenical Council and the Church Constitution]
21 (1985), H. 4 [Dogmatik – Die Lehrautorität der Gläubigen]
➤ 180. (1985) / 4 [Dogma – The Teaching Authority of the Believers]
22 (1986), H. 1 [Oecumene – Christentum zwischen den Weltreligionen]
➤ 183. (1986) / 1 [Ecumenism – Christianity Among World Religious Editorial Introduction]
22 (1986), H. 3 [Kirchliches Recht – Kirchliche Wirklichkeit]
➤ 185. (1986) / 3 [Church Order – Canon Law – Church Reality]
22 (1986), H. 6 [Sonderheft – Synode 1985 – eine Auswertung]
➤ 188. 1986 / 6 [Special Issue – Synod 1985: An Evaluation]
26 (1990), H. 1 [Sonderheft – Sonderheft zur Vorbereitung des INTERNATIONALEN THEOLOGISCHEN KONGRESSES zum Thema: »Auf der Schwelle zum dritten Jahrtausend«]
➤ (1990) / 1 [Special Issue – On the Treshold of the Third Millenium]
26 (1990), H. 2 [Oecumene – Ethos der Weltreligionen und Menschenrechte]
➤ (1990) / 2 [Ecumenism – The Ethics of World Religions and Human Rights Editorial]
27 (1991), H. 5 [Religionssoziologie – *Rerum novarum* 100 Jahre später]
➤ (1991) / 5 [Sociology of Religion – *Rerum novarum*: One Hundred Years of Catholic Social Teaching Editorial]
29 (1993), H. 1 [Exegese/ Kirchengeschichte – Messias und Messianismus]
➤ (1993) / 1 [Scripture – Messianism through History. Editorial]
29 (1993), H. 2 [Theologie der Dritten Welt – Christus in Asien?]
➤ (1993) / 2 [Third World Theology – Any Room for Christ in Asia? Editorial]
31 (1995), H. 3 [Liturgik – Leib und Sinnlichkeit in der Liturgie]
➤ (1995) / 3 [Liturgy and the Body. Editorial]

Concilium Oecumenicum Vaticanum (Hgg.), Zweites Vatikanisches Konzil. Dogmatische Konstitution über die Kirche. Authentischer lateinischer Text. Deutsche Übersetzung im Auftrag der deutschen Bischöfe. Mit einer Einleitung von Joseph Ratzinger, Münster 1965.

Congar, Yves, Der Laie, Stuttgart 1957 (frz.: Jalons pour une théologie du laicat, Paris 1952).
> *Congar, Yves*, Lay People in the Church. A study for a theology of laity, transl. by. Attwater, Donald, London 1957.

Congar, Yves, Die Lehre von der Kirche, in: HDG III 3c: Von Augustinus bis zum Abendländischen Schisma; 3d: Vom Abendländischen Schisma bis zur Gegenwart, Freiburg i. Br. 1971 (frz.: L' Église / 2. De Saint Augustin à l'époque moderne, Paris 1970).

Congar, Yves, Die Tradition und die Traditionen, übers. v. Simon-Roux, Hildegard, Mainz 1965 (frz.: La tradition et les traditions, Paris 1960).
> *Congar, Yves*, Tradition & traditions: the Biblical, historical, and theological evidence for Catholic teaching on tradtition. Introduction by Patrick Madrid, San Diego, CA/MA 1966.

Congar, Yves, D ' une »Ecclésiologie en gestation« à Lumen Gentium Chap. I et II, FZPhTh 18 (1971), 366-377. (= Pesch, Otto Hermann / Hans-Dieter Langer (Hgg.), Kirche im Wachstum des Glaubens. Festgabe Mannes Dominikus Koster zum siebzigsten Geburtstag, FZPhTh 18 (1971), Heft 1-2.

Congar, Yves / Küng, Hans / O 'Hanlon (Hgg.), Konzilsreden, Einsiedeln 1964.
> *Congar, Yves / Küng, Hans / O 'Hanlon* (ed.), Council speeches of Vatican II, Glen Rock, N.J. 1964.

Congar, Yves, Laie, in: *Fries, Heinrich* (Hg.), Handbuch theologischer Grundbegriffe, II, München 1963, 7-25.

Congar, Yves, Ökumenische Bewegung, in: LThK VII (1962), 1128-1137.

Cyprian, De Oratione Dominica (Über das Gebet des Herrn) 23: PL 4, 553.
> *Cyprian*, An exposition on the Lord's Prayer [De Dominica oratione]. By St. Cyprian the Martyr Bishop of Carthage Translated from the Latin, London 1702 [Online-Ressource].

D 'Costa, Gavin, Das Pluralismus-Paradigma in der christlichen Sicht der Religionen, ThG 30 (1987), 221-231.
> *D 'Costa, Gavin*, The Pluralist Paradigm in a Christian Theology of Religions, Scottish Journal of Theology 30, 21, 1986, 211-224.

Decker, Bruno, Schriftprinzip und Ergänzungstradition in der Lehre des hl. Thomas von Aquin, in: *Brosch, H. J.* (Hg.), Schrift und Tradition, Essen 1962, 191-221.

Decker, Bruno, Sola Scriptura bei Thomas von Aquin, in: *Lenhart, L.* (Hg.), Universitas. Dienst an Wahrheit und Leben. Festschrift für Bischof Albert Stohr, Mainz 1960, I, 117-129.

De consecratione episcopi sine canonica provisione (»Über die Weihe ohne rechtsgültigen Auftrag«) vom 9.4.1951, AAS 43 (1951).

Denziger, Heinrich, Enchiridion symbolorum definitionum et declarationum de rebus fidei et morum. Kompendium der Glaubensbekenntnisse und kirchlichen Lehrentscheidungen. Lateinisch-Deutsch, hg. v. Hünermann, Peter, Freiburg i. Br.-Basel-Rom-Wien [37]1991.

Denzler, Georg, Der Dialog im Verständnis Papst Pauls VI, in: *Seckler, Max,* u.a. (Hg.), Begegnung. Beiträge zu einer Hermeneutik des theologischen Gesprächs (Festschrift für Heinrich Fries), Graz 1972, 779-789.

Denzler, Georg, Die Geschichte des Zölibats, Freiburg i. Br. 1993.

Denzler, Georg, Die verbotene Lust. 2000 Jahre christliche Sexualmoral, München 1988.

Denzler, Georg (Hg.), Lebensberichte verheirateter Priester. Autobiographische Zeugnisse zum Konflikt zwischen Ehe und Zölibat, München 1989.

Dionne, Robert J., The Papacy and the Church. A Study of Praxis and Reception in Ecumenical Perspective, New York 1987.

Dombes, Groupe des (Hg.), Maria in Gottes Heilsplan und in der Gemeinschaft der Heiligen, Frankfurt-Paderborn 1998.
➢ *Blancy, Alain / Jourjon, Maurice / the Dombes Group* [transl. by *O'Connell, Matthew J.*], Mary in the Plan of God and in the communion of the saints: toward a common Christian understanding, New York 2002.

Dominikanerprovinz Teutonia [Hg.], Wort und Antwort: Zeitschrift für Fragen des Glaubens 37 (1996), H. 2: Maria.

Döring, Heinrich, Grundriss der Ekklesiologie. Zentrale Aspekte des katholischen Selbstverständnisses und ihre ökumenische Relevanz, Darmstadt 1986.

Drewermann, Eugen, Kleriker. Psychogramm eines Ideals, Olten-Freiburg i. Br. 1989.

Dulles, Avery, Lehramt und Unfehlbarkeit, in HFTh 4 (1988), 153-178.

Dunde, Siegfried Rudolf (Hg.), Müssen wir an der katholischen Kirche zweifeln?, Gütersloh 1993.

Ebeling, Gerhard, Erwägungen zum evangelischen Sakramentsverständnis, in: ders., Wort Gottes und Tradition. Studien zu einer Hermeneutik der Konfessionen, Göttingen 1964, 217-226.
> *Ebeling, Gerhard* [transl. by *Hooke, S. H.*], The Word of God and Tradition: Historical studies interpreting the divisions of Christianity, Philadelphia 1968 / London 1968.

Ebeling, Gerhard, Dogmatik des christlichen Glaubens III, Tübingen 1979.

Ebeling, Gerhard, »Sola Scriptura« und das Problem der Tradition (1963), in: ders., Wort Gottes und Tradition. Studien zu einer Hermeneutik der Konfessionen, Göttingen 1964, 91-143.
> *Ebeling, Gerhard* [transl. by *Hooke, S. H.*], The Word of God and Tradition: Historical studies interpreting the divisions of Christianity, Philadelphia 1968 / London 1968.

Eberts, Gerhard, Das Zweite Vatikanische Konzil und was daraus wurde, Aschaffenburg 1985.

Eicher, Peter, Hierarchie, in: NHthG II, ²1991, 330-349.

Eicher, Peter (Hg.), Neue Summe der Theologie, Bd. 3: Der Dienst der Gemeinde, Freiburg i. Br. 1989, 2. Teil: Umkehr zur Ökumene, 185-236 (*Weinrich, Michael / Hoffmann, Joseph*).

Eicher, Peter (Hg.), Neues Handbuch theologischer Grundbegriffe, 5 Bde., erweiterte 2. Aufl., München 1991, Bd. 4, 98-115 (*Wiedenhofer, Siegfried*).

Eicher, Peter, Offenbarung. Prinzip neuzeitlicher Theologie, München 1977.

Eicher, Peter, Offenbarung. Zur Präzisierung einer überstrapazierten Kategorie, in: *Bitter, Gottfried / Miller, Gabriele* (Hgg.), Konturen heutiger Theologie. Werkstattberichte, München 1976, 108-134.

Eickelschulte, Dietmar, Kirchenamtlicher »Dialog«, WuA 10 (1969), 185f.

Einig, Maternus, Latein für Touristen und Gastarbeiter, WuA 8 (1967).

Einig, Maternus, Der heutige Mensch und die Liturgie (Christliches Leben heute 3), Augsburg 1968.

Elliot, Lawrence / Graef, Heinz, Johannes XXIII. Papst der Güte, Papst des Friedens, Freiburg i. Br. [u.a.] 1978.
> *Elliot, Lawrence,* Johannes XXIII. I will be called John, Freiburg i. Br. [et.al.] 1978.

Emeis, Dieter / Sauermost, Burkard (Hgg.), Synode – Ende oder Anfang. Ein Studienbuch für die Praxis in der Bildungs- und Gemeindearbeit, Düsseldorf 1976.

Emminghaus, J.H., Tiara, in: LThK X (1965), 177f.

Erharter, Helmut / Rauter, Horst Michael (Hgg.), Von der Missionierung zur Evangelisierung. Zur Zukunft der Kirche in Amerika und Europa, Wien-Freiburg i. Br. 1992.

Evangelische Kirche Deutschlands (Hg.), Christen und Juden II. Zur theologischen Neuorientierung im Verhältnis zum Judentum. Eine Studie der Evangelischen Kirche in Deutschland, Gütersloh 1991.

Evangelisch-Lutherische Kirche Deutschlands (Hg.), Lehrverurteilungen im Gespräch. Die ersten offiziellen Stellungnahmen aus den evangelischen Kirchen in Deutschland, Göttingen 1992.

Fabry, Heinz-Joseph, u.a., Bibel und Bibelauslegung. Das immer neue Bemühen um die Botschaft Gottes, Regensburg 1993.

Fahey, Michael, Joseph Ratzinger als Ekklesiologe und Seelsorger, Concilium 17 (1981), 79-85.
> *Baum, G.* [ed.], Joseph Ratzinger as Ecclesiologist and Pastor, Concilium [North American edition] 141 *Neo-Conservatism: Social and Religious Phenomenon* (January 1981), 76-83.

Figl, Johann, Atheismus als theologisches Problem. Modelle der Auseinandersetzung in der Theologie der Gegenwart, Mainz 1977.

Finkenzeller, Josef, Die Lehre von den Sakramenten im Allgemeinen (HDG IV/ 1a-b), Freiburg i. Br. 1980/81.

Fischer, Hermann, Rezeption in ihrer Bedeutung für Leben und Lehre der Kirche. Vorläufige Erwägungen zu einem unklaren Begriff, ZThK 78 (1990), 100-123.

Forte, Bruno, La Chiesa – icona della Trinità. Breve ecclesiologia, Brescia 1984.
> *Forte, Bruno*, The Church, icon oft he Trinity: an introduction to ecclesiology, Manila / Philippines 1990.

Frieling, Reinhard, Der Weg des Ökumenischen Gedankens. Eine Ökumenekunde, Göttingen 1992.

Frieling, Reinhard, Gegen Marx, Bultmann und »manche«. Römische Aspekte zur Befreiungstheologie, MdKI 35 (1984),

Frieling, Reinhard, Hoffnungsschimmer. Vatikanisches Gutachten zu »Lehrverurteilungen«, in: MdK 44 (1993), Heft 4, 66-69.

Frieling, Reinhard, Mit, nicht unter dem Papst. Eine Problemskizze über Papsttum und Ökumene, MD 28 (1977), 52-60.

Fries, Heinrich, Ärgernis und Widerspruch. Christentum und Kirche im Spiegel gegenwärtiger Kritik, Würzburg ²1968. Ital.: Cristianèsimo e chiesa al vaglio della critica odierna, Brescia 1967.

Fries, Heinrich, Das Petrusamt im anglikanisch-katholischen Dialog, StdZ 200 (1982), 723-738 (Heft 11), in: ders., »Damit die Welt glaube«. Gefährdung, Ermutigung, Erneuerung, Frankfurt am Main 1987, 213-236. Ital.: Affinchè il mondo Creda, Roma 1990; auch in: Theologisches Jahrbuch 1984, hg. v. Ernst, W., u.a., Leipzig 1984, 422-436.
> *Fries, Heinrich*, Anglicans and the Pope. Heinrich Fries reproves the Vatican, in: Tablet 1982, 1124-1127.

Fries, Heinrich, Der ekklesiologische Status der evangelischen Kirchen in katholischer Sicht, MThZ 13 (1962), 85-98; auch in: Aspekte der Kirche, Stuttgart 1963, 123-152.

> *Fries, Heinrich,* The Ecclesiological Status of the Protestant Churches from a Catholic Viewpoint, in: Journal of Ecumenical Studies 1 (1964), 195-212.

Fries, Heinrich, Die kirchliche Rezeption der Ergebnisse theologischer Gespräche zwischen katholischen und evangelischen Theologen, in: ders., Dienst am Glauben. Aufgaben und Probleme theologischer Arbeit, München 1981, 74-93.

Fries, Heinrich, Ein Glaube. Eine Taufe. Getrennt beim Abendmahl? Offene Fragen, Graz 1971.

Fries, Heinrich, Einheit in Sicht? Die Ökumene, 20 Jahre nach dem Konzil, in: StdZ 203 (1985), 147-158; auch in: Ökumenisches Forum. Grazer Hefte für Ökumene Nr. 7, Graz 1985, 65-81; nachgedruckt unter dem Titel: Zum gegenwärtigen Stand der Ökumene aus katholischer Sicht, in: ders., »Damit die Welt glaube«. Gefährdung, Ermutigung, Erneuerung, Frankfurt am Main 1987, 177-196.
> *Fries, Heinrich,* Unity in view? Twenty years after the Council, in: Theology Digest 33 (1986), 107-111.

Fries, Heinrich / Rahner, Karl, Einigung der Kirchen – reale Möglichkeit (Quaestiones Disputatae, Bd. 100), Freiburg i. Br.-Basel-Wien 1983 (Sonderausgabe mit Nachwort über die Diskussion ²1986).
> *Fries, Heinrich / Rahner, Karl,* Unity of Churches. An actual possibility, Philadelphia-New York 1985.

Fries, Heinrich, Fundamentaltheologie, Graz 1985.
> *Fries, Heinrich,* Fundamental Theology, Washington D.C. 1996.

Fries, Heinrich (Hg.), Jesus in den Weltreligionen, St. Ottilien 1982.

Fries, Heinrich, Ökumene statt Konfessionen? Das Ringen der Kirche um Einheit, Frankfurt am Main 1977.

Fries, Heinrich / Pesch, Otto Hermann, Streiten für die eine Kirche, München 1987.

Fries, Heinrich, Wandel des Kirchenbild und dogmengeschichtliche Entfaltung, in: MySal IV / I, 223-285. Ital.: Mutamenti Dell' Imagine Della Chiesa Ed Evoluzione Storico-Dogmatica, in: Mysterium Salutis, L' Evento salvifico nella communita di Gesu Cristo, Brescia 1972, 267-346.

Gabriel, Karl, Christentum zwischen Tradition und Postmoderne, Freiburg i. Br. 1992.

Galli, Mario von / Moosbrugger, Bernhard, Das Konzil und seine Folgen, Luzern – Frankfurt am Main 1966.

Ganoczy, Alexandre, Ecclesia ministrans. Dienende Kirche und kirchlicher Dienst bei Calvin, Freiburg i. Br. 1968.

Gaudium et spes, In: Das Zweite Vatikanische Konzil, LThK.E 111 (1986), 241-592 (ebf. in: Erfurter Theologische Studien Bd. 52, Leipzig 1986).

Gertler, Thomas, Jesus Christus – die Antwort der Kirche auf die Frage nach dem Menschsein. Eine Untersuchung zur Funktion und Inhalt der Christologie im ersten Teil der Pastoralkonstitution »Gaudium et spes« des Zweiten Vatikanischen Konzils (Erfurter Theologische Studien Bd. 52), Leipzig 1986.

Goldmann-Posch, Ursula, Unheilige Ehen. Gespräche mit Priesterfrauen, München 1985.

Goldstein, Horst, »Selig ihr Armen«. Theologie der Befreiung in Lateinamerika... und in Europa?, Darmstadt 1989.

Görres, Albert (Hg.), Ehe in Gewissensfreiheit, Mainz 1969.

Goltz, Hermann, Tauwetter in europäisch-ökumenischer Eiszeit? KEK/CCEE in Santiago, ÖR 41 (1992), 66-74.

Gorski, Horst, Die Niedrigkeit seiner Magd. Darstellung und theologische Analyse der Mariologie Luthers als Beitrag zum gegenwärtigen lutherisch-römisch-katholischen Gespräch, Frankfurt am Main-Bern 1986.

Greinacher, Norbert / Küng, Hans (Hgg.), Katholische Kirche – wohin? Wider den Verrat am Konzil, München 1986.

Greiselmann, Josef Rupert, Die Heilige Schrift und die Tradition. Zu den neueren Kontroversen über das Verhältnis der Heiligen Schrift zu den nichtgeschriebenen Traditionen, Freiburg i. Br. 1962.

Greshake, Gisbert / Lohfink, Gerhard, Naherwartung – Auferstehung – Unsterblichkeit. Untersuchungen zur christlichen Eschatologie, Freiburg i. Br. [5]1986.

Greshake, Gisbert, Priestersein. Zur Theologie und Spiritualität des priesterlichen Amtes, Freiburg i. Br. ⁵1991.

Grillmeier, Alois, Kommentar zum ersten und zweiten Kapitel der dogmatischen Konstitution der Kirche, in: LThK.E I (Freiburg 1966), 156-209.

Grote, Heiner, Maria heißt: Nicht machen, sondern Empfangen. Eine theologische Besinnung aus biblisch-reformatorischer Sicht, in: Im Lichte der Reformation (Jahrbuch des Evangelischen Bundes) 35, Göttingen 1992, 65-84.

Guardini, Romano, Beten im Gottesdienst der Gemeinde, Mainz 1982.

Guardini, Romano, Die Mutter des Herrn, Mainz ²1990.

Guardini, Romano, Vom Sinn der Kirche, Mainz 1922, Neuaufl. Mainz-München 1990.
  ➤ *Guardini, Romano* [transl. by *Lane, Ada*], The Church and the Catholic; and The Spirit oft he Liturgy, Lodon 1935.

Guardini, Romano, Von heiligen Zeichen, Mainz 1966.
  ➤ *Guardini, Romano* [transl. by Branham, Grace], Sacred Signs, St. Louis 1956.

Halter, Hans, Taufe und Ethos. Paulinische Kriterien für das Proprium christlicher Moral, Freiburg i. Br. 1977.

Hampe, Christoph (Hg.), Die Autorität der Freiheit. Gegenwart des Konzils und Zukunft der Kirche im ökumenischen Disput, 3 Bde., München 1967.

Hänggi, M., Meßerklärungen, in: LThK VII (1962), 330f.

Harding, Meyer / Urban, Hans Jörg / Vischer, Lukas (Hgg.), Dokumente wachsender Übereinstimmung (I). Sämtliche Berichte und Konsenstexte interkonfessioneller Gespräche auf Weltebene 1931-1982, Paderborn-Frankfurt am Main 1983, 127-190.
  ➤ *Harding, Meyer* [ed.; et. al.], Growth in agreement. Reports and agreed statements of ecumenical conversations on a world level, New York 1984.

Häring, Bernhard, Das Gesetz Christi. Moraltheologie, dargestellt für Priester und Laien, Freiburg i. Br. 1954.

➤ *Häring, Bernhard*, [trans. by *Kaiser, Edwin G.*], The law of Christ: moral theology for priests and laity, Vol. 1, General moral theology, Cork 1963.

Häring, Bernhard, Eine katholische Theologie? J. Ratzinger, das Trauma vom Hans im Glück, in: *Greinacher, Norbert / Küng, Hans* (Hgg.), Katholische Kirche – wohin? Wider den Verrat am Konzil, München 1986, 241-248.

Häring, Bernhard, Frei in Christus. Moraltheologie für die Praxis des christlichen Lebens, II, Freiburg i. Br. 1980.

Häring, Bernhard, Meine Erfahrung mit der Kirche. Einleitung und Fragen von Gianni Licheri, Freiburg i. Br. 1989.
➤ *Häring, Bernhard* [transl. by Swidler, Leonard], My witness for the church, New York 1992.

Häring, Hermann / Kuschel, Karl-Josef (Hgg.), Hans Küng. Neue Horizonte des Glaubens und Denkens, München 1993.
➤ *Häring, Hermann / Kuschel, Karl-Josef* (ed.), Hans Küng: new horizons for faith and thought, New York 1993.

Hasler, August Bernhard, Pius IX. (1846-1878), päpstliche Unfehlbarkeit und I. Vatikanisches Konzil. Dogmatische Durchsetzung einer Ideologie, Stuttgart 1977.

Hasler, August Bernhard, Rom-Wittenberg-Genf. Kirchenamtlicher Dialog in der Krise, in: *Seckler, Max*, u.a. (Hgg.), Begegnung. Beiträge zu einer Hermeneutik des theologischen Gesprächs (Festschrift für Heinrich Fries), Graz 1972, 389-401.

Hasler, August Bernhard, Wie der Papst unfehlbar wurde. Macht und Ohnmacht eines Dogmas, München 1979.
➤ *Hasler, August Bernhard*, How the Pope became infallible: Pius IX and the politics of persuasion, Garden City/ N.Y. 1981.

Haustein, Jörg, Entmythologisierung einer Zauberformel. Schreiben der Glaubenskongregation über die Kirche als Communio, MdKI 43 (1992), 61f.

Hebblethwaite, Peter [übers. v. Müller, Wolfdietrich] Johannes XXIII. Das Leben des Angelo Roncalli (1984), Zürich 1986.
➤ *Hebblethwaite, Peter*, John the twenty (XXIII.). Pope of the council, London 1984.

Hebblethwaite, Peter, Paul VI., London 1995.

Helbing, Hanno, u.a., Interkommunion. Hoffnungen – zu bedenken. Ökumenische Beihefte zur Freiburger Zeitschrift für Philosophie und Theologie, Nr. 5, Fribourg (Schw.) 1971.

Hengsbach, Friedhelm / Catholic Church, National Conference of Catholic Bishops [Dt. Übers. d. Anm. von Radbert Kohlhaas], Gegen Unmenschlichkeit in der Wirtschaft (Economic justice for all). Der Hirtenbrief der katholischen Bischöfe der USA »Wirtschaftliche Gerechtigkeit für alle« aus deutscher Sicht kommentiert von Friedhelm Hengsbach, Freiburg i. Br. 1991.

Hengsbach, Friedhelm / Emunds, Bernhard / Möhring-Hesse, Matthias (Hgg.), Jenseits katholischer Sozialethik. Neue Entwürfe christlicher Gesellschaftsethik, Düsseldorf 1993.

Henrich, Franz, Die Bünde katholischer Jugendbewegung. Ihre Bedeutung für die liturgische und eucharistische Erneuerung, München 1968.

Herms, Eilert, Einheit der Christen in der Gemeinschaft der Kirchen. Die ökumenische Bewegung der römischen Kirche im Lichte der reformatorischen Theologie. Antwort auf den Rahner-Plan, Göttingen 1984.

Herms, Eilert, Einigkeit im Fundamentalen. Probleme einer ökumenischen Programmformel, ÖR 37 (1988), 46-66.

Herms, Eilert, Von der Glaubenseinheit zur Kirchengemeinschaft. Plädoyer für eine realistische Ökumene, Marburg 1989 (Aufsätze 1984-1989).

Hertz, Anselm / Korff, Wilhelm, u.a. (Hgg.), Handbuch der christlichen Ethik III: Wege ethischer Praxis, Freiburg i. Br.-Gütersloh 1982.

Hick, John, Gott und seine vielen Namen, Altenberge 1985.
➢ *Hick, John* [transl. by Wahle, Irmgard], God has many names, ed. by Kirste, Reinhard, Soest 1985.

Hick, John, [übers. v. Ulrich Hühne], Jesus und die Weltreligionen, in: ders., Wurde Gott Mensch? Der Mythos vom fleischgewordenen Gott, Gütersloh 1979, 175-194.
➢ *Hick, John* [ed.], The myth of God incarnate, Gütersloh 1979.

Hick, John, Religiöser Pluralismus und Erlösung, in: *Kirste, R. / Schwarzenau, P. / Tworuschka, U.* (Hgg.), Gemeinsam vor Gott. Religionen im Gespräch, Hamburg 1990.

Hilberath, Bernd Jochen, Abendmahlsgemeinschaft – Station auf dem Weg zur Kirchengemeinschaft? Thesen aus katholischer Sicht, Cath 43 (1989), 95-116.

Hilberath, Bernd Jochen, Ist der christliche Absolutheitsanspruch heute noch vertretbar?, in: *Hilberath, Berd Jochen / Linden, Christopher* (Hgg.), Erfahrung des Absoluten – Absolute Erfahrung? Beiträge zum christlichen Offenbarungsverständnis, Düsseldorf 1990, 105-131.

Hilberath, Bernd Jochen, Theologie des Laien. Zu den Spannungen zwischen dem Zweiten Vatikanischen Konzil und der Laien-Instruktion, StdZ 217 (199), 219-282.

Hintzen, Georg, Das reformatorische Abendmahl aus katholischer Sicht. Überlegungen zur Auslegung von UR [= Unitatis redintegratio = Ökumenismusdekret] 22, Cath 40 (1986), 203-228.

Höfner, Josef, u.a., Evangelisch-katholische Abendmahlsgemeinschaft?, Regensburg-Göttingen 1971.

Horst, Ulrich, Die Kirchenkonstitution des II. Vatikanums. Versuch einer historischen Einordnung, MThZ 35 (1985), 36-51.

Horst, Ulrich, Zwischen Konziliarismus und Reformation. Studien zur Ekklesiologie im Dominikanerorden, Rom 1985.

Hünermann, Peter (Hg.), Das II. Vatikanum – christlicher Glaube im Horizont globaler Modernisierung. Einleitungsfragen, Paderborn – München 1998.

Hünermann, Peter, Droht eine dritte Modernismuskrise?, HerKorr 43 (1989), 130-135.

Hünermann, Peter, Volk Gottes – katholische Kirche – Gemeinde. Dreiheit und Einheit in der Ekklesiologie des Zweiten Vatikanischen Konzils, ThQ 175 (1995), 32-45.

Internationale lutherisch/ Römisch-katholische Kommission (Hgg.), »Das geistliche Amt in der Kirche« (1981), in: DWÜ 1, 329-357 (Nr. 75-77: Dokumente wachsender Übereinstimmung I).

Internationale lutherisch/ Römisch-katholische Kommission (Hgg.), »Einheit vor uns« (1984), in: DWÜ 2, 487-504 (Nr. 92-148: Dokumente wachsender Übereinstimmung II).

Internationale lutherisch/ Römisch-katholische Kommission (Hgg.), Erklärung »Kirche und Rechtfertigung«. Das Verständnis der Kirche im Licht der Rechtfertigungslehre, Paderborn-Frankfurt 1994, 91-118.

Israel, P., Art. Dekret, in: LThK III (1959), 205.

Jäckel, Karin, Sag keinem, wer dein Vater ist. Das Schicksal von Priesterkindern. Zeugnisse - Berichte – Fragen, Recklingshausen 1992.

Jaeger, Lorenz, Das ökumenische Konzil. Die Kirche und die Christenheit, Paderborn 1960.
> *Jaeger, Lorenz* [transl. by *Littledale, A.V.*], The ecumenical council, the Church and Christendom, London 1961.

Jedin, Hubert, Kleine Konziliengeschichte. Mit einem Bericht über das Zweite Vatikanische Konzil, Freiburg i. Br., 6.Aufl., 1990.
> *Jedin, Hubert* [transl. by *Graf, Ernest*], Ecumenical Councils of the Catholic Church. An historical outline, Edinburgh & London 1960.

Jedin, Hubert, Das Zweite Vatikanische Konzil. Dokumente und Kommentare, in: LThK.E III (Freiburg i. Br. 1966-1986), 610-623.

Jedin, Huber, Das Zweite Vatikanische Konzil, in: ders. (Hg.), Handbuch der Kirchengeschichte, Bd. VII: Die Weltkirche im 20. Jahrhundert, Freiburg i. Br. 1979, 97-151.
> *Jedin, Huber / Dolan, John / Aubert, Roger* [et. al.], [transl. by *Becker, Peter*], History of the Church, Vol. 7: The Church between revolution and restoriation, London 1980.

Jüngel, Eberhard, Das Sakrament – was ist das? Versuch einer Antwort, in: *Jüngel, Eberhard / Rahner, Karl,* Was ist ein Sakrament? Vorstöße zur Verständigung, Freiburg i. Br. 1971, 7-61.

Jüngel, Eberhard, Die Kirche als Sakrament?, ZThK 80 (1983), 432-457.

Jüngel, Eberhard, Metaphorische Wahrheit. Erwägungen zur theologischen Relevanz der Metapher als Beitrag zur Hermeneutik einer narrativen Theologie (1974), in: ders., Entsprechungen: Gott – Wahrheit – Mensch. Theologische Erörterungen, München 1980, 103-147.

Justenhoven, Heinz-Gerhard, Francisco de Vitoria zu Krieg und Frieden, Köln 1991.

Kampling, Rainer, Tradition, in: NHthG, Bd. 5, ²1991, 169-182.

Käsemann, Ernst, Zur ekklesiologischen Verwendung der Stichworte »Sakrament« und »Zeichen«, in: *Groscurth, Reinhard* (Hg.), Wandernde Horizonte auf dem Weg zu kirchlicher Einheit, Frankfurt am Main 1974, 199-136.

Kasper, Walter, Der Gott Jesu Christi, Mainz 1982.
  ➤ *Kasper, Walter* [transl. by O'Connell Matthew J.], The God of Jesus Christ, London 1984.

Kasper, Walter, Die apostolische Sukzession als ökumenisches Problem, in: *Pannenberg, Wolfhart* (Hg.), Lehrverurteilungen – kirchentrennend? III: Materialien zur Lehre von den Sakramenten und vom kirchlichen Amt, Freiburg i. Br. – Göttingen 1990, 329-349.

Kasper, Walter, Die bleibende Herausforderung durch das II. Vatikanische Konzil. Zur Hermeneutik der Konzilaussagen (1986), in: ders., Theologie und Kirche, Mainz 1987, 290-299.
  ➤ *Kasper, Walter,* Theology and church, New York 1989.

Kasper, Walter, »Die Kirche in der Welt von heute«. Über die Möglichkeiten kirchlicher Weisung in einer pluralen Welt, in: *Kessler, Michael / Pannenberg, Wolfhart / Pottmeyer, Hermann J.* (Hgg.), Fides quaerens intellectum. Beiträge zur Fundamentaltheologie. Max Seckler zum 65. Geburtstag, Tübingen 1992, 268-287.

Kasper, Walter, Die Lehre von der Tradition in der Römischen Schule, Freiburg i. Br. 1962.

Kasper, Walter, Evangelisierung und Neuevangelisierung. Überlegungen zu einer neuen pastoralen Perspektive, in: *Neuner, Peter / Wagner, Harald* (Hgg.), In Verantwortung für den Glauben. Beiträge zur Fundamentaltheologie und Ökumenik (Festschrift für Heinrich Fries zum 80. Geburtstag), Freiburg i. Br. 1992, 231-244.

Kasper, Walter, Kirche als communio. Überlegungen zur ekklesiologischen Leitidee des II. Vatikanischen Konzils, in: ders., Theologie und Kirche, Mainz 1987, 272-289.
  ➤ *Kasper, Walter,* Theology and church, New York 1989.

Kasper, Walter, Schrift – Tradition – Verkündigung, in: ders., Glaube und Geschichte, Mainz 1970, 159-186.

Kasper, Walter, Theologie und Kirche, Mainz 1987.
➤ Kasper, Walter, Theology and church, New York 1989.

Kasper, Walter (Hg.), Zukunft aus der Kraft des Konzils. Die außerordentliche Bischofssynode '85. Die Dokumente mit Kommentar von Walter Kasper, Freiburg i. Br. 1986.

Kaufmann, Franz-Xaver, Kirche begreifen. Analysen und Thesen zur gesellschaftlichen Verfassung des Christentums, Freiburg i. Br. 1979.

Kaufmann, Franz-Xaver / Zingerle, Arnold (Hgg.), Vatikanische Perspektiven, Paderborn-München 1996.

Kaufmann, Ludwig / Klein, Nikolaus, Johannes XXIII. Prophetie im Vermächtnis, Fribourg (Schw.)/ Brig 1990.

Kehl, Medard, Die Kirche. Eine katholische Ekklesiologie, Würzburg 1992.

Keißig, Manfred (Hg.), Maria die Mutter unseres Herrn. Eine evangelische Handreichung. Erarbeitet und verantwortet vom Arbeitskreis der gliedkirchlichen Catholica-Beauftragten der Vereinigten Evangelisch-Lutherischen Kirche Deutschlands und des Deutschen Nationalkomitees des Lutherischen Weltbundes (Catholica-Arbeitskreis), Lahr 1991.

Keller, Max, Theologie des Laientums, in: MySal IV/2 (1973), 393-421.

Kern, W. / Pottmeyer, H.J. / Seckler, M. (Hgg.), Traktat Offenbarung, in: HFTh II, Freiburg 1985.

Kern, W. / Pottmeyer, H.J. / Seckler, M. (Hgg.), Traktat Theologische Erkenntnislehre, in: HFTh IV, Freiburg/Basel/Wien 1988.

Kertelge, Karl, Die Wirklichkeit der Kirche im Neuen Testament, in HFTh III: Traktat Kirche, 97-121.

Kliem, Richard, Der Lektorendienst. Werkbuch, Freiburg i. Br. 1990.

Klinger, Elmar, Armut – eine Herausforderung Gottes. Der Glaube des Konzils und die Befreiung des Menschen, Zürich 1990.

Klinger, Elmar / Wittstadt, Klaus (Hgg.), Glaube im Prozeß. Christsein nach dem II. Vatikanum, Freiburg i. Br. 1984.

Klinger, Kurt, Ein Papst lacht. Anekdoten um Johannes XXIII. (Herdertaschenbuch 616), Freiburg i. Br. 1977.

Klinger, Kurt, »Geistliches Tagebuch«, Freiburg i. Br. 1964.
> *Klinger, Kurt,* »Geistliches Tagebuch«. Mit einem Nachwort von *Hannah Arendt:* Der christliche Papst. (Herdertaschenbuch 304/305), Freiburg i. Br. ^{9}1965.

Klinger, Kurt, Wir sind die Kirche. Das Konzil als kirchliche und gesellschaftliche Herausforderung, StdZ 115 (1990), 345-352.

Knapp, Markus, Glaube – Liebe – Ehe, Würzburg 1999.

Knitter, Paul F., Ein Gott – viele Religionen. Gegen den Absolutheitsanspruch des Christentums, München 1988.
> Gekürzte Übers. von: *Knitter, Paul F.,* No other Name? A critical survey of Christian attitudes toward the world religions, American Society of Missiology Series 7, Orbis 1985.

Koch, Kurt, Gelähmte Ökumene. Was jetzt zu tun ist, Freiburg i. Br. 1992.

Koch, Traugott, Das Problem des evangelischen Kirchenverständnisses nach dem Augsburger Bekenntnis, in: *Lohse, Bernhard / Pesch, Otto Hermann* (Hgg.), Das »Augsburger Bekenntnis« von 1530 damals und heute, München-Mainz 1980, 125-143.

Köhler, Oskar, Bewußtseinsstörungen im Katholizismus, Freiburg i. Br. ^{3}1973.

Köhler, Oskar, Jugendbewegung, in LThK V (1960), 1181f.

Kongregation für den Klerus u.a., Instruktion zu einigen Fragen über die Mitarbeit der Laien am Dienst der Priester (15. August 1997), hg. v. Sekretariat der Deutschen Bischofskonferenz (= Verlautbarungen des Apostolischen Stuhls 129), Bonn 1997.

Kongregation für die Glaubenslehre, Erklärung »Dominus Jesus«. Über die Einzigartigkeit und Heilsuniversalität Jesu Christi und der Kirche (6. August 2000), hg. v. Sekretariat der Deutschen Bischofskonferenz (= Verlautbarungen des Apostolischen Stuhls 148), Bonn 2000.

König, Franz (Hg.), Die bleibende Bedeutung des Zweiten Vatikanischen Konzils, Düsseldorf 1986.

Koster, Mannes Dominikus, Der Glaubenssinn der Hirten und der Gläubigen (1949), in: ders., Volk Gottes im Werden. Gesammelte Studien, hg. v. *Langer, Hans-Dieter / Pesch, Otto Hermann*, Mainz 1971, 131-150.

Koster, Mannes Dominikus, Ekklesiologie im Werden, Paderborn 1940. (nachgedruck in: ders., Volk Gottes im Werden. Gesammelte Studien, hg. v. *Langer, Hans-Dieter / Pesch, Otto Hermann*, Mainz 1971, 195-272.)

Koster, Mannes Dominikus, Ist die Frage nach der Corredemptio Mariens richtig gestellt? (1959), in: ders., Volk Gottes im Werden. Gesammelte Studien, hg. v. *Langer, Hans-Dieter / Pesch, Otto Hermann*, Mainz 1971, 59-112.

Koster, Mannes Dominikus, Von den Grundlagen der Kirchengliedschaft (1950), in: ders., Volk Gottes im Werden. Gesammelte Studien, hg. v. *Langer, Hans-Dieter / Pesch, Otto Hermann*, Mainz 1971, 115-130.

Koster, Mannes Dominikus, Zum Leitbild von der Kirche auf dem II. Vatikanischen Konzil. Ein ekklesiologischer Diskussionsbeitrag (1965), in: ders., Volk Gottes im Werden. Gesammelte Studien, hg. v. *Langer, Hans-Dieter / Pesch, Otto Hermann*, Mainz 1971, 172-194.

Krätzl, Helmut, Im Sprung gehemmt. Was mir nach dem Konzil noch alles fehlt, Mödling 1999.

Krauss, Meinold (Hg.), Ich habe einen Traum. Visionen und Wirklichkeiten, Stuttgart 1978.

Kreiner, Armin, »Hierarchia veritatum«. Deutungsmöglichkeiten und ökumenisch Relevanz, Cath 46 (1992), 1-30.

Kremer, Jakob (Hg.), Aufbruch des Zweiten Vatikanischen Konzils heute, Innsbruck 1993.

Kühn, Ulrich / Pesch, Otto Hermann, Rechtfertigung im Disput. Eine freundliche Antwort an Jörg Bauer auf seine Prüfung des Rechtfertigungskapitels in der Studie des Ökumenischen Arbeitskreises Evangelischer und Katholischer Theologen: »Lehrverurteilungen – kirchentrennend?«, Tübingen 1991.

Küng, Hans, Christsein, München 1974.

Küng, Hans / Ess, Josef van / Stietencron, Heinrich von / Bechert, Heinz, Christentum und Weltreligionen. Hinführung und Dialog mit Islam, Hinduismus und Buddhismus, München 1984.

Küng, Hans, Das Judentum. Die religiöse Situation der Zeit, München 1991.
➤ *Küng, Hans* [transl. by Bowden, John]: Judaism: the religious situation of our time, London 1992.

Küng, Hans, Die Kirche, Freiburg i. Br. 1967 (Neuausgabe ³1985).
➤ *Küng, Hans* [transl. by Ockenden, Ray and Rosaleen], The church, London 1967.

Küng, Hans, Existiert Gott? Antwort auf die Gottesfrage der Neuzeit. München 1979.
➤ *Küng, Hans* [transl. by Quinn, Edward], Does God exist? An answer for today, Garden City, N.Y. 1980.

Küng, Hans (Hg.), Fehlbar? Eine Bilanz, Zürich 1973.

Küng, Hans, Kirche im Konzil, Freiburg i. Br. 1963, erw. ²1964.
➤ *Küng, Hans* [transl. by Hastings, Cecily / Smith, N.D.], The living church. Reflections on the Second Vatican Council, London & New York 1963.

Küng, Hans, Konzil und Wiedervereinigung. Erneuerung als Ruf in die Einheit, Freiburg i. Br. 1960, ⁷1964.
➤ *Küng, Hans* [transl. by Hastings, Cecily], The Council, reform and reunion, New York 1961.

Küng, Hans, Strukturen der Kirche, Freiburg i.Br. 1962; München 1987.
➤ *Küng, Hans* [transl. by Attanasio, Salvator], Structures of the church, London 1964.

Küng, Hans, Unfehlbar? Eine Anfrage, Zürich 1970.
➤ *Küng, Hans* [transl. by Quinn, Edward], Infallible? An inquiry, Garden City, N.Y 1971.

Kuss, Otto, Der Römerbrief, Regensburg 1957/59.

Larentzakis, Grigorios, Maria in der orthodoxen Kirche. OeFo Nr. 11, 1988, 25-42.

Lécuyer, Joseph / Wulf, Friedrich / Cordes, Paul-J. / Schmaus, Michael, Art. Dekret über Dienst und Leben der Priester, LThK.E III (1968), 127-239.

382

Lehmann, Karl, Dogmatische Vorüberlegungen zum Problem der »Interkommunion«, in: ders., Gegenwart des Glaubens, Mainz 1974, 229-273.

Lehmann, Karl / Pannenberg, Wolfhart (Hgg.), Lehrverurteilungen – kirchentrennend? I.: Rechtfertigung, Sakramente und Amt im Zeitalter der Reformation und heute, Freiburg i. Br.-Göttingen 1986.
> *Lehmann, Karl, / Pannenberg, Wolfhart* (ed.), [transl. by Kohl, Margaret], The condemnations of the Reformation Era: do they still divine?, Minneapolis 1990.

Lell, Joachim, Evangelische Fragen an die römisch-katholische Kirche, Göttingen 1967.

Lell, Joachim, Mischehen? Die Ehe im evangelisch-katholischen Spannungsfeld, Gütersloh 1967.

Lexikon für Theologie und Kirche, 2. Aufl., Ergänzungsbände I-III: Das Zweite Vatikanische Konzil. Dokumente und Kommentare, Freiburg i. Br. 1966-1968 (LThK.E).

Lien, Fu-Long, Die Ekklesiologie in der Theologie Karl Rahners. Mit besonderem Hinblick auf das Problem der interkulturellen und interreligiösen Vermittlung des Christentums, Hamburg 1990.

Lies, Lothar, Ökumenische Erwägungen zum Abendmahl, Priesterweihe und Meßopfer, ZkTh 104 (1982), 385-410.

Listl, Joseph / Müller, Hubert / Schmitz, Heribert (Hgg.), Handbuch des katholischen Kirchenrechts, 2. Aufl., Regensburg 1999.

Lohfink, Gerhard, Jesus und die Kirche, in: HFTh III: Traktat Kirche, 49-96.

Lohfink, Gerhard, Kirchenträume. Reden gegen den Trend, Freiburg i. Br. 1982.

Lohse, Bernhard, Martin Luther. Eine Einführung in sein Leben und sein Werk, München ³1997.
> *Lohse, Bernhard,* Martin Luther: An introduction to hif life and work, Clark 1987; originally published: Philadelphia 1986.

📖 Bibliography 383

Löser, Werner, Das Einheits- und Ökumenismusverständnis der römisch-katholischen Kirche, in: ders. (Hg.), Die römisch-katholische Kirche (= Die Kirchen der Welt XX), Frankfurt am Main 1986, 331-345.

Loewenich, Walther von, Der moderne Katholizismus, Witten ⁴1959 (neu überarbeitet ³1970).
> Loewenich, Walther von [transl. by. Fuller, R.H.], Modern Catholicism, London 1959.

Lüning, Peter, Ökumene an der Schwelle zum dritten Jahrtausend, Regensburg 2001.

Luther, Martin, De captivitate Babylonica ecclesiae praeludium (»Von der babylonischen Gefangenschaft der Kirche: ein Vorspiel«): WA 6, 497-573: 501-526.

Lutherischer Weltbund / Katholische Kirche, Gemeinsame Erklärung zur Rechtfertigungslehre, Paderborn-Frankfurt 1999.
> The Lutheran World Federation / The Roman Catholic Church / The Pontifical Council for Promoting Christian Unity, Joint Declaration on the Doctrine of Justification, Michigan-Cambridge 2000.

Manemann, Jürgen / Metz, Johann Baptist (Hgg.), Christologie nach Auschwitz. Stellungnahmen im Anschluß an Thesen von Tiemo Rainer Peters, Münster-Hamburg 1998, ²2001.

Manns, Peter, Zur Lage der Ökumene nach dem Luther-Jahr, in: ders. (Hg.), Martin Luther »Reformator und Vater im Glauben«, Stuttgart 1985, 293-366.

Marcus, Marcel / Stegemann, Ekkehard W. / Zenger, Erich (Hgg.), Israel und Kirche heute. Beiträge zum christlich-jüdischen Gespräch, Freiburg i. Br. 1992.

Margull, Hans Jochen, Zeugnis und Dialog. Ausgewählte Schriften, Hamburg 1992.

Maron, Gottfried, Auf dem Wege zu einem ökumenischen Lutherbild. Katholische Veröffentlichungen zum Lutherjahr 1983, ThR 50 (1985), 250-283.

Maron, Gottfried, Evangelischer Bericht vom Konzil. Zweite Session, Göttingen 1964; Dritte Session, 1965; Vierte Session, 1966 (Bensheimer Hefte 23, 26, 31).

Maron, Gottfried, Kirche und Rechtfertigung. Eine kontroverstheologische Untersuchung, ausgehend von den Texten des Zweiten Vatikanischen Konzils, Göttingen 1969.

Maron, Gottfried, Zum Gespräch mit Rom. Beiträge aus evangelischer Sicht, Göttingen 1988.

Marquardt, Friedrich-Wilhelm, Das christliche Bekenntnis zu Jesus, dem Juden. Eine Christologie, 2 Bde., München 1990/92.

Martini, Carlo Maria, Perspektiven für Kirche und Welt. Ein Gespräch mit dem Mailänder Kardinal, München – Zürich – Wien 1993.

Martini, Carlo Maria, »Wir sind Kirche«. Das Kirchenvolks-Begehren in der Diskussion, Freiburg i. Br. 1995.

May, Georg, Religiöses Leben in vorkonziliarer Zeit, in: Der Fels 7 (1976), 267.

Mensching, Gustav, Die Religion. Erscheinungsformen, Strukturtypen und Lebensgesetze, Stuttgart 1959.

Mieth, Dietmar, Geburtenregelung. Ein Konflikt in der katholischen Kirche, Mainz 1990.

Mieth, Dietmar, Gewissen / Verantwortung, in: NHthG Bd. 2, 221-231.

Mirbt, Carl / Aland, Kurt (Hgg.), Quellen zur Geschichte des Papsttums und des römischen Katholizismus, I, Tübingen ⁶1967, Nr. 760.

Möhler, Johann Adam, Symbolik oder Darstellung der dogmatischen Gegensätze der Katholiken und Protestanten (1832), hg. v. *Geiselmann, Josef Rupert*, Köln-Olten 1958.
   ➤ *Möhler, Johann Adam*, Symbolism: or, exposition of the doctrinal differences between Catholics and Protestants as evidenced by their symbolical writings, London 1843.

Moeller, Bernd, Klerus und Antiklerikalismus in Luthers Schrift An den christlichen Adel deutscher Nation von 1520, in: *Dykema, Peter A. / Obermann, Heiko A.* (Hgg.), Anticlericalism in Late Medieval and Early Modern Europe, Leiden-New York-Köln 1993, 353-365.

Moeller, Charles, Einleitung in die Pastoralkonstitution, in: LThK.E III (1968), 242-279.

Moltmann, Jürgen, Kirche als Communio, Concilium 29 (1993 / 1 Exegese/ Kirchengeschichte – Messias und Messianismus), 94-95.
> Moltmann, Jürgen, The Church as Communion, Concilium 29 (1993/ 1 Messianism through History Table of Contents), 136-138.

Mörsdorf, Klaus, Art. Bischofsdekret, LThK.E II (1967), 127-249.

Mörsdorf, Klaus, Die Rechtssprache des Codex Iuris Canonici, Paderborn 1937.

Mörsdorf, Klaus, Codex Iuris Canonici, in: LThK II (1958), 1244-1249.

Mörsdorf, Klaus / Rahner, Karl, Kirchengliedschaft, in: LThK VI (1961), 221-225.

Mühlen, Heribert, Die Lehre des Vaticanum II über die »Hierarchia veritatum« und ihre Bedeutung für den ökumenischen Dialog, in: ThG1 56 (1966), 303-335.

Müller, Alois, Marias Stellung und Mitwirkung im Christusereignis, in: MySal III/2 (1969), 393-510.

Müller, Alois / Sattler, Dorothea, Mariologie, in: Schneider, Theodor (Hg.), Handbuch der Dogmatik II, Düsseldorf 1992, 155-187.

Müller, Gerhard Ludwig, Was heißt: Geboren von der Jungfrau Maria? Eine theologische Deutung, Freiburg i. Br. 1990.

Müller, Hubert / Pottmeyer, Hermann J. (Hgg.), Die Bischofskonferenz. Theologischer und juridischer Status, Düsseldorf 1989.

Müller, Michael, Die Lehre des hl. Augustinus von der Paradiesehe und ihre Auswirkungen in der Sexualethik des 12. und 13. Jahrhunderts bis Thomas von Aquin, Regensburg 1954.

Murphy, Francis Xavier, Vatikantheologie: Tatsachen und Erfindung trennen, in: National Catholic Reporter, 24. Februar 1984.

Mußner, Franz, Maria. Die Mutter Jesu im Neuen Testament. Geleitwort von Kardinal Ratzinger, St. Ottilien 1993.

Neumann, Johannes, Synodales Prinzip. Der größere Spielraumim Kirchenrecht, Freiburg i. Br. 1973.

Neuner, Peter, Alfred Loisy (1857-1940), in: *Fries, Heinrich / Kretschmar, Georg* (Hgg.), Klassiker der Theologie II: Von Richard Simon bis Dietrich Bonhoeffer, München 1983, 221-240.

Neuner, Peter, Kirchen und kirchliche Gemeinschaften, MThZ 36 (1985), 97-109.

Neuner, Josef, Art. Priesterausbildung, LThK.E II (1967), 309-357.

Neuner, Peter, Ökumenische Theologie. Die Suche nach der Einheit der christlichen Kirchen, Darmstadt 1997.

Niederstein, Peter, Christen am Runden Tisch. Ermutigungen zur ökumenischen Bewegung, Zürich 1990.

Niewiadomski, Jozef / Palaver, Wolfgang (Hgg.), Dramatische Erlösungslehre. Ein Symposion, Innsbruck 1992.

Noonan, John T., Empfängnisverhütung. Geschichte ihrer Beurteilung in der katholischen Theologie und im kanonischen Recht, Mainz 1969, 661-668.
➤ *Noonan, John T.,* Contraception. A History of Its Treatment by the Catholic Theologians and Canonists, Cambridge (Mass) [2]1967.

Novak, Michael, Der Geist des demokratischen Kapitalismus, Frankfurt am Main 1992.
➤ *Novak, Michael,* The Spirit of Democratic Capitalism, London 1991.

Ökumenischer Rat der Kirchen, Kommission für Glauben und Kirchenverfassung (Hg.), Die Diskussion über Taufe, Eucharistie und Amt 1982-1990. Stellungnahmen, Auswirkungen, Weiterarbeit, Frankfurt am Main-Paderborn 1990.

Ökumenischer Rat der Kirchen (Hg.), Es begann in Amsterdam. Vierzig Jahre Ökumenischer Rat der Kirchen (Beiheft zur Ökumenischen Rundschau Nr. 59), Frankfurt am Main 1989.

Oertel, Ferdinand (Hg.), Erstes Echo auf Humanae vitae. Dokumentation zur umstrittenen Enzyklika über die Geburtenkontrolle, Essen 1986.

Oesterreicher, Johannes, Declaratio de Ecclesiae habitudine ad Religiones non-christianas [Nostra aetate] – Erklärung über das Verhältnis der Kirche zu den nichtchristlichen Religionen, lateinisch/deutsch, in: LThK.E II (1967), 405-495.

Ohlig, Heinz, Weltreligion Islam. Eine Einführung, Mainz 2000.

Panagopoulos, Joannis, Die Orthodoxie im Gespräch mit Martin Luther, in: *Geißer, Hans Friedrich,* u.a., Weder Ketzer noch Heiliger. Luthers Bedeutung für den ökumenischen Dialog, Regensburg 1982, 175-200.

Panagopoulos, Joannis, Luther außerhalb des Luthertums: Orthodoxe Sicht, Concilium 12 (1976), 497-501.

Pannenberg, Wolfhart, Erwägungen zu einer Theologie der Religionsgeschichte, in: ders., Grundfragen Systematischer Theologie, Göttingen 1967, ²1971, 252-295.
➢ *Pannenberg, Wolfhart* [transl. by Kehm, George H.], Basic Questions in theology, Vol.2, London 1971.

Pannenberg, Wolfhart / Lehmann, Karl (Hg.), Lehrverurteilungen – kirchentrennend? III: Materialien zur Lehre von den Sakramenten und vom kirchlichen Amt, Freiburg i. Br.-Göttingen 1990.
➢ *Pannenberg, Wolfhart / Lehmann, Karl* (Hg.) [transl. by Kohl, Margaret], The condemnations of the Reformation era: do they still divide?, Minneapolis 1990.

Pannenberg, Wolfhart / Schneider, Theodor (Hgg.), Lehrverurteilungen – kirchentrennend? IV: Antworten auf kirchliche Stellungnahmen, Freiburg i. Br.-Göttingen 1994.

Pannenberg, Wolfhart, Systematische Theologie I, Göttingen 1988.
➢ *Pannenberg, Wolfhart* [transl. by Bromiley, Geoffrey W.], Systematic theology, Vol. 1, Edinburgh 1991.

Pannenberg, Wolfhart / Schneider, Theodor (Hgg.), Verbindliches Zeugnis, 3 Bde., Freiburg i. Br.-Göttingen, I: Kanon – Schrift – Tradition, 1992; II. Schriftauslegung – Lehramt – Rezeption, 1995; III: Schriftverständnis und Schriftgebrauch, 1998.

Panikkar, Raimond [übers. v. Tepe, Georg] Der neue religiöse Weg. Im Dialog der Religionen leben, München 1990.
➢ *Panikkar, Raimond,* The intrareligious dialogue, New York 1978.

Papandreou, Damaskinos, Verwirrung im Geflecht der bilateralen Dialoge, Una sancta 40 (1985), 309-311.

Papst Johannes Paul II., Enzyklika »Ut unum sint«. Über den Einsatz für Ökumene (25.05.1995), hg. v. Sekretariat der Deutschen Bischofskonferenz (= Verlautbarungen des Apostolischen Stuhls 121), Bonn 1995.

Pemsel-Maier, Sabine, Rechtfertigung durch Kirche? Das Verhältnis von Kirche und Rechtfertigung in Entwürfen der neueren katholischen und evangelischen Theologie, Würzburg 1991.

Persson, Per Erik, Repraesentatio Christi. Der Amtsbegriff in der neueren römisch-katholischen Theologie, Göttingen 1966.

Pesch, Otto Hermann, Begriff und Bedeutung des Gesetzes in der katholischen Theologie, JBTh 4 (1989), 171-214.

Pesch, Otto Hermann, Bilanz der Diskussion um die vatikanische Primats- und Unfehlbarkeitsdiskussion (1979), in: Dogmatik im Fragment. Gesammelte Studien, Mainz 1987, 206-252.

Pesch, Otto Hermann, Bußfeier und Bußgeschichte (1976), in: Dogmatik im Fragment. Gesammelte Studien, Mainz 1987, 362-376.

Pesch, Otto Hermann, Das Gebet, Mainz 1980.

Pesch, Otto Hermann, Das Gesetz. Kommentar zu Thomas von Aquin, Summa Theologiae I-II 90-105 (DThA Bd. 13), Graz 177, 682-716.

Pesch, Otto Hermann, Der junge Mann aus Nazaret – Retter aller Menschen? Zum »Universalanspruch« des Christentums, in: *Thomassen, Jürgen* (Hg.), Jesus von Nazaret. Neue Zugänge zu Person und Bedeutung, Würzburg 1993, 102-130.

Pesch, Otto Hermann, »Der mitgehende Anfang«. Die Bedeutung von Bibel und Bibelauslegung für Glaube und Theologie, in: *Fabry, Heinz-Joseph*, u.a., Bibel und Bibelauslegung. Das immer neue Bemühen um die Botschaft Gottes, Regensburg 1993, 117-145.

Pesch, Otto Hermann, Der Stellenwert der Kirche. Lehren aus dem Luther-Jahr, in: *Roepke, Claus-Jürgen* (Hg.), Luther ´83. Eine kritische Bilanz, München 1984, 16-53.

Pesch, Otto Hermann, Die Canones des Trienter Rechtfertigungsdekretes: Wen trafen sie? Wen treffen sie heute?, in: *Lehmann, Karl* (Hg.), Lehrverurteilungen

– kirchentrennend? II: Materialien zu den Lehrverurteilungen und zur Theologie der Rechtfertigung, Freiburg i. Br. – Göttingen 1989, 243-282.

➢ *Pannenberg, Wolfhart / Lehmann, Karl* (Hg.) [transl. by Kohl, Margaret], The condemnations of the Reformation era: do they still divide?, Minneapolis 1990.

Pesch, Otto Hermann, Die »Gemeinsame Erklärung zur Rechtfertigungslehre«. Probleme und Aufgaben, OeFo 2001.

Pesch, Otto Hermann, Die Unfehlbarkeit des päpstlichen Lehramtes. Unerledigte Probleme und zukünftige Perspektiven, in: *Häring, Hermann / Kuschel, Karl-Josef* (Hgg.), Hans Küng. Neue Horizonte des Glaubens und Denkens, München 1993, 88-128.

➢ *Häring, Hermann / Kuschel, Karl-Josef* (Hgg.), Hans Küng: new horizons for faith and thought, New York 1993.

Pesch, Otto Hermann, Dogmatik im Fragment. Gesammelte Studien, Mainz 1987, 206-252.

Pesch, Otto Hermann, Ehe im Blick des Glaubens, in: CGG 7 (1981), 8-43; 76-81.

Pesch, Otto Hermann / Peters, Albrecht, Einführung in die Lehre von Gnade und Rechtfertigung, Darmstadt ³1994.

Pesch, Otto Hermann, Erträge des Luther-Jahres für die katholische systematische Theologie, in: *Manns, Peter* (Hg.), Zur Bilanz des Lutherjahres, Stuttgart 1986, 81-146.

Pesch, Otto Hermann, Frei sein aus Gnade. Theologische Anthropologie, Freiburg i. Br. 1983.

Pesch, Otto Hermann, Gemeinschaft beim Herrenmahl. Plädoyer für ein Ende der Denkverweigerungen, in: *Hilberath, Bernd Jochen / Sattler, Dorothea* (Hgg.), Vorgeschmack. Ökumenische Bemühungen um die Eucharistie, Mainz 1995, 539-571.

Pesch, Otto Hermann, Gerechtfertigt aus Glauben. Luthers Frage an die Kirche, Freiburg i. Br. 1982.

Pesch, Otto Hermann, Gesetz und Gnade, in: CCG 13 (1981), 8-77.

Pesch, Otto Hermann, Heute Gott erkennen, Mainz ³1988.

Pesch, Otto Hermann, Hinführung zu Luther, Mainz ²1983.

Pesch, Otto Hermann, »Ketzerfürst« und »Vater im Glauben«. Die seltsamen Wege katholischer »Lutherrezeption«, in: *Geißer, Hans-Friedrich,* u.a., Weder Ketzer noch Heiliger. Luthers Bedeutung für den ökumenischen Dialog, Regensburg 1982, 123-174.

Pesch, Otto Hermann, Kirchliche Lehrformulierung und persönlicher Glaubensvollzug (1973), in: Dogmatik im Fragment. Gesammelte Studien, Mainz 1987, 266-293.

Pesch, Otto Hermann, Leben vor Gott, in: *Feiner, Johannes / Vischer, Lukas* (Hgg.), Neues Glaubensbuch. Der gemeinsame christliche Glaube, Freiburg i. Br. 1973, ¹⁹1993, 360-392.

Pesch, Otto Hermann, Rechtfertigung und Kirche. Die kriteriologische Bedeutung der Rechtfertigungslehre für die Ekklesiologie, ÖR 37 (1988), 22-46.

Pesch, Otto Hermann, Rechtfertigung und Reformation. Von der reformatorischen Grundkenntnis zur »Unterscheidungslehre«, bibel und kirche 47 (1992), 140-149.

Pesch, Otto Hermann, Rezeption ökumenischer Dialogergebnisse. Ungeschützte, aber plausible Vermutungen zu ihren Schwierigkeiten, ÖR 42 (1993), 407-418.

Pesch, Otto Hermann, Rom und Genf. Die »Weltkirche« und der »Weltrat der Kirche«, WuA 21 (1980), 76-80, 100-104.

Pesch, Otto Hermann, Sprechender Glaube. Entwurf einer Theologie des Gebetes, Mainz 1970.

Pesch, Otto Hermann, Theologie der Rechtfertigung bei Martin Luther und Thomas von Aquin. Versuch eines systematisch-theologischen Dialogs, Mainz ²1985.

Pesch, Otto Hermann, Thomas von Aquin. Grenze und Größe mittelalterlicher Theologie. Eine Einführung, Mainz ³1993.

Pesch, Otto Hermann, Über die Verbindlichkeit päpstlicher Enzykliken. Dogmatische Überlegungen zur Ehe-Enzyklika Papst Pauls VI. (1969), in: Dogmatik im Fragment. Gesammelte Studien, Mainz 1987, 253-265.

Pesch, Otto Hermann, Verbindlichkeit und Toleranz. Religionsfreiheit im Christentum?, in: *Ahrens, Theodor* (Hg.), Zwischen Regionalität und Globalisierung. Studien zu Mission, Ökumene und Religion, Ammersbek bei Hamburg 1997, 73-98.

Pesch, Otto Hermann, Zum gegenwärtigen Stand der Verständigung [über Luther], Concilium 12 (1976), 534-542.

Petersen, Birte, Theologie nach Auschwitz? Die Krise der christlichen Theologie angesichts der Shoah, Berlin 1996.

Pfammatter, Josef / Furger, Franz (Hgg.), Theologische Berichte II: Zur neueren christologischen Diskussion, Zürich 1973.

Pfammatter, Josef / Christen, Eduard (Hgg.), Was willst du von mir, Frau? Maria in heutiger Sicht, Zürich 1992.

Pfürtner, Stephan H. / Heierle, Werner, Einführung in die katholische Soziallehre, Darmstadt 1980.

Pfürtner, Stephan H., Kirche und Sexualität, Reinbek 1972.

Pfürtner, Stephan H., Sexualfeindschaft und Macht. Eine Streitschrift für verantwortete Freiheit in der Kirche, Mainz 1992.

Philips, Gérard, Die Geschichte der dogmatischen Konstitution „Lumen gentium", in: LThK.E I. (Freiburg 1966), 139-155.

Plate, Manfrede, Das deutsche Konzil. Die Würzburger Synode, Bericht und Deutung, Freiburg i. Br. 1975.

Pottmeyer, Hermann Joseph, Die zwiespältige Ekklesiologie des Zweiten Vatikanums - Ursache nachkonziliarer Konflikte, TThZ 92 (1983), 272-83.

Pottmeyer, Hermann Joseph, Geeignetes Signal für den Willen der Kirche zum Ökumenismus? Anmerkungen zum Schreiben »Über einige Aspekte der Kirche als Communio«, KNA-ÖKI 29, 15. Juli 1992.

Pottmeyer, Hermann Joseph, Kirche als Communio. Eine Reformidee aus unterschiedlichen Perspektiven, StdZ 117 (1992), 579-589.

Pottmeyer, Hermann Joseph, Normen, Kriterien und Strukturen der Überlieferung, in: HFTh IV (Freiburg – Basel – Wien 1988), 124-152.

Pottmeyer, Hermann Joseph, Vor einer neuen Phase der Rezeption des Vaticanum II. Zwanzig Jahre Hermeneutik des Konzils, in: ders., u.a. (Hg.), Die Rezeption des Zweiten Vatikanischen Konzils, Düsseldorf 1986, 47-65.

Pottmeyer, Hermann Joseph, Was ist eine Bischofskonferenz?, StdZ 206 (1988), 435-446.

Quadt, Anno, Evangelische Ämter: gültig – Eucharistiegemeinschaft: möglich, Mainz 2001.

Rahner, Karl, Anonymes Christentum und Missionsauftrag der Kirche, in: ders., Schriften zur Theologie IX, Zürich 1970, 498-515.
> *Rahner, Karl*, Anonymous Christianity and the missionary task of the Church, in: *Rahner, Karl* [transl. by Bourke, David John], Theological investigations, Vol. 12, Confrontations. 2, London et. Al. 1974, 161-178.

Rahner, Karl, Chancen der Priestergruppen, StdZ 185 (1970), 172-179.

Rahner, Karl, Der Glaube des Christen und die Lehre der Kirche, StdZ (1972), 3-19; ebf. in: ders., Schriften zur Theologie VI, Zürich 1965, 262-285; ebs. a.a.O. XII, 550-559; XV, 152-168.
> *Rahner, Karl*, The faith of the Christian and the doctrine of the Church, in: *Rahner, Karl* [transl. by Bourke, David John], Theological investigations, Vol. 14, Questions in the Church, the Church in the world, London et. al. 1976, 24-46.

Rahner, Karl, Das kirchliche Lehramt in der Autoritätskrise, in: ders., Schriften zur Theologie IX, Zürich 1973, 339-365.
> *Rahner, Karl*, The teaching office of the Church in the present-day crisis of authority, in: *Rahner, Karl* [transl. by Bourke, David John], Theological investigations, Vol. 11, Confrontations. 1, London et. al. 1974, 3-30.

Rahner, Karl, Das Konzil – ein neuer Beginn. Vortrag beim Festakt zum Abschluss des II. Vatikanischen Konzils im Herkulessaal der Residenz in München am 12. Dezember 1965, Freiburg i. Br. 1966.

Rahner, Karl, Der Traum von der Kirche, in: ders., Schriften zur Theologie XIV, Zürich 1980, 355-367.
> *Rahner, Karl*, Dream of the Church, in: *Rahner, Karl* [transl. by Quinn, Edward], Theological investigations, Vol. 20, Concern for the Church, New York et. al. 1981,133-142.

Rahner, Karl, Die bleibende Bedeutung des II. Vatikanischen Konzils, in: ders., Schriften zur Theologie XIV, Zürich 1980, 303-318.
➤ *Rahner, Karl,* The abiding significance of the Second Vatican Council, in: *Rahner, Karl* [transl. by Quinn, Edward], Theological investigations, Vol. 20, Concern for the Church, New York et. al. 1981, 90-102.

Rahner, Karl, Die Gliedschaft in der Kirche nach der Lehre der Enzyklia Pius ' XII. »Mystici Corporis Christi«, in: ders., Schriften zur Theologie II, Zürich 1954, 7-94.
➤ *Rahner, Karl,* Membership of the Church according to the teaching of Pius XII's encyclical "Mystici Corporis Christi", in: *Rahner, Karl* [transl. by Kruger, Karl H.], Theological investigations, Vol. 2, Man in the church, London et. al. 1966, 1-87.

Rahner, Karl, Die unvergängliche Aktualität des Papsttums, in: ders., Schriften zur Theologie XVI, Zürich 1984, 249-270.
➤ *Rahner, Karl,* The perennial actuality of the papacy, in: *Rahner, Karl* [transl. by Donceel, Joseph], Theological investigations, Vol. 22, Humane society and the Church of tomorrow, London et. al. 1991, 191-207.

Rahner, Karl, Die zwiespältige Ekklesiologie des Zweiten Vatikanum – Ursache nachkonziliarer Konflikte, TThZ 92 (1983), 272-283.

Rahner, Karl, Einheit der Kirche – Einheit der Menschheit, in: ders., Schriften zur Theologie XIV, Zürich 1980, 382-404.
➤ *Rahner, Karl,* Unity of the Church – unity of mankind, in: *Rahner, Karl* [transl. by Quinn, Edward], Theological investigations, Vol. 20, Concern for the Church, New York et. al. 1981, 154-172.

Rahner, Karl, Exegese und Dogmatik, in: ders., Schriften zur Theologie V, Zürich 1962, 82-111.
➤ *Rahner, Karl,* Exegesis and dogmatic theology, in: *Rahner, Karl* [transl. by Kruger, Karl-H.], Theological investigations, Vol. 5, Later Writings, London et. al. 1966, 67-93.

Rahner, Karl, Grundkurs des Glaubens. Einführung in den Begriff des Christentums, Freiburg i. Br. 1976.
➤ *Rahner, Karl* [transl. by Dych, William V.], Foundations of Christian faith: an introduction to the idea of Christianity, New York 1978.

Rahner, Karl, Jesus Christus in den nichtchristlichen Religionen, in: ders., Schriften zur Theologie XII, Zürich 1975, 370-383.

➢ *Rahner, Karl,* Jesus Christ in the non-Christian religions, in: *Rahner, Karl* [transl. by Kohl, Margaret], Theological investigations, Vol. 17, Jesus, man, and the Church, London et. al. 1981, 39-50.

Rahner, Karl, Kirche, Kirchen und Religionen, in: ders., Schriften zur Theologie VIII, Zürich 1967, 355-373.
➢ *Rahner, Karl,* Church, Churches and religions, in: *Rahner, Karl* [transl. by Bourke, David], Theological investigations, Vol. 10, Writings of 1965-1967, London et. al. 1973, 30-49.

Rahner, Karl, Kirche und Atheismus, in: ders., Schriften zur Theologie XV, Zürich 1983, 139-151.
➢ *Rahner, Karl,* The Church and atheism, in: *Rahner, Karl* [transl. by Riley, Hugh M.], Theological investigations, Vol. 21, Science and Christian faith, London et. al. 1988, 137-150.

Rahner, Karl, Kirche und Sakrament, Freiburg i. Br. 1960.

Rahner, Karl, Art. Kirchenkonstitution, in: LThK.E I (1966), 210-259.

Rahner, Karl, Kleines Fragment »Über die kollektive Findung der Wahrheit«, in: ders., Schriften zur Theologie VI, Zürich 1965, 104-110.
➢ *Rahner, Karl,* A small fragment "on the collective finding of truth", in: *Rahner, Karl* [transl. by Kruger, Karl-H. and Boniface], Theological investigations, Vol. 6, Concerning Vatican Council II, London et. al. 1969, 82-88.

Rahner, Karl / Vorgrimler, Herbert (Hgg.), Kleines Konzilskompendium. Sämtliche Texte des Zweiten Vatikanums mit Einführungen und ausführlichen Sachregister (Herderbücherei Bd. 270), Freiburg i. Br. 1966.

Rahner, Karl, Kontinuität und Innovation in der Ekklesiologie des II. Vatikanums, in: *Alberigo, Giuseppe / Congar, Yves / Pottmeyer, Hermann Josef* (Hgg.), Kirche im Wandel. Eine kritische Zwischenbilanz nach dem Zweiten Vatikanum, Düsseldorf 1982, 89-110.

Rahner, Karl, »Mysterium Ecclesiae«, in: ders., Schriften zur Theologie XII, Zürich 1975, 482-500.
➢ *Rahner, Karl,* »Mysterium Ecclesiae«: On the declaration made by the Congregation for the Faith on the doctrine of the Church, in: *Rahner, Karl* [transl. by Kohl, Margaret], Theological investigations, Vol. 17, Jesus, man, and the Church, London et. al. 1981, 139-155.

Rahner, Karl, Priestertum der Frau?, in: ders., Schriften zur Theologie XIV, Zürich 1980, 208-223.
> *Rahner, Karl*, Woman and the Priesthood, in: *Rahner, Karl* [transl. by Quinn, Edward], Theological investigations, Vol. 20, Concern for the Church, New York et. al. 1981, 35-47.

Rahner, Karl, Theologische Grundinterpretation des II. Vatikanischen Konzils, in: ders., Schriften zur Theologie XIV, Zürich 1980, 287-302.
> *Rahner, Karl*, Basic theological interpretation of the Second Vatican Council, in: *Rahner, Karl* [transl. by Quinn, Edward], Theological investigations, Vol. 20, Concern for the Church, New York et. al. 1981, 77-89.

Rahner, Karl, Über das Latein als Kirchensprache, in: ders., Schriften zur Theologie V, Zürich 1962, 411-467.
> *Rahner, Karl*, Latin as a church language, in: *Rahner, Karl* [transl. by Kruger, Karl-H.], Theological investigations, Vol. 5, Later writings, London et. al. 1976, 366-416.

Rahner, Karl, Über den Absolutheitsanspruch des Christentums, in: ders., Schriften zur Theologie XV, Zürich 1984, 171-184.
> *Rahner, Karl*, Christianity's absolute claim, in: *Rahner, Karl* [transl. by Riley, Hugh M.], Theological investigations, Vol. 21, Science and Christian faith, London et. al. 1988, 171-184.

Rahner, Karl, Über die Heilsbedeutung der nichtchristlichen Religionen, in: ders., Schriften zur Theologie XIII, Zürich 1978, 341-350.
> *Rahner, Karl*, On the importance of the non-Christian religions for salvation, in: *Rahner, Karl* [transl. by Quinn, Edward], Theological investigations, Vol. 18, God and revelation, London et. al. 1983, 288-295.

Rahner, Karl, Über die Schriftinspiration, Freiburg i. Br. 1958.

Rahner, Karl, Vergessene Anstöße dogmatischer Art des II. Vatikanischen Konzils, in: ders., Schriften zur Theologie XVI, Zürich 1984, 131-143.
> *Rahner, Karl*, Forgotten dogmatic initiatives of the Second Vatican Council, in: *Rahner, Karl* [transl. by Donceel, Joseph], Theological investigations, Vol. 22, Humane society and the Church of tomorrow, London et. al. 1991, 97-105.

Rahner, Karl, Zur theologischen Problematik einer »Pastoralkonstitution«, in: ders., Schriften zur Theologie VIII, Zürich 1967, 613-636.

396 *Pesch* THE PREHISTORY OF THE SECOND VATICAN COUNCIL

> *Rahner, Karl,* On the theological problems entails in a "pastoral constitution", in: *Rahner, Karl* [transl. by Bourke, David], Theological investigations, Vol. 10, Writings of 1965-1967.2, London et. al. 1973, 1965-1967, 293-317.

Rainer, Michael J. (Hg.), »Dominus Jesus«. Anstößige Wahrheit oder anstößige Kirche? Dokumente, Hintergründe, Standpunkte und Folgerungen, Münster – Hamburg 2001.

Raiser, Konrad / Sattler, Dorothea (Hgg.), Ökumene vor neuen Zeiten. Für Theodor Schneider, Freiburg i. Br. 2000.

Ratzinger, Joseph, Das Konzil auf dem Weg. Rückblick auf die zweite Sitzungsperiode, Köln 1964.

Ratzinger, Joseph, Das neue Volk Gottes. Entwürfe zur Ekklesiologie, Düsseldorf 1969.

Ratzinger, Joseph, Der Geist der Liturgie. Eine Einführung, Freiburg i. Br. 2000.
> *Ratzinger, Joseph* [transl. by Saward, John], The spirit of the liturgy, San Francisco 2000.

Ratzinger, Joseph, »Der Weltdienst der Kirche. Auswirkungen von Gaudium et spes im letzten Jahrhundert«, in: Bauch, Andreas / Glässer, Alfred / Seybold, Michael (Hgg.), Zehn Jahre Vaticanum II, Regensburg 1976.

Ratzinger, Joseph, Die erste Sitzungsperiode des Zweiten Vatikanischen Konzils, Köln 1963.

Ratzinger, Joseph, Die letzte Sitzungsperiode des Konzils, Köln 1966.

Ratzinger, Joseph, Die Tochter Zion. Betrachtungen über den Marienglauben der Kirche, Einsiedeln 1977.
> *Ratzinger, Joseph* [transl. by McDermott, John M.], Daughter Zion: meditations on the church's Marian belief, San Francisco 1983.

Ratzinger, Joseph / Grillmeier, Aloys / Rigaux, Béda, Dogmatische Konstitution über die göttliche Offenbarung, LThK.E II (1967), 497-583.

Ratzinger, Joseph, Entgegnung zu Theodor Schneider, Römisch (und) Katholisch, ÖR 39 (1990), 318-320.

Ratzinger, Joseph, Ergebnisse und Probleme der dritten Konzilsperiode, Köln 1965.

Ratzinger, Joseph, Kirche, Ökumene und Politik. Neue Versuche zur Ekklesiologie, Einsiedeln 1987.
 ➢ *Ratzinger, Joseph*, Church, ecumenism and politics: new essays in ecclesiology, Slough 1988.
 ➢ *Ratzinger, Joseph* [transl. by Miller, Michael J., et. al.], Church, ecumenism and politics: new endeavors in ecclesiology, San Francisco 2008.

Ratzinger, Joseph, Luther und die Einheit der Kirchen. Fragen an Joseph Kardinal Ratzinger, IkaZ 12 (1983), 568-582.

Ratzinger, Joseph, Salz der Erde. Christentum und katholische Kirche in der Jahrtausendwende, Stuttgart 1996.
 ➢ *Ratzinger, Joseph* [transl. by Seewald, Peter], Salt of the earth: Christianity and the Catholic Church at the end of the millennium, San Francisco 1997.

Ratzinger, Joseph, Schriftauslegung im Widerstreit. Zur Frage nach Grundlagen und Weg der Exegese heute, in: ders. (Hg.), Schriftauslegung im Widerstreit, Freiburg i. Br. 1989, 15-44.

Ratzinger, Joseph, Theologische Prinzipienlehre. Bausteine zu einer Fundamentaltheologie, München 1982.
 ➢ *Ratzinger, Joseph*, Principles of Catholic theology: building stones for a fundamental theology, San Francisco 1987.

Ratzinger, Joseph, Zur Lage des Glaubens. Ein Gespräch mit Vittorio Messori, München-Zürich-Wien 1984.
 ➢ *Ratzinger, Joseph* [transl. by Attanasio, Salvator; Harrison, Graham], The Ratzinger report: an exclusive interview on the state of the Church. Joseph Ratzinger with Vittorio Messori, San Francisco 1985.

Rendtorff, Rolf / Henrix, Hans Hermann (Hgg.), Die Kirchen und das Judentum. Dokumente von 1945 bis 1985, Paderborn-München ²1989.

Repgen, Konrad, Der Bischof zwischen Reformation, katholischer Reform und Konfessionsbildung (1515-1650), in: *Berglar, Peter / Engels, Odilo* (Hgg.), Der Bischof in seiner Zeit. Bischofstypus und Bischofsideal im Spiegel der Kölner Kirche. Festgabe für Joseph Kardinal Höffner, Erzbischof von Köln, Köln 1986, 145-314.

Rice, David [übers. v. Maass, Hans-Joachim], Kirche ohne Priester. Der Exodus der Geistlichen aus der katholischen Kirche, München 1991.
  ➤ *Rice, David*, Shattered vows. Exodus from the Priesthood, Belfast 1991.

Richter, Klemens (Hg.), Das Konzil war erst der Anfang. Die Bedeutung des II. Vatikanums für Theologie und Kirche, Mainz 1991.

Richter, Klemens / Lengeling, Emil Joseph / Angenendt, Arnold / et. al. (Hg.), Liturgie – ein vergessenes Thema der Theologie? (Quaestiones disputatae 107), Freiburg i. Br. ²1987.

Richter, Klemens, Liturgiereform als Mitte einer Erneuerung der Kirche, in: ders. (Hg.), Das Konzil war erst der Anfang, Die Bedeutung des II. Vatikanums für Theologie und Kirche, Mainz 1991, 53-74.

Riedel-Spangenberger, Ilona, Zwischen Kollegialität und Zentralismus, Archiv für kath. Kirchenrecht 158 (1989), 457-475.

Rieske-Braun, Uwe (Hg.), Konsensdruck ohne Perspektiven? Der ökumenische Weg nach »Dominus Jesus«, Leipzig 2001.

Romeo, A., L' enciclia »Divino afflante Spiritu« e le »opinions novae«, Divitas 4 (1960), 387-456.

Rosenstein, Gustav, Die Stunde des Dialogs. Begegnungen der Religionen heute, Hamburg 1991.

Ruether, Rosemary Radford [übers. v. Berger, Ulrike], Maria. Kirche in weiblicher Gestalt, München 1980.
  ➤ *Ruether, Rosemary Radford*, Mary, the feminine face of the church, Philadelphia 1977.

Rynne, Xavier, Letters from Vatican City, New York-London 1963.
  ➤ Rynne, Xavier [übers. v. Lindemann, Helmut], Die zweite Reformation. Die erste Sitzungsperiode des Zweiten Vatikanischen Konzils. Entstehung und Verlauf, Köln-Berlin 1964.

Sacrosanctum Oecumenicum Concilium Vaticanum II: Constitutiones, Decreta, Declarationes. Cura et studio Secretariae Generalis Concilii Oecumenici Vaticani II, Romae, Typis Polyglottis Vaticanis 1974 = Edito anni 1966.

Sattler, Dorothea, Gelebte Buße. Das menschliche Bußwerk (satisfactio) im ökumenischen Gespräch, Mainz 1992.

Schäfer, Klaus, Nochmals: Zum Thema Priestergruppen, StdZ 185 (1970), 361-378.

Schäfer, Klaus, Zum Thema Priestergruppen, StdZ 185 (1970), 34-46.

Schaeffler, Richard, Die Wechselbeziehungen zwischen Philosophie und katholischer Theologie, Darmstadt 1980.

Schatz, Klaus, Vaticanum I 1869. 1870, 3 Bde., I: Vor der Eröffnung; II: Von der Eröffnung bis zur Konstitution »Dei Filius«; III: Unfehlbarkeitsdiskussion und Rezeption, Paderborn 1992-1994.
Schauf, Heribert, Christus, das Haupt seiner Kirche, Cath 16 (1962), 38-58.

Schauf, Heribert, Der Geist Christi und die Kirche, Cath 15 (1961), 70-76.

Scheeben, Matthias Joseph, Handbuch der katholischen Dogmatik, I (= M. J. Scheeben, Gesammelte Schriften, hg. von Josef Höfer, III), Freiburg 1948, 211-241.
> *Scheeben, Matthias Joseph* [transl. by Wilhelm, Joseph / Scannell, Thomas B.], A manual of Catholic theology. Based on Scheeben's "Dogmatik", London/ New York ²1899-1901.

Schilson, Arno / Kasper, Walter, Christologie im Präsens. Kritische Sichtung neuer Entwürfe, Freiburg i. Br. ²1980.

Schmaus, Michael, Katholische Dogmatik III/1: Kirche und göttliches Leben im Menschen, München ⁵1958.

Schmaus, Michael, Der Glaube der Kirche V/1: Das Wesen der Kirche, St. Ottilien ²1982.

Schmidt, Stjepan, Augustin Bea. Der Kardinal der Einheit, Graz 1989.
> *Schmidt, Stjepan,* Augustin Bea, the cardinal of unity, New Rochelle, N.Y. 1992.

Schnackenburg, Rudolf, Die Kirche im Neuen Testament, Freiburg i. Br. 1961.
> *Schnackenburg, Rudolf* [transl. by O'Hara, W. J.], The Church in the New Testament, Montreal 1965.

Schnackenburg, Rudolf, Neutestamentliche Theologie. Der Stand der Forschung, München ³1965

> *Schnackenburg, Rudolf* [transl. by Askew, David], New Testament Theology today, New York 1963.

Schneider, Theodor, Auf seiner Spur. Ein Werkstattbuch, hg. v. Alois Moos, Düsseldorf 1990.

Schneider, Theodor (Hg.), Der verdrängte Aufbruch. Ein Konzils-Lesebuch, Mainz 1985.

Schneider, Theodor, Gemeinsames Priestertum und kirchliches Amt, in: ders., Auf seiner Spur. Ein Werkstattbuch, hg. v. Alois Moos, Düsseldorf 1990, 336-345.

Schneider, Theodor (Hg.), Handbuch der Dogmatik, 2 Bde., Düsseldorf 1992.

Schneider, Theodor, Römisch (und) Katholisch? Eine ökumenische Situationsbeschreibung aus römisch-katholischer Sicht, ÖR 39 (1990), 29-45.

Schneider, Theodor, Zeichen der Nähe Gottes. Grundriß der Sakramententheologie, Mainz ⁵1987.

Schillebeeckx, Edward, Christliche Identität und kirchliches Amt. Plädoyer für den Menschen in der Kirche, Düsseldorf 1985.
> *Schillebeeckx, Edward*, The church with a human face: a new expanded theology of ministry, New York 1985.

Schockenhoff, Eberhard, Das umstrittene Gewissen. Eine theologische Grundlegung, Mainz 1990.

Schoonenberg, Piet, Hierarchia veritatum, TTh 8 (1968), 293-298.

Schulte, H./ Pieper, J./ Raskop, H. [Übers.], Thomas-Fibel. Des hl. Thomas von Aquin Erläuterungen zum Apostolischen Glaubensbekenntnis, zum Vaterunser und zu den Zehn Geboten, München 1979.
　　Deutsche Version zu: *Aquin, Thomas von*, In Symbolum Apostolorum, scilicet »Credo in Deum« exposito, Art. 9: ed. Marietti, Opuscula Theologica II, Turin 1954, Nr. 972.

Schütte, Heinz, Kirche im ökumenischen Verständnis – Kirche des dreieinigen Gottes, Paderborn-Frankfurt am Main ²1991.

Schütte, Heinz, Ziel: Kirchengemeinschaft. Zur ökumenischen Orientierung, Paderborn 1985.

Schwab, Wolfgang, Entwicklung und Gestalt der Sakramententheologie bei Martin Luther, Frankfurt am Main-Bern 1977.

Schwager, Raymund (Hg.), Christus allein? Der Streit um die pluralistische Religionstheologie, Freiburg i. Br. 1996.

Schwager, Raymund, Dem Netz des Jägers entronnen. Das Jesusdrama nacherzählt, München 1991.
➢ *Schwager, Raymund* [Williams, James G.], Jesus of Nazareth: how he
    understood his life, New York 1998.

Schwager, Raymund, Kirchliches Lehramt und Theologie, ZkTh 111 (1989), 163-182.

Schwartländer, Johannes / Bielefeld, Heiner, Christen und Muslime vor der Herausforderung der Menschenrechte, hg. v. der Wissenschaftlichen Arbeitsgruppe für weltkirchliche Aufgaben der Deutschen Bischofskonferenz, Bonn 1992.

Seckler, Max, Der Begriff der Offenbarung, in: HFTh II (1985), 60-84.

Seckler, Max / Kessler, Michael, Die Kritik der Offenbarung, in: HFTh II (1985), 29-59.

Seckler, Max, Der Papst und der Krieg, ThQ 171 (1991), 130-131.

Seckler, Max, Die Theologie als kirchliche Wissenschaft – ein römisches Modell (1969), in: ders., Im Spannungsfeld von Wissenschaft und Kirche. Theologie als schöpferische Auslegung der Wirklichkeit, Freiburg i. Br. 1980. 62-84.

Seckler, Max, Glaubenssinn, in: LThK IV (1960), 945-948.

Seckler, Max, Katholisch als Konfessionsbezeichnung (1965), in: ders., Die schiefen Wände des Lehrhauses. Katholizität als Herausforderung, Freiburg i. Br. 1988, 178-197; 254-260.

Seckler, Max, Kirchliches Lehramt und theologische Wissenschaft, in: ders., Die schiefen Wände des Lehrhauses. Katholizität als Herausforderung, Freiburg i. Br. 1988, 105-135; 230-241.

Seckler, Max, Religionsfreiheit und Toleranz. Die Erklärung über die Religionsfreiheit des Zweiten vatikanischen Konzils im Kontext der kirchlichen Toleranz- und Intoleranzdoktrinen, ThQ 175 (1995), 1-18.

Seckler, Max, Theologie als Glaubenswissenschaft, in: HFTh IV (1988), 180-241.

Seckler, Max, Theologie der Religionen mit Fragezeichen, ThQ 166 (1986), 164-184.

Seckler, Max, Toleranz, Wahrheit, Humanität, in: *Vogt, Hermann J.* (Hg.), Kirche in der Zeit. Walter Kasper zur Bischofsweihe. Gabe der Katholisch-Theologischen Fakultät Tübingen, München 1990, 126-149; auch in: Kessler, Michael, u.a. (Hgg.), Konfliktherd Toleranz? Analysen, Sondierungen, Klarstellungen, Tübingen 2002, 123-150.

Seckler, Max, Über den Kompromiß in Sachen Lehre (1972), in: ders., Im Spannungsfeld von Wissenschaft und Kirche. Theologie als schöpferische Auslegung der Wirklichkeit, Freiburg i. Br. 1980, 99-103; 212-215.

Seeber, David Andreas, Das Zweite Vaticanum. Konzil des Übergangs (Herder-Taschenbuch 260/261), Freiburg i. Br. 1966.

Sekretariat der Deutschen Bischofskonferenz (Hg.), Bischöfe zum Frieden (Stimmen der Weltkirche 19), Bonn 1983, 5-130.

Sekretariat der Deutschen Bischofskonferenz (Hg.), Bischofssynode, Sonder-Versammlung für Europa: Damit wir Zeugen Christi sind, der uns befreit hat. Erklärung mit lateinischem Originaltext (= Verlautbarungen des Apostolischen Stuhls 103), Bonn 1991.

Sekretariat der Deutschen Bischofskonferenz (Hg.), Enzyklika Centesimus annus seiner Heiligkeit Papst Johannes Paul II. an die verehrten Mitbrüder im Bischofsamt, den Klerus, die Ordensleute, die Gläubigen der katholischen Kirche und alle Menschen guten Willens zum hundertsten Jahrestag von Rerum novarum (= Verlautbarungen des Apostolischen Stuhls 101), Bonn 1991.

Sekretariat der Deutschen Bischofskonferenz (Hg.), Erklärung der Glaubenskongregation: Persona humana (Sexualmoral) (= Verlautbarungen des Apostolischen Stuhls 1), Bonn 1975.

Sekretariat der Deutschen Bischofskonferenz (Hg.), Erklärung der Kongregation für die Glaubenslehre zur Frage der Zulassung der Frauen zum Priesteramt (= Verlautbarungen des Apostolischen Stuhls 3), Bonn 1976.

Sekretariat der Deutschen Bischofskonferenz (Hg.), Instruktion der Kongregation für die Glaubenslehre über einige Aspekte der »Theologie der Befreiung« (= Verlautbarungen des Apostolischen Stuhls 57), Bonn 1984.

Sekretariat der Deutschen Bischofskonferenz (Hg.), Instruktion der Kongregation für die Glaubenslehre über die christliche Freiheit und die Befreiung (= Verlautbarungen des Apostolischen Stuhls 57), Bonn 1986.

Sekretariat der Deutschen Bischofskonferenz (Hg.), Kongregation für die Glaubenslehre: Instruktion über die kirchliche Berufung des Theologen (= Verlautbarungen des Apostolischen Stuhls 98), Bonn 1990, Nr. 32-40.

Sekretariat der Deutschen Bischofskonferenz (Hg.), Kongregation für die Glaubenslehre: Schreiben an die Bischöfe der katholischen Kirche über einige Aspekte der Kirche als Communio (= Verlautbarungen des Apostolischen Stuhls 107), Bonn 1992.

Sekretariat der Deutschen Bischofskonferenz (Hg.), Laborum exercens (=Verlautbarungen des Apostolischen Stuhls 32), Bonn 1981.

Sekretariat der Deutschen Bischofskonferenz (Hg.), Nachsynodales Apostolisches Schreiben Pastorem dabo vobis (»Ich werde euch einen Hirten geben« [Jer 3,15]) über die Priesterbildung im Kontext der Gegenwart (= Verlautbarung des Apostolischen Stuhls 105), Bonn 1992, Nr. 29.

Sekretariat der Deutschen Bischofskonferenz (Hg.), Papst Johannes Paul II. in Deutschland, 15.-19. November 1980 (= Verlautbarungen des Apostolischen Stuhls 25 A), Bonn 1980, 169-174.

Sekretariat der Deutschen Bischofskonferenz (Hg.), Schreiben der Kongregation für die Glaubenslehre zu einigen Fragen der Eschatologie (= Verlautbarungen des Apostolischen Stuhls 11), Bonn 1979.

Selge, Kurt-Viktor, Evangelischer Bericht vom Konzil. Erste Session (Bensheimer Hefte 27), Göttingen 1965.

Semmelroth, Otto, Die Kirche als Sakrament des Heils, in: My Sal IV/1 (1972), 309-356.

Seybold, Michael, Unfehlbarkeit des Papstes – Unfehlbarkeit der Kirche, in: *Denzler, Georg* (Hg.), Papsttum in der Diskussion, Regensburg 1974, 102-122.

Sieben, Hermann Josef, Vom Apostelkonzil zum Ersten Vatikanum. Studien zur Geschichte der Konzilsidee, Paderborn 1995.

Söll, Georg, Mariologie (HDG II/4), Freiburg i. Br. 1978.

Staffa, Dino, L' unità della fede e l' unificazione dei popoli, nel magisterio del Sommo Pontefice Giovanni XXIII, Divinitas 6 (1962), 3-12, bes. 21-31.

Stehle, Hansjakob, Verlegene Formeln, DIE ZEIT Nr. 43, 16. Oktober 1992, 12.

Stehle, Hansjakob, Wo steht Gott am Golf?, DIE ZEIT Nr. 5, 25. Januar 1991, S. 14, Kolumne »Weltbühne«.

Stellungnahme der Synode der Evangelischen Kirche im Rheinland, 12. Januar 1993, MdKI 44 (1993), 37.

Stirnimann, Heinrich, Marjam. Marienrede an einer Wende, Fribourg/Schw. 1989.

Stockmeier, Peter, Kirche unter der Herausforderung der Geschichte, in HFTh III (1986), 122-152.

Suttner, Ernst Chr. (Hg.), Eucharistie – Zeichen der Einheit. Erstes Regensburger Ökumenisches Symposion, Regensburg 1970.

Swidler, Leonard / Connor, Patrick (Hgg.), »Alle Katholiken haben das Recht ...« Freiheitsrechte in der Kirche. Mit einer Einführung von Norbert Greinacher, München 1990.
> *Swidler, Leonard / Connor, Patrick (ed.)*, A Catholic bill of rights, Kansas City: Sheed & Ward, 1988.

Swidler, Leonard, Die Zukunft der Theologie. Im Dialog der Religionen und Weltanschauungen, Regensburg-München 1992.
> *Swidler, Leonard*, After the Absolute: The Dialogical Future of Religious Reflection. Minneapolis: Fortress Press, 1990.

Tavard, George H., Geschichte der Ökumenischen Bewegung, Mainz 1965 (frz. 1961).

➤ *Tavard, George H.* [transl. by Hughes, Royce W.], [Petitie histoire du mouvement oecuménique.] Two Centuries of Ecumenism, London 1961.

Thils, Gustave / Theodor, Schneider, Glaubensbekenntnis und Treueid. Klarstellungen zu den »neuen« römischen Formeln für kirchliche Amtsträger, Mainz 1990.

Timpe, Nicolaus, Das kanonistische Kirchenbild vom Codex Iuris Canonici bis zum Beginn des Vaticanum Secundum (Erfurter Theologische Studien Bd. 36), Leipzig 1978.

Thurian, Max (Hg.), Ökumenische Perspektiven von Taufe, Eucharistie und Amt, Frankfurt am Main-Paderborn 1983.
➤ *Thurian, Max / World Council of Churches* (ed.), Ecumenical perspectives on baptism, eucharist and ministry, Geneva 1985.

Trippen, Norbert, Theologie und Lehramt im Konflikt. Die kirchlichen Maßnahmen gegen den Modernismus im Jahre 1907 und ihre Auswirkungen in Deutschland, Freiburg i. Br. 1977.

Tromp SJ, Sebastianus, Corpus Christi quod est Ecclesia, I: Introductio Generalis, Rom 1937; II: De Christo Capite, Mystici Corporis, Rom 1960; III: De Spiritu Christi Anima, Rom 1960.

Trummer, J., Art. Konstitutionen, in: LThK VI (1961), 505.

Tyrell, George, Christianity at the Crossroads, London 1907.
➤ *Tyrell, George*, Das Christentum am Scheideweg, München-Basel 1959.

Ullrich, Lothar, Dialog und Identität. Philosophische und theologische Aspekte, in: *Ernst, Wilhelm / Feiereis, Konrad* (Hgg.), Denkender Glaube in Geschichte und Gegenwart, Leipzig 1992, 320-341.

Uptrup, Klaus-Meyer zu / Jungo OSB, Michael (Hgg.), Lima-Liturgie. Vertont von Maxime Kovalevsky, Stuttgart-Mainz 1990.

Urban, Hans Jörg, »Damit die Welt glaube«. Der ökumenische Prozess im Dienst des christlichen Zeugnisses, Paderborn 2000.

Utz, Arthur F. / Groner, Joseph-Fulko (Hgg.), Aufbau und Entfaltung des gesellschaftlichen Lebens. Soziale Summe Pius` XII., 3Bde., Fribourg (Schw.) 1954-1961.

Utz, Arthur F. / Galen, Brigitta von (Hgg.), Die katholische Sozialdoktrin in ihrer geschichtlichen Entfaltung. Eine Sammlung päpstlicher Dokumente vom 15. Jahrhundert bis in die Gegenwart, 4 Bde., Aachen 1976.

Valeske, Ulrich, Hierarchia veritatum. Theologiegeschichtliche Hintergründe und mögliche Konsequenzen eines Hinweises im Ökumenismusdekret des II. Vatikanischen Konzils zum zwischenkirchlichen Gespräch, München 1968.

Verscheure, J., Katholische Aktion, in: LThK VI (1961), 74-77 und/ oder in HKG VII (1979), 310-313.

Vischer, Lukas, Wie weiter – nach den ersten zehn Jahren?, in: *Békés, Gerard / Vajta, Vilmos* (Hgg.), Unitatis redintegratio 1964-1974. Eine Bilanz der Auswirkungen des Ökumenismusdekretes, Frankfurt am Main 1977, 141-157.
  ➢ *Békés, Gerard / Vajta, Vilmos* (ed.), Unitatis redintegratio 1964-1974: the impact of the decree of Ecumenism [International Ecumenical Colloqium, 19th to 22nd November 1974 in Sant' Anselmo in Rome], Roma 1977.

Volk, Ernst, Mahl des Herrn oder Mahl der Kirche?, KuD 31 (1985), 33-64.

Volken, Laurenz, Jesus der Jude und das Jüdische im Christentum, Düsseldorf 1983.

Vorster, Hans, Geht es wirklich nur so? Die Glaubenskongregation zur Kirche als Communio, ÖR 41 (1992), 464-475.

Wächter, Lothar, Art. Dekret, in: LThK³ III (Freiburg 1995), 70.

Wagner, Harald, Das Amt vor dem Hintergrund der Diskussion um eine evangelisch-katholische Grunddifferenz, Cath 40 (1986), 39-58.

Wagner, Harald, Das Verständnis von Offenbarung im Zweiten Vatikanischen Konzil und bei Rudolf Bultmann, in: *Jaspert, Bernd* (Hg.), Rudolf Bultmanns Werk und Wirkung, Darmstadt 1984, 396-407.

Wagner, Harald, Die eine Kirche und die vielen Kirchen. Ekklesiologie und Symbolik beim jungen Möhler, München 1977.

Wagner, Harald, Johann Adam Möhler. Fakten und Überlegungen zu seiner Wirkungsgeschichte, Cath 43 (1989), 195-208.

Waldenfels, Hans, Das Christentum im Streit der Religionen um die Wahrheit, in: HFTh II (1985), 241-265.

Waldenfels, Hans, Der Gekreuzigte und die Weltreligionen, Einsiedeln 1983.

Waldenfels, Hans, Faszination des Buddhismus. Zum christlich-buddhistischen Dialog, Mainz 1982.

Waldenfels, Hans, Religion in China, StdZ 201 (1983), 95-109.

Waldenfels, Hans, Religionen als Antwort auf die menschliche Sinnfragen, München 1980.

Walf, Knut, Einführung in das neue katholische Kirchenrecht, Zürich 1984.

Walf, Knut, Kirchenrecht (Leitfaden Theologie 13), Düsseldorf 1984.

Walf, Knut, Zur Debatte. Themen der Katholischen Akademie in Bayern 14 (1984) Nr. 1, 16.

Weinzierl, Erika (Hg.), Der Modernismus. Beiträge zu seiner Erforschung, Graz-Wien-Köln 1974.

Welty, Eberhard, Herders Sozialkatechismus II: Der Aufbau der Gemeinschaftsordnung, Freiburg i. Br. ²1957.
> *Welty, Eberhard* [trans. by Kirstein, Gregor], A handbook of Christian social ethics, Vol. 2: The structure of the social order, New York 1953.

Wendebourg, Dorothea, Das Amt der Ämter, Zeitschrift für evangelisches Kirchenrecht, 45 (2000), 1-37.

Werbick, Jürgen, Kirche. Ein ekklesiologischer Entwurf für Studium und Praxis, Freiburg i. Br. 1994.

Weß, Paul, Ihr alle seid Geschwister. Gemeinde und Priester, Mainz 1983.

Wiedenhofer, Siegfried, Das katholische Kirchenverständnis. Ein Lehrbuch der Ekklesiologie, Graz 1992.

Wiederkehr, Dietrich, Das Prinzip der Überlieferung, in: HFTh IV (1988), 100-123.

Wiederkehr, Dietrich, Ekklesiologie und Kirchen-Innenpolitik. Protokoll einer Re-lecture der Kirchenkonstitution von Vaticanum II, in: *Kessler, Michael* u.a. (Hgg.), Fides quaerens intellectum. Beiträge zur Fundamentaltheologie (Max Seckler zum 65. Geburtstag), Tübingen 1992, 251-267.

Wiederkehr, Dietrich (Hg.), Wie geschieht Tradition?, Freiburg i. Br. 1991.

Wiederkehr, Dietrich (Hg.), Sensus fidei – consensus fidelium, Freiburg i. Br. 1993.

Wikenhauser, Alfred, Einleitung in das Neue Testament, Freiburg i. Br. 1952.
> *Wikenhauser, Alfred* [trans. by Cunningham, Joseph], New Testament introduction, New York 1958.

Wilckens, Ulrich, Maria, Mutter der Kirche (Joh 19,26f.), in: *Kampling, Rainer / Södling, Thomas* (Hgg.), Ekklesiologie des Neuen Testaments. Für Karl Kertelge, Freiburg i. Br. 1996, 247-266.

Wolf, Hubert / Arnold, Claus (Hgg.), Die deutschsprachigen Länder und das II. Vatikanum, Paderborn – München 2000.

Wolfinger, Franz, Die Rezeption theologischer Einsichten und ihre theologische und ökumenische Bedeutung, Cath 31 (1977), 202-233.

Wulf, Friedrich, Theologische Phänomenologie des Ordenslebens, in: MySal IV/2 (1973), 450-487.

Zehner, Joachim, Der notwendige Dialog. Die Weltreligionen in katholischer und evangelischer Sicht, Gütersloh 1992.

Zirker, Hans, Christentum und Islam. Theologische Verwandtschaft und Konkurrenz, Düsseldorf ²1992.

Zulehner, Paul M., Kirche – Anwalt des Menschen. Wer keinen Mut zum Träumen hat, hat keine Kraft zum Kämpfen, Freiburg i. Br. 1980.

Zulehner, Paul M., Wider die Resignation in der Kirche. Aufruf zu kritischer Loyalität, Wien-Freiburg i. Br. 1989.

ABKÜRZUNGEN

AAS	Acta Apostolicae Sedis. Commentarium Officiale [Offizielles Gesetzes- und Verordnungsblatt des Papstes und der Römischen Kurie]. (in Latin, English, French, German, Italian, Polish)
BSLK	Die Bekenntnisschriften der evangelisch-lutherischen Kirche. Hg. im Gedenkjahr der Augsburgerischen Konfession 1930, Göttingen 1930, überarbeitet [6]1967 u.ö. ➤ The Book of Concord: the confessions of the Evangelical Lutheran Church, ed. by *Tappert, Theodore G.*, Philadelphia 1959. ➤ The Book of Concord: the confessions of the Evangelical Lutheran Church, ed. by *Kolb, Robert and Wengert, Timothy J.* [transl. by *Charles Arand* [et.al.]], Minneapolis 2000.
Cath	Catholica (Münster). Vierteljahrsschrift für ökumenische Theologie.
CGG	Christlicher Glaube in moderner Gesellschaft. Enzyklopädische Bibliothek in 30 Teilbänden, hg. v. *Böckle, Franz / Kaufmann, Franz-Xaver / Rahner, Karl / Welte, Bernhard*, Freiburg i. Br. 1980-1982.
CIC	Codex Iuris Canonici. Lateinisch-deutsche Ausgabe des CIC 1983, Kevelaer 1983. ➤ Codex Iuris Canonici. The Code of Canon Law in English translation, ed. by the Canon Law Society of Great Britain and Ireland, London [et. al] 1983.
Concilium	Concilium. Internationale Zeitschrift für Theologie. (Deutsche Ausgabe). 1965-. ➤ Concilium. International journal for theology, New York 1965-.
DH	*Denzinger, Heinrich*, Enchiridion symbolorum definitionum et declarationum de rebus fidei et morum. Kompendium der Glaubensbekenntnisse und kirchlichen Lehrentscheidungen. Lateinisch-Deutsch, hg. v. Hünermann, Peter, Freiburg i. Br.-Basel-Rom-Wien [31]1991 [36. verbess. Aufl. von DS mit unverändertem Textbestand, aber erweitert um eine Auswahl aus den Texten des Zweiten Vatikanischen Konzils].
Divinitas	Divinitas. Pontificae academiae theologicae Romanae commentarii.

DS	*Denzinger, Heinrich*, Enchiridion symbolorum definitionum et declarationum de rebus fidei et morum. 32. erw. und verbess. Aufl. von *Schönmetzer, Adolf*, Barcelona-Freiburg i.Br.-Rom 1963, u.ö. [deutsch in DH].
DThA	Die Deutsche Thomas-Ausgabe. Vollständige, ungekürzte deutsch-lateinische Ausgabe der Summa theologica [des Thomas von Aquin]. Übersetzt und kommentiert von Dominikanern und Benediktinern Deutschlands und Österreichs. Hg. von der Philosophisch-Theologischen Hochschule Walberberg bei Köln, noch nicht abgeschlossen, Heidelberg-Graz-Wien-Köln (inzwischen Graz-Wien-Köln), 1933ff. ➤ Summa Theologiae: Latin text and English translation, introductions, notes, appendices and glossaries, ed. by Gilby, Thomas [et. al.], Cambridge 1964-1981.
FZPhTh	Freiburger Zeitschrift für Philosophie und Theologie (Fribourg/Schweiz).
HDG	Handbuch der Dogmengeschichte, hg. v. *Schmaus, Michael / Grillmeier, Alois / Scheffczyk, Leo / Seybold, Michael*, 4 Bde. in Faszikeln, noch nicht abgeschlossen, Freiburg i. Br. 1951ff. ➤ The Herder History of Dogma, ed. by Schmaus, Michael / Grillmeier, Alois, London 1964-.
HerKorr	Herder-Korrespondenz, Monatshefte für Gesellschaft und Religion (Freiburg. i. Br. 1946-). ➤ Herder correspondence: a monthly review for the Christian world, New York / London / Dublin, 1963/1.1964-7.1970.
HFTh	Handbuch der Fundamentaltheologie, 4 Bde., hg. v. *Kern, Walter / Pottmeyer, Hermann Josef / Seckler, Max*, Freiburg i. Br. 1985-1988, erw. Tübingen ²2000.
HKKR	Handbuch des Katholischen Kirchenrechts, hg. v. *Listl, Josef / Müller, Hubert / Schmitz*, Heribert, Regensburg 1983.
IkaZ	Internationale katholische Zeitschrift Communio, Freiburg i. Br. 1972-. ➤ Communio: international catholic review, Washington, D.C. 1.1974-.
JBTh	Jahrbuch für biblische Theologie (Neukirchen / Vluyn 1.1986-).
KNA	Katholische Nachrichten Agentur GmbH.

K A N N-ÖkI	KNA, Ökumenische Information.
KuD	Kerygma und Dogma: Zeitschrift für theologische Forschung und kirchliche Lehre (Göttingen 1955-).
LThK	Lexikon für Theologie und Kirche, Zweite, völlig neu bearb. Aufl., hg. v. *Höfer, Josef / Rahner, Karl*, 10 Bde. und 1 Registerband, Freiburg i. Br. 1957-1965.
LThK.E	LThK, 3 Erg.Bde.: Das Zweite Vatikanische Konzil, Konstitutionen, Dekrete und Erklärungen, lateinisch und deutsch, Kommentare, Freiburg i. Br. 1966-1968.
MdKI	Materialdienst des Konfessionskundlichen Institutes des Evangelischen Bundes, Bensheim.
MThZ	Münchner Theologische Zeitschrift.
MySal	Mysterium Salutis. Grundriß heilsgeschichtlicher Dogmatik, hg. v. *Feiner, Johannes / Löhrer, Magnus*, 5 Bde. in 7, Zürich 1965-1975.
NHthG	Neues Handbuch theologischer Grundbegriffe, hg. v. *Eicher, Peter*, 2. erw. Aufl. 5 Bde., München 1991.
NR	*Neuner, Josef / Roos, Heinrich*, Der Glaube der Kirche in den Urkunden der Lehrverkündigung. Neubearb. von *Rahner, Karl / Weger, Karl-Heinz*, Regensburg ⁹1971. ➤ *Neuner, Josef / Dupuis, Jacques*, The Christian faith in the doctrinal documents oft he Catholic Church, Bangalore 1973.
OeFo	Ökumenisches Forum – Grazer Hefte für Ökumene (Graz 1978-).
ÖR	Ökumenische Rundschau (Frankfurt am Main 1965-).
ÖRK	Ökumenischer Rat der Kirchen (Weltrat der Kirchen). ➤ The World Council of Churches
PG	Migne, J.P. (Hg.), Patrologia, Series Graeca, 161 Bde., Paris 1857-1866.
PL	Migne, J.P. (Hg.), Patrologia, Series Latina, 217 Bde., Paris 1878-1890.
StdZ	Stimmen der Zeit (München).
Suppl	Supplementum [zur Summa Theologiae des Thomas von Aquin].

412 Pesch THE PREHISTORY OF THE SECOND VATICAN COUNCIL

ThG	Theologie der Gegenwart. Informationsorgan für wissenschaftliche und praktische Theologie (Hennef/Sieg, Erfurt 1994-).
ThGl	Theologie und Glaube. Zeitschrift für den katholischen Klerus (Paderborn 1908-1943; 1982-).
ThLZ	Theologische Literaturzeitung: Monatsschrift für das gesamte Gebiet der Theologie und Religionswissenschaft (Leipzig-Göttingen 1876-).
ThQ	Theologische Quartalschrift, hg. v. Professoren der Katholischen Theologie an der Universität Tübingen (Tübingen 1819-).
ThR	Theologische Rundschau (Tübingen 1897-).
TTh	Tijdschrift voor theologie (Nijmegen 1896-).
TThZ	Trierer Theologische Zeitschrift: Pastor bonus, hg. v. der Theologischen Fakultät Trier in Verbindung mit dem Katholisch-Theologischen Fachbereich der Universität Mainz, Trier 1947-.
WA	Weimarer Ausgabe = D. Martin Luthers Werke, Kritische Gesamtausgabe, Weimar 1983ff.
WuA	Wort und Antwort. Zeitschrift für Fragen des Glaubens (Wahlberberg-Mainz 1960-).
ZEE	Zeitschrift für Evangelische Ethik: Kommentare, Studien, Berichte, Diskussionen (Gütersloh Jg. 1/20. 1957/1976. 1977-).
ZkTh	Zeitschrift für katholische Theologie, hg. v. der Theologischen Fakultät der Universität Innsbruck (Innsbruck 1877-).
ZThK	Zeitschrift für Theologie und Kirche (Tübingen 1891-). ➤Journal for theology and the church, New York 1965-[1970].

INDEX